Sir Frederick Banting

Portrait by Curtis Williamson. Courtesy University of Toronto.

F. G. Banting. M.D.

Sir Frederick Banting

LLOYD STEVENSON, M.D.

The Ryerson Press ~ Toronto
Charles C Thomas ~ Springfield, Ill.

7/10/44

Published December, 1946

Revised, March, 1947

FOR

WILLIAM ROBERTSON BANTING

The Story of his Father's Life

PRINTED AND BOUND IN CANADA
BY THE RYERSON PRESS, TORONTO

Acknowledgments

WHEN HAROLD NICOLSON penned his advice on "How To Write A Book," or specifically how to write a biography, he advised preparing an abstract of the standard work on the subject and adding fresh materials marginally. With this as a guide, composition would be greatly simplified.

In writing a biography of Sir Frederick Banting, this facility has been denied me. I have had to dig up my materials where I could find them. I am therefore unfeignedly and deeply grateful to the members of Sir Frederick's family and to his many friends and colleagues who have helped me with reminiscences, letters, photographs and drawings and with constructive criticism. Friendly critics who have read the manuscript in whole or in part have saved me from many errors.

I am perhaps most deeply indebted, for their assistance, to Dr. G. E. Hall, Dr. C. C. Lucas, Dr. E. C. Black, Dr. C. J. Mackenzie, Mr. A. Y. Jackson and Miss Sadie Gairns, although many others, as listed below, have been helpful and encouraging. Dr. Lucas and Dr. Black very kindly prepared for me a memorandum on Sir Frederick's contributions to aviation medicine research. I have made extended use of the information contained in this memorandum and have reproduced parts of it almost verbatim. This section, supplemented with other material, has been checked for accuracy and security by Dr. Hall, who was closely concerned with aviation medicine research, and by Dr. C. J. Mackenzie, President of the National Research Council. Other portions of the book have been verified in a similar manner by those best acquainted with the facts. I have not always been able to reconcile differences of opinion and recollection and have consequently been forced to neglect some part of their advice. I must take responsibility for the book as it stands.

My thanks are also due to Lady Banting (Dr. H. E. Banting); Mr. Thompson Banting; the late Mr. Nelson Banting; Professor E. W. Banting; Mr. W. R. Banting; the late Mrs. M. R. Banting; Dr. F. W. W. Hipwell; the late Dr. Angus McKay; Mrs. Catherine O'Neil; Mr. T. S. H. Graham; Dr. C. C. Miller; the late Dr. Velyien E. Henderson; Dr. Duncan Graham; Dr. G. W. Ross; Dr. C. A. Rae; Dr. Gordon Cameron; Dr. C. A. Wells; Dr. E. H. Hutchinson; Dr. W. W. Barraclough; Dr. W. E. Gallie; Mr.

v

Walter Cowan; Lieut.-Col. L. C. Palmer; Miss Blodwen Davies; Dr. W. P. Tew; Dr. G. A. Ramsay; Dr. F. R. Miller; Dr. F. J. H. Campbell; Dr. J. W. Crane; Dr. W. L. Robinson; Dr. J. B. Collip; Dr. C. H. Best; Dr. W. R. Campbell; Dr. J. A. Gilchrist; Dr. G. H. A. Clowes; Dr. Seale Harris; Dr. Harry G. Armstrong; Dr. E. F. Burton; Mr. Bertram Brooker; Mr. John D. Robins; Mr. J. W. McLaren; Mr. Arthur Lismer; Mr. Napier Moore; Mr. William Colgate; Wing Commander C. B. Stewart; the late Sir William Mulock; Dr. Frank Adams; Dr. G. H. Stevenson; Dr. E. P. Joslin; Dr. Bruno Mendel; Dr. D. A. Irwin; Dr. E. J. King; Dr. C. S. Wilson; Dr. Norman M. Wrong; Mr. Herbert I. Kurtz; General A. G. L. McNaughton; Dr. H. J. Cody; Sir Henry Dale; Mrs. Edmund MacDonald; Mrs. Helen C. Brown; Miss Frances Loring; Miss Ethel Sullivan; Miss Elsie G. Sumner; Mr. Emanuel Hahn; Mr. C. A. G. Matthews; Mr. Wilfred Rowland Childe; Mr. Vilhjalmur Stefansson; Dr. George Hunter; Dr. Lillian A. Chase; Dr. C. F. Code; and Dr. Lorne Pierce.

A number of those mentioned have very generously given me permission to quote from their writings or to reproduce photographs or works of art. For permission to use copyright material I am also indebted to the following: Messrs. William Morrow and Company, Inc.; Messrs. W. B. Saunders Company; Messrs. Robert M. McBride and Company; Messrs. Houghton Mifflin Company; the Macmillan Company, Ltd.; Random House, Inc.; the University of Toronto Press; the Royal Society of Medicine; *The Edinburgh Medical Journal; The Canadian Medical Association Journal; Surgery, Gynecology and Obstetrics; The British Medical Journal; The Lancet; The Journal of Bone and Joint Surgery; The American Journal of Psychiatry; The New York State Journal of Medicine; Canadian Business; The Canadian Geographical Journal; The Toronto Star;* and *The Toronto Evening Telegram.* These are the publishers of the principal sources for quotation or reproduction; together with these, the sources of shorter excerpts are specifically acknowledged in footnotes.

My wife has given me invaluable help by checking references and quotations, by patient scribing and by the substantial labour of preparing the index; she is directly responsible for much of whatever good has been retained, whatever bad has been discarded. For the past two years she has entertained the shade of Sir Frederick as a household guest.

L. G. S.

Foreword

To some, Banting was known and will be remembered as a quiet young farm boy who made a name for himself in medical research—a source of pride to his native Alliston. To others, he was known and will be remembered as a rugged, yet shy medical student at the University of Toronto, whose name became, through his great discovery, synonymous with medical research in Canada, an example and inspiration to all future generations of medical students. To the battle tired, the wounded and the sick soldiers under his care as a battalion medical officer in 1916-1918, he will be remembered as a kindly, sincere and sympathetic doctor, whose courage and skill under shell fire won him a Military Cross. That such a man should later, through similar sincerity of purpose, courage in the face of great difficulties, and devotion to the needs of his fellow men, ease the suffering of countless millions, was simply to continue his rôle as a distinguished humanitarian.

To a very few, Banting was known, and will be remembered, as a young, impoverished surgeon in the city of London, who, through those dreadfully discouraging days of trying to build up a practice, instructed in physiology and anatomy at the University of Western Ontario, and, to pass many dreary hours of waiting for patients who did not come, became a constant reader of medical journals and conceived the idea which eventually led to the control of diabetes.

To his colleagues of the insulin era, he may be recalled as a determined, wilful and not infrequently difficult young investigator, who, in spite of the lack of scientific training, gave insulin to the world and, in that ever dominant spirit of appreciativeness and abundant unselfishness, shared his honours in the days of his triumph.

To yet others, Banting was a great scientist, a disappointed and disillusioned man, a national leader of medical research, the possessor of rare scientific talents, an unsociable creature or a simple outdoor man, depending upon the point-of-view and judgment of the particular critic.

To me, who had the opportunity of being closely associated

with him from 1929 until his death, Banting was, above all else, a great man, respected for his abilities, loved for his weaknesses, admired for his humility and venerated for his achievements. Not a great scientist, as scientifically trained people appreciate the word, he was primarily a stimulator of science and scientific thought—a symbol of medical research. Generous to a fault at times, this big, kind-hearted, modest friend guided his fellow-workers to obtain the training which had been denied to him, and in the process men were developed.

Known by countless persons, but understood by too few, Banting has been portrayed by the young author of this biography as he was and as he should be remembered—a man of many talents, of many moods, of many traits and of many interests, a man immortalized long before his death, the recipient of innumerable international honours, yet a man possessed of the finest degree of humility, a great Canadian.

G. E. HALL,
Dean of Medicine.

University of Western Ontario,
London, Ont.
May 15, 1946.

Foreword to the Second Edition

The publication of this second edition offers the opportunity of correcting certain misprints and minor errors that crept into the first edition. I am grateful to the librarians of the Medical School Library, University of Western Ontario, for their assistance in making the Bibliography more complete.

L. S.

Table of Contents

List of Illustrations

Frontispiece: F. G. BANTING, M.D.

xi

Prologue

ALTHOUGH the name Banting (also spelled, in the older records, Benting or Bentinck) appears to have originated in Holland, Sir Frederick's immediate forebears were all of British extraction. His grandfather, John Banting, was an Englishman who lived in the north of Ireland. There he married and became the father of a numerous family. About the middle of the last century he moved to Canada. One of his sons, William Thompson Banting, born March 31, 1849, was the scientist's father.

Sir Frederick's father, whose influence over him was profound, became a respected farmer, a trustee in the Methodist Church, a teacher in the Sunday School and a member of the choir. He was earnest, hard-working, kindly. He was so exceptionally devout that some of his younger acquaintances have retained the mistaken impression that he was a lay preacher.

In March, 1931, Sir Frederick wrote in his diary:

"Some religious people have philosophy of a true nature developed out of their religion. The philosophical aspect of religion has appealed to them. My father, who was born eighty-two years ago today, did not have the educational background to study philosophy and possibly it did not come within his scope of reading, but he had a philosophy of broadmindedness, toleration and work that was as ideal as that of the best."

The other side of the house was Scottish. William Thompson Banting was married on January 28, 1879, at Thompsonville, to Margaret Grant, whose parents, Alexander Grant and Sarah Ann Squire, were both of Scottish blood.

Margaret Grant was a remarkable woman, dowered with the rare combination of evangelistic piety and genial wit. She became the mother of five children: Nelson, Thompson, Kenneth, Esther and Frederick, all but the youngest born at Thompsonville, where the family made their first home. Her affection for her youngest son, Frederick, an affection which he always fully and warmly returned, she never allowed to take on the appearance of favouritism; yet as the youngest child (four years junior to Esther, who was next older) he required her attention longer than

xiii

the rest, and she never gave up watching over him. The story of their relationship is one of the pleasanter aspects of his life, which was not infrequently clouded by unhappiness and distrust. Whoever tried to discourage him, whoever met his zeal with indifference, whoever mistrusted the likelihood of success, his mother's faith and good humour were never failing. It is just possible, however, that her influence was too deep and strong, too all-pervading. It has been suggested that his behaviour in certain relationships of his adult life was determined by a mother-fixation. The evidence on which this assumption rests is by no means conclusive. Many of those who knew him best are of the opinion that his father had a greater hold over him than his mother.

It is clear, at any rate, that Banting was bound to his parents by stronger ties than those of ordinary filial affection. He stood erect on his own feet, tough-minded and manly, but he never stepped entirely clear of the lengthening shadow of the elder Bantings. Their works and ways went with him to the end.

In 1885, the Bantings moved from the neighbourhood of Thompsonville to the neighbourhood of Alliston. When giving up the Thompsonville farm they had intended to journey to the west, but a change in circumstances forced them to alter their plans.

From about 1880 until well into the present century, the Canadian West appeared to popular imagination as the happy land of dream. Frustration and disappointment elsewhere only required removal to the Eden west of the Great Lakes, to be transformed into rosiest hope. At a somewhat later period, when the westward movement was still strong, when the climate seemed kinder than ever and the crops were so enormous that great additional manpower was needed to gather them in, the stalwart sons of William Thompson Banting, like many other Ontario boys, spent varying periods in the West, depending on the size of the harvest, and the duration of the railways' annual Harvester Excursions. The third son, Kenneth Banting, afterwards succumbed to the lure and settled permanently. But it was only a whim of fate which prevented the fortunes of the entire family from being transferred to this land of promise.

In that momentous year of 1885, Louis Riel, the impetuous rebel chieftain who had been exiled from Canada for heading an armed uprising of the Métis sixteen years before, returned to his old battleground and started fresh disasters by exploiting a genuine grievance of the Métis in the matter of land settlements. The Métis were few in number, but the Indians whom he was gradually rallying to his support were many, and the government in Ottawa saw the need for swift action. On March 17, Riel formed a provisional government with himself as president. Troops were at once despatched from eastern Canada; more were recruited in the fear that the rising might grow in menace. To those who would join this punitive expedition offers of free land were extended.[1]

One of those attracted to the gathering force was William Thompson Banting. As already related, he gave up his farm at Thompsonville and made preparations to leave for the west. But on May 13 of the same year, just as he was ready to enlist, the rebels were soundly beaten at Batoche; two days later Riel himself was captured. The forces of the insurgents melted away; the rebellion fizzled out. Farmer Banting, in a rural phrase, had "come to a stand." Should he go West on his own account or should he return to farming in Ontario? After some consideration he decided to remain in Ontario. His old place at Thompsonville had been rented to someone else. For a short time he "worked a place" near Beeton, but he continued to look for a new site and finally selected a farm in the second concession of Essa township, about two miles from the town of Alliston. Here he settled, with his wife and four children, and here, on November 14, 1891, another son was born, to be christened Frederick Grant Banting.

And the ironical Fates, who happened to be looking on, half smiled, half frowned.

[1]This supposed offer of free land is part of the story told in the family. I can find no record of such an offer and am informed on good authority that it was never made. In 1885 western land was so easily obtained that the promise of a free grant would have been little to the purpose. Perhaps Banting's father thought of participation in the campaign as a prelude to a western move already contemplated.

PART I
A Boy's Will

I remember the gleams and glooms that dart
Across the schoolboy's brain;
The song and the silence in the heart,
That in part are prophecies, and in part
Are longings wild and vain.
    And the voice of that fitful song
    Sings on, and is never still;
    A boy's will is the wind's will,
And the thoughts of youth are long, long thoughts.

HENRY WADSWORTH LONGFELLOW.

1

THE MORNING sunlight lay warmly on the sidewalks of Victoria Street in Alliston, Ontario. Townsfolk and countryfolk were intermingled happily, and no one seemed to hurry. It was a pleasant Saturday morning just before the turn of the century, and the somnolence of the country town was undergoing a weekly disturbance. The rattle of wheels, the clopping of hooves, the cheerful murmur of voices filled the street, and repeated good-mornings fell on the air with a clear and dewy sound, echoing blandly along the pavements from lip to lip.

In this good-natured and leisurely throng there was one small focus of unhappiness. Closely dogging the footsteps of a pleasant-faced but resolute woman in a long, dark dress, trotted a disconsolate little boy of seven or eight. He seemed to be executing a doleful sort of dance. When his mother stopped to speak to a friend or glance at a store window, the boy stood very close beside her, trying to edge in behind her skirt, as if from excessive shyness; when she moved on again he matched his short steps to her longer ones, and followed her like a shadow, turning with her as she turned, and shuffling sidewise to keep behind her whenever she seemed about to pause. His body was taut with the most acute self-consciousness; his round little face was pink with embarrassment. If someone spoke to him he was put so thoroughly out of countenance that he stammered. He was trying, though not with complete success, to hide from passers-by, and especially from the mocking eyes of his contemporaries, his misfortune and his shame: he was wearing a pair of high-buttoned boots with Cuban heels, heels that increased his stature by an inch but depressed his spirit immeasurably, for these boots were obviously intended for a *girl*.

The bitterness of an undeserved degradation swelled in his heart. He did not feel the warmth of the sunshine. He did not share with his schoolfellows the joy of the week-end's release. His whole unhappy consciousness was centred miserably on his fancy, effeminate boots. Why should he, alone among so many, be

1

singled out for disgrace? Simply because his sister, Esther Banting, four years his senior, had outgrown her boots before they
showed signs of wear, and the thrifty elder Bantings had bestowed
them on their youngest child, Frederick, in order not to waste
good shoe leather. Did no one understand what humiliation was
imposed upon him? No one. On school days he could discard
his boots as soon as he was out of sight of home, picking them up
again on the way back. But when his mother took him to town
with her, what could he do? And in the winter, when he would
be forced to wear them to school because of the cold, where could
he look for comfort? His mind grew dark with distress. He was
beginning to feel, for the first time in his life,

> the heavy and the weary weight
> Of all this unintelligible world.

He was very glad, therefore, when the shopping expedition was
over and they started for home. Perched in the buggy beside his
mother, he kept his legs painfully twisted in the shadow under
the seat, as much out of sight as possible, until the Bantings'
shambling old mare, Betsy, had taken them beyond the limits of
the town. Then he breathed more easily; his muscles slackened
in relief; he sighed gently, and straightened to look around him.

The gratuitous shame of Esther's boots was presently almost
forgotten in the delights of the countryside. They turned north
on the dusty "third," and clattered over the plank bridge that
spanned the River Boyne. The water rippled quietly among the
stones, in the soft and various shadows of overhanging trees. A
short distance downstream two boys were fishing from the bank.
Fred half rose from his seat, and called to them, and waved. Then
he remembered his boots, and sat down abruptly. Betsy jogged
onward with her unequable gait, and the fishermen vanished
behind.

The road was now steadily, though never sharply, uphill, an
extended grade of one in six, so that after a few minutes one could
look back at a broadening prospect of panelled green, the wheat
and oats and the broad, clovered acres of Simcoe County.

A few minutes more, and they turned in at their own gate, a
collie with an eloquent tail loping down from the house to meet
them.

The Banting home was a simple farmhouse on this third concession line of Essa township. It was built on the crest of a gentle hill, commanding a distant view of Alliston. To the west, along the horizon, stood the worn and misty profiles of the Blue Mountains; to the east, at a distance of about fifteen miles, was Lake Simcoe; between the Banting farm toward the north and the main road from Cookstown to Alliston on the south, meandered the sluggish stream called the Boyne, to empty near Nicholston into the Nottawasaga; the trees which lined its banks were clearly seen from the yard. The house was of white frame, a storey-and-a-half, built on a sprawling, L-shaped plan, with broad windows. It was in the downstairs front bedroom that Frederick, the youngest of five children, had been born.

Once free of his hated boots, Fred was out-of-doors again "like a shot." There wanted nearly two hours to dinnertime, and he headed toward the river. Sunlight warmed him; the wind ruffled his hair. He pulled a piece of Timothy grass and put it between his teeth. His emancipated feet began to skip.

Scout Island, a high, grassy island in the Boyne, had been the scene of a thousand games—games of warfare and siege, and sometimes games of pirates. But now and then it was better to lie in the grass, or where the young ferns were sprouting like green quills, and merely watch the clouds drift by at enormous heights, great bales of whiteness, or ragged shapes of grey like mossy branches, or merely straggling wisps of vapour. And then thoughts drifted over as well, and these were more varied in shape and colour than the clouds. There were plans and dreams and hopes, and also memories (of the day before yesterday perhaps) though fewer of these; there was the sad and persistent shadow of Esther's boots; presently, as the sun reached its zenith and the day wore on toward afternoon, there was a tantalizing vision of various delicious foods. Then a vague and misty idea suddenly condensed at a point, and the boy threw away his sprig of grass, and started once again for home.[1]

[1]There is a happy and characteristic epilogue to the story of Esther's boots. When Mrs. Banting discovered that other children were teasing her "Freddy" about his boots, she immediately bought him a new pair, properly masculine in style.

2

In the familiar calendar pictures of the barefoot boy, and in the exuberant paintings of Norman Rockwell, which for years have graced the covers of the *Saturday Evening Post,* the boy is almost invariably portrayed in the company of a dog. The dog usually has one ear lifted,

> Quick raised to ask which way we go,

and looks at his master with shining alertness. Boy and dog are companions and friends. They have the same inquisitive energy and the same delight in movement. The master is not too exacting, and the dog is thoroughly devoted and completely uncritical.

We always had a dog at home on the farm (wrote Banting many years later, and we may imagine the reflective smile which played on his lips as his pencil traced the words).[2] During my first eighteen years of life we were never without one. During this time there were three who were intimate friends of the family in general, and of myself in particular. Of these three, the second, who was known as Collie, stands out in my memory above the others, because of his friendship, his intuitive intelligence, his bravery, and his sympathetic understanding.

Old Collie never left the farm. His sense of responsibility never allowed him to roam about the country or visit the town two miles away, or even chase the elusive rabbits along the river bank, about forty rods distant from the line fence. He usually fought with the neighbours' dogs when they trotted along at the heels of the visiting neighbour.

Collie had his own house under the cherry tree in the back yard. It was lined in winter with an old buffalo robe and had a little porch which prevented the snow from blowing in. The only time he ever went into our house was during a thunderstorm in the summer time. With the first sound of thunder, he would put his nose to the kitchen door, and paw and whine until he was let in. When admitted, he went into a dark landing off the

---

[2] All quotations attributed to Banting are from longhand manuscripts found among his papers.

back stairs; when the storm was over, he stood by the door until he was let out.[3]

Despite Collie's timidity at the rumble of thunder, he was a staunch guardian of the household.

Mother was never afraid when Collie was around. There were in those days many tramps and peddlers who came to beg or to sell. They were very undesirable characters as a rule, and when the men were in the back field and mother was alone, it was sometimes a disagreeable experience to have to go to the door and turn such men away. One tramp went right into the house and could hardly be persuaded to leave. But this was not the case if Collie were around. Ordinarily he was the most amiable of dogs. But he could smell a tramp, and his hair would rise, and he would give warning of his intentions with a growl and savage bark. He always took up a position immediately in front of mother, as a protector, and kept between her and the uninvited guest.

One of these uninvited guests was discovered by Mrs. Banting in the barn, half way down the ladder from the loft, where he had spent the night. He explained that he had had no intention of stealing, but had only wanted a place to sleep. He was walking, had no funds, and was hungry. Mrs. Banting took him in and fed him, and as he was leaving, he insisted on making her a present of a drinking mug, which he had picked up at a village bar; it was the only thing he had. This mug was pounced on by Fred, who used it thereafter for his own, while the visitor was seen through the gate by the watchful and ever suspicious Collie.

At the same time (wrote Banting) we had a very large black cat who was domiciled in the warm stable, and whose duty it was to keep mice out of the bins of grain. If the cat ventured to the house, there were two black streaks followed by a cloud of dust, and Collie would return with his tongue out and a grin on his face, while the cat regained his breath perched on the gate-post of the barnyard.

But if Collie was master of the house, the cat was master in

[3]Banting wrote two short pieces on his dog, both scribbled in pencil on sheets of foolscap. I have taken the liberty of combining sentences from both.—L. S.

the stable. When the men went down to do the chores of a cold winter night, the dog nearly always followed and entered the barn. He was met by the cat, who did not flinch. Collie very meekly crawled under the grindstone, which was just inside the feed-room door, and if he ventured out, the cat would walk menacingly toward him and Mr. Collie would return to safety under the grindstone.

Only on one occasion was Collie ever known to go down the road beyond the corner of the farm. This is how it occurred:

About half a mile from our house there was the old river where we all learned to swim and fish in summer, and skate, play shinny, and trap in the winter. There were many logs and stumps frozen in the ice, but very often, on a clear, cold, moonlight night in winter, when the ice was free of snow, the girls and boys of the neighbourhood, and even some from town, would gather for a skate. A large, old-fashioned fire was kindled, and the party sat around on logs, skated, and gathered wood. Before the party broke up, the fire sometimes melted through the ice to be automatically extinguished. The younger ones could not stay so late, but often passed the place next morning on the way to school and saw the hole in the ice.

My sister and I attended such a party one night, and just as we were about to take off our skates, Collie came rushing up, barking and running back and forth. It was so strange we knew something serious had happened. We took off our skates and did not even wait to lace our boots, but hurried home after Collie, who kept running back to us and jumping against us. We ran, but when we were half way home, Collie ran on ahead. He came rushing up to meet us at the gate, jumping up and licking our faces.

At last we reached the house. Mother was away and father was alone in the house. He was always troubled with corns; they arose from wearing the old wooden-peg boots as a boy. He had got ready for bed, had then soaked his feet in hot water by the kitchen stove, while he read another chapter in his book, keeping the water hot by periodic additions from the kettle. When his feet were thoroughly soaked, he pared his corns and applied a new remedy which some kind soul had said would cure. A few minutes after the application he began to experience a burning sensation. This increased to a terrific pain. He decided to get to bed, but the pain was so severe that he could scarcely move. He

then had cramps in his legs. He succeeded in crawling part way
to his room, pushing the lamp along the floor in front of him.
He could not suppress the groans of pain. The faithful dog
heard, and though he was never known to go so far away, he
came down to the river to tell us. We understood, and arrived
in time to wash away the drug, and relieve the most severe pain.

3

Banting's earliest years were as happy as may be, but he had
a serious bent, and was always inclined to look at the world rather
soberly; in his mother's phrase, he was usually "not very jolly."
An habitual Quakerish gravity sat oddly on his youthful
shoulders. Somewhere at the back of his eyes, however, a sly
sense of fun was lurking.

Simple necessary duties were never lacking. There is an
ancient and honourable device by which farm boys are first made
acquainted with Duty in such a way that the grim lady seems
almost prepossessing. A young farm boy is permitted, for instance,
to ride home from the field of an evening on the back of one of
the work horses. Presently he is allowed to help remove the harness, and later on he has the rare privilege of unharnessing the
horse by himself. Imperceptibly, privilege becomes duty. In
Banting's own phrase: "Work began as a special form of play."
Probably the element of play disappeared rather early. Duty, as
such, and without a cosmetic disguise, was a familiar figure on the
Banting homestead. There was nothing casual or lukewarm in
the Banting Methodism. The constant religious atmosphere
necessarily made its impression.

Morning worship was an invariable family custom. Immediately after breakfast Mr. Banting would read a portion of scrip-
ture from the *Home Readings*. Then the whole family would
kneel while he led them in prayer. The ceremony was concluded
with the Lord's Prayer, recited in unison.

Church attendance was a matter of course. When his feet
did not yet reach the floor, Fred sat up in church and behaved

himself; any inclination to wriggle about was stopped short by a quickly outstretched hand.

One sat as still as one could and tried to be attentive. That was hard; sermons were always full of such big words. It was all impressive and mysterious, but after a time one lost interest. A wandering eye observed with pleasure the stained margins of the pointed church windows, one red, the next one green, the next yellow, the next blue. When the sun got up a little higher, the light that fell through a blue-bordered window to the east cast a streak of its blueness on platform and pulpit, and on the black-clad figure of the minister. The presence and position of this streak of colour varied with the length of the service.

After what seemed endless waiting (and very creditable patience) the sermon at last was over, and it was time to sing again. That was much better; Fred liked to sing. Father liked to sing too; in Thompsonville he had been a member of the choir. His strong voice was lifted now in one of the stirring Methodist hymns. Fred, watching and listening, admired his father tremendously.

Sunday School in the afternoon was assembled in a square auditorium, surrounded on three and a half sides by a balcony, which was divided into classrooms; there were classrooms too in the space below the balcony; these were separated from each other and from the main room of the school by heavy curtains. In the auditorium was a platform with a red carpet, a pair of massive carved chairs with red plush upholstery, and a little table with a bell. Backed by a tall pointed window, presided over by a dignified superintendent, this was nearly as impressive as the church. Father taught a class in the school, and the presence of his tall, bearded figure, although breathing kindness, was an added restraining influence that suppressed any notion of mischief.

Perhaps a part of a Sunday afternoon might be whiled away with a book. *The Means of Grace, Pilgrim's Progress,* or *Proverbial Philosophy* of Dr. Martin Tupper (a lengthy versified treatise in four series)—these books which were favourites with his father were probably not quite to Fred's taste as yet, though we may imagine him turning the leaves of Bunyan's allegory while he admired the pictures of the Giant Despair, and was perhaps sufficiently intrigued by the vigorous engraving of the fight with Apollyon to read the story of that wonderful engagement.

(He was afterwards to follow for himself a pathway where giants were met with, and where there were lions, not always chained, in the way.) Scott and Dickens and Thackeray were also found on these shelves, and a well-thumbed edition of Wordsworth.

From girlhood to old age, Fred's mother was fond of keeping scrapbooks. The later scrapbooks are collections of newspaper clippings of articles about her famous son, but a page or two remain to us also of one which she made as a girl. It contains, among jokes and news items, a number of sentimental poems ("When the Song's Gone Out of Your Life," etc.) a new translation of Paul Gerhard's famous hymn, beginning "O Head! blood-stained and wounded," and ten doggerel verses, entitled "The Book Agent and the Farmer." The first of these ten verses makes reference to a religious book which was immensely popular sixty years ago, and ran through many editions.

"Will you order the Looking-Glass, friend"—said he,
Turning over the leaves so the Farmer might see.
"It is next to the Bible in worth; far ahead
Of the trashy work that you last year read."

It is very doubtful if "trashy" reading of any kind was ever permitted in the Banting home. The *Bible Looking-Glass* (the same so highly commended by the Agent in the rhyme) seems to have been a favourite. A thick, green volume, still carefully cherished, it was handled so often that the stout binding wore out along the back, and had to be reinforced with a piece of red-flowered print. The full title is comprehensive:

THE BIBLE LOOKING-GLASS, REFLECTOR, COMPAN-
ION AND GUIDE TO THE GREAT TRUTHS OF THE
SACRED SCRIPTURES, AND ILLUSTRATING THE
DIVERSITIES OF HUMAN CHARACTER AND THE
QUALITIES OF THE HUMAN HEART, PROFUSELY
ILLUSTRATED BY OBJECT TEACHING PICTURES,
showing the PAIN *and* MISERY *resulting from* VICE *and the*
PEACE *and* HAPPINESS *arising from* VIRTUE.

Perhaps the young Frederick, like so many thrill-hungry boys in the days before the advent of moving-pictures, consumed dime novels on the sly, but it is quite apparent that the reading provided for him at home was very solid fare.

Nevertheless, *hors d'oeuvres* were plentiful. Both of his parents were fond of reading for amusement as well as for edification. They commonly sat in the kitchen of an evening after supper and read aloud to each other by turns. The book was usually a sentimental novel, and the children were allowed to "listen in," provided they had finished their homework. Young Fred contrived to listen regardless. Immediately above the kitchen was the bathroom, which contained no stove or other heating device; a hole had therefore been cut in the kitchen ceiling to permit the surplus of warm air to rise to the bathroom. Crouched close beside this hole, or lying prone, propped on his elbows with his chin in his hands, Fred gazed down into the warm glow of the kitchen, watched the changing humours on the faces of his father and mother and listened intently while one or other of them read. Fred's father was a warm-hearted man, easily moved. When he came across a harrowing passage (the foreclosure of the mortgage, the death of the invalid child, the all-too-late repentance of the culprit who was more weakling than villain) his spectacles would grow misty, his voice uncertain, and he would surrender the book to his wife, who could read it serenely with less outward sign of emotion. Next they would laugh together. Then hurry on to an approaching climax in the story. Then pause to discuss the outcome, speaking of the characters as if they were real persons, perhaps acquaintances or friends.

Fred watched and listened from his eyrie in the room above. The yellow light of the coal-oil lamp shone kindly on his parents below, gleamed on the white pages of the book and on the polished utensils of the kitchen. It was a magic world, remote from everything else, warm and genial and inviolate. And yet it reached far out to the ends of the earth and gathered the romance and adventure of many lands into a snug, domestic compass, to be examined and relished by the fireside.

It was a picture Fred never forgot. It became a symbol, a standard. He liked the stories; also he was curious and he hated to miss things; but most of all he was interested in his parents. He could wonder about them, could even laugh at them a little. Yet when he told the story in later years it was always with warmth of admiration and affection, and often—yes, it was unmistakable—often with a shade of envy.

4

An interesting side-light on the household arrangements is given us by the youngest son's description of the procedure of soap-making. Incidentally, the boy who helped to stir the pot seems to have shown a lively interest in the method. This was his first lesson in chemistry. He writes:

During the winter, in the frugal farm household, all the fat of the beef, lamb or pork was saved, and in the spring the leech was set up to make soft soap. The leech consisted of a hollowed-out log about four feet long, sawed off evenly at each end. A platform was built of logs covered with sloping boards, and the hollow log stood upright on the platform; it was tilted forward so that the lye would run off, and held in place by a wire from two posts. A little straw was placed in the bottom to act as a filter and hold the ashes back, and then the hole was filled up with hardwood ashes, water was allowed to seep through, and the lye was collected in a tub, or more frequently a sawed-off barrel. The lye was then put into a large black pot and the fat added. Under the pot was built a fire for the few succeeding days, and the contents stirred with a stick from time to time, until the thick, gelatinous, ropy soap was finished. The leech was usually set up behind the chip yard, and chips, knots, and wood that was not suitable for the stove were burned. Soft soap was an ideal cleaner for wood, and the tables and chairs were spotless; even the doorstep and floor were clean enough to eat off.

The proverbial juxtaposition of godliness and cleanliness was evidently realized in thorough-going style.

5

Since there was less to be done on a farm in the winter, winter was the time when all went to school regularly, provided of course that the roads were not blocked with snow. In the spring, and more especially at harvest time (when even the blacksmith's assistant deserted the smithy to take a job on a farm) there was more work to be done than there were hands to do it, and the older boys were forced to take frequent "holidays" from their schooling. Fred's early education, thanks to his position as the youngest of the family, was less frequently interrupted.

After morning worship, he was off to school on the old mare called Betsy. Betsy was capable of a singular gait, something between a canter and a gallop, and away she would go, Fred clutching her mane with one hand, his books with the other. Out of the lane and down the road, over the plank bridge that crossed the Boyne, up the hill and around to the right on the highway; down the main street of Alliston (Victoria Street) then left on Church Street; past the Town Hall, with its belfry where the pigeons fluttered, then to the right again at the third corner, and there was the school.

The school was a two-storey building, which contained a primary department (or "public school" as it is called in Ontario) on the ground floor, and a secondary department, the continuation school, upstairs. It was built of red brick, with white bricks around the windows and in a vertical column at each corner. In front was a square tower. This was surmounted by a bell, so placed that it was nearly invisible from the ground; at regular intervals, however, it always reminded one of its presence, and its double-noted clangour seemed very loud and imperative if one chanced to be late.

Dismounting in the yard, Fred would dismiss the faithful Betsy with a slap on the rump, and off she would go again, straight back on the road she had come, as unerring as a homing pigeon.

It is not very certain that Fred was fond of school. He did his work conscientiously, but he did not excel. At any rate, no medals came Fred's way at Alliston. One of his teachers afterwards told reporters: "Banting was not a remarkable scholar. He was not brilliant and we would not have picked him for one on whom fame should settle. But of this we were invariably sure —he would always give his best effort to whatever he tried to do. As a result he was proficient in all his studies, but outstanding in none."

In Madame Curie's brief biography of her husband, the distinguished physicist, Pierre Curie, she describes his early difficulties in school.

Pierre's intellectual capacities (she wrote) were not those which would permit the rapid assimilation of a prescribed course of studies. . . . The difficulty he experienced in following such a programme was usually attributed to a certain slowness of mind. . . . I think, however, that this belief was not entirely justified. It seems to me, rather, that already from his early youth it was necessary for him to concentrate his thought with great intensity upon a certain definite object, in order to obtain a precise result, and that it was impossible for him to interrupt or to modify the course of his reflections to suit exterior circumstances. It is clear that a mind of that kind can hold within itself great future possibilities. But it is no less clear that no system of education has been especially provided by the public schools for persons of this intellectual category.[4]

Banting's mind was no doubt radically different, in many respects, from that of the youthful Curie, but this paragraph might have been written of him with equal truth. The diversity of the school curriculum, and the necessity of memorizing great numbers of facts not familiarized by use were the barriers which kept him from early distinction, and indeed from any great display of capacity during his college years. Languages seemed especially difficult; words slipped away from a mind which was essentially curious about *things;* the arbitrary rules of syntax he found hard to retain. But his thoroughness, his spirit, his inquisitive turn of thought kept him nicely afloat. He was not brilliant, but he was average or better; he was safe. More than that, he was dogged. And the brilliant, facile minds which slipped lightly over difficulties and did not know they were there, missed something; the difficulties slowed him down, but they also set him to thinking. His method was not a quick and shallow assimilation, exhibited in fluent recitals from his books, but a slow mulling over in his mind of everything that was offered him for study. Some of it he retained; some of it he forgot; most of it, at any rate, he thought about.

[4]*Pierre Curie,* by Marie Curie. Translated by Charlotte and Vernon Kellogg, New York, The Macmillan Company, 1923, pp. 33-34.

6

Another aspect of his nature, one which became increasingly evident in later years, was his marked artistic ability. This seems to have been the one positive talent which he displayed in early life. It "ran in the family," for his mother's sister, Elizabeth Grant (afterwards Mrs. Pulford) was an amateur painter, while his oldest brother, Nelson, was very skilful with pencil and chalk, and the third brother, Kenneth, was considered by the rest of the family to be the most gifted artist of all. This familial talent was employed in serious efforts, dignified by frames; it was also used in making comic sketches and caricatures. When a visiting cousin came near to tumbling from a cherry tree, but managed at the last moment to hang on by her toes, one of the boys pictured her predicament in a clever water-colour. It shows the startled little girl in upside-down consternation, her pigtails swinging, her skirts around her shoulders, her pantaloons much in evidence; from a branch overhead a robin is looking at her quizzically.

Young Fred, too, was soon making sketches of trees and houses and farm animals. He even attempted portraiture, with comic effect if not always comic intention. Grown a little older and more skilful, he produced pen-and-ink cartoons in imitation of those he saw in magazines. These he inserted in frames which had been used for photographs or mottoes, and presented them to members of the family as gifts. Later on he tried his hand at painting. A picture still exists which is believed to be the first he ever attempted in oils. In default of canvas he used a piece of thin cardboard, apparently the side of a carton. The scene is boldly painted, and shows two blue hills against a yellowish sky, the bushes at their base reflected in a sheet of water; in the foreground is a wooded shore, a rowboat moored at its edge. This picture was carefully framed by the artist, but is neither signed nor dated. It is thought that he made it while still in public school, using oil paints belonging to his aunt. He presented it to his oldest brother and his sister-in-law as a Christmas gift.

Preoccupied with his work at college, he abandoned his paint-

Courtesy Mr. Thompson Banting.

MR. AND MRS. W. T. BANTING, SIR FREDERICK'S PARENTS

ing, and did not find time to return to it until after the war, when he again painted landscapes in oils, being especially attracted by the scenes of New Ontario and northern Quebec. The productions of his boyhood represent the type of landscape to be found near Alliston, but they seemed to be imaginary compositions, assembled on the instant and rapidly painted.

Not all of his time was occupied with study, chores, holiday jaunts and artistry. He found energy, too, for athletics. He was "into everything"; he played hard and he enjoyed the game. He seems to have lacked something of the fierceness of the competitive spirit, but nevertheless he was an excellent soccer player, noted for tremendous power. He played hockey and baseball as well. A photograph of the Alliston High School baseball team, taken at this time, shows a group of earnest young men in baseball uniforms with "AHS" across the chest, and handsome striped stockings; as sober as the best of them, Fred Banting is distinguished by his unruly hair, which protrudes gaily from under the peak of his particoloured cap. This was the year that the Alliston team, coached by the school principal, H. V. Laughton, won the league championship.

Fred presently came into possession of another uniform of which he had still better reason to be proud. Some years before the future soldier-scientist discovered an interest in science, he was enrolled in the Alliston company of volunteers, and donned the Queen's uniform for the first time.

7

His interest in medicine, as a way of life and a means of service, rather than as a science, was early aroused. His own words tell us how this came about.

On the way home from school one day, I stopped to look at two men who had just commenced the first row of shingles on the roof of a new house. As I watched, the scaffolding on which they stood suddenly broke. The two men fell to the ground and were badly injured. One man did not move; the other moved his arms and then was still. I ran for the doctor. He came in a few minutes. His presence was a relief for everyone. I watched every movement of those skilful hands as he examined the injured men, and tended to cuts, bruises and broken bones.

In those tense minutes I thought that the greatest service in life is that of the medical profession. From that day it was my greatest ambition to become a doctor.

This dawning interest, capped by an impulsive resolution, received added strength from sharing it with his cousin, Fred Hipwell, whose father was the druggist in Alliston, and who had been planning a career in medicine almost as long as he could remember. The boys talked together of their ambitions, in the confidence that nothing could interfere. Except, of course, that Fred Hipwell's parents wished him to be a clergyman, and Fred Banting's parents had the same plans for him. Medicine or divinity: which was it to be? The boys decided to compromise. They would be medical missionaries, like David Livingstone.

Apparently divinity was to come first. In 1910, when they graduated from High School in Alliston, they went down to Toronto together and registered at Victoria College.

A curious postscript remains to add. Among Banting's schoolmates at Alliston were two unfortunate children who died of infantile diabetes, a disease which is swifter and more terrible than the same "sugar sickness" in adults. One of them was a favourite playfellow who lived not far from the Banting home and with whom Fred often went backward and forward to and from school. The death of a playmate is a shocking and inexplicable event to a child, innocent as he is of the ways of death and sadly puzzled by its dreadful finality. If the impression seems quick to pass, it nevertheless leaves a vague shadow somewhere in the mind, which fades more slowly and is perhaps never quite erased. Banting long remembered this double tragedy and not infrequently referred to it. The later course of his life naturally reanimated this memory, turning a misty ray of light on the distant and pathetic figures, dwindling across the years, of the luckless little victims of a then unchallenged killer.

PART II

The Class of Seventeen

He showed me that the lines of a good helve
Were native to the grain before the knife
Expressed them, and its curves were no false curves
Put on it from without. And there its strength lay
For the hard work.

"The Axe-Helve," ROBERT FROST.

It occurred to me when we were puffing up the hill and the train was speeding along away below that the engine with all its power could not go up that slushy, soft, snowy road as fast as we could. Power is useless unless directed in the proper channel. People have different powers and the big question in life must be—"Are we on the right road for travel?" We will certainly not get far in our given time unless we have chosen the road that is fitted to our particular locomotive.

BANTING'S DIARY, *March 21, 1931.*

1

"IN VAIN did the wrath of Heaven destroy the old tower of Victoria College," reported the *Varsity* (the tower having been damaged by lightning) "for it now stands more defiant than ever, only awaiting the glaring tiles. The new residences now present a respectable appearance. . . . The exterior of South Hall has been decorated by a fresh coat of paint, and the interior by a flourishing contingent of freshettes."

Neither the residences nor their "flourishing contingent" had any part in the plans of Freshman Banting. Together with Hipwell, he took lodgings at 351 Huron Street. As for the freshettes, Banting was too painfully shy to think of making a date. He was unable to dance. Sometimes, in the throes of bashfulness, he even felt unable to talk. Besides, and this was more important, he was imbued with that earnestness of purpose which his Methodist upbringing and his dedication to the ministry imposed upon him.

But was he really dedicated to the ministry? This question returned to perplex him more and more frequently. He began to feel that he would never be suited to the work. His most engrossing interests lay elsewhere. However, he would wait and see what the year might bring forth. Subconsciously, perhaps, his decision was already made. He had come to Victoria at the instance of his parents. His own inclination, if given free rein, would have taken him at once to the Medical School. But for the time being it was held in check. Would self-control outlast the year? He was not an Ernest Pontifex, coerced into orders against his will. He had made no strenuous protest against his parents' choice. Yet almost at once he began to grow restive.

Coincidentally, Hipwell too was feeling the powerful attraction of the healing art. Their community of interest, the interaction of their consenting minds, disposed the cousins toward the same endeavour. When a pair of boys want to climb a high board fence, one of them "boosts" the other, who in turn reaches a hand to assist his friend, and between them they are very soon over. The metaphysical fence that separated Banting and Hipwell from the shining fields of medicine was after all not very

19

high. They looked at the fence and they looked at each other. Was the outcome really in doubt?

This seems to be the proper place to record the corollary of Banting's rejection of the life of a cleric. He eventually drifted away from the Methodism of his early youth, but the transition occurred gradually and without shock, leaving his inherited ethical code intact. For the greater part of his college life he continued to go to church, partly from habit, and partly, perhaps, from the wish to please his parents. His weekly letter to his mother frequently told of church attendance. How long the more orthodox attitude of his childhood inwardly persisted we can only conjecture.

With faithful regularity, he wrote a letter home every Sunday, a habit he continued for many years. Though carefully preserved by his mother, most of his letters of this period have since been destroyed. They were mostly brief and factual, recording the incidents of his day-to-day existence, but one exception to this rule has survived. It consists of fifteen four-line stanzas of doggerel verse, concluding with the matter-of-fact couplet,

> Time to close and go to bed.
> That's all for now. Yours truly, Fred.

A bashful and distinctly bucolic young man, Banting learned gradually to relish new amusements, particularly the theatre. But this was not enough to explain a mediocre record at Victoria. He had not yet fully made up his mind about his career. Hesitation lasted for a year and a half, while he obtained the standing necessary to enter medicine.

At the beginning of his sophomore year, 1911, initiation was unusually violent. His classmates were merciless to their successors. Six students were fined and President Falconer warned the rest in a letter to the college paper. What part Banting took in these proceedings is rather uncertain. Probably a minor one.

Something more to his taste was the annual "Bob," a festivity so named from the fact that it had always terminated (at least in the original Victoria College at Cobourg) with a collection for

Robert the Janitor. Originally it consisted of a few songs and recitations, but gradually it developed into a more elaborate function in which the freshmen were "intellectually hazed" by the sophomores. The "Bob" had lapsed for a year because of the growth of rowdyism, and the faculty had considered the advisability of banning it. But in 1911 it was taken over by the Union Literary Society and reverted to its original form, consisting of a series of skits (a courtroom scene, where freshmen were "tried" for being fresh, a burlesque of a faculty meeting, etc.) and a selection of songs.

> The boast of scholarship, the speaker's power,
> And all that tends to make a man a snob,
> Awaits alike th' inevitable hour;
> The paths of Freshmen lead but to the Bob.

Banting had a rich and powerful baritone voice, and he promptly found a place for himself in the Vic Glee Club, under the direction of Mr. E. R. Bowles. The Club gave concerts at the College, and in Methodist churches in the city; in February it went on tour. On February 2 the *Varsity* reported: "Members of the Vic Glee Club are smiling broad and happy smiles these days. The annual tour has been announced and all are looking forward to a jolly time." On February 12: "The members of the Glee Club are away. A notice posted at the foot of the stairs ordered them to bring skates, toothbrush, smiles and music." They were off on a five-day tour, visiting Hamilton and St. Catharines. Their success was chronicled by a *Varsity* reporter:

They dropped into Hamilton Friday at 6.00. The concert in the Zion Tabernacle was heard by a large crowd and much appreciated. They took the 2.30 train to St. Kitts on Saturday, and walked into that city as smug and benign as a mission class out for an airing. Saturday night was spent skating on the rink, and getting acquainted with the young ladies of the town. The evening was a huge success. So successful, in fact, that one young man failed to turn up for any of the services on Sunday. . . . The Club sang three times on Sunday. . . . Monday was spent in sight-seeing at the Falls and bobbing. No casualties. A full house heard the Monday evening concert. Tuesday evening was spent in skating with the Hamilton young ladies and playing hockey on Ryerson Rink.

Notwithstanding sporadic amusements such as these Banting's career at Victoria was destined to be dull, and therefore to be short-lived. The curriculum did not interest him. His French was disastrous, his Latin worse. He had already decided that the "angelic conjunction of Medicine with Divinity" (as Cotton Mather called it) was not for him. Medicine alone compelled his attention.

He announced his decision at Easter, refusing the kindly offer of the Rev. A. P. Addison, the Methodist minister of his home-town church, to negotiate for him with his father. His parents, he knew, were reasonable and understanding, and would not try to force him into the ministry when he did not hear the "call." The difficulty was that the longer and more expensive course he had selected would be a very serious drain on their resources. Yet they received his announcement without reproaches. Perhaps they had half expected it. At any rate he returned to the farm for the balance of the year, and all reference to the matter was dropped. In the autumn of 1912, he returned to college, this time to register as a student of medicine. And again he was accompanied by Hipwell.

At the first turning-point in his life, he had taken the right road. "It is an incontrovertible truth," wrote Dean Swift, "that no man ever made an ill figure who understood his own talents, nor a good one who mistook them."

2

The historian of "onety-seven" begins his Chronicle with a note of the pride which characterized his class (and it was, in truth, a remarkable class). He carries the story forward with a rush:

The soft balmy zephyrs of the clear days of the early fall of 1912 conspired with the workings of Destiny to bring out the banner class of the University. We left the plough, counter, ledger, high school book, or little red schoolhouse on the half concession, and wended our several ways to the Mecca of our desires, which turned out to be a plain white brick building in the factory style of architecture. . . . The memories of the first few days are those of frantic searches for rooms ("modern conveniences, moderate rates") . . . the intricacies of the trails to the lecture rooms, the urgent appeals for a leader against the ancient tribe who previously possessed the lands, and a final morning of soft soap, blood, flour, blacking, Soph, Freshie, mud and yells.

Into this joyful fracas stepped Constable Christie, and order was restored. Another quieting influence is represented to the historian's mind by the parallelogram of forces: work had commenced. Knowledge proceeded to unroll her ample page to their somewhat startled eyes and the boys found themselves busy. "We learned to speak guardedly of molecules," writes the historian, "to converse wisely about gastropods . . . and to distinguish the sphenoid and the structures passing through the foramen magnum." He remembers that some paid fines for "weights out of order." Then the glory of onety-seven again breaks forth from the record:

Athletically, we led the way, beating our howling adversaries of the second year in several pitched battles, gory and muddy, working our way through rugby, association and hockey . . . "magno cum laude." Best of all, when the nights of smoke, stale restaurant pie and mutual quizzes had passed away, we emerged into our sophomority, lean and scarred, but still going strong.

In these athletic glories, Banting had his share. His best feats were accomplished in rugby football, in which he played the position then referred to as right scrim. The game as he played it had evolved part way from its original form toward a likeness of present-day rugby, but there were still nine men on the line, and little passing, so that ruggedness was a greater desideratum than speed. Banting at this time weighed close to one hundred and seventy pounds, with no spare flesh, and as a classmate expressed it, "he could look after himself very nicely." Although he never aspired to Varsity rating and confined himself to interyear and interfaculty competition, he was better known as an athlete than as a scholar. His toughness of fibre and tremendous physical endurance were presently to be called upon in grimmer battles overseas, in a war that was still preparing.

In their second year the gladiators of onety-seven outdid themselves, winning eighty-five per cent. of the interfaculty game credits. Across the playing fields of the Toronto campus was heard the gleeful chant,

> We're the Meds of onety-seven,
> We're the best this side of heaven!

They were successful socially too. "Our Hallowe'en dance," says the historian complacently, "was graced by Toronto's fairest (our 'janes') and smoothest (us)." But though Banting was ready for anything in the way of sport, he shied away from dances. Hipwell and Beaumont Cornell and a number of others undertook to improve his education in the amenities, but with poor success. He balked. He was awkward and shy. Besides he was busy. Still, there were interludes of fun, and it was about this time that he began to show his interest in a certain attractive young woman with whom he afterwards had an intermittent romance, "now you see it, now you don't," for many years. Long rambles in the country, occasional theatre dates, occasional parties. His life was not all work; yet it was certainly more stolid than the "norm."

The anatomy of the head and neck had been completed in the first year, together with elementary courses in the basic sciences. The class now continued in anatomy, and added such work-demanding studies as organic chemistry and bacteriology. "We mastered the volutions of the peritoneum with keen discernment," says the angel of the records, "revelled in the vagaries of Ethyldiprophylazoalphoaminobenzene, and also thought in terms of gram-positive and extra-cellular cocci. Was it any wonder, gentle reader, that the masters of our fates with one accord cried, "Enough! Pass on! Show us the next!"

Banting carried along consistently, as he had done in Alliston, somewhere near the middle of the class, or a little above. He was an average, grade-C student. But his mind was now ascending to a new height of interest, and the half-heartedness of his brief career in Arts was over. There were flickering indications that he was not to be typed as a "plodder" and dismissed from notice. When a number of students asked the technician in histology to prepare tissue sections for them, they were advised to "take a tip from this fellow, Banting," who for some time had been preparing his own.

It was not then so common as it has since become for a medical student to possess a microscope, but Banting was one of the more fortunate. He cherished a shining, brass-finished Leitz, purchased through the T. Eaton Co. for $57.50; in the use of this instrument he developed sufficient enthusiasm, and hence sufficient skill, to rank as a good amateur microscopist, especially in the study of the blood. His friends recall that he was forever pricking his finger to make blood films, which he stained in various ways and studied with great care. This led him to further elementary studies in hematology, ranging beyond the requirements of the course.

In the third and fourth years, his partners in physiology and pharmacology found him a shade too energetic. They remember that his interest in experiments far surpassed his interest in food, and that lunch was a matter of small importance when compared with the fascinating results of injecting picrotoxin into a rabbit, or testing the reflexes of the spinal animal. A game of snooker might be suggested as a pleasant noon-hour diversion, but Banting was never deterred. He wound up the kymograph and pithed another frog, or he patiently adjusted the pointers which traced the record of his experiment on smoke-blackened paper. Sorry, but he was much too busy for pool; too busy, on occasion, to take time out for a sandwich. The stimulus of absorption kept him hard at work. He was curious to see what would happen when he painted a nerve ganglion with nicotine and then tickled the proximal end of the nerve with a gentle current. Or he was anxious to get a cannula in place, dissect out the heart, and try to make it behave normally when perfused with Ringer's solution. Time enough to eat when he had finished the experiment.

Banting, like most students, tried a number of different boarding houses. He settled, finally, at 63 Gloucester Street, the home of Mrs. Catherine O'Neil, where he remained until graduation, and to which he returned for a brief stay after the war. He shared a room with an old friend from Alliston, T. S. H. (Sam) Graham, who was a student of mathematics. Fred Hipwell lived next door, at No. 65.

Banting and the O'Neils became fast friends. Mrs. O'Neil was an Irish Catholic, a widow with two daughters. Her home was old-fashioned and comfortable. In the front parlour was a fireplace of green and white tiles with brass andirons, and for many years after he had left the house, the mantel bore a photograph of Banting, flanked by two china figurines in pink and blue pastel. There was sufficient reason for the high regard which Mrs. O'Neil bestowed on him. Her kindliness won him to respond, and he was prolific with ideas for helping her. When he went home to Alliston for a week-end, he always returned to 63 Gloucester Street laden with vegetables from the farm. Mrs. O'Neil was enchanted. "All washed and lovely," she would say, picking the scrubbed carrots from the basket, and her eyes would shine with pleasure.

She was disappointed in him only once—when he took to smoking. The first year he stayed with her, he returned from his Christmas holidays with the cigarette habit. Mrs. O'Neil was saddened. "What did your mother say to you?" she inquired reproachfully. His mother had been disappointed too. She had said: "Is it necessary? Well, if you must, I suppose it's not such a bad vice as some." But Mrs. O'Neil shook her head. She felt it was only right when she heard that Nelson and Thompson Banting had each been presented with a desk on his twenty-first birthday, while Kenneth and Fred, who had taken up smoking, were allowed to pass *their* twenty-first birthdays without this acknowledgment of manhood. The elder Bantings thought so too. They did not relent.

The most important element in Banting's life at this time, as for the next thirty years, was work. Graham in one corner of the room, Banting in another, they laboured night after night, and once the evening's grind was well begun, seldom exchanged a word. Sam studied algebra or calculus. Fred studied anatomy or physiology. The room was quiet with the heavy, ponderable quiet of concentrated thought.

Dr. F. W. W. Hipwell, in the course of a brief memoir of his cousin and friend, has this to say:

Fred considered the study of medicine very seriously. The hours of work were hard and long. Often he took those of us, seemingly more frivolous, to task for our shortcomings. But it was done invariably in that kindly and sincere way of his own, and without rancour. . . . He particularly enjoyed the study of anatomy. I recall his pride in the possession of a three-volume Sabotta McMurrich. When clinical years followed, his determination to practice surgery was well established.

If work, as Osler said, is the master-key to medicine, then Banting always had the key.

But fun had its place as well. One evening when Graham was out on an errand, Banting and Anna O'Neil hatched a plot. They bundled up a pillow and some old clothes and put them under the coverlet on Sam's bed. Then they arranged a blonde wig on his pillow, with the pigtail lying across one "shoulder" of the dummy. Anna put a dress on one of the chairs and a pair of high-heeled shoes under the edge of the bed. They shaded the light and withdrew to the parlour. When Sam returned from his errand, Banting was buried in a newspaper, Anna and her mother were busy with their sewing. Sam remarked that it looked like a thaw outside, and went off to his room to study. He was back again in a moment.

"Mrs. O'Neil," he said in a low tone, "there's someone in my room. There's a *woman*, Mrs. O'Neil. She's asleep in my bed." And while Fred and Anna bit their tongues and said nothing, the amazed Mrs. O'Neil, who was not a party to the plot, hurried off upstairs to investigate. Banting's laughter was huge and robust and infectious; we may imagine that the success of this Tom Brown joke sent it echoing through the house.

They tell another story about him. *Si non e vero. . . .* It seems that he was walking one day along Queen Street, when he noticed smoke issuing from a second-floor window above a store on the opposite side. He dashed across the street and into the store, located the stairway, and with no by-your-leave, bounded lightly upstairs to the bed-sitting-room above, where he snatched a blazing curtain from the window, dropped it on the floor, and smothered the fire with a quilt from the bed. To the astonished mistress of the house and store, who came panting upstairs after him, he explained what he had done, and gravely apologized for possible damage to the quilt. It is not unlikely that this story has an element of truth. One would like to believe that it is true.

3

The teaching staff of the medical school and the associated hospitals was a brilliant one. Banting, like his fellow students, drank at many fountains. They studied biology under the direction of Professor Bensley; they essayed inorganic chemistry with the aid of Professor Lang, who was "trade-marked" by immaculate spats and the habit of slowly scratching his ruddy countenance with one long finger as he talked; they listened with attention to the sprightly lectures of Professor (afterwards Sir John) McLennan, who taught them physics.

For Banting's choice, the most memorable of his pre-clinical teachers was J. Playfair McMurrich. (Was this preference the cause or the effect of his particular liking for anatomy?) The learned anatomist, tranquil and dignified, talked of the structures of the human body and their mutual relationships with an easy-paced manner, a thoughtful deliberation, that projected on the student's mind an unmistakable image; rather it seemed like a three-dimensional fact, a tangible possession. The professor not only expounded the facts of anatomy, but reasoned anatomically. And from the depths of an astonishing erudition, he drew the passages of medical history which so often embellished his lectures. He was distinguished also as an author and editor (*Leonardo da Vinci the Anatomist,* Sobotta's *Atlas and Textbook of Human Anatomy,* etc.).

A. B. McCallum, professor of biochemistry, was such an assiduous worker that the students supposed him to live in the medical school: he was seldom seen elsewhere. A prophet unawares, he once suggested, while lecturing to the class of seventeen, that the secret of the body's ability to utilize sugar was probably to be found in the islets of Langerhans in the pancreas, and that perhaps a member of the class might some day discover that secret, to the glory of himself and onety-seven. This oddly intuitive remark was perhaps elaborated or repeated, for several of Banting's classmates afterwards recollected most distinctly how the professor had "called the play." No doubt he made the same suggestion to other classes, little foreseeing the ultimate event.

James McKenzie was professor of pathology, Irving Cameron

of surgery, and Alexander McPhedran of medicine. Duncan Graham, who afterwards succeeded to the chair of medicine, was at this time teaching bacteriology. Velyien Henderson was professor of pharmacology. B. P. Watson headed the department of obstetrics and gynæcology.[1] George W. Ross, an intimate friend of Banting's in later years, taught therapeutics. But although Banting would afterwards mention some half dozen names with resurgent pleasure, only one man inspired in him the whole-hearted admiration of the disciple. This pre-eminent teacher, Banting's counsellor and friend through many years, was Clarence Leslie Starr, the then Surgeon-in-Chief of the Hospital for Sick Children. And since a man incontinently reveals the bias of his mind and the aim of his spirit in his selection of a hero, it will be well to pause at the shrine. Other men have had several heroes, often strangely unlike, but Banting, in this important formative period, had only one.

Starr was the son of a country doctor, and from his earliest childhood was keenly interested in the treatment of the sick. The experience of these early years left a deep impression on him which showed itself constantly in his attitude towards patients and in the ideals which he endeavoured to inculcate in his students.

He was graduated with honours from the Medical School in Toronto in 1890. He then spent a year and a half as house-surgeon at the Hospital for Ruptured and Crippled in New York under the tutelage of Wm. T. Bull and Virgil P. Gibney. During this period he received the degree of M.D. at Bellevue Hospital Medical School. From New York he went to England and Germany where he studied with Howard Marsh, D'Arcy Power, John Caird, and Hoffa.

Upon his return to Toronto in 1894 he was appointed to the staffs of the General Hospital and the Hospital for Sick Children. In the former he engaged in general surgery but in the latter he limited himself at first to the surgery of deformities.

In 1911 he was appointed Surgeon-in-Chief at the Hospital for Sick Children and was given the task of re-organizing the surgical staff. This gave him his first opportunity to demonstrate his remarkable ability as an organizer and administrator. By slow degrees he surrounded himself with young men, trained in

[1]Afterwards Professor of Obstetrics and Gynæcology at Columbia University.

both general and orthopædic surgery, each of whom he considered
capable of suceeding ultimately to the post of surgeon-in-chief.
He had no patience with a system which, for the sake of getting
the day's work done, fills hospital appointments with men of poor
abilities who cannot be expected to compete for ultimate advancement.   Such a high standard means, of course, that the staff
must be small and probably work very hard, but for young men
he considered this no disadvantage.[2]

Banting eventually served an interneship at the Sick Children's but meantime he encountered Dr. Starr in the rôle of a
clinical teacher of surgery.   As a teacher, Starr was superb.   He
was of the type that wins the limitless admiration of its juniors.
He had none of the grudging intellectual pride that engenders a
fearful wariness in students, but displayed, on the contrary, a rare
gift for arousing in them a consuming love of their art.   His mind
was clear, practical, and penetrating.   He was all but universally
loved for his infinite willingness and broad humanity.   A keen
diagnostician and a master surgeon, he was also an articulate and
genial instructor.
    Banting's choice of orthopædic surgery as the field of his
special interest was probably inspired, and certainly confirmed,
by his association with Starr, who appears to have taken a particular liking to this burly, assiduous student with the earnest
desire to learn.   The master's professional dignity was qualified
by an engaging twinkle and a ready smile.   Under his stimulating
influence, Banting's interest in surgery took root and fructified;
he was beginning to find himself in the medical scheme of things,
beginning to picture his future.   Dr. Starr was his pattern of
professional conduct, his mentor in the surgical art, and through
the tangle of subsequent perplexities, a wise and faithful friend.
That Starr should be drawn so strongly to the younger man is
evidence not only of his kindliness but also of his fine discernment, for he was impatient of mediocrity and Banting was not
numbered among the upper ten in academic honours.   But Starr
was not deceived.   He was justified of his faith.

[2]*The Journal of Bone and Joint Surgery*, 11: 406-407.

W. T. BANTING FAMILY GROUP WHEN FRED WAS ABOUT FIVE YEARS OF AGE

KENNETH BANTING   NELSON BANTING   THOMPSON BANTING

MR. W. T. BANTING   MRS. W. T. BANTING   FREDERICK BANTING

ESTHER BANTING

4

While work had been proceeding in its usual round, an ominous shadow had stolen over the world, and over the green lawns of Toronto's campus. Suddenly the citizens of the world's democracies looked up, in horror and surprise, to see the magnitude and realize the menace of the warlike power that stood over them.

"Our third year opened," writes the class historian, "under a strain and shadow. Exponents of a barbaric philosophy had turned the world into a shambles." The first World War had begun.

It is interesting to see, in turning over the pages of the *Varsity*, in the year preceding the war, how earnestly the problems of statecraft and foreign relations were debated. A Toronto graduate of the class of ninety-one, the late Professor Stephen Leacock of McGill, afterwards wrote of his own college days that

> Empire had no further reach
> Than to round out an after-dinner speech,
> Or make material from which John A.
> Addressed us on our Convocation Day.

If the pages of the college paper may be taken as a fair indication, Empire was a livelier issue in 1913 and the first half of 1914, perhaps because the reality of the threat to its existence was vaguely and uneasily realized. In December, 1913, Sir Wilfrid Laurier, at a dinner in Convocation Hall, declared, "Europe is a war camp!" and warned of the danger to democracy. But the air was full of warnings, and University students, like other citizens, preferred, on the whole, to think of pleasanter things. There was, however, an element in the student body concerned to deprecate what they considered to be "jingoistic imperialism" and the Toronto *Mail and Empire* accused the University of fostering sedition, a charge which was hotly denied. The cause of the *Mail's* editorial excitement was the International Polity Club, devoted to pacifism, which met in January to discuss the British Liberal revolt against increased armament expenditure, a movement the Club members strongly endorsed. Also the

Varsity had solemnly declared: "Patriotism . . . is little more than the petty prejudice of a primitive mind."

On the other side of the picture, there were discussions of "the obligation of University men to serve the state in proportion as the state has served them"; Sir John Willison and Mr. N. W. Rowell (afterwards Mr. Justice Rowell) treated the Polity Club to a broader view of imperial relations; in the March elections at University College, the "Conservative Party" urged the formation of an Officer's Training Corps. But the unquenchable student editorialist airily observed: "Patriotism . . . is emotional humbug."

The turn of events was soon to show that all of this supposedly "seditious talk" was merely the spindrift of restless minds, and that patriotism, as a valid and compelling motive, was no less vigorous in the University than in the country at large. The callow editorial writer, amazingly transfigured, was seen on the lawn of University College in the King's uniform, stoutly shouldering a rifle. The same sort of talk had been heard at Oxford and Cambridge. It was a symptom of the disordered times, and was hushed by the first touch of reality. "The Divine Irony," wrote Professor Maurice Hutton, "had smiled on our pacifism; fed it, encouraged it, until we were certain of it, and then in a moment taken it all away, and left us with a sense only of our utter blindness and our inordinate capacity of self-deception."

The outbreak of war transformed the life of the campus. The construction of Hart House was suspended. Courses were accelerated. From four to six, squads of students were rigidly drilled, most of them unfortunately, without arms. The historian of onety-seven wrote: "Awkward squads, and shrill-voiced officers, serious with their new honours, encountered one on every side." From the *Varsity*, Wednesday, September 30: "Professors De Champ, Balbaudand and Bibet will be absent this session, as they have joined their colours and are now at the front." Again from the historian: "Several of our boys left us at the sound of the first bugle. Owen, McKeough, Wigle, Price, McLinton and others we have never seen since. . . . Groups of men were slipping away silently day by day and returning in khaki. The map of Europe with battling armies would be visualized involuntarily at lectures or lab. We saw No. 2 Casualty Clearing Station manned entirely by the best of our seniors, and bade good-bye to over twenty of our own class before spring. The Base Hospital was organized, and took away dozens of our most capable clinicians and associates."

Again from the *Varsity*, Wednesday, September 30:

There is about to be organized in the University of Toronto a Canadian Officers' Training Corps. . . . Pending the granting of authority by the Militia Department for the organization of the Corps, the Rifle Association has handed over its entire equipment and machinery for the enrolling and drilling of the students. Thus it is hoped that, when the formal organization takes place, there will be at least nine or ten companies already virtually organized. . . .

A number of the younger men on the University staff are now drilling every day, with a view to qualifying as instructors, and around them have rallied quite a considerable body of students, who expect also to become instructors or non-commissioned officers.

One of these students was Banting. He had been restrained with difficulty from joining the C.E.F. as a private of infantry. He was working against the collar, for he wished to be off to the wars. The best he could do at the moment was to become a drill sergeant. An extremely tough sergeant he became, and meanwhile he threw himself upon his studies with augmented energy.

In the spring of 1915 he worked for a time as a dresser in the camp at Exhibition Park, succeeding his friend, Gordon Cameron, who had gone overseas. There he performed his first surgical operation, using his scalpel by special permission on a severe case of quinsy, but only with great trepidation and after anxious study of the pertinent page in Foote's *Minor Operations*. The result was satisfactory.

In the summer he accompanied the rest of the C.O.T.C. for training exercises at Niagara. "At the close of a shortened term," says the historian, "we signed several yards of official-looking documents, filled our water bottles, rolled our greatcoats à la Hipwell, boarded the *Cayuga*, and had a strenuous two weeks at Niagara Camp. Our lines were daily inspected by such notables as Edis and Shorten, while McTavish made good at the mess tent. 'Soda' was everywhere in evidence, and his warlike chest

and guttural accents steeled our nerves in ferocious charges, and
made our shooting the standard in the camp. Hardened by such
manœuvres, shining from frequent inspections . . . we were
received back home with great applause."

The man among his seniors at Niagara whom Banting particularly admired, and one of the few with whom he later became
intimate, was Colonel T. B. Richardson. Among other interests
they shared was a liking for amateur carpentry and cabinet-
making. Richardson made Banting a present of a chair of his
own manufacture, and possibly the younger man's enthusiasm for
such work, for which, however, he was to have little time for
many years, dated from this association. In 1935, Colonel
Richardson, looking back at the old camp, recited his versified
"Homage" to Banting at a public dinner, beginning with the
stanza:

>Across a vale of twenty years
>A youth of stalwart mien, intent,
>At old Fort George anon appears
>Staff-Sergeant, there on duty bent.

Duty took him back again to Toronto. "Our military life still
persisted in our senior year, and received great stimulus from our
comrades who returned from the front, late in the year, to finish
their course." C. A. Rae, J. S. Crawford, E. A. Broughton, R. M.
Harvie, and a dozen others resumed their studies after nearly a
year of active service. Crawford had gone overseas with the
First Canadian Contingent, and passed unscathed through Ypres,
Festubert and Givenchy. Broughton and Harvie had spent the
winter of 1915-16 in the "University of Salonica" (a base hospital) in Greece. But there were others who did not return.
Major W. S. McKeough, who enlisted as a lieutenant with the
18th Battalion and won rapid promotion, was killed in the Somme
offensive. Lieutenant Harold H. Owen died while covering
the retreat of his men, the remnant of a shattered platoon. Wigle,
Price, McLinton and others never rejoined the class.

The pace was now accelerated still more. The fourth year
was finished at the end of April, 1916, and fifth year work was
commenced on the first day of May. After a short respite in
July, a special military summer session speeded the class toward
graduation through August days which the historian describes

as "long, glaring and breathless." Though every effort was made to prevent curtailment of any part of the work, the diary of a member of onety-seven records a rather meagre number of classes. Busy surgeons and internists sometimes failed to appear at their appointed times, and the gaps in the ranks of the teaching staff were not always easy to fill. Somehow the class contrived to learn what their examiners expected them to know, and passed examinations of the usual difficulty with more than the usual credit.

On December 4, the final "results" were ready in the office. Hipwell borrowed an automobile, and with half a dozen others, including Banting, drove down with impatient speed for an interview with Miss Jamieson, the Secretary. The reports were satisfactory—more than satisfactory—and the long grind was over.

"Congratulations, doctor!"

"Congratulations!"

It is not difficult to imagine their elation, their sense of relief, their pride, and above all, their eagerness to get on with the job for which every one of them had been preparing. Of the seventy-two members of the class, four were women, and two of the men were not physically fit for the service. The remaining sixty-six joined the armed forces at once. The Class of Seventeen, though soon to be scattered to the four winds, remained unified in spirit: so far as lay in the power of its members, the "gang" was intact. By courtesy of the College of Physicians and Surgeons of Ontario, the graduates were enabled to take the Council Examinations before Christmas, and proceed immediately to their military duties.

The class was separating. Sadly the historian wrote:

No more will we see "Jeff" with his hairy band of Profs. do a "Hielan' fling" on Daffydil Night. Vitch, "Fin," "Happy," Reddick, Thompson and dozens of others will juggle dances no more. Fuller is through arguing medicine. Tommy White's sparkling epigrams and anecdotes are already falling on other ears.

Banting was one of the first to join. He enlisted on December 5, 1916, as a lieutenant in the Canadian Army Medical Corps. During his four years at the Medical School, his habits had been neither very solitary nor very gregarious. He had made some good friends: Cecil Rae, Gordon Cameron, "Archie" Wells, "Scotty" McKay, Beaumont Cornell, and perhaps as many more. He had played hard and worked harder. Academically, he had not distinguished himself, but the foundation so laboriously laid proved firm and enduring.

The stage now darkened. The coming act, more lurid and more violent, would prove his qualities the more conclusively.

PART III

The First Campaign: 1916-1919

Shall the Earth
Remain the gainer for the centuries
Of toilsome groping upward—Justify
Him, who created? Shall Democracy,
Gazing men frank and fearless in the eyes,
Still lead her peaceful cohorts down the years
To ever widening freedom? Shall our Chiefs
Be Prophets, Sages, Servers of their kind—
'Gainst pestilence and ignorance our wars—
Our meed of victory—the Common Good?
Or shall the shadow of the Iron Hand
Blacken the Earth? Shall Medieval night
Engulf our dawn—Torn from a Lister's hand
The knife goes back to Cain! Shall all we piled,
Stone after stone for painful centuries
Fall crashing into chaos, while the guns
Roar sullen requiem?

From a poem entitled "Neutral," written by Laura Carter in August, 1914, and widely reprinted. This poem was a favourite with Banting, who subsequently met the author, daughter of General Carter of yellow fever fame, during a visit to Jamaica in 1924.

1

THE USUAL PERIOD of officer training followed enlistment. It was unexciting but necessary, and probably a welcome change from academic life. This interval was brief. Medical officers were needed overseas, and infantry drill and administrative procedures were learned in short order.

His embarkation leave was something of an ordeal for Banting, who hated farewells and fought shy of emotional demonstrations. He paused to see friends in Toronto and dropped in on Mrs. O'Neil, who was of course delighted beyond measure. The old lady urged him to cut short his stay in the city and hurry on to Alliston, that not a moment of the last days with his family might be lost. Happy days they must have been, despite the shadow of farewells and the atmosphere of tension, of dissembled sadness and assumed jocularity, which such occasions provoke. Did he find time for a cross-country ramble, for a look at the quiet face of the Boyne? Did he notice again, with altered interest, the things he had been accustomed to see since childhood? The aspect of the house, the fields, the road to town. People he knew on the street with words and ways he remembered. Hipwell's drugstore with its stirrup-shaped sign over the door. The Windsor Hotel, with its second-storey bay window and its queer, triangular dormers. Latimer's carriage works at the corner of Paris Street, with its weather-smeared notice, "Tires set, hot or cold." What were his thoughts as he stood on the station platform and waited for the train which should carry him away to undreamed-of adventures, perhaps to death?

His ship cleared from Quebec early in the year but before it put to sea in good earnest for a crossing there was a long delay at Campbellton, New Brunswick. In this town on the south bank of the Restigouche River at the head of deep water navigation, with the picturesque Sugar Loaf Mountain looming behind it, units of the C.A.M.C. and a heavy siege battery from London and Guelph arrived on February 26, 1917, to take up barracks. Through an oversight on the part of the authorities, no word of their coming had been given and no arrangements had been made for food. Local citizens fed their hungry visitors and many of the men were housed in Campbellton homes. The interlude in Campbellton was prolonged for many weeks, and Banting had an opportunity to see a part of Canada he had never before visited.

When the ocean journey was eventually resumed, it was uneventful. No submarines were encountered and the weather was forbearing. Just as the convoy steamed into the mouth of the Mersey, however, one of the ships struck a submerged object with a most sickening jolt and tremor, and there was a momentary fear that the waters were mined. Nothing happened; no mines were discovered; and the ships continued safely to their anchorage.

Banting's first destination was the C.A.M.C. depot at Westenhanger, in Kent. From there he was ordered to The Granville Canadian Special Hospital at Ramsgate. This was a stroke of luck. His ambition in life was to become a surgeon, specifically an orthopædic surgeon, and the fates now dropped him with obliging acquiescence square in the middle of a rich field of surgical effort.

It is difficult to assign a date to the establishment of the Canadian orthopædic centre, as the special kind of work therein performed developed gradually in various places. A special hospital for orthopædic cases was opened at Ramsgate, November 15, 1915, with Lieutenant-Colonel W. L. Watt in command, but it was devoted rather to treatment which afterwards became more peculiar to convalescent camps and command depots. It was only after its removal to Buxton in October, 1917, with Lieutenant-Colonel J. T. Clarke still in command, that orthopædic work was especially developed.[1]

Colonel Murray MacLaren was in command of this hospital during Banting's residency, while Colonel E. C. Hart was A.D.M.S. of the district of Buxton. Probably the most distinguished member of the staff, at any rate in retrospect, was W. E. Gallie, destined to succeed eventually to the chair of surgery at Toronto, where he followed C. L. Starr. A brilliant and ingenious surgeon, he became famous for his "living suture" operation for the repair of hernias, an operation performed with special instruments of

---

[1] *The Medical Services* (official history of The Canadian Forces in The Great War, 1914-19) by Sir Andrew Macphail. Ottawa, 1925.

his own design. His chief characteristics—suavity, acumen, tremendous industry and a generous interest in his staff—had the effect of inspiring those around him with his own perseverance and dispassionate zeal.

Banting worked hard at Buxton, studying with characteristic diligence, while friends who were less persevering, or less ambitious, spent their leisure in excursions into the English countryside and to near-by centres starred by Baedecker. Dr. W. W. Barraclough, a classmate who was also stationed at Buxton, remembers as Banting's only extravagance his collector's fondness for English china, which took him to all the china shops within reach and sometimes used up his spare cash disastrously. An odd hobby for a bachelor. But paradoxically his chief diversion was study. He was preparing himself with dogged energy for the examinations of the Conjoint Board; success at these examinations would entitle him to the degrees of M.R.C.S. and L.R.C.P., honours much to be coveted by the rising surgeon. This praiseworthy endeavour, an uncommon mark of ambition at any time and a very unusual undertaking for a young soldier, was seconded by the teaching efforts of his seniors, especially Gallie, who even contrived to provide him with subjects for dissection. Another classmate of Banting's at The Granville Special Hospital, Dr. E. H. Hutchinson, has vivid recollections of Gallie's remarkable willingness to go out of his way to be helpful to the novitiates, and of how his untiring zeal proved a constant and restoring stimulus. Between the stimulus and the response, in so far as Banting was concerned, no shadow fell. His strength kept pace with his purpose. As for diversions, he was little beguiled. The fact that he had become engaged before proceeding overseas helped to keep him "in line"; perhaps it accounted also for his interest in English china.

Despite unsurpassed opportunities for learning the basis and rationale of surgery and for assisting at operations, Banting was not wholly content. He was not, for one thing, much charmed with his location. ("I had rather be a lamp-post in Folkestone than Mayor of Buxton," he wrote.) For another, he was anxious to get into action. As a young man of fighting age he felt that he ought to be in France.

The opportunity soon came. He went over to France with the 13th Field Ambulance. And now at last he was in the thick of

it. He was ministering to the wounded, easing the pangs of the
dying. Whether or not such experience in front-line surgery is
good training for the surgeon is a question by no means closed
to doubt. Harvey Cushing has expressed the opinion that the
speed which is often necessitated by pressure of work and unfavourable circumstances tends inevitably to produce careless work.
Life is despairingly cheap and death is ever present however well
the work be done, and the atmosphere is therefore unlikely to
generate that watchful solicitude which is seen in times of peace.
Scrupulous niceties of technique are often impossible. This in
itself constitutes a challenge to the conscientious medical officer;
without the resources of a well-equipped hospital to back his
efforts, he must frequently rely on self-discovered ingenuity. Without consultants, pressed for time, for basic necessities, for life
itself, he must learn to trust his own judgment, to do what he
feels must be done, and to do it quickly. He must find within
himself the powers and conclusions to make good the deficiency.
Whatever it may offer to the surgeon, and there is reason to
think that it provides him, in some respects at least, an opportunity unparalleled in peace, such an experience is a profound
and terrible one for the human, an education in pity, in fortitude,
and in decision.

Banting's training had been good, but when better trained
and far more experienced men were often hard put to it to know
what to do, he felt less than completely confident; felt, indeed,
like the great Ambrose Paré on his first campaign, "a fresh-water
surgeon." But his native capacities were more than adequate
and his will to succeed, to do his work well, was irreproachable.
The advice which he wrote many years afterwards, to his son,
William, took the form of a precept which he strove always to
observe himself: "Never leave a job half-done."

There are many men living today in Canada, veterans of the
Canadian Army Overseas, who bear witness to his skill. One
of them, whose leg Banting amputated in France, is now a technician in The Banting Institute in Toronto. There are others
who owe to his judgment and courage limbs that were not amputated. In this respect he was both conservative and daring;
conservative in the literal sense of refusal to amputate, daring
in the assumption of the risk involved. Seldom was his judgment
at fault. As an orthopædist, he was a credit to his teachers. As

an orthopædist, he saved his own arm from the saw and prevented the abrupt termination of his career. But that is another story.

The tales that are told of Banting's wartime adventures are numerous and mostly apocryphal. For instance, it has frequently been asserted in the newspapers that he won the Military Cross for cleaning out a machine-gun nest single-handed, and an assortment of picturesque details has been added to embellish the story. The fact is that he once walked coolly into an enemy dugout, armed with nothing more deadly than a swagger stick, and emerged with three German prisoners. This seems to be the basis of the story of the captured machine-gun nest.

He was accompanied on this occasion, as on most others, by his devoted batman, a British Columbian named Kels, who considered his job, despite its dangers, "the cushiest job in the war," since it entailed little marching. He was a courageous and hard-working soldier whom Banting held in affectionate regard, and they served together during the greater part of Banting's career in France. Many are the tales which Banting would tell in after years of the valour and ingenuity of the batman. Of how Kels could always manage to find somewhere the things which no one else could find—essential items of equipment said to be out of stock, small luxuries hard to obtain under the chaotic conditions of warfare—as well as many clever makeshifts and substitutes. Of how Kels once surprised the party by serving mushrooms with the bully beef, mushrooms which he had picked in the battle area, of how Kels would appear, disappear and reappear, always in the right place at the right moment, always ready for emergencies, always cool under fire.

Then there was the occasion when they moved to a new site, formerly occupied by the enemy, and Banting forbade them the use of a well in the vicinity, fearing that it might be poisoned. He went away to attend to something else and found on his return that Kels had lined up a trio of captured "Jerries," whom he had found lurking near by.

"I think you'll find that well is all right, sir," said Kels with assurance.

"How come?" asked Banting.

"Because," explained Kels, nonchalantly brandishing a pistol, "because I made every one of them drink at least a quart of the water."

"You see what I mean," Banting would say in relating this story. "There was only one Kels. Just one."

When the Germans were driven out of their trenches north of the Canal du Nord, the 13th took over some of their dugouts for dressing stations. Each dugout had two doors, the one in front protected by a parapet, the one in the rear more exposed. Since the fighting had now moved on beyond the dugouts, the doors were the wrong way about. One night, when the duel of the big guns was raging, Major L. C. Palmer and Banting were standing in one of those unprotected doorways, watching the fireworks, when a runner dog, a large German shepherd, came trotting up, probably looking for its master who had formerly occupied the diggings. Such a dog was always a difficult brute to handle, for it had been trained to permit the approach of no one except its master. When it saw the two strangers in the doorway, it squared its legs, drew back its lips from gleaming teeth, and commenced a steady growl. Palmer reached for his revolver, but the dog was too quick for him. It slipped past his legs and into the dugout. There were standing orders to kill or if possible to capture these dogs because of the messages they carried, and the two men followed it down.

The day had been hot and sultry. The dog stood in a corner of the dugout which was lit by a flickering candle; the poor beast was fierce and menacing still, its hackle erect and its muscles tensed, but it was panting and evidently distressed. The dugout contained a supply of bottled water, and keeping a sharp eye on the dog, Major Palmer picked a bottle from a wicker panier, and poured a part of the contents on the floor. The dog came forward cautiously and lapped it up.

Palmer and Banting then went back to the top of the steps to watch the shooting and breathe the evening air. Presently the dog joined them and stood quietly beside them. Suddenly, like a thing demented, it uttered a piercing and terrible yell and hurled itself down the steps. A moment later, as they turned to look down, a large shell, which neither of them had heard in the air, exploded directly in front of them. A part of the trench was caved in and the men were thrown to the ground, thoroughly frightened but by a lucky freak of fate quite unhurt.

A shellburst, even so close a call as this, was hardly a novelty. They agreed, with some chagrin, that the sudden cry of the dog had been more startling than the explosion. Next day the Intelligence sent men to rope the animal, and two of the gallant officers of the 13th were glad to see the last of it.

Banting was presently transferred to the 44th Battalion, and the official history of the unit contains the following paragraph:

Captain F. G. Banting, Medical Officer of the 44th, goes forward with the attack—and, with his medical detail, establishes the first dressing station in Drury Quarry. His work is beyond praise. Pressing into service a captured German medical detail he works incessantly throughout the operations—clearing hundreds of wounded in addition to the men of his own unit. He is recommended for the Military Cross in recognition of his services with the unit.[2]

This remarkable feat, often recounted, is thus vouched for officially. Banting performed prodigies of valour and endurance, an omnipresent fury of whirlwind energy. "Have you seen Condé?" somone asked Turenne at the close of a battle. "I must have seen a dozen Condés," was the reply, "he multiplies himself." So with Banting. He was everywhere. He never rested. So long as a wounded man remained on the field he could not let himself stop. On this and like occasions he was a grim taskmaster, but no one of his men worked harder than he.

If, however, the recommendation for a Military Cross was actually made at this time, it apparently was not approved. In any case, the feat for which his decoration was awarded was of later date.

At Quatre Vends, in 1917, Banting rejoined the 13th Field Ambulance, commanded by Lieutenant-Colonel W. H. K. Anderson. His immediate superior was the second-in-command, Major (now Lieutenant-Colonel) L. C. Palmer, an able surgeon with whom he was later associated in the first case of diabetic gangrene to be treated successfully by a combination of insulin injections and surgery.

But that was still hidden in the future, and the surgery of aid posts and dressing stations had few refinements and many difficulties. The autobiographies of country doctors are full of

[2]Six thousand Canadian men, being the history of the 44th Battalion Canadian Infantry, 1914-19.

stories of "kitchen surgery"; of how intricate and dangerous operations have been performed at short notice, with a minimum of equipment, yet carried off triumphantly. But the working conditions of the M.O's in France and Flanders were often infinitely worse than anything that can be imagined in the most squalid farm community. A Regimental Aid Post (R.A.P.) was established in the most convenient position close to the line. John McCrae, a Canadian M.O. who won lasting fame as the author of the universally quoted "In Flanders Fields," worked at a post so close to the fire that wounded soldiers occasionally tumbled at his feet. Dressing stations were sometimes not much better. A farmhouse, a barn, even a dugout might be transformed into some semblance of an operating theatre. By daylight when possible, by any lamp available, often a smoky lantern, when the uneasy darkness fell, these men fought an intense and unceasing battle against injury, disease and death. They were constantly exposed to the danger of enemy action. Battle casualties in the medical corps were higher than in any other arm of the service. They worked for long hours without rest. Yet the quality of their work was such that neither the voluntary recruiting system, nor even the draft, brought as many men to the trenches as were returned to them again, after injury or sickness, by the Medical Corps.

The fire of heavy guns kept the harassed soldiers forever watchful. The long whistle of a shell would certainly end with an explosion (except for the occasional "dud") but would the explosion be an "overhead," in which case one should remain standing, or a "ground burst," when it was better to lie flat? The 13th had an Italian stretcher bearer named Joe, who possessed the rare and enviable ability to distinguish the two types of shell by the sound they made in their trajectory. When a shell signalled its coming, therefore, Joe laconically translated its message for his comrades close at hand, who acted accordingly. This remarkable man, who had joined the 13th with his brother Lucille in British Columbia, where the unit was formed, had another peculiar distinction: he had been awarded two D.C.M's in a single day, one the Distinguished Conduct Medal, the other a District Court Martial.

In the entire unit there was only one man who never acquired the listening attitude which characterizes the front-line soldier.

Courtesy Mrs.
Catherine O'Neil.

Courtesy Mr. Thompson Banting.

Above: SERGEANT BANTING AND THREE COMPANIONS IN THE C.O.T.C.
Left to right: F. G. BANTING, C. E. WILSON, F. W. W. HIPWELL,
T. S. H. GRAHAM.

Centre: AS A MEDICAL STUDENT.

Below: ON GRADUATION FROM HIGH SCHOOL.

One day when the Germans were giving the Canadian lines a "blacksmithing," Major Palmer observed with amazement that his latest junior officer was sitting in a trench, apparently oblivious to the cannonade, reading a book. On nearer approach, he saw, with increased surprise, that Banting was engrossed in a pocket manual of anatomy. Although he saw frequent repetitions of this episode in the days that followed, he never quite became accustomed to the sight. Studying under fire was a "new one."

In the intervals of active duty, when the unit was not in an advanced position, Banting endeared himself to his comrades in the ranks by joining in their soccer games, and the young man of Alliston upheld the honour of Ontario among the boys from B.C. He was instrumental in obtaining equipment for volleyball, and the agile bearers took to the game with zest.

Early in the autumn of 1918 the battle was carried to the enemy with increasing power and determination. Allied forces were poised to strike and the Second Battle of Cambrai, begining toward the end of September, was one of the crucial actions of the War.

Zero hour on the 27th of September was 5.20 a.m., when the barrage opened and the troops went forward to the attack. . . .

The 4th Canadian Division made the attack on the right, with the 44th and 46th Battalions, while the other two battalions of the brigade, the 50th and 47th, were in close support and ready to push through. The bearers of No. 13 Field Ambulance worked with this brigade with squads detailed to each battalion, while the motor and horsed ambulances rendezvoused on the Pronville-Inchy road . . . immediately the troops went forward. (Banting was detailed for a time, as we shall see, to the 44th Battalion.)

. . . The first wounded were cleared through a collecting post in the last end of Inchy . . . to which point ambulance cars got through quite early in the morning, and cleared to Quéant by the Pronville road. By 10 a.m. the 11th and 12th Brigades had passed forward accompanied by their respective field ambulance bearer parties, and at this time No. 13 Field Ambulance in charge of the collecting post at Inchy, moved forward to Quarry Wood. . . .

Owing to the deep penetration effected on the left front of the Corps by the 11th (British) and the 1st Canadian Divisions, attempts to push forward there on the 28th were checked by flanking fire; on the right the 3rd and 4th Canadian Divisions attacked at 6 a.m. in conjunction with the XVII Corps. . . .

The 4th Canadian Division, on the 28th, employed the 10th Brigade on a two battalion front, the 50th and 47th going in first, and the 46th and 44th continuing the advance later in the day. No. 13 Field Ambulance bearers were clearing, and during the early part of the day made use of the medical posts established the evening before. Thus wounded were evacuated by horsed ambulance and wheeled stretcher from the forward area to the Quarry just west of Bourlon village, where they were taken over by motor car and lorry. In the afternoon, as the battalions had pushed north-east of the main road, a clearing post was established in Lilac Farm . . . from which point motor ambulances and lorries cleared towards evening, taking the wounded out by way of the main road to just east of Marquion, then south to Inchy. On this front during the day casualties were quite heavy, but by the early part of the night the wounded were all out. Several casualties occurred among the C.A.M.C. personnel; one ambulance wagon was destroyed and the driver killed by shell-fire.[3]

Major Palmer, with Banting and several other junior officers, operated the clearing post (actually it was a dressing station) at Lilac farm, which was not far distant from Cambrai, still in enemy hands. As Colonel Snell has stated there were several casualties among the C.A.M.C. personnel, with the result that Palmer and Banting soon found themselves the only officers at the station. With the aid of a number of very competent sergeants they continued the work. Their station was a partly wrecked barn, and in the centre of the barnyard a misguided artillery officer had set up an 18-pounder, which was firing over the ridge pole at the Germans, who were then in retreat. The fire was apparently effective. At any rate, the enemy determined to put the gun out of action. The A.D.S. drew a hornet's nest about their ears and shells at once began to fall in the vicinity, to the alarm not only of the Canadians but of a number of

[3]A. E. Snell, C.M.G., D.S.O., B.A., M.B., Colonel, R.C.A.M.C., *The C.A.M.C. With the Canadian Corps During the Last Hundred Days of the Great War*, published by authority of the Hon. E. M. Macdonald, Minister of National Defence, Ottawa, 1924; p. 163; pp. 166-167; p. 169; p. 171.

German prisoners who were being held in the farmhouse adjoining.[4] The Germans were using "whiz-bangs," so called because there was no premonitory whistle before the explosion, only a whiz and a bang, and if the shell scored a hit, more work for the survivors. Even Joe, with his uncanny ability at gauging the ways of gunfire, was baffled by the "whiz-bang."

The first shell to do damage landed squarely in the yard at the moment when a German major happened to be standing on the back steps of the farmhouse. A piece of shrapnel caught him under the chin, and when the firing was over it was discovered that the unhappy major had been neatly and horribly beheaded. Another fragment from the same shell wounded Banting on the outer side of the right forearm. The enemy had a battery of four guns, and everyone at Lilac Farm ducked for whatever cover he could find until the other three shells had landed. Then they emerged to survey the harm and succour the casualties.

In the shelter of a brick wall, Major Palmer examined Banting's arm. The steel had penetrated deeply, severing the interosseous artery. His sleeve was soaked with blood. By means of a tourniquet the bleeding was controlled, and Palmer removed the fragment of shrapnel and applied a field dressing.

"It's the clearing station for you," he said, as he adjusted the bandage, "there's an ambulance waiting, and you're going back in it."

"Don't send me out," said Banting earnestly, "you're short-handed now, and I hate to leave. This is only a superficial wound. I'll be all right. I'm just getting to know the boys and I can't run out on them for a scratch."

The Major was about to insist. A message arrived while he spoke. He was ordered to go up to Cambrai, which had just been taken, and establish a new dressing station. He hesitated. Banting was the only remaining officer. But Banting was in a state of shock, pale from loss of blood and haggard from overwork.

[4]"The Germans at that time had a perfect right to fire on us as they could not have known it was a Red Cross Station, and besides our own artillery . . . had planted a gun in the court-yard of the farm, which was firing from the centre of our dressing station. I ordered them out, and they said, 'We will only be here a few minutes,' as they were firing just so many rounds; they moved out quickly."—Dr. Palmer, personal communication.

"You get back to the C.C.S.," said the Major firmly, "there are good sergeants here who can do the dressings. I'm going on to Cambrai."

The battle was shifting and uncertain, and the day was not yet won. No sooner had Palmer reached the town than the Germans counterattacked, and the defenders withdrew. The Major, who had been hunting about for a suitable site for his new A.D.S., was forced to hide in a cellar. In the street above him he could hear the heavy tramp of the German infantry, and the curt commands of the officers.

Fortunately the enemy did not hold the town long enough to institute a search for stragglers. In his cellar hideout he was undisturbed. Shortly after midnight the British again advanced, and in the seesaw battle which ensued, the Germans were once more dispossessed. About four o'clock in the morning Palmer re-appeared at Lilac Farm. He had left it not later than eleven, and had therefore been gone for at least seventeen hours.

In the wreckage of the barn, among the wounded and dying, he found his indomitable junior, Captain Banting, who had taken a wound most men would have thought disabling, still standing grimly on his feet, still dressing wounds.

Palmer's first reaction was anger. His order had been disobeyed.

"I thought I told you to get out of here," he shouted. He was dead tired, and he was not disposed to be pleasant.

"Nobody else to do it," said Banting.

"The sergeants could have done it," said the Major fiercely. "Now get out. Get into that ambulance and get out."

Reeling with weakness and fatigue, Banting reached the ambulance and climbed up to the front seat beside the driver. Car and driver were both regulars of the 13th. Banting nodded to the man beside him, and at once fell asleep.

The heavily loaded ambulance jolted off through the darkness. The road had been frequently and severely pounded. It was shell-pocked and uneven. He awoke in pain, his arm throbbing excessively. The jarring trip might be expected to bring on a fresh hæmorrhage, for he had a field dressing only, and no tourniquet. The clot held good for most of the way, but just as the car pulled up at the C.C.S., the bleeding began. Completely exhausted, he swooned. Willing hands carried him to a cot.

The blood was staunched, a needle of morphine relieved the pain and his wound was freshly dressed. Mercifully he slept.

For this display of fortitude, following on many days of hard and skilful work, Major Palmer recommended Banting for the Military Cross. The recommendation was confirmed by Colonel Anderson and forwarded to the authorities in London, where, in due course, it was accepted.[5]

At the casualty clearing station he was told that he would probably be evacuated to England. This moved him to further protest, but without effect. The decision would be made farther back. He bade good-bye to the anxious and solicitous Kels and started on his way to the base hospital. During all this time, as he recalled later, "I had nothing to eat except a piece of angel cake which had come in a parcel to one of the boys." Later he got a cup of chocolate and some biscuits.

He was transferred to another hospital and between one and two o'clock in the morning was taken to the operating room for debridement (the cleansing of a wound with excision of devitalized tissue). To his great relief he found that the anæsthetist was a man he knew and trusted. "I wasn't fussy about who did the operation," he said afterwards, "but I was particular about the man who administered the anæsthetic."

[5]The official citation is to be found in the *Canada Gazette*, Vol. 53, Part I, 1919: July-Sept. Supplement, Sept. 20, 1919, Page 13. It reads as follows: "Capt. Frederick Grant Banting, 13th Fld. Amb., C.A.M.C. Near Haynecourt on September 28th, 1918, when the medical officer of the 46th Canadian Battalion was wounded, he [Banting] immediately proceeded forward through intense shell fire to reach the battalion. Several of his men were wounded and he, neglecting his own safety, stopped to attend to them. While doing this he was wounded himself and was sent out notwithstanding his plea to be left at the front. His energy and pluck were of a very high order."

It should be explained that Haynecourt is only about two miles from Lilac Farm. The discrepancies in the two versions of the story, the bald citation and the detailed narrative given above (which is based on information received from Dr. Palmer) have drawn the following comment from the latter: "It is quite true that Dr. Banting was sent to replace Dr. Dunlop who was killed while looking out of a window in a shattered home, when he was hit by shrapnel. The ambulance always made the replacements when a Medical Officer was hit and Banting was sent to replace him. Later Banting joined me at Lilac Farm, a short distance up from Haynecourt, where we had the advanced dressing station of the 13th Canadian Field Ambulance. It was there that Banting was hit. . . ."

Hours later, when he was well "out" and the nausea had passed, he became conscious of someone moving around his bed, of hands tucking him in. That would be a nursing sister. He did not open his eyes. His left hand groped for a cigarette. Someone put a cigarette between his lips; someone applied a light to it. He drew in gratefully.

"Are you warm enough now, sir?" said a familiar voice. "You were cold a little while ago and I got an extra blanket from another bed." Banting opened his eyes. Standing beside him in the darkness who should it be but Kels? Kels, to whom he had said good-bye many miles farther forward, many hours previously. Kels to be sure. Who else could look after him so well?

There was the crisp rustle of a starched uniform. The batman vanished. As soon as the nurse had passed out of earshot, he reappeared. "He was like the cat in the storybook," said Banting later, "he could disappear into thin air and then materialize suddenly from nowhere. A sort of trick he had."

Although the stubborn casualty disputed it with bitterness, the order to evacuate him to England was not reversed. As he was being carried into the ambulance train he heard once again the voice of his genie. This time it said in ingratiating tones: "Just put that officer over here, sergeant, will you please?"

The invaluable Kels: he had selected a section with a window so that Banting could recline and watch the scenery as he travelled. Nor was that all. During the journey Kels somehow managed to find hot water for shaving, somehow got hold of a recent English newspaper, somehow contrived to perform other minor miracles. Somehow, anyhow. Just leave it to Kels.

At Calais, however, the final farewell was said.

"I won't try the channel, sir," said Kels.

"But I think he could have worked it," said Banting later, "Kels could go anywhere."

The faithful batman must have been A.W.L., but his misdemeanour if not exactly condoned was at least overlooked; his self-assigned mission accomplished, he mysteriously reappeared in his unit at the front.

Within a few days of sustaining his wound Banting was transferred to England aboard a hospital ship and taken to the No. 1 General Hospital in Manchester. He promptly telegraphed Dr. Gallie at Buxton to come to see him. Colonel MacLaren authorized the visit, and Gallie went to Manchester the same day. He found Banting with his right arm bandaged; he had a moderate elevation of temperature and a corresponding increase in pulse rate. The wound on the dorsum of the forearm was infected and there was a slight ulnar nerve lesion. It was the nerve lesion which was worrying Banting. He was reassured, however, when Gallie expressed the opinion that the nerve had not been severed and that full recovery of function would undoubtedly take place. The infection was not considered serious and Gallie cabled to Mrs. Banting in Alliston to inform her that her son was out of danger.

About a fortnight later the wounded Captain was transferred once again to Buxton. Sometime during the interval he apparently suffered a turn for the worse and the story is told that his surgical attendants actually proposed to amputate his arm, which he firmly refused to permit. This story is variously related but the central facts seem well attested; Dr. Gallie, who examined the wound when Banting first arrived at Manchester, who saw it again at Buxton, and who would almost certainly have been called in consultation had an amputation been seriously considered, is inclined to question the truth of the story, or at least the reality of any indication to amputate. Whatever the indication and whatever the circumstances, the fact emerges that at some time the question arose as to whether or not it would be advisable to use the saw, and that the decision not to do so was Banting's. A good right arm was thereby salvaged, and the threat to his later surgical career averted.

In private conversation in later years he liked to tell the tale himself, but various of his auditors give various differing versions of what he said. One blessed listener, however, wrote down the gist of the story immediately after hearing it and the following account derives from this source.

A convoy of wounded officers arrived at the English hospital at one o'clock in the morning, Banting among them. He had not had a chance to take a bath for many days and he longed for nothing so much as a tubful of hot water and a cake of soap. Wandering down a corridor, he found an empty bathroom. There was a board across the bath and on this he rested his wounded arm, swathed in bandages, while he enjoyed the luxury of hot water and soap, scrubbing himself awkwardly with his left hand. Meanwhile the nursing sisters had found him missing from his bed and were afraid that he had "escaped"; consequently a scolding awaited him on his return. Although he explained and apologized, they were not appeased; baths were officially administered, they pointed out, by the nurses, unless a patient had a special "privilege."

This was on a Wednesday. Orders were that no wounds could be dressed until the chief surgeon had examined them. The chief surgeon, a retired man who was a "dug-out" for the war, did not arrive until Sunday. (This seems to imply that the wound was not dressed in the meantime, which is certainly not true, since Dr. Gallie had seen it and pronounced the condition not alarming; likewise it is hardly credible that the interval of complete *laissez-faire* could have been so long; what is true, certainly, is that Banting thought there was too much delay in attending to it.) When ultimately examined by the chief surgeon the wound was found to be infected. Seizing the end of the packing with forceps, the surgeon ripped it out, a common enough practice (although the best men are the gentlest) but one which in this case caused acute pain and even more acute indignation. The surgeon passed on to another case and a new dressing was applied by a nurse. Subsequently there was a moderate hæmorrhage, and for this reason and also with a view to extending the wound and improving drainage, the patient was taken to the operating room. Again there is recorded a complaint of undue roughness before the anæsthetic was administered. Following this operative procedure, no more dressings were done for some days and Banting finally decided that he had been forgotten; he therefore took over the direction of his treatment himself, indignantly refusing a later suggestion that the arm should be amputated.

To anyone familiar with the ordinary routine of hospitals, this sounds like a wild yarn, invented by someone who wished to "dramatize" simple events. Would a nursing sister in a large general hospital disregard the orders of the attending surgeon and carry out the directions of the patient, even although the latter were a medical officer? It is hard to credit. Yet in seeking further evidence on this point, the following sentences were discovered in a letter written by Banting in 1929: "When there is too much hurry and flurry, treatment sometimes becomes sloppy, especially when men are overworked. In my own case, during the war, I was forced to take over and give the orders myself." There it rests.

During his stay in hospital he was sometimes troubled at night by horrifying dreams. Battle experiences recurred to plague him. It seems that in one of his periods of relief from the line, after he had been for about two weeks in a forward area, he was sent out along a sunken road in an ambulance of wounded. In daylight the road was subject to the fire of German snipers. At night it was heavily shelled. As they sped on through the darkness, shells whistled over them. But suddenly there was another sound, a roaring, trampling, battering sound, drawing quickly nearer. The driver pulled up and flashed on his lights. Banting was sitting beside him on the driver's seat. In that instant of brilliant light they saw pounding toward them from the blackness a double team of horses drawing a wagon load of ammunition. With a wild rattle of harness, a screech of iron wheels and a clatter and crunch of hooves, the teams were reined to a stop. The front pair of horses had separated; the rear team had crowded up between them; the wagon tongue projected over the radiator of the ambulance.

One night in hospital, when Banting had dropped off into a troubled sleep, he dreamed of his mother. She was visiting him at the front line in France. He was taking her from point to point. Suddenly down a darkened road rushed the foaming and thunderous teams with the wagon load of ammunition, straight upon her. He flung out his arms and shouted.

His wounded arm was flung across the bed. He was sweating, terrified, struggling to awake. He found himself in the silent, spacious darkness of a peaceful hospital ward, many miles from fighting and alarums. He sank back on his pillow, breathing heavily. Only a dream. But how vivid and frightening!

The dreams soon passed; the passage of time and the improvement of his health engendered better sleep; better sleep produced better health. His wound was healing. The return to Buxton and the resumption of activity were salutary.

The nightmare of war itself was soon to reach an end. His prolonged convalescence in England was not long completed when hostilities ceased.

After the usual transfers, shuntings and delays, he sailed once more for Canada where his postponed career awaited him.

PART IV

London Interlude

One man's disillusion may be another man's inspiration, the spirit of one may be permanently maimed by accidents of fate which spread the wings of another.

As I Remember Him, HANS ZINSSER.

The seer's hour of vision is short and rare among heavy days and months.

RALPH WALDO EMERSON.

In retrospect, great discoveries seem to have long been written on the sky.

JOHN HOMANS.

A man with a conviction is worth twelve men with interests.

J. S. MILL.

1

THE YEAR of Banting's life which followed his discharge from the army was a continuation of the orthopædic training which he started in England, but with a narrowing and deepening of his interests. A great variety of material, medical and surgical, passed through the wards of the Sick Children's Hospital in Toronto where he now resumed his work under C. L. Starr. But paramount in surgical interest was the mechanical correction of childhood deformities—the crooked backs, the club feet, the twisted, distorted, spastic limbs.

It was a year devoted to quiet work. For a part of the time, Banting lived again in his old quarters at 63 Gloucester Street, watched over by Mrs. O'Neil. But not many hours in the twenty-four found him absent from the hospital. His appetite for work, now fed on the employment he best loved, grew more voracious than ever. Dr. Frank Adams, a classmate who was also a resident at the Sick Children's during this period, remembers little to be said of Banting other than that he was quietly and constantly industrious. What Starr expected and required of his residents we have already seen: he was an exacting master, and in Banting he found a responsive pupil.

During the time of Banting's residency, Dr. Bruce Robertson was doing his pioneer work in blood transfusion at the Hospital. At the present time, when transfusion is common and many thousands of persons have had the experience of donating blood, it is rather difficult to realize how comparatively recent is the development and widespread use of a practical procedure for the purpose. In the first World War many lives were lost from shock and hæmorrhage which might have been saved by transfusions of plasma or whole blood. Banting had seen this for himself and he was therefore a keenly interested assistant in the work being done by Dr. Robertson. He himself was often a donor and a number of sickly children, including a little pickaninny with a gleaming grin, in whom he took a special interest, received transfusions of his blood.

His liking for children, of all sizes and colours, was warm and genuine. To the infants, the toddlers and the older boys and girls at "Sick Kids' " he was the kindest of physicians and the gayest of companions. If their elders sometimes thought him dour, the "kids" knew better; they found him the very spirit of fun. They loved the nicknames he gave them, they loved his stories and his sly banter, they loved his jokes. And he in turn worked for and watched over them with a zeal "beyond the call of duty."

Meantime his pre-war romance was resumed. It seems to have been a tense and not-quite-happy association, although the probability is that it would have worked out well under different circumstances. It persisted, with many "final" breaks and many fresh beginnings, throughout the year in London which followed, and even after his return to Toronto. He had given the young lady a diamond ring which she wore for a time and returned to him, then accepted again, then returned again. During the intervals of estrangement Banting wore the ring on his watchchain and occasionally used the diamond to scratch a slide in the laboratory; his associates could thus keep themselves more or less informed of his current status. The diamond was ultimately rejected.

In the early summer of 1920, Banting and his friend, Dr. W. P. Tew, who had been the class president in their final year at college, decided to try their luck in practice in London. Next to Windsor, it was the largest city in Western Ontario, and had the added advantage of being a university town, the seat of an excellent medical school. The Medical School of the University of Western Ontario[1] was then struggling to keep up its standards in cramped, inadequate quarters, with insufficient laboratory space, in the old building on Waterloo Street. But a fine new building, designed to the specifications of its able dean, Dr. Paul McKibben, was nearing completion at a more desirable site on Ottaway Avenue (South Street), directly opposite the Victoria Hospital. There were capable surgeons in London, Dr. Hadley Williams and Dr. W. J. Stevenson among others, and Professor Starr, the *doyen* of Toronto Surgeons and Banting's friend and adviser, heartily approved his proposed move.

Banting accordingly wound us his affairs in Toronto and went down to London about the first of July. Tew remained at the

---

[1] Then called Western University. The name was changed in 1923.

Burnside (the obstetrical department of the Toronto General Hospital) until the end of August, so that Banting arrived in the city alone, and almost friendless. T. S. H. Graham, his former room-mate at 63 Gloucester Street, who had become principal of a London Collegiate, was one of the few to welcome him.

Almost immediately on his arrival, Banting bought a house. It was a large white-brick residence at 442 Adelaide Street N., but was perhaps, for his purpose, a none-too-fortunate site. He bought it from Mr. Rowland Hill, a shoe merchant, with the understanding that Mr. Hill should continue to occupy it for about a year, while the builders were completing his new home. Banting, meanwhile, was to have a bedroom, and the use of the front parlour for an office. The money for the purchase was in part borrowed from his father, who also supplied him with brown-varnished office furniture. (The desk and chair he continued to use for the rest of his life.)

So he opened his new office, with a sign on the lawn reading

DR. F. G. BANTING

and the same inscription on a brass plate screwed to the door. Then he sat down in his brand new chair, and waited for his first patient.

Perhaps he was a little too sanguine. Perhaps a new doctor, with no reputation whatever so far as London was concerned, with few friends and no important connections, should hardly expect a sudden rush of business. Very well: he could wait. He reached to the bookshelf and took down a book. It was a text-book of anatomy. On the flyleaf was his name, a drawing of a field-gun with several soldiers grouped around it, the word "Cambrai," and a date. He turned the pages leisurely, then fixed on a certain portion to master, and compelled his fleeting attention. Soon his whole mind was absorbed in a familiar, yet arduous task. The vertical crease, denoting concentration, appeared between his brows. The office clock struck the hour, and Banting, heedless, turned a page, but turned it backward in order to re-read the section he had just completed. This was a characteristic gesture. It was the old, laborious method of his college days, patient and thorough. Years afterward he was to write: "It is not within the power of the properly constructed human mind to be satisfied."

Banting's hoped-for practice was long in appearing. He had expected to do special work in orthopædic surgery, but unfortunately specialism (which is chiefly a post-war phenomenon) had not yet developed in London to any marked degree. Dr. Tew's observation, "Everybody did everything," was almost literally true. Dr. George Ramsay, who afterwards became the city's leading orthopædist, was still engaged in a general surgical practice. A few important orthopædic cases, especially those from out of town, were sent to Starr or Gallie or Robertson in Toronto. None of them, and this seemed galling to the ambitious young doctor on Adelaide Street, were sent to Banting. He began to feel that London's physicians, like Mr. Pilgrim and Mr. Pratt in *Janet's Repentance*, were in league against the newcomer. But of course the battle was only just begun, and there can be little doubt that if his peculiar star had not beckoned him to another field, he would in the end have realized his surgical ambitions. Professor Best has since remarked of his chief that the difficulties of his insulin research "were surmounted with a dogged perseverance which would have achieved results in any line of endeavour." His short stay in London was hardly a fair test of his potential capacities as a practitioner.

To augment the returns from his practice (and in later years he liked to relate that these reached the grand total of nothing at all during his first twenty-eight days in London), and also as a means of furthering his desire of knowledge adequate for a fellowship, he secured a position as an instructor at the medical school, where he taught anatomy, physiology and clinical surgery. Students of the period remember this quiet, energetic, earnest young teacher, a little diffident perhaps, but friendly enough, and a good man to answer a question. In the side room off the anatomy laboratory, he performed dissections of his own. His demonstrations in physiology showed an expert hand with the scalpel, a faculty for managing apparatus, and a clear exposition of functional problems. His work as a teacher was definitely successful, but his mind was clouded with dissatisfaction.

At last he found an outlet for his energies which pleased him better. Professor F. R. Miller, a brilliant graduate of Toronto and Munich and a well-known neurophysiologist, was chief of the

F. G. Banting

SURGERY, GYNECOLOGY AND OBSTETRICS

AN INTERNATIONAL MAGAZINE, PUBLISHED MONTHLY

VOLUME XXXI   NOVEMBER, 1920   NUMBER 5

THE RELATION OF THE ISLETS OF LANGERHANS TO DIABETES WITH SPECIAL REFERENCE TO CASES OF PANCREATIC LITHIASIS

By MOSES BARRON, M.D., MINNEAPOLIS, MINNESOTA
From the Department of Pathology, University of Minnesota, Minneapolis, Minnesota

ANY reference to the pancreas as secreting a hormone necessary for the utilization of sugar by the tissues of the body is, misleading, as that function is, accurately speaking, exercised by only a very small portion of the organ, the so-called "islets" of Langerhans; so that what is generally understood as the relation of the pancreas to diabetes is rather the relation of the islets to that disease. And yet it should not be overlooked that in spite of a great abundance of proof from experimental and clinical studies, it has not been universally accepted that the deficiency of either the pancreas as a whole or of the specific portion of it, the islets, in diabetes mellitus.

The purpose of this paper ... be... examples of typical changes in ... cases of true diabetes to ...fering ...tailed study of the histopath... ...andu- case of pancreatic lithiasis... ...ference to the islets, and to ... Lan- ...dings with those recorded in ... been ...obtained in experimental ... ...ducts in animals. Such a comb... hese ...inical and experimental cases ... ...dvantage because of the simila... mall the spontaneous and the induced... Pancreatic lithiasis is a very ... or ...tion. Only a relatively small num... have been recorded in the literat... ore Graaf speaks of it as early as 166...

gagni and Cawley recognized the condition in 1765 and 1778 respectively. Opie (35) found two cases in 1,500 autopsies. Rindfleisch (39) found 3 cases in a series of 2,000 autopsies. Zesas (45) in 1905 collected only about 70 cases from the literature. Of these, 7 had been diagnosed clinically. Einhorn (10) states that the clinical recognition of this disease is exceedingly rare; much rarer than the very rare condition itself. In our own laboratory, this was the first case found in a series of several thousand autopsies ... in the lack of communi... Gall-stones are ... ...bladder with excretory ducts; instead, they are in intimate relation with the lymphatics.

REVIEW OF THE LITERATURE

Experimental ligation of ducts. The study of this rather complex organ in its relation to diabetes has led to extensive experimental work. Arnozan and Vaillard (2) ligated the pancreatic ducts in rabbits and found that within 24 hours the ducts became dilated, the epithelial cells were desquamated, and there were protoplasmic changes in the acinic cells. At the seventh day there was beginning round cell infiltration, and at the fourteenth day a great deal of the parenchyma had been replaced by connective tissue. The authors thought that the sclerosis was due to the retained secretion. Ssobolew (44) ligated the ducts in rabbits, cats, and dogs. He found a

By permission of Surgery, Gynecology and Obstetrics.

Above: THE FIRST PAGE OF DR. MOSES BARRON'S PAPER, IN WHICH BANTING FOUND HIS INSPIRATION.

It was while reading this paper that he conceived the idea that the "hypothetical hormone" might be extracted from a duct-ligated pancreas.

Below: THE PARAGRAPH, MARKED BY BANTING, FROM WHICH HE DERIVED HIS IDEA FOR THE INSULIN RESEARCH.

Photographed in the library of the Medical School, University of Western Ontario.

Physiology Department at "Western"; Professor Miller invited Banting to assist him in a research problem, an investigation of the results of cerebellar stimulations, and Banting seized the chance with avidity. Here was a problem on the frontiers of knowledge, a chance to probe into the unknown in the company of a practised explorer.

A review of the literature showed conflicting views on the excitability of the cerebellar cortex. The eminent Sir Victor Horsley and his co-workers denied its existence. Some investigators, true, had been able to produce effects that seemed due to cortical excitation, but Horsley attributed these responses to the escape of current to other regions. Professor Miller and his young associate attacked the question anew. They tried to exclude the cause of former confusions, using a method designed to make it practically certain that no physical spread could occur. Their conclusion, in the face of no small authority which maintained the contrary, was that the cerebellar cortex is definitely excitable, a thesis since confirmed by other workers, and by the later researches of Professor Miller himself. Banting was thus initiated into the ways of medical research, and took his first step on a thorny path, a path he was destined to pursue for life, and to make an easier passage for some who followed.

And still, as he once expressed it to an acquaintance, "the patients stayed away in droves," and he had time enough and to spare. Miss Sullivan, the librarian at the Medical School, soon recognized him as the most frequent visitor in the reading room. Dr. F. J. H. Campbell (with whom, and with Colonel and Mrs. Shannon, he sometimes beguiled an evening at bridge) invited him to summarize for the Journal Club the recent literature on blood transfusion. He assumed the task with his usual energy, gave it much time and thought, and prepared an exhaustive abstract, which he read before the members of the Club. It was about the same time that he was associated with Dr. Ramsay in the first blood transfusion to be completed successfully in the London area; the multiple syringe method was used and the patient, a child with a severe anæmia, ultimately was restored to a fair degree of health.

Restlessly, Banting returned again to his office, walked up and down, smoked cigarettes, studied pathology, or anatomy, and waited. He looked out of the window and waited. When the long day had worn itself to a dreary remnant, he went out to dinner.

Dr. J. W. Crane, Professor of Pharmacology, had introduced him at the Shakespeare Club, where he made the acquaintance of Miss Mary Healy, a professional painter. Perhaps it was in this way that his half-forgotten interest in painting was now revived. As he walked one day along Dundas Street, he happened to notice in a shop window a display of paints and brushes and a small portable easel. He paused to look at them, and was seized by the impulse to try his hand at making pictures, something he had not attempted, except for an occasional pencil sketch, since his boyhood. He carried his purchases home and began to experiment with colours. This was the beginning of a pleasant and profitable apprenticeship, and a life-long source of pleasure. Such are the uses of boredom.

But the waiting, the boredom, the long, dull days were nearly over. Days soon became too short, for the tempo of Banting's life was to be hastened suddenly. The indicator was moving over from half-speed to full.

2

On October 30, 1920, Banting conceived an idea, the compulsion of which drove him onward to fame. It was an idea which changed his own career profoundly, and its eventual fruition, as everyone knows, has made life possible, and bearable, for millions of diabetics. The above-mentioned date is the Bastille Day in mankind's struggle against an ancient and terrible disease. The trumpet was sounded for a frontal assault.

It was not a unique idea. It was not even a new idea. But its moment in time had come. Progress in the collateral sciences had provided the means for attainment; the stage was set for the reappearance of a simple but brilliant hypothesis.

"Many ideas grow better," said the Autocrat, "when transplanted into another mind than in the one where they sprang up." Banting's idea was not precisely a transplant; rather the same conjunction of facts which produced it, as early as 1906, in the mind of Lydia de Witt, now evolved it afresh, and this time it grew. This time the auspices were favourable.

He had stopped at the library before leaving the Medical School on that momentous October day, and had examined the November copy of *Surgery, Gynecology and Obstetrics*. The first article in the journal was a twelve-page account of "The Relation of the Islets of Langerhans to Diabetes, with Special Reference to cases of Pancreatic Lithiasis," by Dr. Moses Barron of Minneapolis. Banting was to talk to his students the following day on the functions of the pancreas. He took the journal home with him.

About nine o'clock that evening he telephoned Dr. Tew. "I wish you would come down to the house if you are free," he told him, "I have something I want to show you." The two friends read over portions of Dr. Barron's paper together, and discussed its implications at some length. Banting was interested especially in a certain paragraph in Barron's review of the literature of his subject; he drew a vertical line beside it with his pen and underlined a part of it. After Dr. Tew had gone home, Banting continued to ponder this paragraph on the experimental ligation of ducts.

"Arnozan and Vaillard," he read, "ligated the pancreatic ducts in rabbits and found that within twenty-four hours the ducts became dilated, the epithelial cells were desquamated, and there were protoplasmic changes in the acinic cells . . . at the fourteenth day a great deal of the parenchyma had been replaced by connective tissue. . . . Ssobolew ligated the ducts in rabbits, cats, and dogs. He found a gradual atrophy and sclerosis of the organ with relatively intact islets and no glycosuria."[2]

More evidence to the same effect was cited, and Dr. Barron pointed out the similarity between the degeneration which occurs

[2]Glycosuria: the excretion of sugar in the urine. Although the presence of sugar does not necessarily indicate diabetes, it is one of the characteristic signs of the disease. Thomas Willis (d. 1675) recognized the sweetness of the urine, "as if there has been sugar and honey in it," and in 1775 Dobson evaporated diabetic urine and recovered sugar; forty years later the chemist Chevreul identified the sugar excreted by diabetics with the sugar of grapes (glucose).—L. S.

in the pancreas following experimental ligation of the ducts, and the blocking of the ducts by gallstones.

This meant, then, that tying off the pancreatic ducts caused atrophy of the whole gland *except a very small portion, the "islets" of Langerhans,*[3] *which many scientists believed to be the source of the hypothetical diabetes-preventing hormone,* the hormone necessary for the utilization of sugar by the tissues of the body. When the ducts were securely tied, *most* of the gland atrophied, yet no glycosuria resulted. It had been proved by von Mehring and Minkowski, in 1889, that removal of the entire pancreas from a dog was invariably followed by all the symptoms of severe diabetes, terminating with death from inanition in the course of two or three weeks. Obviously, therefore, the part of the gland which prevented the disease was the same part which remained almost intact many weeks after tying the ducts. Banting knew that attempts to follow up the work of Minkowski, and treat diabetes by the administration of fresh pancreas or extracts of the gland by mouth (in the same way as it had been found possible to do with thyroid preparations when the thyroid gland was deficient) had all been unavailing. Extracts were not much more successful when injected beneath the skin or directly into the circulation. It was easy to explain that pancreatic preparations given by mouth were destroyed in the stomach or duodenum. Why were the extracts equally useless when injected?

Banting may be imagined as saying to himself: "The main part of the pancreas (excluding the islets) produces a powerful digestive ferment. Extracts have been made from the *whole* gland. Perhaps that powerful ferment has destroyed the hormone from the islets during the process of extraction. But if the ducts are tied off and the main part of the gland allowed to atrophy, while the islets are practically undamaged, perhaps extraction

[3]"I would commend to students of medicine Paul Langerhans' thesis, presented in 1869, and reprinted in English in 1937 with an introductory essay by Dr. H. Morrison. This young man, as a medical student, discovered the structures which were later named in his honour by Laguesse, the islands of Langerhans. Langerhans had no knowledge of the actual function of the islets and indeed it was not until a year after his death that von Mehring and Minkowski proved that complete removal of the pancreas invariably produces diabetes in some species of animals."—C. H. Best, "Hormonal and Dietary Factors in Pancreatic Tissue," the Banting Memorial Lecture, 1945.

would give us the hormone without interference from the ferment."[4]

Certainly his reasoning was something after this fashion. What we do know definitely is this: at about two o'clock in the morning, Banting wrote in a small black notebook the words which contained the germ of his idea. "Tie off pancreas ducts of dogs. Wait six or eight weeks. Remove and extract."

"We do not know whence ideas come," he told a Chicago audience at a later time, when the value of his own idea had been proven beyond doubt,[5] "but the importance of the idea in medical research cannot be overestimated. From the nature of things ideas do not come from prosperity, affluence and contentment, but rather from the blackness of despair, not in the bright light of day, nor the footlights' glare, but rather in the quiet, undisturbed hours of midnight, or early morning, when one can be alone to think. These are the grandest hours of all, when the imagination is allowed to run riot on the problem that blocks the progress of research, when the hewn stones of scientific fact are turned over and over, and fitted in so that the mosaic figure of truth, designed by Mother Nature long ago, be formed from the chaos."

This figure of speech is peculiarly apt, when used, as of course he was using it, with reference to his own midnight vigil in London. The "hewn stones of scientific fact" relating to diabetes and the rôle played in that disease by the pancreas, were many, but as yet no one had fitted them together to form "the mosaic figure of truth."

In the surveys of the work which preceded his own, given by Banting in a number of his addresses, there is no mention of the investigations of Lydia de Witt. Despite a very wide acquaintance with the literature of the subject, he seems unaccountably to have overlooked her work. Otherwise, he would certainly have mentioned it: he always gave a full share of credit to the "lone grey

---

[4]As we shall see again later on, this conception was not wholly correct. The digestive ferments of the pancreas must be activated in the bowel before they attain their destructive power; also the islet tissue of the gland *is* affected, although much more slowly than the acinar tissue, by ligation of the duct.—L. S.

[5]F. G. Banting, "Medical Research," Ann. Clin. Med., 3: 565-572, March, 1925.

company before the pioneers," particularly to E. L. Scott, who had come closer than anyone else to solving the problem. Lydia de Witt, however, had approached it in the same manner as Banting. Basing her experiments upon the observation made by Schulze, Ssobolew, and others, that complete atrophy of the glandular structures of the pancreas is caused by ligating the duct, while the islands of Langerhans remain relatively unaffected, she made extracts of the islet tissue of cats, and found that they had no digestive powers, but possessed distinct glycolytic properties.[6] This remarkable work was done in 1906, and is an excellent example of the way in which science sometimes turns up a diamond, then passes by oblivious. Banting knew a diamond when he saw one and as we shall presently see, he was a very diligent and alert prospector.

The work of the other pioneers has been briefly summarized by their successor and scientific heir, the discoverer of insulin:

In 1889, von Mehring and Minkowski observed that the complete removal of the pancreas produced a severe and fatal diabetes in days.[7] Five years previous to this, Vaillard and Arnozan had tied the tubes leading from the pancreas and found that the animals did not become diabetic but that the pancreas shrivelled up. Other investigators, using a microscope, found that certain cells of the pancreas—the islands of Langerhans—were not involved, but that it was the other cells which disappeared. [Actually the Langerhans cells *were* involved, but to a lesser degree.]

Minkowski was the first to conceive the idea that an extract of the minced pancreas injected into a diabetic dog might relieve the symptoms. Caparelli, Battistini and Vanni prepared extracts

[6]It is not true that the islet tissue is entirely unaffected. This was Lydia de Witt's conception, and also Banting's. It has since been shown, however, that the islets share to a minor degree the degeneration which takes place in the rest of the gland, and that a duct-tied gland actually contains less insulin than a normal gland.

[7]"Von Mehring died in 1908, but Minkowski lived for ten years of the insulin era and was appointed Chairman of the German Insulin Committee, which received as a gift all the rights which the University of Toronto had acquired in Germany as a result of the discovery. . . . Minkowski, one of the great students of diabetes, died in 1931, but his wife lived to be a victim of Nazi oppression. It is a source of gratification to all of us that funds made available by the Insulin Committee of the University of Toronto played a part in her rescue."—C. H. Best, "Hormonal and Dietary Factors in Pancreatic Tissue."

and reported favourable effects, but their results were not confirmed. Unfortunately the injections were accompanied by pronounced toxic effects, which overshadowed any benefit derived.

Following the discovery by Schafer that an extract of the thyroid administered to sufferers from thyroid insufficiency relieved symptoms, a large group of observers, including White, Mackenzie, Wills and Sibley, endeavoured to supply the deficient hormone in diabetes mellitus by giving extracts of the pancreas. Their results were not conclusive. Zuelzer, in 1908, by use of an alcoholic extract of the pancreas, obtained favourable results in five cases of diabetes mellitus, but unfortunately toxic results made the continued use of the extract impossible.

Following the discovery by Diamare and Rennie that the islet cells exist separate from the other cells in bony fishes, Rennie and Fraser fed the principal islets of these fish to diabetics, but were unable to show beneficial results. They found this substance too toxic for injection purposes. The search for the elusive hormone was not given up, however. Kleiner, Murlin, Scott and Paulesco continued the physiological investigations on laboratory animals.

In 1912, E. L. Scott prepared alcoholic extracts of the pancreas, and showed that these extracts sometimes relieved certain of the symptoms of diabetes in animals. He endeavoured to tie off the pancreatic ducts and to extract the remnant of the pancreas after it had digested the remaining cells [the method previously employed by Lydia de Witt] but unfortunately his operation was not followed by complete disappearance of the cells.

This was probably due to the fact that his ligatures were tied so tightly that they caused sloughing of the underlying tissue. Fibrin—the blood clot—was deposited on the surface and the tube was re-established. Furthermore, Scott was not satisfied with the methods of estimating the percentage of sugar in the blood, and consequently left the problem, which he almost solved, in order to obtain more precise methods.

In 1913, Murlin prepared alkaline extracts of the pancreas and also of the small intestine, and demonstrated that they reduced the elevated blood sugar of diabetic dogs. However, he found that this result could be obtained by the administration of alkalies alone, and the investigation was abandoned. After the war Murlin resumed his investigations and found that the administration of perfusates of the pancreas was followed by an elevation of the respiratory quotient.[8] Thus he could restore to the diabetic animal some of its lost power of burning carbohydrates.

However, despite the many investigations, in 1920, so vague were facts, that even so great an authority as J. J. R. Macleod stated in his textbook that there is as yet no proof of the existence of the internal secretion of the pancreas, and that there is no proof against the theory that the islet cells are detoxicating centres.

Concerning the solution of the problem he states: "This consists in seeing whether the symptoms which follow removal of the pancreas are removed and a normal condition re-established, when means are taken to supply the supposed missing internal secretion to the organism; if they should be, conclusive evidence would be furnished that it is by 'internal secretion,' and not by 'local influence' that the gland functionates."

Professor Artur Biedl of Vienna, on the other hand, had stated in his textbook, *The Internal Secretory Organs* (1913), that the existence of an internal secretion of the pancreas had been absolutely proved by Forschbach's parabiotic experiments.

Some authorities believed the islets to be of essentially the same nature as the rest of the gland, perhaps secreting tubules temporarily modified for the purpose of supplying an internal secretion. Others, agreeing that the islets were of the same nature as the rest of the gland, insisted that they must have the same function and that they formed one of the ferments of the pancreatic juice. Still another group of observers regarded the islets as definite and distinct organs, having no connection (except a community of embryonic origin) with the secreting tubules of the pancreas. To read the chapter on the pancreas in a textbook of twenty years ago (such as the second edition of Swale Vincent's *Internal Secretion and the Ductless Glands,* published in 1922, but written before the discovery of insulin was announced) is to wade in a tangle of argument, through which it is quite impossible, despite the best efforts of the author, to find a clear path.

[8]Respiratory Quotient (R.Q.): $\dfrac{\text{Volume of } CO_2 \text{ produced}}{\text{Volume of } O_2 \text{ used.}}$

In a healthy, starved animal the R.Q. rises when carbohydrates (such as sugar) are administered, since carbohydrate is being oxidized. This is not true of a diabetic animal, which cannot use carbohydrates.—L. S.

"When doctors differ, who shall decide?" The doctors were differing with a vengeance. These men were experts in vegetative physiology. They were trained research workers. They had given the question much thought, and they had performed innumerable experiments. Who could foresee that the North-West Passage to a clearer understanding, and to an effective treatment for diabetes, would be discovered by a surgeon?

Banting had not yet acquired any extensive knowledge of the literature. He had read an article in a journal, and he had had an idea. He could not be sure what value that idea might prove to have. The important thing was that he believed his hypothesis to be true, and he felt a consuming desire to put it to the test. Increasingly, as he thought about it, the conviction was borne upon him that he had grasped the skirts of happy chance. He meant to hold on.

3

Professor Miller, to whom Banting confided his inspiration, was somewhat dubious. He did not fail to appreciate the simple but cogent arguments which supported the idea, but vegetative physiology was not his special work. He had devoted himself for years to the physiology of the nervous system, and had made important contributions to knowledge in that extremely difficult province. He wanted Banting's assistance in further work on the brain. Banting now appeared with a problem of his own in endocrinology. Dr. Miller, though pleased to see this evidence of the inquiring mind, refused to undertake direction of the necessary experiments. He advised his young assistant to consult Professor Macleod of the University of Toronto.

Banting received the same advice from Dr. Crane and Dr. Ramsay. Dean McKibben was not prepared to promise, on behalf of the Board of Governors, the salary which Banting demanded for a research appointment, and he too advised him to confer with Dr. Macleod. Macleod had done a great deal of work on carbohydrate metabolism. He would be eminently qualified to judge the worth of the idea, and if experiments were undertaken to test it, his guidance would be invaluable.

Banting, the young man with the idea, accordingly made an appointment with Macleod, and one week-end he drove off to Toronto in his rattletrap Ford. The first interview was unsatisfactory. Macleod was not impressed. He pointed out the vast amount of work which had already been done, the many attempts to isolate the internal secretion of the pancreas (if such a thing existed) and the handicap which Banting would experience from his lack of training in research. Acutely disappointed, Banting once more pondered the question from every angle, but retained his stubborn conviction that his idea was worth a trial. Next day he returned to the attack. He felt that he had somehow failed to "put across" exactly what he had in mind, and this time he arrived in the Professor's office with a black-and-white statement of what he believed and why, and what he proposed to do about it. Perhaps this clarification was all that was needed. Perhaps the very force of his determination swept away demur. In any event Macleod agreed, with something less than enthusiasm, to provide him with a place to work for eight weeks at the conclusion of his London appointment. He was to have an undergraduate assistant and an allotment of ten dogs.

It is easy to be wise after the event. It is easy to say that Professor Macleod should have recognized initiative and ardour and have set them to work without delay, backed by his full support. We must remember that Macleod was better acquainted with the difficulties of such work than was Banting. A man who has seen a score of expeditions come to grief on the slopes of Everest, pauses to think before he equips yet another to try the steep ascent.

Having obtained this measure of support, Banting resigned his position at "Western." Some of his friends doubted the wisdom of the break. Many warring impulses no doubt strove within him, but the master impulse told. The young woman to whom he was engaged, and who was at this time teaching school in a town close to London, broke off the engagement, and this probably contributed to his sense of crisis. His cherished idea had now become an *idée fixe* and he saw little chance of it blossoming without a change of site. Right or wrong, he felt that the treatment he received in London was ungenerous and unjust. He must get on with his new work. He was impatient to begin. He

would conquer, as Alexander did, "by not delaying." He wanted
to operate on his dogs at once, so that the glands would have time
to atrophy and there would be no further delay when he reached
Toronto. Macleod ruled, however, that the whole experiment
must be conducted with Banting's immediate supervision, and he
was therefore forced to wait. Wait he did, but with gnawing
impatience and mounting eagerness. Would the time never
come?

Meanwhile, as he wrote later:

I whiled away the spare time at the out-patient department of
the hospital. Here I saw a little boy of five or six years who had
no foot. The condition is very rare and it was called a congenital
amputation. . . . The little lad was very self-conscious and always
kept his deformity hidden behind the good leg under the chair.
Here was a problem. I thought of all the soldiers who had ampu-
tations, so I made a plaster cast of the leg and took it to a shoe-
maker who made a laced cuff of strong leather. I then got a pair
of light, strong side arms of steel and a small wooden foot made
at the workshop. The father brought the unused shoe and we
put it on the brace. I shall always remember the look on the
boy's face when he stood up in his new outfit. He walked—then
he ran—then he jumped on it and could not take his eyes off it.
Instead of tucking it under the chair, he put it out for everyone
to see. The whole thing only cost me a few dollars and I was
more pleased than the boy. Years later Sir Robert Jones, the
greatest British orthopedic surgeon, visited London and examined
and commented [favourably] on the splint.[9]

But whatever Banting's talents of this kind, other things were
in store for him. Early in the spring of 1921 he gave up "practice" and returned to Toronto.

[9]Quoted by Leonard W. Brockington, LL.D., in "The Doctor's Example,"
address delivered at Convocation for conferring degrees in Medicine, University of Western Ontario, March 27, 1946.

ON THE 30TH OCTOBER. 1920. FREDERICK GRANT BANTING ORIGINATED THE HYPOTHESIS THAT THE FAILURE THERETOFORE TO ISOLATE THE INTERNAL SECRETION OF THE PANCREAS HAD BEEN DUE TO ITS DESTRUCTION BY THE FERMENTS LIBERATED DURING THE PROCESS OF EXTRACTION.

HE DEVISED AN EXPERIMENTAL METHOD BY WHICH THIS DESTRUCTION COULD BE AVOIDED AND THE INTERNAL SECRETION (NOW KNOWN AS INSULIN) OBTAINED.

IN MAY. 1921. BANTING AND CHARLES HERBERT BEST. BOTH GRADUATES OF THE UNIVERSITY OF TORONTO. CONDUCTED IN THIS ROOM THE EXPERIMENTS WHICH CULMINATED IN THE ISOLATION OF INSULIN.

Courtesy Professor C. H. Best.

INSCRIPTION FROM THE PLAQUE ON THE WALL OF THE LABORATORY WHERE THE INSULIN RESEARCH WAS BEGUN

The hypothesis mentioned has not been confirmed on closer examination. See pages 67n., 68n., 96.

V

The Magic Islands

A fixed idea is like the iron rod which sculptors put in their statues. It impales and sustains. A great man is absorbing because he is himself absorbed.

TAINE.

Genius is initiative on fire.

HOLBROOK JACKSON.

Imagination is but a free thinking. The imaginative are blessed with a facility in the association of facts. High latent force develops when such a man is faced with a perplexing problem, and wide spark gaps are bridged.

F. G. BANTING.

1

THE GREAT ADVENTURE was beginning.[1] The exploration which would eventually discover, groping through a conflux of mists, the ineffable secret of the islands of Langerhans was putting out with dubious preparation. With little more than the idea,

The trenchant thought that cuts a pathway clear,

the long quest was being undertaken boldly.

Banting's qualifications as an investigator of carbohydrate metabolism appeared meagre. Searching intelligence, restless curiosity, unending endurance and resilience—all these were his in more than common measure. In technical training he was deficient. Were his natural qualities, together with such training as he had had, sufficient to outweigh this defect?

Mr. H. G. Wells many years ago remarked that to be trained in research is a contradiction in terms. The truth, or half-truth, of this assertion is incontestable. But the unknown is always and forever approached along charted tracks of the known, and the question resolves itself to this: how much is it necessary to know? Banting subsequently stated that had he been familiar with all the complexities of the subject as revealed (or perhaps better to say, obscured) in the voluminous literature, he might never have had the courage to attempt his own research.[2] To the question "How much is it necessary to know?" no general or conclusive reply is possible. Robert Koch was a country doctor, whose education was probably much inferior to Banting's, yet no one man, with the glittering exception of Pasteur, has given modern medical science such a powerful impetus. Pasteur himself was a chemist and knew little or nothing about medicine. It will be

[1]Unless otherwise specified the quotations attributed to Banting are from his "History of Insulin," *Edinburgh M.J.*, 36: 1-18, Jan., '29. This is the famous Cameron Lecture. Unless otherwise specified quotations attributed to Best are from "Reminiscences of the Researches which led to the Discovery of Insulin," *C.M.A.J.*, 47: 398-400, Nov., '42.

[2]Nevertheless, by the time he actually began his experiments he was very well versed, according to Professor Henderson, in the literature of the whole field.

remarked at once, however, that the science of bacteriology was first developed, almost invented, by these illustrious scientists. There was no one with better credentials: no one could claim to be a specialist in bacteriology. Pasteur and Koch therefore worked in a virgin field (if early workers who did little more than scratch its surface be left out of account) while the acre which Banting chose to till was already well worked over, and regarded as unproductive. Was an ordinary doctor, with some surgical experience, the right man for the job? In May, 1921, it would hardly have seemed that he was.

Work was commenced on May 16. It had been arranged that Banting should have ten dogs and the use of a laboratory for eight weeks. This allotment of time and material must later have seemed naïve. Scores of dogs and many months of intensive effort were afterwards devoted to the work.

Professor Macleod had mentioned to his senior class in physiology that a young surgeon, a Toronto graduate, had returned to the University to carry out investigations aimed at determining the true function of the pancreatic islets (which some believed to be detoxifiers, a defence against certain organic poisons) and isolating the antidiabetic hormone which other authorities thought they produced. It happened that two members of the class, C. H. Best and E. C. Noble, had been engaged during the past term in experimental studies of Piqûre (puncture) or Claude Bernard diabetes,[3] a type of sugar sickness produced by damaging in experimental animals (in this case turtles) a certain centre in the brain—the floor of the fourth ventricle. They had acquired in this way a better understanding of carbohydrate metabolism and certain special skills in the performing of the necessary tests. If the young surgeon required collaboration in his work he might look to these young physiologists to provide it.

"Mr. Best and Mr. Noble," wrote Banting, "were appointed as assistants, each to give four weeks. The tossed a coin to decide who would give the first four weeks, and Mr. Best won the

[3] It was shown by Claude Bernard, using rabbits, that puncture with a sharp stilette at a certain spot on the floor of the fourth ventricle was immediately followed by an excessive secretion of urine which contained abundance of sugar. Refer to C. Bernard, *Leçons de Physiologie experimentale* (Paris), 1885, p. 296; *Systéme nerveux* (Paris), 1857, p. 397.

toss. At the end of the four weeks, however, Mr. Noble did not return and Mr. Best stayed with me."[4] Did ever Lady Luck provide an ambitious young man with such a singular opportunity! How Best converted this opportunity to use and glory Banting was always the first to relate. Best at this time was a recent graduate in physiology and biochemistry, having just obtained his B.A. He was engaged in scholarship work in physiology and had been recommended by Macleod principally because he would be able to assist Banting in the determination of the sugar content of blood and in other necessary chemical procedures. (Probably the earliest written account of the insulin research is contained in the letters which this slender, fair-haired boy was posting to his fiancée while the work was in progress. These letters have naturally never been published but must surely, begging the pardon of their author and recipient, be unique among love letters. It is interesting also to learn that the young man's paternal aunt, Miss Anna Best, had been a nurse at the Massachusetts General Hospital when Dr. E. P. Joslin, later a world-famed authority on diabetes, was a houseman, and had subsequently developed the disease herself and been one of Joslin's early patients. She died of diabetes only a few years before insulin became available.)

Following the programme laid down in Banting's midnight memorandum, they first ligated the pancreatic ducts of a number of dogs. This seemed relatively simple. The next step, the production of experimental diabetes, was considerably harder, and Banting's special training and ability as a surgeon, which might seem at first thought almost irrelevant, enabled him to surmount a major difficulty. To "depancreatize" a dog, that is to remove the pancreatic gland surgically and thus produce, after the example of Von Mehring and Minkowski, a condition of experimental diabetes, is by no means easy.

[4]Drs. Best and Noble agree that the coin-tossing story is a fiction, invented by a newspaper reporter and repeated here by Banting without inquiry. Noble was not in the best health at the time and his home being close to Toronto he left at once for a holiday. Best's home was far away in the Maritimes and he had previously decided to spend the summer working in Toronto. Noble returned later on and took an important part in the developmental work which followed the discovery. His name appears on many of the later papers.—L. S.

Writes Professor Best:

Banting's modesty was apparent from the very start of the investigations. Our first problem was to look over the literature in the attempt to get a better idea of the various operative procedures which had been used in work on the pancreas. Professor Macleod informed me that Banting felt he would have to depend entirely upon me for the translation of articles in the French literature. I found, however, that when I secured the publications of Hédon and other French workers in this field, that Banting's knowledge of French was of the same order as my own. We translated these articles together and the information secured provided a basis for our first attempts to produce the diabetic state upon which we wished to study the effects of the pancreatic extract. The operating facilities, however, were not satisfactory during the hot summer months of 1921 and we eventually abandoned the Hédon procedure of removing the pancreas in two stages and adopted a technique, which Banting developed, for complete pancreatectomy at one operation.

This somewhat laconic narrative of the initial work fails to picture the galling disappointment which was theirs when their precious dogs died of shock and infection, and also their triumph when the newly devised operation proved successful. Working in a small inferno of a laboratory, and sometimes also on the roof of the building, bathed in sweat and supposing themselves pressed for time, their efforts assumed as much drama and anxiety as if their subjects had been human patients desperately ill. And human lives (did they perhaps divine it?) were indeed at stake.

In the various accounts of his experiments which Banting has left, it is impossible to miss the presence of another motive. The dogs which he used, so to speak, as guinea pigs, were never for him mere living materials for his investigations. He was never so soft-hearted as to sacrifice the interests of science to sentiment, but the dogs were always spared unnecessary pain and it is pleasant to learn that his attempt to isolate a potent extract was speeded by the wish to save his diabetic dogs. His anxiety for their welfare, which he carried to a length which may seem preposterous to those who are more grimly "scientific," makes the campaign conducted against him at a later date by the anti-vivisectionists in Toronto, appear all the more absurd. Some account of individual dogs that went through heroic adventures in topsy-turvy metabolism will presently appear. But every dog he used was more than a "number" or a "case" or an "experimental subject" to Banting: every one was a canine personality and every one was distinguished in the notebooks by some peculiarity of breed or appearance. There was dog 92, a yellow mongrel designated as a "collie-hound"; there was dog 409, a likeable Irish terrier; there was dog 55, "a big clumsy white bull mongrel, female, wt. 14 kilos." (The numbers, by the way, were purely arbitrary, perhaps the number of a cage, perhaps a date, perhaps neither.) Every dog without exception was a friend and co-worker.

Banting and Best performed the first pancreatectomies on normal dogs to familiarize themselves with the blood and urinary findings and general clinical behaviour of the dogs following this operation. They could hardly hope to keep their first subjects alive long enough to benefit from their hypothetical extract. While they waited for degeneration of the acinar cells of the pancreas to take place in the dogs whose pancreatic ducts they had tied, they perfected the technique of pancreatectomy and studied the signs, symptoms and bio-chemistry of experimental diabetes.

On July 6, they chloroformed two of the dogs whose pancreatic ducts they had ligated seven weeks before. "To our great disappointment," writes Banting, in the Cameron Lecture already quoted, "it was found that the pancreas was not degenerated. Careful examination showed that the ligature was still present in a bulbous sac in the course of the duct. It was therefore necessary to operate on all the duct-tied dogs a second time and to exert particular care as to the tension put on the ligatures. If the ligature was applied too tightly gangrene developed immediately underlying the ligature and serous exudate laid down on the surface over the ligature resulted in the recanalization of the duct. If applied too loosely the duct was not blocked. We therefore in some cases applied two or three ligatures at different tensions. In re-operating we found some of the dogs had fairly well degenerated glands but it was decided to leave these another two weeks."

Further disappointment. Further delay. With seven of their eight weeks gone, they discovered that most of their work would have to be done again. They had hardly begun. This second difficulty in surgical technique Banting afterwards believed to be the reason for the failure of E. L. Scott's experiments. Once again it was demonstrated how great was the value of surgical training to an experimental physiologist.

By the twenty-seventh of July a depancreatized dog was ready; a duct-tied dog was also ready; the stage was set for the most crucial experiment of all. From this point onward the pace of the work was accelerated. The changes to be studied required not weeks but hours, even minutes, to become apparent. If an internal secretion of the pancreas existed, it must now be proved. Banting was about to take the final step in the programme which he had outlined for himself in London.

A duct-tied dog was chloroformed. Banting and Best, clad in their customary white cotton gowns, stood over it. With decisive strokes of his practised scalpel Banting opened the abdominal cavity and displaced the stomach to reveal the shrivelled remnant of the pancreas. This he removed. The degenerated gland was chopped into small pieces in a chilled mortar and frozen in brine. The mass was ground up and about 100 c. c. (a little more than three ounces) of saline were added. Of this extract 5 c. c. were administered intravenously to the depancreatized dog. Samples of blood were taken at half-hour intervals and analyzed for sugar content. It was shown that the blood sugar had fallen from 0.200 to 0.11 per cent. in two hours, and at the same time the clinical condition of the dog was much improved.

"The intense excitement and pleasure with which we watched the depth of colour in the sugar reagent fade as the blood sugar . . . became reduced under the action of insulin is difficult to describe," writes Best.

Here was the first proof that Banting's midnight inspiration had not been an empty dream, that he had not started on a fool's errand, that his work was not to be fruitless. But was it really proof? Was it proof positive? Most certainly not. Some error in the experiment, some factor not considered, might be responsible for this appearance of success. Many repetitions, many control experiments, many checks and safeguards, would be necessary to verify the result. Suppose, for instance, that this effect were not specific. Suppose that extracts of liver, of spleen, or of other organs, might produce a transient fall in blood sugar. What about blood dilution? Suppose the reagents used in testing for blood sugar were imperfect. Suppose that the result was obtainable only under special conditions. (Professor Macleod on his return from Edinburgh brought further doubts and objections, but by that time Banting and Best had considered and eliminated almost all of them.) No, the case was far from proved. Yet what exultation must have swelled in their hearts when they saw their dejected dog rapidly brighten and improve after the injection of their mysterious extract, and when the chemical tests confirmed their observation that its diabetes was less severe.

The improvement was of short duration; the dog soon relapsed into as grievous a state as before. But the fleeting, miraculous change, the surge of life that had entered its veins with their extract was at once the reward and the stimulus of their exertions. Their drudgery was lightened by a glimpse of delectable mountains, a promise of victories to come. Banting's faith was unshakable, but the stoutest faith may sometimes ask for a sign.

2

"Subsequent experiments," we read further, "were very successful and we consistently observed that the administration of this extract of degenerated pancreas resulted in the marked lowering of blood sugar, the diminution of sugar excretion, and phenomenal improvement in the general condition of completely diabetic dogs. The administration of a single large dose of this material often changed a listless, semi-comatose diabetic dog into a bright, active animal. Visitors to our working quarters during the months of August and September were greatly impressed with the remarkable effects of this extract—Professor C. L. Starr and Dr. George Young were among the first to witness a demonstration of the beneficial effects of the extract containing the long-sought-for internal secretion of the pancreas. The kindly interest and help of Professor Henderson was of inestimable value at this stage."

But we have left the story in the middle of July. Many difficulties were to be met and overcome before these triumphs were insured. To borrow a resounding sentence from Thomas Carlyle, "mountains of impediment were hurled aside." Let us turn now to the testimony of Best.

The blood sugar estimations, in which the Myers and Bailey modification of the Lewis-Benedict method were used, ran smoothly throughout the investigations but we had some preliminary difficulties with D-N ratio.[5] Banting had understood from Professor Macleod that the D-N ratio of the completely depancreatized dog must be 3.65 to 1 before a maximum degree of diabetes could be assumed. Actually, this ratio is the one which may be obtained in phloridzinized animals, but it is never exhibited for prolonged periods by the completely depancreatized dog.[6] After a great deal of discussion of the results of the glucose and nitrogen estimations a search of the literature revealed the above-mentioned facts and Banting was then happy to proceed with the injections of extract into animals which had a much lower D-N ratio. The results in the notebooks show that very definite lowering of blood sugar, decrease of sugar excretion, and improvement in the general condition of the diabetic animals, were secured in July, 1921. Even more definite results were obtained in August. . . .

Banting continues the history:

We may here mention another difficulty which arose with the early stage of the work, namely, obtaining samples of blood and the administering of extracts. In some physiological laboratories, in order to obtain samples of blood, the animal was anæsthetized, a large vein exposed by an incision through the skin, and a cannula tied into the vein. When the sample was obtained, the vein was ligated and the skin sewn up. It can be readily seen that when a few samples of blood had thus been taken the veins would be all used up. Furthermore the repeated administration of the anæsthetic was deleterious to the health of the dog, and caused in itself an elevation in the blood sugar. The first dog which died was carefully dissected and a map of all superficial veins was made.

[5]Ratio of dextrose (glucose) to nitrogen; also called G-N ratio. Urinary glucose was thought to come only from protein, this ratio being a measure of the conversion. The theory is out of date. The ratio is not constant.—L. S.

[6]Phloridzin is a chemical poison which, when given to animals in large doses, causes a diseased condition resembling diabetes.—L. S.

It was found that by careful technique a fine needle could be inserted into the vein of a dog as into the vein of a human, and repeated samples of blood obtained for analysis or repeated injections made. By using the same hole in the skin each time there was but little inconvenience to the dog.

In this connection it may be of interest to mention the general methods used in the care and handling of the animals. Not only from the humane standpoint but also to obtain the best results the experimental animal must be treated as a human in hospital. Good food, plenty of water, and a clean roomy cage are essential. The same rigid antiseptic routine must be carried out in the case of the dog as in the case of the human.[7] With kindly and gentle treatment practically all dogs can be made into pets and allowed the privilege of running about the laboratory except when specimens of urine are necessary.

To give an example, we had a dog about the laboratory for a number of weeks. The first thing in the morning the dog was allowed out of the cage. At this time the animal quarters were in the attic of the Medical Building, the laboratory in which we worked was two floors below. The dog was taken down to the laboratory and left loose about the room. When a sample of blood was required she willingly responded. She was put on the table on her side, a towel was put over her head, and the vein was distended by an elastic band. When blood had been obtained the towel was removed and the dog jumped up looking for her reward—a piece of meat. As soon as she got that she was off the table and running around the room again till the next sample was wanted.

Finally the dog had its pancreas removed. By the administration of extract from five degenerated pancreases the dog was maintained in good condition for eight days. At the end of this time we had used up all the available supply of what we then called "isletin." The severe symptoms of diabetes became evident.

About three o'clock in the morning while watching the development of terminal symptoms, it suddenly occurred to me that it might be possible to get rid of the toxic materials associated with the products of the acinous cell in another manner. Our former experiments had clearly shown that if we could but get

[7]"The animals were nursed as carefully as the somewhat limited facilities permitted, and each one was indelibly printed in our memories by virtue of some specific point which the observations on it established."—Best. For instance, dog 92 was the first to suffer insulin shock. This will be mentioned later.—L. S.

rid of these products a non-toxic beneficial extract could be prepared.[8] It was hoped that the old classroom experiment of injecting secretin[9] to stimulate the production of pancreatic juice could be continued long enough to exhaust the acinous cells.

The following morning a normal dog was anæsthetized and while Mr. Best extracted secretin from its intestinal mucosa a cannula was placed in its pancreatic duct. For four hours secretin was continuously injected and pancreatic juice was collected. At the end of this time no more juice was secreted in spite of the continued injection of secretin. The vagi[10] were then stimulated below the diaphragm and a few more drops of pancreatic juice were obtained. The exhausted pancreas was then rapidly removed, frozen, minced and extracted. This extract was carefully administered to the depancreatized dog. Even before the blood sugar results were obtained the dog showed clinical improvement insomuch that it began to clear its eyes, take more interest in the surroundings and within three hours was walking about the cage. I shall never forget the joy of opening the door of the cage and seeing this dog, which had been unable to walk, jump to the floor and run about in its normal fashion. For the three succeeding days the dog was maintained in good condition by the use of this extract. Unfortunately we were not able to obtain complete exhaustion in later experiments, and extracts made from incompletely exhausted glands were not so effective and the dog rapidly sank and died twenty days after the pancreas had been removed.

The exhausted gland extracts were not practical, but they served as contributory evidence in favour of the main theory of obtaining extracts of the island cells free from the products of acinous cells.

[8]Banting and Best then believed that it was essential to eliminate trypsin, a digestive ferment from the acinous cells. The proteins other than insulin were precipitated by their efforts to get rid of trypsin and in so doing they eliminated the real offenders, at least to a considerable degree.—L. S.

[9]Secretin(e): "A hormone formed by the epithelial cells of the duodenum under the stimulus of acid contents of the stomach, the office of which is to incite pancreatic secretion."—Stedman's *Medical Dictionary*.

[10]The vagus nerves (from a Latin root meaning "wandering," so called because of the extensive distribution of the nerves). These nerves are important elements of the autonomic nervous system, and their stimulation produces, among other effects, increased secretion of pancreatic ferments.— L. S.

A classroom experiment performed by Banting while a student in the same building only a few years previously was thus repeated in a modified form to aid him in his epochal research. The intensity and devotion with which he performed such experiments in his student days was remarked upon in an earlier chapter. This good work, of a type which must have seemed elementary and perhaps pointless to some of the other medical students, was now paying dividends. Although the exhausted gland extracts, as Banting himself pointed out, were not practical, and this phase of his investigations proved unimportant, the method was of theoretical interest and the idea illustrates the manner in which the mind of the research scientist correlates apparently unrelated facts and attempts to make capital of their affinity.

Banting's account of the experiment also illustrates an earlier statement that he regarded every dog as a friend and patient. This particular dog was number 92, the yellow "collie-hound," and was relatively a veteran in the business, since she had lost her pancreas at 4.00 p.m. on August 11, had been kept fairly healthy with the early extracts, had been the subject for a preliminary study of the effects of overdosage and was finally drafted again for a trial of the extract of secretin-exhausted gland, although as Banting made clear, this idea was really conceived in an effort to save her life. The account to be seen in his own handwriting in the original notebooks (some of the notes are in his hand, some in Best's) is even more vivid.

19 August, '21. Dog decidedly worse. Will not respond to snapping of fingers. Lies down nearly all the time. Does not lick wounds. If raised to her feet she lies down again. Appears very weak. Pus gathering in inner canthus of eyes. Eyes look sunken. Dog appears very tired.

21 August, 10.00 a.m. Dog in excellent condition. Wounds . . . are all licked clean. Eyes bright. No pus in corners. Dog tried to jump out of cage. When put on floor she ran around smelling, and sat down to scratch neck. Wounds are evidently not sore as she can run and even tried to stand on hind legs with her forelegs against me, but was too weak. Her spirits are excellent. She gets up and wags tail on our approach (before the extract was given she could not even be made to rise by snapping fingers, etc.).

2.00 p.m. Dog jumped out of cage to floor, about 2½ feet, lit on forefeet and did not fall. She is in excellent spirits.

Next day she suffered an anaphylactic shock from extract of partially exhausted cat pancreas and for about five minutes she hung between life and death while Banting and Best worked feverishly to save her. Thereafter the extracts so produced proved less effective in staving off the ravages of diabetes (it was very difficult to exhaust a gland completely) and poor 92 took a turn for the worse.

August 25. Dog very weak. Hungry, thirsty. Can hardly stand up. Staggers when she tries to walk. . . .
August 26, 6.00 a.m. Dog very, very weak. Refuses meat. Has only passed about 200 c. c. urine during night. Seems to be extremely tired. Had two good drinks of water when the dish was put under her nose. The only movement she made was to raise her head and feebly wag tail. Lies stretched out on her side and cannot be roused by affection.
6.00 p.m. Dog improved as compared to this morning. Able to stand and walk when put on her feet but does not move unnecessarily. Refuses meat. Drinks very little.
August 31. Dog died during night.

The post-mortem revealed pus in the right pleural sac and bilateral pneumonia. Infection had flourished because the diabetes was very imperfectly controlled. Dog 92 was a casualty in an important action and did not die in vain. But the "biography" recorded in Banting's notes reveals not only keen observation but real and active sympathy and an affection that was more than "scientific."

The continuing experiments called for many more than the ten dogs originally obtained from Professor Macleod. "There are some notes in this first book," writes Professor Best (with reference to the first of the notebooks in which the collaborators recorded their findings) "which remind me of the fact that the supply of animals was not always satisfactory. Suggestions have been made by poorly informed authors that dogs were appropriated from the street with very little ceremony. This is not true, but there were occasions when we made a tour through various parts of the city and bargained with owners of animals. They were paid for by funds which we took from our own pockets. This money may have come from the sale of Banting's automobile. Neither of us received a stipend during the summer of 1921 and for a time I used funds which he loaned me. A part of this money certainly came from the sale of his Ford car."

The interest and assistance of Professor Velyien Henderson, head of the Department of Pharmacology, has already been mentioned. Professor Henderson states:

My early association with [Banting] during the early days of the discovery of insulin was in the first instance due to the fact that he was worrying about the surgical problem of ileus, and as I was doing some experimental work on intestinal movements, he came up to my laboratory from Professor Macleod's during his spare time. He naturally discussed his own work with me and this continued during the following year when he became a member of my Department.

Later in the year, after Macleod's return from Edinburgh, it was Henderson who gave Banting a position in the University with a salary, which, though small, was sufficient for his needs and enabled him to continue with his work. By fortunate coincidence a demonstrator in pharmacology resigned from the University staff to work in the Ontario Department of Health. Having paid three months of his salary, Henderson had enough left over to make a place for Banting. The latter was required to teach pharmacology about two days a week and was free to devote the rest of his time to research. In point of fact he did very little teaching and Professor Henderson apparently regarded his job as a research appointment since he insisted that Macleod should write a letter to the University authorities stating it to be his belief that Banting's experiments were likely to lead to worthwhile results. But again we are ahead of the story: as Best's reminiscences make clear the research team was financially close to the wind during that strenuous summer.

These notebooks (continues Best) have brought back many other memories—of meals prepared in the night over the Bunsen burner, of a minor operation performed on a friend balanced precariously on the animal operating table, and of the many long chats with Banting about what the future might hold when unlimited amounts of insulin would be available.

The extract, by the way, had not yet been dubbed with its present name but was still called "isletin."

To begin again at the point where we left the actual research, we turn once more to the Cameron Lecture. Banting writes:

Experiments with degenerated gland extract and exhausted gland extract showed that these extracts produced lowering of blood sugar, disappearance of sugar from urine, increased utilization of intravenous glucose in the depancreatized dog and marked clinical improvement with increased duration of life.

It was then inevitable that a more practical means of obtaining extract must be found if progress was to be made. Laguesse had found that there were relatively more islet cells in the pancreas of a new-born than in the adult pancreas. The first idea was to extract the pancreas of new-born animals. It seemed reasonable to conclude that the pancreas of a partly developed fœtus might contain even more abundant islet cells. It was finally conjectured that if one could obtain the pancreas of a fœtus at the end of the first third of pregnancy that the internal secretion of the islet cells would be present since other internal secretions (e.g., epinephrin) are present at this stage of development. At the same time, it seemed reasonable to conclude that since digestion is not called into play till after the birth of the animal that there would not be powerful digestives present in the fœtus.[11] Having been born and raised on the farm, and being familiar with stock-breeding, I knew that cattle are frequently bred before fattening in order to make them better feeders. There would therefore be plenty of fœtal calves at the abattoirs. The next morning at nine o'clock, having obtained sterile instruments and containers, Mr. Best and I proceeded to the abattoir where we obtained the pancreases of nine fœtal calves varying from three to fours months' gestation.

An extract was made and carefully administered intravenously to a depancreatized dog on November 19, 1921. Following the injection the blood sugar fell from 0.33 to 0.17 in one hour. This result was confirmed by subsequent injections. We were thus

[11]Banting speaks here as if this had all been a matter of conjecture except for the discovery made by Laguesse of the relatively more abundant islet cells in the pancreas of a new-born animal. It had been demonstrated by Ibrahim, however, that the pancreas of the ox up to the fourth month of intrauterine life contains no active proteolytic enzyme (i.e., digestive ferment) while the experiments of Carlson and Drennan seemed to indicate the presence of a substance producing hypoglycæmia (low blood sugar).—L. S.

able to maintain an adequate supply of the active principle of the islands of Langerhans with no expense to the laboratory, and in quantities which provided for repeated trials and various extractions. It was found that the active principle could be extracted from the fœtal gland with acetone and alcohol, and that it was not destroyed by chloroform or ether.

3

We have now followed the investigations through three principal stages. The first stage was that in which Banting pursued the idea which had started him in quest of the elusive extract —the process of duct ligation and subsequent extraction of the gland. The second stage was the emergency production of the extract from a pancreas exhausted by the injection of secretin and the stimulation of the vagus nerves until the acinar cells were worn out and only the islet cells remained active. The third stage was that just described, in which fœtal glands, containing as yet little or no active acinar tissue, were employed as the source of "isletin." The first two methods were strictly laboratory procedures. Though of great scientific interest they were incapable of large-scale repetition. The third method was more productive than the others, but here again the supply of raw material was obviously limited. If the work were to have larger implications and results of practical value it was obviously necessary that attention should be turned to the pancreas of adult animals. Just how much progress, then, had been made?

As we have seen, Von Mehring and Minkowski, by their discovery that removal of the pancreas produces diabetes, precipitated a tremendous flurry of research work and numerous attempts had been made, from 1889 onward, to devise methods for extracting the active principle of the gland. These numberless efforts had been attended with varying degrees of success, and indeed Zuelzer's experiments were considered so satisfactory that his method was patented by the Schering Company of Berlin, who undertook the preparation of his extract on a commercial scale. But all methods, Zuelzer's included, had eventually to be abandoned and the problem was left unsolved.

Banting had approached it with a view to eliminating toxic factors by getting rid of the digestive elements of the gland in one way or another, and had succeeded in reaching his objective by no less than three different routes. No one of these routes, however, was broad enough for heavy traffic; no one of the methods would produce the extract in more than infinitesimal amounts. He had proved the existence of an internal secretion of the pancreas beyond all cavil or dispute, and had succeeded in isolating it in a form that was pure enough for limited use. He had, to change the figure, struck oil, but only a trickle of oil. How could he step up production to the point where it would attain clinical significance? There was only one sufficient source for the material —the pancreas of the adult animal. And here he was faced again with the problem which had baffled so many others. Was it not after all an impossibility to make a whole gland extract free of poisonous impurities? This was an admission which Banting's stubborn spirit refused to make. When he had gone thus far, no power in hell or heaven could prevent him from attempting more. General Grant at Vicksburg expressed the famous resolve that he would "fight it out along these lines if it takes all summer." Banting was now midway in his great campaign of the magic islands and was fully determined to "fight it out along these lines" without regard to time or difficulty.

As a matter of fact, the work did not proceed in an orderly sequence beginning with the first method and ending with the whole gland extractions. As early as August 17, 1921, studies were made of the effect of whole fresh gland extracts and a page from the first notebook shows that on this date a very definite fall in blood sugar was obtained with an extract made up in Ringer's solution, and with one which had been acidified. The alkaline extract apparently did not produce any definite effect. It will be noted from dates already given that this work was left over for the time while other courses were followed. Much information was secured concerning the properties of the extract and its effect upon diabetic animals. It was found that sugar given with the extract was retained to a much greater extent than was the case when it was administered in the absence of the extract. Injection of the extract into depancreatized animals was found invariably to be followed by a prompt and decided fall in the percentage of sugar in the blood, the extent and duration of the fall varying with the amount of extract injected. The reduced blood sugar was accompanied by a diminished excretion of sugar in the urine, and comparison of the sugar balance following the administration of a known amount of sugar when the extract was given and withheld showed that depancreatized animals recovered some of their lost power of utilizing carbohydrate under the influence of the injections. Similarly prepared extracts of liver and spleen were proved to have no such effects, and it was found that the administration of an active pancreatic extract by the mouth or by the rectum did not reduce the sugar content of the blood as it did when given intravenously or subcutaneously. Incubation of the extract with pancreatic juice resulted in the complete destruction of the active material.

At an early phase in the work, the collaborators were interested in the result of overdosage. This is recorded by Best as follows:

On August 14, 1921, an experiment was made to investigate the effect of what we then considered to be an overdose of the extract. The blood sugar was lowered from 0.22 per cent.—a definite diabetic level—to the hypoglycæmic figure of 0.06. The insulin shock reaction, now so well known, was then observed for the first time, and dog 92 suffered its effects. . . . A little later this experiment was repeated and a note was made that the animal with a low blood sugar appeared much brighter after the administration of glucose.

When Professor Macleod returned from Europe in September he observed the effects of the administration of the extract. Banting has written:

In view of the great importance of the fundamental observation that the active principle of the extract exerted a definite influence upon the blood sugar and sugar secretion of diabetic animals, he advised us to secure even more results along this line.

This they did, and the extraction of fœtal glands was one of the steps which followed.

Henderson had suggested that the results obtained in their first successful experiments might be explained by a blood dilution factor. They performed experiments to eliminate this possibility. Macleod, on his return from abroad, made the same suggestion, and on being told that it had already been done he insisted on having these experiments repeated under his direction to make sure that there had been no mistake.

The crucial problem of producing extracts from the whole gland of the adult beef was undertaken afresh. As a matter of fact, a highly potent extract was prepared before Macleod's return. The first extracts made from the whole adult gland were extracted with alcohol removed by distillation in vacuo at low temperature. An effective product was secured by extraction with alcohol and acid. Then, as if their luck had suddenly turned, Banting and Best found themselves unable, after repeated attempts over a period of about a week, to produce a satisfactory extract. This inexplicable turn of events was most discouraging. Had they deluded themselves? Were their previous good results due merely to a fortuitous chance? Had they now to confess that somehow, despite the utmost care, mistakes had crept into their experiments, and that they, like the others before them, had been beaten and chagrined? The evidence that their work was good was by now too imposing to admit of serious doubt. Yet something was definitely wrong. If they could make a good extract once, why could they not make it again?

Professor Henderson, wise in the way of research, helped them with the solution of their problem. First he asked each of them to write down as nearly as he remembered exactly what had been done on the day of the first successful extraction. Comparison of the two accounts helped little. Neither of them could recall more than that they had used a piece of gland of specified size from the tail of a pancreas, and had extracted it with alcohol and acid. The amounts and exact concentrations of the reagents had not been recorded since the experiment was only a preliminary trial. Henderson advised that they should cut a pancreas into sections and make two series of extractions: in one series they were to use a fixed amount of alcohol, varying within rather wide limits the amount of acid; in the other series they were to keep the acid constant and vary the alcohol. The importance of the relative acidity and of the concentration of alcohol was soon

Courtesy Professor C. H. Best.

Above: BANTING AND BEST with the first dog to be kept alive by insulin.
Below: LEONARD THOMPSON, first patient to receive insulin, January 11, 1922.
(Photograph taken ten years later.)

apparent as they were not long in finding the right combination.[12] Various percentages of alcohol were used for the extraction and it was found that the active principle was not soluble above ninety per cent. The importance of the degree of acidity may be judged from the fact that another investigator reached the same point by a somewhat similar line of reasoning but failed to obtain the right pH in his extractions and so missed the opportunity to isolate insulin.

The first phase of the adventure of the magic islands, the islands of Langerhans, was now drawing to a close. Much experimental work remained to be done and the contributions of Collip and others in purifying the extract have still to be recorded. But a passage had been found through the reefs of difficulty; one dog had been kept alive for seventy days without a pancreas by giving it daily injections of various extracts. Was the whole gland extract safe for human use? The toxic effects which had rendered Zuelzer's preparation useless had to be expected also from this one; had, indeed, been observed in experimental animals. The next job, then, was to purify it.

4

On January 11, 1922 (records Banting) the first patients were treated with extract in the Toronto General Hospital. Following the injections there was a typical lowering of blood sugar and a slight decrease of the sugar in the urine. But since the percentage of protein in the extracts was high, a sterile abscess developed at the point of injection.

These results were not as encouraging as those obtained by Zuelzer in 1908. He and his associates reported their results in six cases of diabetes mellitus treated with a pressed juice of pancreas which had been extracted with alcohol and evaporated to dryness. The residue was redissolved in salt solution. Following

---

[12]This is the story as told by Professor Henderson. Professor Best's recollection is that this difficulty arose, and was solved in somewhat the manner described, at a much later date, after Collip had made his contribution and had turned to other work. The temporary inability to produce insulin was experienced during the phase of the work being done at the Connaught Laboratories. In any case it was soon overcome.

the intravenous injection of this extract in five diabetic patients who were kept on a fairly constant diet, the excretion of acetone, diacetic acid and sugar in the urine decreased or entirely disappeared. An improvement in the general conditions of all patients treated was observed following the injections. The intravenous injection of this extract in these five cases was accompanied by severe chills, fever and occasionally by vomiting.

In 1909, Forschbach, working in Minkowski's Clinic, reported two cases treated with Zuelzer's extract. One was not improved by the extract and the other showed a slight temporary reduction in the excretion of sugar. Owing to its extreme lability and the severe toxicity following its administration the extract prepared by Zuelzer did not come into general use in the treatment of diabetes mellitus.

Our results in the human were, however, sufficiently encouraging to change the whole trend of the research. Professor J. J. R. Macleod abandoned his work on anoxæmia and turned almost his whole laboratory staff on to the problems of the physiological activity of this pancreatic extract.

Dr. J. B. Collip was given the problem of chemical refinement, and in a short time he was able to run the scale of fractional precipitation from 60 to 90 per cent. alcohol and thereby succeeded in producing a less toxic and more active product.

Best and Borschacht, an accomplished biochemist, had done alcoholic fractionations to get rid of trypsin, not knowing that it had to be activated before it would destroy insulin, but in so doing they had removed much of the inert protein. Collip stepped up the percentage of alcohol and removed the greater part of it, thus producing a practical extract. Fractionations had previously been discontinued at 65 per cent. because at this point the trypsin, for which tests were performed, had been elimated. (Who first suggested the use of alcohol is not clear. Professor Henderson was always insistent that the idea had been Banting's. Professor Best asserts that when he and Borschacht were doing fractionations, Banting recalled that the suggestion had originally been made to him by Macleod, although he had forgotten it in the meantime. It is not a point of great importance since the method had already been tried by earlier workers.)

It was plain, none the less, that expert collaboration was needed. "Research in medicine is specialized," Banting wrote later,[13] "and as in all organized walks of life, a division of labour is necessary. In consequence a division of labour in the field of insulin took place." Professor Collip was called upon to assist.

It would be well at this time to summon Collip himself to the stand and hear from this distinguished investigator his own account of his part in the work.[14]

Banting and the writer (he tells us) first met in the early Spring of 1921 in the office of Professor J. J. R. Macleod in the Department of Physiology of the University of Toronto, under whom we had both come to work. That day there began a close association between us, and although this was for a time strained by certain misunderstandings, it grew closer with the passing years. I recall quite vividly how impressed I was with Banting and his problem, which was nothing less than a frontal attack on the pancreas to obtain its elusive internal secretion. My own problem, the effect of pH upon the blood sugar, seemed insignificant by comparison, but I had come to work with a man, whereas Banting had a problem which even at that time superseded such things as personalities and graduate training. I feel that I was very fortunate to have been a worker in Macleod's laboratory at the time that Banting started his first investigations and to have known of the progress of this work at first hand. He was most anxious that I should become a co-worker with him. I assured him that I would be delighted to do this, but that I would have to wait until my revered Chief, Professor Macleod, said the word. Some weeks later, at a time when Banting's early experiments, in which he had been assisted by C. H. Best (now Professor Best), had in my opinion established completely the existence of insulin, Dr. Macleod asked me to join in the work. The part which I was able to contribute subsequently to the work of the team was only that which any well-trained biochemist could be expected to contribute, and was indeed very trivial by comparison with Banting's contribution.

It would seem in retrospect, and reviewed dispassionately from a neutral corner, that Collip's ultimate estimate of his own contribution errs equally in the opposite direction from an excess

[13]F. G. Banting, M.B., "Canada's Record in Research," *MacLean's Magazine*, November 15, 1924.

[14]J. B. Collip, "Frederick Grant Banting, Discoverer of Insulin," *The Scientific Monthly*, 52: 472-474, May, '41.

of modesty. His work was after all the capstone of the whole investigation, short of producing insulin in commercial quantity —a problem which required the combined efforts of many workers. It marks the first major advance beyond the point attained by Zuelzer; and if the stage was set for Collip's arrival, if "any well-trained biochemist" could have done as much, this should not be allowed to detract from his credit for producing a usable extract. The same difficulty had presented itself on previous occasions and had been left unresolved. Other advances, achieved by other scientists in the meantime, provided Collip with better weapons. Of these he made capital use. Details of the methods employed hold little interest for the general reader. For those concerned with such matters, an account of the preparation of the earlier extract (Banting and Best) and also of the preparation of the extracts as used in the first clinical cases (J. B. Collip) may be found in the *Transactions of the Royal Society of Canada.* (Vol. 16, Section V, 1922.)

A relatively pure extract (not so good as later preparations) resulted from Collip's fractional precipitation method. Could the same thing be done on a grand scale? "Unfortunately," states Banting, "when Dr. Collip endeavoured to do this on a large-scale production, he encountered serious difficulties. After a few months' delay Mr. Best took up the problem of production and refinement and he . . . [continued] in charge of the production of insulin in the Connaught Laboratories at the University of Toronto. He and those associated with him are responsible to a very large extent for many refinements now used in the manufacture of insulin."

Those associated with him included Fitzgerald, Defries, Scott, and a number of others who, on this score at least, are largely unknown to fame except among those familiar with the research and the whole story of the development of insulin. Collip was provided facilities by Professor Fitzgerald and Professor Defries of the Connaught Laboratories. A little later Mr. E. C. Noble, Drs. J. Hepburn and J. K. Latchford began work on insulin under the direction of Professor Macleod in the department of Physiology. Other names which are not undeserving our notice must necessarily be passed by in an account which gives chief regard to the central figure. But at every stage of the work Banting and Best received help and sustenance from other workers. The discovery of insulin followed in the genealogy of events from studies which had gone before; it was aided by contemporary efforts both in Toronto and elsewhere; and its crowning development was made possible only by the united and co-operative exertions of many scientists in many lands. It is not to be supposed that insulin sprang full-armoured and ready for immediate use from the head of a Jove-like Banting. Science provides our best examples of concerted team-work, of "sequent toil all tending toward one goal." For instance, whoever may have suggested the use of alcohol, the idea of using strong acid (for Banting and Best had used weak acid originally) was the idea which ultimately solved most of the remaining problems and it originated not in Toronto but in the United States (Walden and Shaffer).

Banting's relations with his chief, Professor Macleod, were not of the happiest, and there seems no reason now for concealing the fact. The original announcement of the discovery came from Macleod, a fact which his juniors did not relish. The announcement was so worded that those who heard it were left with the impression that most of the praise was due the Professor. He was lauded accordingly. Far from any desire to steal the commendation rightfully belonging to others, Macleod, already heaped with honours, was following in complete innocence the tradition in which he had been nurtured.[15] In the German universities of his day, and Germany was then the magnetic centre of world science, the accomplishments of the laboratories were always proclaimed under the name of the laboratory director, regardless of who had performed the experiments. A passing nod, sufficient approbation, was given to the actual workers. Macleod himself, as a younger man, had experienced the underdog's chagrin at the high-handedness of this Germanic custom. If he felt its injustice then, as no doubt he did, he had apparently forgotten. The vista was altered when seen from the top of the hill. Those who knew him best never seriously questioned his good faith, but this had no effect on Banting's hot and immediate anger. The Teutonic notion of what should constitute a proper allotment

[15]The sentences which follow are perhaps liable to misinterpretation. Professor Collip, who was closely associated with Macleod, points out that no one could less resemble the autocratic German professors, whose students leaped to attention on their approach. Macleod, though dignified, was genial and human, never the martinet.

of recognition (a conception to be considered later when dealing with Banting's management of the Institute), fared badly when transplanted to the democratic environment of Canada, and having followed the course of Banting's patient and arduous struggle, we can hardly wonder at his swift indignation. What stirs our perplexity and gives rise to a certain feeling of embarrassment is the grudging persistence of his dislike, the depth and duration of his animosity, which long survived the general recognition of his own high deserts. It is possible that there were other circumstances of which we know nothing, but the spectacle of the young man turning away in anger from the old one, refusing for years to speak to him, cannot be said to add to our admiration for Banting. He was, among his other qualities, a lasting hater.

There is also the fact to be considered that at the first scientific meeting in New Haven where the discovery was announced (it had previously been presented to the Toronto Academy of Medicine but not immediately publicized) Macleod was the chairman and his summation followed the remarks of Banting and Best. Both scientific and press reporters hailed the president of the American Physiological, the already famous scientist (granted that he had given them the clue). On the next public occasion of a scientific nature, a meeting of the American Association of Physicians in Chicago, Macleod was constrained to present the case by a rule of the Association which requires that a paper on which a member's name appears shall be read by the member, rather than by one of the "outside" collaborators; Banting and Best being non-members of the Association at that time.

Old bitterness is better forgotten, and the details of their disagreement can be of little interest. Nevertheless, to make perfectly clear the paramount credit in the discovery which is due to Banting, it is worth while to consider in what degree Macleod contributed to the work. So far as the present investigation has been able to discover, Professor Macleod is deserving of the gratitude of the diabetic and the plaudits of the world for diverting a part of his laboratory facilities from other work (and there were many demands upon him); for making available to Banting the useful collaboration of C. H. Best, J. B. Collip and other workers; for insisting on the verification of the initial work and the repetition of certain control experiments; for advice on technical problems; and for the value of his great prestige in assuring the validity of the results, and explaining the theoretical implications to fellow scientists. These were important contributions which it is not desired to minimize. "Under his direction," wrote Banting, "various problems were allotted to pairs of workers and an unparalleled amount of information was gained in a comparatively short time." But the helping hand was not the creating hand, and popular opinion has not been unjust to Macleod in reserving its greatest acclaim for his young colleague, who cannot be fairly designated, as he has been, Macleod's "assistant."

For the part played by the other chief participants, their own testimony will suffice. Dr. Best has written of Banting's "generosity" in sharing with him the credit for the discovery of insulin. That Banting himself assigned "equal credit" to Best is a well-known fact; that he was generous in so doing is Professor Best's candid admission. Certainly no other single collaborator approaches the stature of Best, and Banting, who was in the surest position to know, never wavered in his loyalty to his co-worker. Secondary questions, such as who first suggested the use of acidified alcohol for preparing the extract (an obvious thing to do and not original with either of them) have been brought in dispute by others, but are not deserving of serious attention.[16] The duct-tied gland, the secretin-exhausted gland, the non-acinous fœtal gland were all of them concepts of the senior partner. What more could any man covet than the equal credit which Banting assigned, and what would be gained by a nicer balancing of points, a fractious quibbling over details? Professor Collip, likewise, makes no demand on the predominant rôle which some of his admirers have claimed for him, and his own estimate of the value of his contribution has already been cited.

These comparisons are brought forward without reference to personalities and without the wish to detract from the well-

[16]"Banting argued that as he had used fœtal tissue which was too old to contain merely islets, and as secretin-exhausted pancreas could not be free from enzymes, the use of acid and alcohol to reduce enzymatic activity must succeed and did in the first case tried, but it was a struggle to produce active extracts regularly from beef pancreas. This step-like progress was not due to blind intuition, but to a sound and thorough knowledge of the literature of diabetes and a critical sifting of the facts from the doubtful. The thoroughness of his knowledge was not revealed to all with whom he was in contact and he was misjudged by some in consequence."—Professor Velyien E. Henderson.

deserved celebrity of Banting's colleagues, each of whom has carried on important researches of his own and has notable achievements in science to his credit. The discovery of insulin was, as we have seen, an example of superb team-work, and Banting could not have made a practical, usable extract without assistance. But the captain of the team and the player who carried the ball was undoubtedly Banting. The greater share of the fame for the discovery fell to him, and Fame, who is notoriously fickle and unfair, for once was entirely just.

The consummation of the whole research, the production of a safe and potent extract in commercial quantity, was the work of no one man, of no one group of men. Banting resumes the story.

During the spring of 1922 (he writes) Dr. Best succeeded in producing quantities of insulin sufficiently large and sufficiently purified to prove thoroughly the value of insulin to diabetic patients. A large number of hopeless, severe diabetics began to come to Toronto. It was the ideal of all those associated in the work to obtain the largest quantities of insulin at the lowest possible price for the rapidly increasing clinical needs.

When the first report of insulin was made at New Haven in December, 1921, Dr. G. H. A. Clowes offered to put the resources of the Eli Lilly Company at our disposal whenever we felt that our laboratory experiments had reached the point at which their practical co-operation might be of benefit. About April, 1922, we accepted his kind offer. From this time the Eli Lilly Company collaborated with us and were of the greatest assistance in the development of the large-scale production. There was an intimate reciprocation of all results between the two laboratories, and in the early days when we were unable to make sufficient insulin for our clinical needs Mr. Lilly and Dr. Clowes were good enough to assist us from their inadequate supply. It is interesting now to look over the telegrams and letters that went back and forth between Toronto and Indianapolis at that time. They recall the terrific pressure under which we were all working in the common endeavour to provide a purified product for widespread distribution. About this time Toronto and Indianapolis were honoured with visits from many distinguished scientists, including Sir Henry Dale. . . . These visitors were particularly interested in the methods of extraction and the large-scale production of insulin.

The correspondence between Toronto and Indianapolis to which Banting refers was enormous; huge files accumulated in both cities. With few exceptions, the interest of these letters, at least to the general reader, is slight, since they are all highly technical. In any case Professor Macleod was a more assiduous letter-writer than Banting. Dr. Clowes has stated[17] that "the truth is I had very little correspondence with him as I made so many visits to Toronto that I saw him on the average of two or three times a month during the first year of insulin. . . . Banting was no letter-writer." Nevertheless a number of letters exist in which we may trace not only the technical developments but also the cross currents of personal differences, the eddying conflicts of judgment and emotion. Such a letter is the following:

August 14, 1922.

DEAR DR. CLOWES:

Your letter of August 11th is received this morning. I was sorry that I did not get the 50 c. c. from Mr. Walden in Boston for we were out of extract three days last week. The 500 c. c. arrived Saturday and is being tested this morning. I was anxious for you to see Drs. Geyelin and Palmer for they were thinking of starting to make it for their own use. And I am glad that you will be able to send them some soon. When Best came back he told me that he had seen Professor Macleod and that Macleod had had a letter from S—— in California and that he was making extract and using it on patients. Best told me that Macleod had sent S—— full details of preparation, and that S—— in his letter had thanked Macleod for "HIS" method and that the results were good. They have given some per rectum. Now I think that Professor Macleod might have spoken to some of us about the matter. Were you aware of it? As regards the reprints of the preparation, I have only sent out two or three because I thought that for the present it was just as well to hold up on some of the methods. A Dr. N—— was up from Pittsburg and wanted to find out all he could. I gave him a reprint and we told him the outlines of the tunnel process but I did not tell him anything and I warned Scott and Best not to give any information that would in any way involve a breach of confidence with you. You may rest assured that as far as I am concerned nothing will in any way get out that will give methods of preparation.

[17]Personal communication.

I appreciate the effort that you are putting forth to help us. The clinic here has not started and will not start for a while yet. In the meantime I am carrying on the best I can. I take the specimens up to Christie Street Hospital. Tomorrow one of the most influential Americans of Washington arrives with his daughter. The patients are doing well. I have not heard from Dr. Joslin. Professor —— is not in favour with the other men forming a committee as he thinks it would not be in keeping with the priority coming from Toronto. I tried to assure him that by this means, and only by it, would the priority come. He has no objections to the men coming at the same time but thinks that a committee should not be formed and that nothing would be gained by having them yet. Unless it be to go over the results we got at Christie Street. You see what I am up against. But never mind—I will overcome the difficulty and make Toronto General Hospital proud of itself in spite of itself. It makes me all the more anxious to see Dr. Woodyatt.

The embryonic pancreas was only tested on depancreatized dogs and as far as they were concerned was the most potent thing tried. I think you are perfectly right in drawing the conclusion that you do regarding their potency [the potency of extracts of embryonic pancreas].

The vacuum pump arrived Friday and was tried out Saturday but there was a leak in the condensor which is being fixed today, and when it is fixed things will start again.

I hope to see you soon. I will go into a few of our best cases when you come and work out the carbohydrate consumption in detail on them. What about stopping over a few hours in Rochester on your way and seeing Williams? I told him that I would speak to you and ask you.

Yours very sincerely,
F. G. BANTING.

Dr. Clowes continues:

I have duplicates of a great many letters I wrote to him but of course these are all very technical. Certain of my letters to Banting in the fall of 1922 are interesting since they indicate the course that I then followed of pledging all clinicians who received insulin for experimental purposes to hold back their publications until such time as Banting and his associates were prepared to get out a series of papers covering their laboratory and clinical work. In one of these letters as early as September,

1922, I mentioned to Banting the fact that I hoped that if we followed this course of distributing material to qualified clinics free of charge, not only in the United States but all over the world, it would result in a rapid appreciation of insulin which should lead to Banting and his associates receiving the Nobel Prize at a very early date. As you know, Banting and Macleod were given the Nobel Prize a year later at what, I believe, was a record for prompt recognition by the Nobel Prize Committee of a great discovery.

To return to Banting's own narrative:

In the autumn of 1922, the product was still extremely impure and we were experiencing great difficulty with deterioration and sensitization reactions. By the middle of November the Eli Lilly Company were first able to effect a very substantial purification and concentration of the product by developing the isoelectric method of precipitation. This product had the added advantage of being reasonably stable. The yields at that time were still very small, but by January (1923), as a result of work carried out in the Connaught Laboratories and the Eli Lilly Company, we were able to provide insulin to about 250 clinicians.

On account of the limited supply of insulin only severe diabetics were accepted for treatment. These were thoroughly investigated with the object of gaining as much information as possible in order to guide the practitioner in the use of insulin when it became available. As soon as the supply became more abundant, it was decided that the Connaught Laboratories should send a limited supply of insulin to diabetic specialists throughout Canada and that the Eli Lilly Company should do the same in the United States.

[This is a story which we have seen repeated in recent years in the careful allotment of a limited supply of penicillin, before mass production, speeded by wartime needs, made it readily procurable.]

In November, 1922, a two-day Round Table Conference was held in Toronto. Diabetic specialists from the United States joined with the Toronto group in considering the future plans. Various clinical problems were allocated for special study to the various centres, and it was agreed to report all preliminary findings in a special "diabetic" number of the *Journal of Metabolic Research*.

Representatives from the various countries came to Toronto for periods of time and were given full details of the preparation and use of insulin. Professor Duncan Graham organized a post-graduate course in the treatment of diabetes and use of insulin at which a large number of doctors attended. Similar schools were established at diabetic centres throughout the United States.

Whilst Banting and his associates were pursuing their researches in Toronto and Dr. George H. A. Clowes and the research staff of the Eli Lilly Company were working in Indianapolis, Dr. Phillip A. Shaffer was working in his laboratory in St. Louis along similar lines and contributed greatly to the general knowledge of the subject.[18] Other workers took up the task in many parts of the world, and information about the properties of insulin grew apace.

In Great Britain, at the National Institute for Medical Research, Hampstead, the scientific staff of the Medical Research Council was seeking to increase the yield of product from the raw material, to simplify, shorten and cheapen the processes of its production, to obtain accurate measurements of potency by reference to a fixed standard of value and finally to find the best methods of securing the bacteriological sterility of the final product. They were in constant communication with the workers at Toronto, both groups giving and receiving full information of new developments and improvements as they occurred. Results obtained were made freely available for the assistance of those engaged in other work. Technical information and small samples of the finished product were so far as possible put at the disposal of approved scientific workers undertaking collateral lines of investigation elsewhere. At various hospitals where the necessary facilities existed for biological and chemical work in the laboratories and for scientific clinical studies, investigation and carefully controlled treatment under suitable safeguards was undertaken in close association with the work of the National Institute. British workers experienced, and helped to surmount, the difficulty of passing from the small laboratory scale of produc-

[18]Shaffer is usually given credit along with Walden for originating the strong-acid method.

tion to large-scale production by mechanical means, without which the product could never become generally available at reasonable cost. (Here again there is an analogy in the story of penicillin, for it was the large-scale production of the latter drug which caused the greatest difficulties.) British-made insulin was first supplied from two sources, namely, the firm of the British Drug Houses, Ltd., in conjunction for this purpose with Messrs. Allen and Hanburys, and the firm of Messrs. Burroughs, Wellcome and Company. These firms undertook the manufacture under agreement with the Medical Research Council.

It should be mentioned that the process developed in Toronto for the production of insulin was patented, and that the substantial sums accruing from this source did not go to Banting or to any other individual or group. A patent was secured in the names of Banting, Best and Collip, but was assigned before issue to the Board of Governors of the University of Toronto. Everywhere in the world, once the initial stage was passed, the process was given away "without strings," except that a fee or royalty was charged by the Connaught Laboratories of the University for testing insulin made in the United States. The Connaught Laboratories, however, did not receive the money. When expenses had been paid, the remainder was divided into two equal parts. One of these was accepted in trust by the Insulin Patent Pool, to be used for purposes of maintaining the patent rights and eventually for further kindred research. The other half of the net proceeds was divided three ways. One-third of it was to be used for research under Banting's direction wherever he might go, so long as he remained in Canada. Another third was similarly earmarked, with the same proviso, for the work of Best and any associates he might designate. The remaining third was to support the research of Collip and his co-workers. The chief object of patenting the process was to prevent the unauthorized manufacture and exploitation of a potentially dangerous drug. Similar safeguards were set up in the United States and Great Britain, and in other countries. The uniform production of a pure and potent extract was thus ensured. At the same time funds were provided for further research and limits were set to the commercialization of insulin. Science is thus sometimes and to some extent self-supporting and self-propagating and does not depend entirely on the beneficence of governments and philanthropic foundations.

We have now followed to completion, short of a technical discussion of methods, the purification and processing of insulin. This development was far from full realization, and no general distribution, even for severe cases, was possible, before clinical trial of the new drug was undertaken. Its value had of course been proved in human cases before large-scale production was attempted. Insulin emerged from the laboratory and made its appearance in hospital wards, and we must now retrace our steps and see in what manner it functioned and what changes it wrought in producing the scientific sensation above described and the widespread search for better methods of manufacture.

Crossing the campus of the University of Toronto and a corner of Queen's Park, crossing College Street at the corner of University Avenue, we come to the massive, yellow-brick buildings of the Toronto General Hospital. The second floor of the old pavilion became the "diabetic floor."

PART VI

The Prophet in the Valley of Bones

The hand of the Lord was upon me, and carried me out in the spirit of the Lord, and set me down in the midst of the valley which was full of bones, and caused me to pass by them round about: and, behold, there were very many in the open valley; and, lo, they were very dry.

And He said unto me, "Son of Man, can these bones live?"

And I answered, "O Lord God, thou knowest."

Again He said unto me, "Prophesy upon these bones, and say unto them, 'O ye dry bones, hear the word of the Lord. Thus saith the Lord God unto these bones: "Behold, I will cause breath to enter into you, and ye shall live: and I will lay sinews upon you, and will bring up flesh upon you, and cover you with skin, and put breath in you and ye shall live; and ye shall know that I am the Lord." ' "

So I prophesied as was commanded: and as I prophesied, there was a noise, and behold a shaking, and the bones came together, bone to his bone. And when I beheld, lo, the sinews and the flesh came up upon them, and the skin covered them above: but there was no breath in them.

Then said He unto me, "Prophesy unto the wind, prophesy, Son of Man, and say to the wind, 'Thus saith the Lord God: "Come from the four winds, O breath, and breathe upon these slain, that they may live." ' "

So I prophesied as He commanded me, and the breath came into them, and they lived, and stood up upon their feet, an exceeding great army.

THE BOOK OF THE PROPHET EZEKIEL.

Top left: MEDALLION BY EMANUEL HAHN, R.C.A.
(Used on the occasion of the opening of the Canadian National
Exhibition in 1923.)
Courtesy the Artist and The Canadian National Exhibition Association.

Centre: DIPLOMA OF THE NOBEL PRIZE AWARD MADE TO BANTING AND
MACLEOD IN 1923.

Top right: COVER OF THE BOUND DIPLOMA WITH BANTING MONOGRAM.

1

IN February, 1923, Dr. F. John Poynton, physician to the University College Hospital, London, and the Hospital for Sick Children, Great Ormond Street, reported on five cases of diabetes mellitus in young children.[1] All five of these cases were treated before insulin became available. All five were treated carefully and thoroughly by the best methods known, chiefly by the restriction and careful balancing of diet. With what result?

CASE I (a boy aged 7): "On admission he smelt strongly of acetone and was comatose. The action of his heart was feeble and his face grey. The abdomen was scaphoid, and the urine contained 2.2 per cent. of sugar. Death was sudden."

CASE II (a boy aged 5½): "On admission (his third admission) he looked ill and drawn, and his urine was loaded with ketone bodies and sugar. There was general abdominal tenderness. In spite of intravenous alkaline injections he died that night in severe convulsions."

CASE III (a girl aged 9): "The third case was of special interest because there had been a history of only one week's illness. . . . After admission she was very quiet and refused her food, and . . . fell into coma with profound collapse . . . she never rallied."

CASE IV (a boy aged 8): "He left the hospital losing ground and in an apparently hopeless condition, but it would have been sheer cruelty to keep him longer away from his home, particularly as we were doing him no good. To my astonishment he then commenced to improve, and though not free from sugar kept well through the winter. . . . Then all his symptoms reappeared. . . . he came to hospital . . . smelling strongly of acetone, breathing deeply, and very drowsy. The urine had a specific gravity of 1032, and contained sugar and great excess of ketone bodies. In spite of every effort he died in coma. . . ."

CASE V (a girl aged 7½): "It was apparent that the last stage was reached, and at urgent request she went home, dying in coma. . . ."

[1]*British Medical Journal:* 1-1923, 277.

The experience gained from these cases (wrote the distinguished Dr. Poynton) was not unexpected, but was very disappointing, for we had all, according to our lights, worked most diligently at them; yet all five died within three years. In all the cases of any duration we invariably went through three stages of thought: first the belief that we were succeeding—a belief which was never confident; then the uneasy feeling that we were losing ground; and finally, the realization that our efforts were fruitless. We protracted the illnesses, but nothing more, and this very partial success was so unsatisfactory from the children's point of view that had not there been always a hope that some new advance might appear, or some unexpected improvement arise, it seemed hardly worth while.

. . . That diet only touched the fringe of the problem seemed also beyond dispute. No doubt our methods were open to criticism—no dietetic therapy could escape this fate—but no criticism would alter, in my opinion, the essential fact that the disease was materially untouched.

The remarkable periods of comparative quiescence, the unexpected outbursts, and the sudden improvements under apparently less favourable surroundings, all pointed to a mysterious hidden hand working against us.

Finally, with new methods in sight, I would venture to repeat that this series of cases may be of some value to those with fewer opportunities to form a clear idea of new results. If, as we all hope, these are much more favourable in the diabetes of the young, they will be seen more clearly against this black background—painted, as it were, at the eleventh hour.

This account reveals, with grim, eloquent economy, the tragic sequence of events in juvenile diabetes. In adults, the outlook was not quite so bad, particularly in the stout, active patient over fifty years of age. But long-continued debility, a life-in-death of starvation, of the "oatmeal cure" or the "potato cure," of dosage with opium and atropine and various preparations of alkalies, progressed only too often into that fatal drowsiness, developing into coma, which closed the history of the diabetic. Or death from intercurrent infection, to which diabetics are peculiarly subject, was common. Like Job, the sore afflicted patriarch of Uz, diabetics were a prey to boils and carbuncles. They died of pneumonia, of tuberculosis, of mastoiditis, of almost any infection which might choose to invade their sick and weary bodies. Eczema, diabetic pruritus, and worse still gangrene, tormented others. A sloughing, gangrenous foot could fill a hospital ward with its nauseating stench; amputation was often imperative, but like all surgical operations, it was fraught with terrible risk for the diabetic, for whom anæsthesia alone was a dangerous ordeal, and whose unhealthy tissues seemed actually to invite the influx of germs; what is more, since diabetes and arteriosclerosis go hand in hand, deficient circulation in the stump often initiated further gangrene—a hopeless cycle. Oedema, cystitis, peripheral neuritis, paralysis, cataracts and sudden blindness were occasional symptoms.

Apart from its terrible complications, diabetes is a long drawn-out and inescapable affliction. It has long been known to medical students as the disease of the three p's—polydipsia (inordinate thirst), polyphagia (inordinate hunger), and polyuria (frequent and excessive urination). Aretæus, many centuries ago, first used the term diabetes, calling it a wonderful affection "melting down the flesh and limbs into urine." He suggested that the disease got its name from the Greek word signifying a syphon. Although many cases are controllable by diet, in many others the course is simply prolonged by dietary means, as in the juvenile cases described by Poynton. In spite of the enormous amount of food consumed when the diet is not restricted, a patient may become rapidly emaciated, a living skeleton. Headache, a feeling of intoxication, thick speech and a staggering gait, may herald the onset of coma. There are also cases "in which, particularly after exertion, the patient is attacked suddenly with weakness, giddiness and fainting; the hands and feet are cold and livid, the pulse small, respiration rapid; the patient becomes drowsy, and death occurs within a few hours."[2] The breathing of a patient in diabetic coma is typical: inspirations and expirations are loud and deep; the patient is said to exhibit "air-hunger." The breath very often has the fruity odour of acetone. The pulse grows weak; the patient gradually fails and dies, sometimes within twenty-four hours.

All this in the absence of insulin. All this . . . transposed into the past tense. All this while the helpless physician stands, or

[2]This vivid description is quoted from the ninth edition of *The Principles and Practice of Medicine,* by Osler and McCrae, published in 1920.

rather stood, with his hands tied and his mind and heart clouded with frustration and despair. All this in the years before Banting.

The words of Poynton have a peculiar dark felicity; written, as he said, at the eleventh hour, they display a vivid consciousness that his grim report, together with similar reports from other sources, marked the end of the old régime in the treatment of diabetes. In the same volume of *The British Medical Journal* the index lists no fewer than a dozen articles, as well as numerous editorial notes, on the subject of insulin, including a report on its clinical use by Banting, Campbell and Fletcher. Nearly a year earlier than this, however, in March, 1922, a preliminary report had appeared in the pages of *The Canadian Medical Association Journal*. It was an account of the effect of pancreatic extracts in the first seven cases of diabetes mellitus in which they were used.

2

On December 2, 1921, a fourteen-year-old boy (L. T.) suffering from diabetes, was admitted to the Medical Wards of the Toronto General Hospital. In the history of this remarkable case, the following record appears:

About December, 1919, he was taken to his family physician because he had been wetting the bed at nights, and also because his ankles became swollen occasionally. One week later, sugar was found in the urine. He states that at this time he was in good health, his appetite was somewhat excessive, but no increased thirst was complained of. Careful dietetic regulation was prescribed and he states that he adhered to this diet fairly well. This his family physician will not confirm. Fasting was also tried, apparently without success. The glycosuria persisted, he began to lose weight; frequency of micturition, both day and night, increased up to the time when his physician recommended admission to hospital.

On admission he was poorly nourished, pale, weight 65 pounds, hair falling out, odour of acetone on the breath . . .

abdomen large and tympanitic. . . . He appeared dull, talked rather slowly, quite willing to lie about all day. Hands show marked xanthochromia.[3] . . . The urine at the time of admission was strongly acid . . . the test for sugar strongly positive . . . tests for ketones strongly positive. . . . Blood sugar 5.8 mg. per c. c.

He was put to bed and was quite content to remain there most of the time. However, when he wished to do so, he was allowed to get up and wander about the ward, which he did very little during the first month. [An outline of his diet, which need not detain us, follows. Suffice to say that it was of the type prescribed by such dietetic authorities as Allen and that the total intake was about 450 calories.][4]

This case was one of severe juvenile diabetes with ketosis. Previous to admission he had been starved without evident benefit. During the first month of his stay in hospital, careful dietetic regulation failed to influence the course of the disease and by January 11 his clinical condition made it evident that he was becoming definitely worse.

So far this story is almost an exact parallel of the cases reported by Poynton, as previously quoted. The sequel, the miraculous sequel, forms an exhilarating contrast.

The extracts given on January 11th were not as concentrated as those used at a later date, and, other than a slightly lowered sugar excretion and a 25 per cent. fall in the blood sugar level, no clinical benefit was evidenced.

Daily injections of the extract were made from January 23 to February 4 (excepting January 25 and 26). This resulted in immediate improvement. The excretion of sugar . . . became much less. On days of treatment, this varied from 7.5 gms. to 45.1 gms. compared with a previous amount well over 100 gms. daily. The acetone bodies disappeared from the urine. The boy became brighter, more active, looked better and said he felt stronger. No extract was given from February 5 to February 15. During this time sugar again appeared in the urine in large amounts along with traces of acetone. Administration of extract

[3] A yellowish pigmentation of the skin not uncommonly seen in diabetes. —L. S.

[4] Dr. O. G. Mills and Dr. G. L. Bird of the Oshawa Clinic, who were then on the interne staff of the Toronto General Hospital, recall that this pathetic little boy was perpetually hungry and had to be closely watched to prevent him from pilfering food from other patients.

in smaller doses after February 16 again resulted in lowered sugar excretion and disappearance of acetone from the urine.

After all the long and disappointing years during which juvenile diabetics were admitted to hospitals with the sign of their doom already written on their faces (the diagnosis being the equivalent of a death sentence) this fourteen-year-old boy, thin and listless, exhaling the deathly, sweetish odour of acetone, came in through the doors of the Toronto General Hospital not to a drowsy death but to new health, new vigour, new life. Like Joseph Meister, whom Pasteur saved from rabies, he was the first of a fortunate host of children, who, thanks to strong deliverance, outfaced the spectre of untimely death, and ran away from him, laughing. Banting, a beneficent piper of childhood's dreams, led these fortunate children from the pale and somnolent regions where they dwelt

> . . . to a joyous land,
> Joining the town and just at hand,
> Where waters gushed and fruit-trees grew
> And flowers put forth a fairer hue,
> And everything was strange and new.

Probably at no other time in his career did Banting feel so fully and indefeasibly the triumph of success.

3

The momentous paper reporting the first clinical trial of insulin concluded with these paragraphs:

Although the other six patients treated by these extracts were all favourably influenced by its administration, particular reference might be made to one . . . a severe case who had been excreting 20 gms. of glucose on a diet containing 10 gms. carbohydrate and 24 hundred calories per day. Following injection of the extract his urine became sugar free, and he obtained complete relief from severe depression and extreme lassitude. Respiratory quotients in this same case showed a definite rise after injection of the extract, confirming the increased utilization of carbo-hydrate.

All patients were improved clinically. It is difficult to put in words what is meant by clinical improvement. Those who have been treating diabetes will have recognized as early signs of improvement a certain change in the skin, the appearance of the eyes, the behaviour of the patient, his mental and psychic activity and the physical evidences, as well as his testimony, of increased vigour and desire to use his muscles. Under present day treat-ment, such improvement occurs in diabetics free from acetone but is undoubtedly more striking in patients recovering from a ketosis. This is the nature of the improvement seen clinically as a result of the administration of these extracts, and, while it is of a temporary nature, we believe that it justifies the hope of more permanent results following more adequate and carefully regu-lated dosage.

This preliminary report was the work of Banting, Best and Collip, and of W. R. Campbell and A. A. Fletcher of the Depart-ment of Medicine. It is notable that reference is made through-out to "pancreatic extracts." In January of the following year the subsequent report already mentioned was published by Bant-ing, Campbell and Fletcher in *The British Medical Journal* under the title "Further Clinical Experience with Insulin (Pancreatic Extracts) in the Treatment of Diabetes Mellitus."[5] At that time over fifty cases of diabetes had been treated with insulin, and some had been under treatment continuously for several months.

Although the most striking results (wrote Banting, Campbell and Fletcher) have been seen in children and young adults, all patients have been benefited by the treatment. Many of the patients have come to the hospital in a state of extreme under-nutrition, suffering from great weakness along with an indisposi-tion to any physical activity. On the first or second day of treat-ment, if sufficient insulin is given, the urine becomes sugar-free, and on the second or third day, ketone-free. These patients become conscious of increasing strength before the end of the first

[5]"Insulin was not the first name used among our group of workers. As early as August, 1921, the word 'isletin' occurs in our notebooks. Pro-fessor Macleod insisted that the internal secretion of the pancreas should be called 'insulin.' Later it was found that Sharpey-Schafer, of Edinburgh, suggested this name about 1910."—Banting.

week. From a state which may be one of discouragement or of profound mental depression they become cheerful and interested. Hunger is replaced by appetite; the thirst is lessened; oedema, which is common in these cases, disappears. Patients find they are less irritable, and state that they begin to sleep well. The expression improves; the skin becomes less harsh and dry; even the hair becomes softer; in fact, the patient loses that appearance which characterizes the diabetic. In ten days a very considerable amount of physical vigour is restored. Some patients have been able to return to work after a month of treatment. The patient's weight frequently increases, and this can be readily brought about by supplying food in excess of the calorie requirement and increased amounts of insulin. One patient, aged 16, who had lost 40 pounds during her three years of diabetes, gained 35 pounds in less than four months. Mild infections are favourably influenced; for example, the pain of a chronic pyorrhœa was relieved by treatment; it recurred when the injections were stopped, and was relieved again when they were continued. Simple catarrhal infections are no longer of serious import. During this time the urine can be kept sugar-free and ketone-free. The morning blood sugars are lower and may approach the normal level. [It was reported that with increased tolerance for carbohydrate the dosage of insulin could be gradually reduced, sometimes to half the original amount.] Certain cases indeed may, after a period of insulin treatment, recover such a degree of tolerance as no longer to require extract to maintain them on a basal diet. . . . We are at present inclined to the opinion that the newly regained tolerance of these patients should be protected for a time by the use of small amounts of insulin.

The treatment of ketonuria, acidosis, and coma was also reported.

Of the 10 cases of complete coma treated four died. The first case of coma was admitted to hospital in February, 1922, and died in April. This case came into the hospital in a state of severe acidosis, markedly emaciated and dehydrated, with a high D-N ratio. Owing to the difficulty in the production of insulin at that time many of the preparations lacked potency and satisfactory treatment was impossible. The patient was treated at intervals with insulin. The acidosis was improved, to return when treatment was discontinued. The case gradually became worse and went into coma; was brought out by large doses of a weak extract;

lapsed again into unconsciousness and died when the supply of extract was exhausted. One other fatal case was effectually brought out of coma but died of pneumonia. In the other two cases, one died with sloughing gangrene of the foot, and the other of complete vasomotor failure. In both these cases coma was relieved by insulin treatment. At the time of death the urine of these patients was free of sugar and ketones; the blood sugar and blood ketones were normal, and glycogen was found in the liver and muscles *post mortem*.

The remaining six cases of coma treated are all living. One has recovered and is now aglycosuric without insulin on a diet about double the basal requirement. The other five patients have remained free of symptoms and the urine free of sugar and ketones under dietetic treatment and the daily administration of insulin.

We are not prepared, at present, to lay down definite rules for the management of diabetics in coma for we believe that with greater opportunities for study more satisfactory methods may be devised for treating this as well as other problems in relation to the disease.

It was reported, however, that the dose employed had been usually far in excess of the requirement, and that the danger of a hypoglycæmia reaction was guarded against by sufficient glucose given intravenously at the same time. The insulin was administered to these patients either subcutaneously or intravenously, followed by subcutaneous injections.

To those who had previously striven, practically unrewarded, with cases of diabetic coma, the results achieved with insulin must have seemed almost incredible, like modern repetitions of the miracle of Bethany, when Lazarus was raised from the dead.

The fatality which occurred when supplies of the extract were exhausted was bitter and ironical for all concerned. Once again a striking parallel may be found in the story of penicillin. When this more recent "miracle drug" was ready for its first clinical trial in the winter of 1941, a forty-three-year-old policeman, suffering from a virulent pyogenic infection, was the first human to receive it.

"Multiple abscesses covered his face and scalp and were spreading to his arms. The microbes had attacked the bones of his head and his eyes. Even his lungs were caught in this grisly sweep of death. Sulfapyridine had failed. It had even complicated matters, causing the patient to break out in a drug rash."[6] Dr. C. M. Fletcher and Dr. Mary Florey, physician-wife of Dr. Howard Walter Florey, who first turned Fleming's discovery to practical account, administered intravenous penicillin. "At the end of twenty-four hours, there was striking improvement." The supply of penicillin, however, was very small. The man's urine was collected and sent back to the laboratory where small amounts of penicillin were extracted from it to add to the waning remnant.

"By the fifth day the policeman was without fever. He was able to eat with good appetite. The abscesses were resolving. But there was no more penicillin. There wasn't so much as a pinhead's worth of the drug—anywhere in the world. It had almost won. But now there was no more. And there could be no more, since there was no way to hurry the mold into producing more.

"With no penicillin to curb them, the bacteria flamed into action. The patient died. . . .

"It would be gratifying to report that the second case was a success, that penicillin triumphed over sure death. But it didn't. This patient, like the first, also died. The minute supply of drug was exhausted mid-way in treatment."

With insulin, twenty years earlier, the same thing had occurred. A patient had been raised from the brink of the grave, but had slipped back to inevitable death when the supply of the drug was exhausted. How hard they all worked in the laboratory to produce it, to produce even a weak extract, in time! But the effort was in vain. Death worked faster.

This points to the tremendous difficulty which was experienced at this time in producing insulin in large enough amounts. For a long time it was absolutely impossible, despite the most strenuous efforts, to produce enough to meet current demands in Toronto, let alone for distribution elsewhere. The discovery of insulin was widely heralded not only in medical journals but in the lay press, and applications for treatment were received in ever increasing numbers. "Among these applications were many

[6]This quotation and the two which follow are taken from J. D. Ratcliff's fascinating book, *Yellow Magic, The Story of Penicillin* (Random House, New York, 1945).

from patients with severe diabetes who had been under observation for long periods on well-controlled diets, but with a gradual failure of tolerance for carbohydrates. In view of the limited quantities of insulin available, the need of these patients for relief and the fact that such patients only can furnish satisfactory data for the establishment of our main propositions, it was decided to confine attention to these severe cases, reserving for future study and treatment the less severe ones. Consequently we are not in a position, at the present time, to furnish any data on a very interesting group of patients whose disease is in the early stage, and who may ultimately show very great degrees of functional repair of the pancreas when the latter is allowed a considerable period of inactivity as a result of treatment."

4

Determination of the dosage of insulin was one of the principal initial problems. We have already seen that Banting and Best were interested at an early period of their research in the possible results of overdosage, and it was remarked that the pancreatic extract produced early in the century by the German investigator, Zuelzer, was withdrawn from the market because of the severe toxic reactions which attended its use. Two types of toxic reaction were demonstrated by the Toronto workers, one due to impurities, the other to too large a dose. In the course of the experiments connected with this work it was discovered that the injection of insulin reduced the percentage of sugar in the blood of a normal rabbit, an observation which suggested a means for testing the relative potency of different extracts and led to the adoption of a method of assay based on the definition that one unit of insulin is the amount which, on subcutaneous injection, lowers a rabbit's blood-sugar by 50 per cent. in one to three hours. This original unit was known as the Toronto unit. Banting and his associates observed, however, that sufficiently large doses of insulin produced in the rabbits severe convulsions which were generally fatal if not controlled by the administration of glucose. The blood-sugar was forced down to too low a level with a convulsion as the result. This observation, and the experience gained from clinical work with a preparation standardized by the original method, led later to the adoption of a new unit which was defined as being one-third of the amount of insulin, in cubic centimetres, required to lower the blood-sugar below 0.045 per cent. and cause convulsions in a rabbit weighing two kilograms, which had been previously fasted for twenty-four hours. This unit, which is approximately one-third of that previously employed, permitted greater latitude in prescribing the remedy.

Toxic reactions (noted the joint authors) may follow the injection of an extract of any animal tissue, owing to its content of protein and split protein products. These reactions have been especially severe in the experience of investigators with pancreatic extracts, and have been the chief obstacle to their introduction for clinical use. Some reactions of this type were produced by injections of the extract first used by us. The present product, however, is practically protein-free, so that with the exception of urticarial eruptions[7] in one, or possibly two, sensitive patients, these occurrences are no longer met with. Insulin administration may be followed by a reaction of another kind, which is the result of the fall in blood sugar (hypoglycæmia). When a single injection is given to a patient there is a rapid fall of blood sugar which reaches a low point in two to eight hours, and tends to return to the original level in twelve to twenty-four. . . .

While the extent of this fall is dependent in a measure upon the amount of insulin and upon the initial blood-sugar level, it cannot be predicted with any great degree of accuracy in an individual patient. In giving a dose, therefore, to render the patient sugar-free it sometimes happens that the blood-sugar falls well below the normal level, and this sudden hypoglycæmia is accompanied by a characteristic train of symptoms. When the blood-sugar percentage falls to 0.07 per cent. under the influence of insulin, the patient becomes aware of it. He may first complain of hunger, or more often a sense of weakness or fatigue, and, especially if it is his first reaction, he is conscious of some anxiety or of what he calls nervousness, or he may even show the signs of a definite neurosis with loss of emotional control, such as crying spells. Almost constantly present is a feeling of tremulousness; actual tremor is rarely seen. The patient may also have some

[7]Skin eruptions in the nature of hives, due to sensitivity to a foreign protein.—L. S.

inco-ordination for fine movements. Vasomotor phenomena are common: pallor or flushing, sometimes one after the other; a sense of heat or chilliness; almost always a profuse sweat. The severity of these symptoms increases with the hypoglycæmia, and the lowering of the blood sugar near to 0.05 per cent. produces very acute distress or even mental disturbances such as confusion and disorientation. A blood sugar of 0.032 per cent. resulted in a state of coma. . . . One patient while asleep passed into a low muttering delirium. . . . One patient was quite irrational while his blood sugar was around 0.06 per cent. On another occasion he became deaf and had difficulty in articulation. This difficulty in articulation has been seen several times. Others have had only a vague feeling of uncertainty which would have passed unnoticed had they not experienced a previous reaction. . . .

These reactions can be relieved by food administration; 50 to 100 c. c. of orange juice has an almost immediate effect in clearing up the symptoms. A better result is obtained with 5 to 25 grams of glucose given with orange or lemon juice.

Unconscious patients were found to respond to a small injection of adrenaline. Once roused, they could be given sugar by mouth. Failing this (and the adrenaline practically never failed to restore consciousness) glucose was given subcutaneously or intravenously.

Special nursing precautions should be taken for the detection of reactions when insulin treatment is first started, when a new preparation is given and when insulin is administered late in the day, as the reaction may occur during sleep. As yet pharmacological assay of the potency of insulin has not been satisfactory, and to this may be attributed the occasional reactions seen when new preparations are used. However, once a patient has had a reaction he is quick to recognize the onset of the next one, and means may be taken to relieve it. Up to the present time no serious mishap has occurred as a result of these hypoglycæmic reactions, but while this is so it is felt that hypoglycæmia constitutes a real source of danger.

There has been little reason since to alter this dictum, though better preparations and superior standardization have improved matters. During many years of experience with the use of insulin it has been found that these reactions are more often annoying than dangerous, provided that the patient and his medical and nursing attendants are well aware of the signs and symptoms of hypoglycæmia and that prompt measures are taken to combat it. Usually the patient realizes that an insulin reaction is impending before there is any unmistakable outward sign of it, and drinking some orange juice or eating a chocolate bar is enough to ward it off. Insulin is best administered about twenty minutes to half an hour before a meal, and patients must be warned that it is dangerous to skip a meal while taking the drug. If they are unwell from other causes and cannot eat at all, or only small amounts, they must continue to take smaller doses of insulin, always guarding against reactions. If they discontinue the use of insulin under such circumstances because of the fear of insulin shock, severe or moderately severe diabetics always run the contrary risk of lapsing into the precomatous state which is rapidly succeeded, if unrelieved, by full diabetic coma. Cases of diabetic coma as seen at present are chiefly due to one of three causes: rapidly onsetting diabetes in children; coma which results from a debauch or dietary indiscretions; and coma following loss of appetite and failure to take insulin because of the fear of reactions.[8] Education of the diabetic patient is therefore all-important. "There is no disease," said Banting, "which requires such an intimate co-operation between the physician and patient." It may be remarked in passing that normal persons who feel "faint from hunger," particularly after physical exertion, are undergoing an experience which is analagous in a minor way to an insulin reaction.

The dosage of insulin is a very important factor in the successful treatment of a patient; on the one hand, we have to fear hypoglycæmic reaction and, on the other, we know that glycosuria will result when the blood sugar rises above the patient's threshold level for excretion of sugar. It is, therefore, not always easy to adjust the conditions so that there is sufficient insulin present to nullify the post-prandial hyperglycæmia,[9] and yet insufficient

[8]Coma also occurs in elderly patients who are unaware that they suffer from diabetes and whose condition slowly worsens until gradually, or sometimes quite suddenly, they sink into a comatose state; in such cases, where acidosis has been present for a considerable time, even heroic doses of insulin frequently fail of a good effect and the prognosis is then hopeless.

[9]Elevation of blood sugar following a meal.—L. S.

to produce a dangerous lowering of the blood sugar. We know, however, that the effect of insulin on blood sugar is not exerted immediately after subcutaneous injection, and therefore we space the injections so that their effect is occurring during the period of assimilation of carbohydrates. This usually means injecting the insulin, at or shortly before, the meal, but instances occur . . . possibly due to delayed, or too rapid, absorption of sugar into the blood stream, the use of meals containing too much high carbohydrate food, etc. . . . in which glycosuria occurs at one time and reaction at another. These, fortunately, are not common, but serve to emphasize the necessity for careful observation of the patient for a period in a hospital before discharging him to the care of his private physician. Further, the initial symptoms of reaction are so specific as to leave no doubt in the mind of anyone who has seen them and the remedy is, fortunately, easy to apply before there is any real danger.

At the end of the preliminary period of observation on a fixed diet the majority of cases of severe diabetes excrete a fairly constant amount of sugar, and this information is most valuable in determining the actual amount of insulin to be employed in treatment. In certain cases, possibly owing to daily fluctuation in tolerance for carbohydrates, the daily excretion of sugar varies and it is impossible to determine the initial dose of insulin. In these cases it is advisable to begin with a moderate dose gradually increasing it until the desired effect is obtained. The amount of insulin used will depend not only on the carbohydrate tolerance of the patient, but on the height and fixity of the blood-sugar level.

Whether we shall in the future permit patients to have higher blood-sugar levels than at present seems advisable is a point on which there is conflicting evidence. At present we are inclined to the belief that more successful results are obtained with regard to the general well-being of the patient, clearing up of minor and even major infections, etc.

While this in the main is still the opinion of experts in the treatment of diabetes, it is now generally agreed that certain patients, particularly those with some degree of heart failure, are better off when they are permitted to maintain blood-sugar levels somewhat higher than normal and to excrete small amounts of sugar in the urine; too zealous treatment with insulin may precipitate a complete cardiac breakdown. This, however, is a refinement of clinical practice which need not concern us in this place.

Owing to the short duration of the effect of insulin it might seem desirable to ingest the carbohydrates at one particular meal and give the extract in relation to this meal, thus avoiding the number of injections—two to three daily sometimes necessary in the severer cases. This, however, is not the case, as the carbohydrate is apparently stored and burned under the influence of the insulin, and during this period the patient feels like a healthy, normal person, and later, when only fat and some protein is available for burning, he gets a mild ketosis and experiences lassitude or fatigue. In our view a prolongation of the period of action is most desirable, and whether this is to be obtained by slowing the rate of absorption or by more frequent injection is a matter for further study.

Obviously the first alternative was the more desirable from the viewpoint of the patient's convenience. How slowing of absorption was accomplished will presently appear.

5

Diabetics are perhaps more subject to infections and gangrene than any other class of patients. In such cases a distressingly high mortality has been observed. Without doubt the more recent dietetic treatment has removed many of the terrors of operation, such as coma, and has even aided in the more rapid clearing up of infections for the less severe degrees of the disease. However, many patients lose a great deal of their carbohydrate tolerance when infection is added to their diabetic condition. And further, the infections are more prone to occur in the more severe cases who do not respond favourably to dietetic treatment. For both types of patients insulin furnishes most valuable assistance in treatment in that it keeps the blood sugar normal—an important consideration in the treatment of infection—enables the patient to utilize carbohydrates, and in consequence, prevents acidosis and removes the danger of post-operative coma. It seems clear that necessary surgical procedures may be undertaken in properly treated cases with practically no more risk than the normal.

In pre-insulin days the diabetic was a poor surgical risk and surgeons strove to avoid operating on patients with the sugar sickness. A crosslight can be thrown on the state of affairs in that era by glancing at an authoritative book, now antiquated, on post-operative care.[10]

It was formerly one of the traditions of surgery that sugar in the urine was an absolute contra-indication to anesthetization. Nowadays, unless we are dealing with an undoubted and progressing case of diabetes mellitus, it is generally considered that with the exercise of proper precautions the risk is slight. [*Unless,* mark you, we are dealing with an undoubted and progressing case of diabetes mellitus!]

The patient should be properly prepared by dieting during as long a period as the nature of the surgical indication will allow, so that the sugar content of the urine is diminished as much as possible. One should take care, however, that the patient is not starved. [But how little short of starvation was the treatment of severe diabetes!] The anesthetic should be carefully and evenly administered. The period of anesthetization, should be as short as possible. Chloroform is contra-indicated on account of its effect on fat metabolism in the liver. Usually in the case of middle-aged glycosurics who have been maintaining an almost constant output of sugar for some years with only slight disturbance to health, with these precautions little need be feared, although if the sugar percentage is high, a protracted etherization may disturb the metabolic balance and lead to fatal results.

In undoubted diabetes, especially in those cases where the sugar cannot be reduced by dieting, operations should be put off as long as possible, and their performance should be as rapid as the surgeon's technique will allow. Carbohydrates should be administered after the operation with the hope of staving off coma. . . .

When the diabetic coma supervenes, it may come on shortly after operation, so that *the patient who has been under ether for twenty minutes, to allow the excision of a carbuncle, may be dead in from four to twelve hours.*[11] Usually it takes two, three or more days for coma to develop. . . .

Recovery from post-operative diabetic coma is rare. The usual treatment of coma in diabetes should be instituted. The patient's bowels should be emptied and injections of sodium

[10]*Surgical After-Treatment, A Manual of the Conduct of Surgical Convalescence,* by L. R. G. Crandon, A.M., M.D., W. B. Saunders, Philadelphia, 1911.

[11]The italics are mine.—L. S.

bicarbonate (6 drams to the pint) should be given under the skin, and fluids, alkaline if well borne, should be forced.

The relative uselessness of such therapy we have already seen, and it is not too fanciful to imagine a certain weariness in Crandon's tone as he enunciates the almost fatalistic words, "The usual treatment of coma in diabetes should be instituted." Better, of course, than doing nothing. Or was it? Poynton at least was a prey to doubts.

With the advent of insulin this danger was, as predicted by Banting, practically abolished in properly controlled cases. The first operation performed upon such a patient with the immense advantage of pre-operative control of the diabetes by insulin was an amputation of a gangrenous foot done by Dr. L. C. Palmer, who, it will be recalled, had been Banting's immediate superior officer in France. Banting directed the medical management of this case, and since the patient was the wife of a well-known politician, the successful result lent a little added prestige, or at least publicity, to the method employed.

Here is the story of the case as told by Banting:

One of the earliest cases we treated (August, 1922) was a woman of sixty-five, who was suffering from an extensive infected gangrene of the left leg. This condition had been progressively extending for a period of four months. . . . After five days' treatment with insulin, combined with a regulated diet, she became free of acetone, almost sugar-free, and her general condition was improved. She was given gas and oxygen anesthesia and an amputation was performed at the junction of the middle and lower thirds of the thigh. Following this operation the wound healed by primary intention except for a small stitch-hole abscess which cleared up in two weeks. The general condition of the patient rapidly improved. The dose of insulin was reduced, and four months after the amputation insulin was discontinued. The patient was kept on a restricted diet at first but gradually the restrictions were removed, and eight months following the operation the patient was allowed to eat whatever she wished, including bread, potato and sugar. For over three years she lived on a liberal diet without insulin, and her death in 1925 was due to pneumonia.

All types of operation were soon being performed with confidence upon diabetic subjects, and it became evident that Banting, the former surgeon, had largely eliminated one of the major difficulties of his confrères.

6

Another benefit which accrued from judicious use of the extract was hailed by the obstetricians. At one time the chances for a diabetic woman to give birth to a living child were not good. As a matter of fact conception was rare; if it occurred, abortion or miscarriage was apt to follow. De Lee took a very gloomy view of the whole situation:[12]

Sterility is common, Lecorche, of 114 cases, finding only 7 gestations. This is due to atrophy of the uterus and ovaries, which also explains the frequent amenorrhea and premature menopause. Abortion and premature labour occur in 33 per cent. of the pregnancies, the fœtuses usually being macerated. The children, if the pregnancy goes to term, often die shortly after birth, the total mortality being 66 per cent. . . .

Without doubt pregnancy has a bad effect on the course of the disease. It may develop a latent diabetes, there being cases where severe symptoms appeared only during successive pregnancies, and others where the disease grew progressively worse each time. . . . Unless treatment is instituted [he might well have said, even though treatment *is* instituted] the sugar in the urine increases, the malnutrition becomes marked, and the nervous system, which, as usual in pregnancy, suffers first from bad influences, begins to show signs of intoxication and acidosis appears. Coma occurs in 30 per cent. of the cases and is almost always fatal. It may be brought on by a very slight shock in pregnancy, but more often during and just after labour. Delivery seems to have even a worse effect than most surgical operations, causing collapse, coma, or sudden death. . . .

True diabetes has a very bad prognosis, Offergeld finding over 50 per cent. mortality, of which 30 per cent. died in coma, the

[12]*The Principles and Practice of Obstetrics,* by Joseph B. De Lee, A.M., M.D., Fourth Edition, W. B. Saunders, Philadelphia, 1925.

others of tuberculosis or coma, within two and one-half years. . . . Of the children, 51 per cent. were stillborn, and even though apparently well at birth, 10 per cent. died within a few days after, and 5 per cent. more before six months, from hydrocephalus and diabetes.

How readily we forget the past! How soon we take for granted the miracles of every day! Digging into the textbooks of yester-year we encounter such discouraged statements, such appalling figures, with a distinct sense of shock. Were things really so bad? Consider De Lee's advice on the management of such a case before the viability of the child:

If a woman comes under treatment with a history of diabetes, and the examination of the urine in the first months show grape-sugar, especially with acidosis, *it is best to terminate the pregnancy at once.* The attempt to carry the patient up to term or even to viability of the child is too perilous—either the shock of delivery brings on coma, or some other nervous shock does it, or the disease aggravates dangerously, and, too often, the child dies *in utero. If the pregnancy is near viability and the symptoms respond to medical treatment, one may try to tide the woman along with a view to improving the child's chances, even though this hope is only too often illusory—the child dies either before or after delivery. Kleinwächter says we should not consider the child at all.*[13]

Discussing the treatment after viability of the child, De Lee had this to say:

Since some cases of simple glycosuria occur at this time, and since *any interference or even natural labour may evoke a terminal complication,* most authorities advise waiting, with medical treatment, and the induction of premature labour only when threatening symptoms arise. *General experience advises the induction of premature labour in all cases when the sugar content of the urine does not diminish under appropriate treatment.* . . . Coma indicates the emptying of the uterus, but the child is almost always dead. . . . *Nursing is not to be permitted. Further child-bearing is prohibited.*

[13]Italics mine.—L. S.

The fourth edition of the lucid volume from which these quotations are drawn contains De Lee's first mention of insulin.

The above was written (he says) before the discovery of insulin. The author has not changed it because the use of insulin in pregnant diabetics is too recent to enable us to draw definite conclusions. We have had enough experience already to say that by its help, together with the usual dietary measures, we will probably be able to carry most of the cases without danger through pregnancy to term.

This conservative footnote was soon withdrawn and in subsequent editions the section was rewritten and his doubts were largely resolved. By 1940, when the seventh edition came off the press, he was able to paint a brighter picture, though adding the guarded and not universally accepted statement that "unfortunately insulin has improved the outlook for the babies very little."

True diabetes if complete [formerly] had a very bad prognosis, Offergeld finding 50 per cent. mortality, of which 30 per cent. died in coma, the others of tuberculosis or coma, within two and one-half years, but insulin and recent dietetics have changed all that. Hansen found a mortality of 17 per cent. for the mothers and 43 per cent. for the babies, but Packham had only 1 death in 17 cases—and this patient had neglected herself. Only 2 babies were lost. Kramer in 665 cases of pregnancy in 530 diabetics showed only 4.2 per cent. mortality, but the fœtal and neonatal mortality reached 5.7 per cent.

Despite the enormous improvement which the quoted figures seem to indicate, he felt himself forced to add:

The prognosis for the baby, at present, can only be improved by delivering it before it dies *in utero*—but this is a precarious procedure.

Here is the summation:

Whereas formerly we performed abortion in the early months, and induced labour after viability of the fœtus, we now can, with insulin and dietetics, almost always maintain the gravida's metabolism on a normal level, and carry the pregnancy to term or near it. Obstetric treatment is instituted when the disease proves rebellious to medical, and a few cases of "insulin resistance" have been reported—perhaps due to the counteraction of other endocrine glands.

A young diabetic is taking a real risk when she marries, but she may have one baby, and possibly two if she will co-operate with her physician. We do not abort multiparas without a thorough trial of all our resources. . . .

It is thus apparent that under the influence of insulin childbirth lost much of its terror and difficulty for the diabetic mother. Although diabetes is still a formidable complication of pregnancy the outlook is no longer so grimly foreboding, and it is not too much to say that it is now the rule and not the exception when all goes well.

7

The original reports on the clinical use of insulin have been quoted at some length because they give a vivid picture of the state of affairs at that time, including the unresolved difficulties and still unanswered questions, and because they rank among the great classics of medical literature. The second paper, in which the first extensive hospital experience was reported, includes a discussion of diet, exercise and various specific considerations, such as the most suitable weight which a diabetic patient should maintain. These are technical matters and are not of primary concern in the present narrative. It must be observed, however, that Banting, Campbell and Fletcher by no means advocated the abandonment of diet therapy. They stressed, in fact, the extreme importance of careful management of the diet. The ground which had been gained, at the cost of much thought, patience, and long-term experience by authorities on diet, especially Allen, was not to be ceded. Many diabetics are controlled today by dietary restrictions alone, and only when such means fail, or when the diet necessary to keep the patient sugar-free is inadequate for his needs, does the conscientious physician resort to insulin.

Had insulin been discovered before the great work of Allen was accomplished, it would have been impossible to utilize it with the same intelligent discretion.   Diet and insulin are complementary methods of reaching the same end, and when both are necessary each must be nicely adjusted in relation to the other.[14]

The earliest practical application of Banting's discovery was made in the wards of the Toronto General Hospital.   While Banting's name heads the list of authors of all published papers on the subject, both scientific and clinical, which emanated from Toronto in the early years of the research (with one exception), the work in the T.G.H. was conducted by others.   These were men more eminently qualified, from the strictly clinical viewpoint, and on the ground of their experience, to treat diabetics; yet Banting was understandably piqued at being forced into a secondary rôle when the child of his genius began to take its first steps.   True, his name was always first in the published observations: this was a point on which he insisted very firmly.   But he was denied an appointment which would rank him equal with the staff physicians at the hospital, and the use of insulin in the wards was not under his direction.   His annoyance over this injustice (if it was an injustice) may seem a mark of the undue sensitivity and ever alert suspicion of which he has sometimes been accused.

It should be remarked that the epochal paper in the *British Medical Journal,* although ostensibly authored by "Banting, Campbell and Fletcher" was actually written by the latter two; moreover Banting kept no detailed protocols on his patients and the only case of his which appeared in the paper was "written up" by Fletcher.   There were several reasons for this.   Banting was extremely busy at the time, since he was engaged in both clinical and laboratory work (the latter at terrific tempo) and there were numerous outside demands on his time because of his growing celebrity.   Also we must remember that he was not an expert clinician; his limited post-graduate training had been surgical rather than medical; he had neither the knowledge nor the experience to take part on equal terms with his colleagues in the early clinical applications of his discovery.   It can hardly be wondered

[14]Joslin, the premier authority on diabetes, believes in acting on the dictum: "Give them what they need to eat and give them the insulin to cover it."

at, then, that Professor Duncan Graham, chief of the Department of Medicine, did not give him an absolutely free hand with patients for whose welfare the Professor was responsible. Banting *did* subsequently receive an appointment which gave him the same status as his two co-workers.

"If I had it to do over again tomorrow," says Professor Graham, "I should do it in exactly the same way." (And there was no one whose judgment Banting relied upon more fully in his years at the Institute; he made few major decisions without consulting Graham. Nor can we fail to note that the latter's name appears on none of the papers mentioned above, although the work in the hospital was done under his supervision.)

Nevertheless Banting was rather disgruntled at the time and in terms of human nature the explanation is not far to seek. In the University laboratories his position was anomalous: he was surrounded by technical experts while he himself might almost have been classed as an inspired amateur; of this he was well aware. In the wards of the hospital he was working side by side with men who had a similar advantage over him in training and experience and who were devoting their full time to clinical medicine; of this too he was fully conscious. On one side of the street he was "no physiologist," "no chemist"; on the other side he was "no clinician." What was he, then? Let us not forget that he was the discoverer of insulin and that both physiologists and chemists before him had "had a go" at *that*. Without his work the laboratories would not have been producing it, the clinicians would not have been administering it. This third, and triumphant, aspect of his position was ranged in his mind beside the other two.

It is plain that his situation was not an easy one and that only a mature and well-balanced personality might have been expected to accept it with complete good humour and judicious calm. Banting's personality was not mature. Neither was he characterized, even in the mellower years of his later life, by judicious calm. He was dynamic, forceful and impatient. He behaved as might have been foretold. He was generous by times and demanding by times. He was not always easy to get along with. Yet all things considered few men in a similar place have reacted so well to sudden eminence.

Some of his friends are of the opinion that his associates at the time might have treated him with greater tact. This is probably true. But tact is a difficult art to practise on a windstorm and it is hard to charm the thunder.

However that may be, he looked about him meantime for other opportunities for clinical research, and the facilities of the Christie Street Hospital were placed at his disposal by the Honourable the Minister Dr. H. Beland, of the Department of Soldiers' Civil Re-Establishment.

Although Banting himself, busily engaged in further laboratory studies and with many other calls upon his time, exercised a general supervision over the work, and Best too was concerned in it, the man in immediate charge at Christie Street was Dr. Joseph A. Gilchrist, a member of the class of seventeen. Gilchrist was a severe diabetic himself and one of the first to receive insulin. Before turning to his endeavours in the military hospital, it will be well worth while to review his own now famous case, admirably related by Banting in the Cameron Lecture.

A close friend and classmate of mine (wrote Banting) found sugar in his urine in November, 1916. In March, 1917, he developed polyuria, polyphagia, polydipsia and marked weakness. He lost one stone in weight in a fortnight. On April 4 he began the Allen treatment, and slowly regained a tolerance of about 200 gms. available carbohydrate. He returned to his army duties in September, 1917, and was able to carry on until March, 1919. His tolerance had decreased during this time to 150 gms. available carbohydrate. Following his discharge from the army in March, 1919, he retrogressed slowly downhill until October, 1921, when a particularly severe form of influenza shattered his tolerance. Up to this time the patient had been mantained practically sugar-free, but after the attack of influenza his tolerance fell to 60 gms. carbohydrate. He began to lose weight rapidly. Thirst, hunger and polyuria returned. His strength diminished, and owing to mental and physical lassitude he found it impossible to continue his work. Glycosuria became persistent and ketone bodies appeared and steadily increased. A distinct odour of acetone was at times noticeable from his breath.[15]

On February 11, 1922, this patient was taken to the Physiology Department of the University of Toronto, and the respir-

[15]When his disease was most severe, just prior to his rescue with insulin, Gilchrist still forced himself to walk a distance of two or three miles daily. —L. S.

atory quotient was found to be 0.74 and unchanged by the
ingestion of 30 gms. of pure glucose.   Then 5 c. c. of insulin
were given subcutaneously, and within two hours the patient's
respiratory quotient had risen to 0.90.   The urine was sugar-
free and he had shaken off his mental and physical torpor.   Following this experiment the patient did not again receive insulin
until May 15, as the product was being further improved.   Since
the latter date, the patient has been constantly on insulin.

During the first six months of insulin treatment it was impossible to maintain him sugar-free, although he received about 120
units per day.   However, he gained in weight and his clinical
condition improved.   About January, 1923, with the improvement in the quality of insulin, the patient became sugar-free with
the exception of one or two occasions.   During the first nine
months he required no reduction in the dose of insulin, but since
that time on the average of every two months he has had a series
of hypoglycæmic reactions which necessitated the reduction of the
dose.   One exception to this occurred in June, 1924, at which
time appendectomy was performed, following a mild attack of
appendicitis.   An increased dose was required to maintain him
sugar-free during this period.   At present he requires but 17
units of insulin, or one-seventh of his original requirement.   His
diet has been practically constant during the whole period of
observation.   All symptoms attributable to diabetes have long
since disappeared.   He has gained two stone in weight, and
apart from the necessity of taking insulin and controlling his diet,
he leads an active, normal life.

There is probably not a person alive who has had more
samples of blood taken from his veins.   He served as a willing
subject for human assay. During the early months of clinical work
every batch of insulin was tested on him.   Different methods of
administration were tried on our "human rabbit"—as he chose to
call himself.   We also worked out the best time for administering the doses of insulin with regard to meals and sleep.   And he
was the first human to experience the effect of an overdose of
insulin.   And because of his medical training he was able to
throw much enlightenment on the subjective as well as the
objective aspect of insulin.[16]

[16]This should not leave the impression that "how to use insulin" was
worked out solely on Dr. Gilchrist.   The early patients at the T.G.H. under
Campbell and Fletcher were "human rabbits" too, and respiratory quotients
and other determinations had been made before he came under treatment.—
L. S.

8

This was the man, then, who undertook the clinical research at Christie Street. No living physician could have had a stronger bond of sympathy and understanding with the diabetic soldiers. "Doctor, heal thyself," says the adage, and a doctor who has healed himself of the same disease that his patients present has the best possible reason for kindly discernment. But if he suffers, yet controls, the same incurable ailment, his fellow feeling for others in like case is thereby doubly strengthened, as is theirs for him. The diabetic veterans at Christie Street recognized in Gilchrist an officer who fought with them and for them, all standing together under fire.

It is not necessary to consider in any detail the results of the work carried out in the military hospital. Important as it was, it was essentially of the same kind as that being done concurrently at the Toronto General Hospital, and formed a part of the extensive investigations which established the proper mode of employing insulin.[17] The paper in which these results were published, in *The Canadian Medical Association Journal* for August, 1923, was one of the few on the anti-diabetic principle in which Banting's name appeared in other than the prime position as chief author. That Gilchrist's name took priority was due to Banting's insistence, Gilchrist having shouldered most of the work. On the same basis, however, Banting might equally well have given precedence to his colleagues at the Toronto General Hospital.

From the establishment of the clinic in May, 1922, each batch of extract varied in potency, owing to difficulties in standardization. Each batch was, therefore, tested by observing the fall in blood sugar in different patients, Gilchrist remaining the principal "human rabbit." This was done in order to ascertain the efficiency of the material. Because of the protein content of the insulin, anaphylactic (allergic) symptoms sometimes followed the initial dose, and the patient was therefore desensitized by the

[17]The clinic at Christie Street was in operation before the clinic at the T.G.H. was opened, but much of the important scientific work at the "General" had already been done. The Christie Street paper was about a year later than the "General" paper; it added nothing of scientific importance.

subcutaneous administration of one unit every twenty minutes, until five units had been given. On the following day he was given the amount of insulin which it was estimated would reduce his blood sugar to the normal level, and subsequent doses to maintain him sugar-free.

Other untoward results sometimes occurred with the early batches of extract.

On injection (wrote Gilchrist, Best and Banting) there is local pain, due to the cresol preservative, but this disappears in from one to three minutes. Following this there may be in some induration at the site of injection which usually passes off in from twelve to twenty-four hours. With some of the earliest lots, this induration persisted as a hard, tense swelling with tenderness, but no local redness or heat. In from seven to ten days these areas, in a few cases, showed signs of redness and fluctuation and proceeded to abscess formation. There was little or no adenitis in the glands draining the area, no fever, and after incision and drainage the abscess cleared up rapidly.

In two patients urticaria and fever occurred, but only persisted for two to three hours. . . . During the last few months many of the objectionable features of the extract have been eliminated. There has been no abscess formation, but little induration, and no urticaria. The pain on injection has been markedly decreased.

Some interesting experiences with hypoglycæmic reaction are recorded.

On one occasion, a patient went down two flights of stairs to the dining room at 5.00 p.m., returned to the ward after his meal, and at 8.00 p.m. was found trying aimlessly to clamber up the wall. He remembered nothing from the time of going to supper till 8.30 p.m. when the ingestion of glucose relieved his symptoms.

A wonderful spirit of camaraderie pervaded the hospital. Men who had felt themselves condemned to a sick and useless existence, if not to death, were given hope and assurance, and at the same time were called upon to take part in a great experiment. The subjects of this experiment were all volunteers, and they seem to have accepted the challenge thus presented not only with courage and good will but with a sort of boyish zest. One man in particular, known as "Old Gil," would beg for more injections than he needed, on the principle that if a little was good more would be better.

Another patient wrote the following account of what he had seen and experienced at Christie Street:

The patients who on admission are frequently dull, depressed diabetics with little hope for the future, soon become bright, cheerful and energetic. The discomfort of hypodermic injections is gladly endured for the benefits accruing from the treatment. Patients who were hardly able to walk a quarter of a mile on the level, and who with difficulty ascended a flight of stairs, are now going for two to three mile walks daily, and enjoying them without fatigue. While in hospital, instead of pessimistically contemplating a down-hill progression to diabetic coma, or a slow starvation, the patients are now engaged in vocational therapy, and vie in friendly rivalry with one another in attempts to make the most finished product. The well-known irritability of the diabetic vanishes, and in its stead is the sunny smile of a patient rescued from a lingering death, who gazes on the future with a feeling of confidence born of his own experience. He has found something which will enable him once again to earn his living. He realizes that he has attained to a diet which although closely regulated will satisfy his hunger and his bodily needs. This change is so noticeable that strangers visiting the wards have remarked upon the contrast in the appearance of patients receiving insulin and those who have not yet commenced treatment.

There was one patient, however, who was an exception to the general rule of cheerful and consistent co-operation. He was cheerful enough, and for periods of perhaps two weeks he was consistent and faithful; but at the end of two weeks he had usually reached his limit. As he was well enough to be up and about he simply took French leave from the hospital and disappeared on a two-day "drunk." When he eventually returned he was always very crest-fallen and contrite—and of course very sick. It was then necessary to begin all over again the effort to control his diabetes. This annoying culprit (the type of diabetic who is the bane of a doctor's life and who often arrives in hospital in diabetic coma) was viewed by his fellow patients as a deserter from the cause. All the rest were heart and soul behind Gilchrist in his battle with the disease, which of course was also their battle.

They were detailed, as it were, to capture a certain objective, which they proceeded to do as nearly "according to plan" as possible.

This story recalls another which illustrates an embarrassment which occasionally befalls the diabetic. Gilchrist unluckily once experienced an insulin reaction on a Toronto street and was arrested on a charge of intoxication. This indignity reaching the ears of his "boys" at Christie Street, they formed a delegation headed by Old Gil which repaired in hot haste to the court house to give impassioned testimony on behalf of the captain. Gilchrist was released with apologies but was bantered unmercifully at the hospital and his name was coupled in jest with the rascally alcoholic.

"We wish to thank the patients," wrote Gilchrist and his colleagues in concluding their paper, "for their unfailing, cheerful co-operation, and faith in the treatment throughout the vicissitudes of the earlier experimental work on insulin."

9

By this time the "insulin rush," one of the most remarkable phenomena of the twentieth century, was well begun. From near and far unhappy diabetics descended on Toronto in hordes, like the year of the locusts. Banting's personal celebrity mounted suddenly on the wings of world-wide publicity. Of that again. What distinguished this sudden outburst of public enthusiasm for a scientific discovery from other similar outbursts was the profound and beneficent change which was all this time occurring in the lives of suffering diabetics. The gratitude of invalids restored to vigour was heart-whole and beautiful. The extent of the change so wrought will inspire, when properly visualized, a sensation of awe. No one, except a restored diabetic, could better appreciate this change than the group of physicians who had made a specialty of treating the disease. For years they had striven, with courage and persistence and with indifferent fortune, to stay the ravages of the terrible sugar sickness. Pre-eminent

among these was Dr. Elliott P. Joslin of Harvard, who had
directed at the New England Deaconess Hospital the care of many
hundreds of diabetics.

Said Joslin many years later:

There is one chapter of the Bible which I like to read. I call
it the Banting Chapter and it was written by the Prophet Ezekiel.

"The hand of the Lord was upon me, and carried me out in
the spirit of the Lord, and set me down in the midst of the valley
which was full of bones,

"And caused me to pass by them round about: and, behold,
there were very many in the open valley; and, lo, they were very
dry.

"And he said unto me, Son of man, can these bones live? And
I answered, O Lord God thou knowest.

"Again he said unto me, Prophesy upon these bones. . . .

"So I prophesied as he commanded me, and the breath came
into them and they lived, and stood up upon their feet, an exceeding great army."

These words show the estimation in which I hold Sir Frederick, the discoverer of insulin, and Charles Best and their many
associates, and indeed all who have the marvellous gift of
prophesy.

But I am neither a prophet nor the son of a prophet, and
in the spring of 1922 I had no prophesy. I wondered what would
happen to my poor diabetics' dry bones, when out of the sky came
word from Toronto . . . that I was one of those to have the
prophesy after all. . . . Ileten.

He went on to describe the case of Miss Mudge.

Miss Mudge, the first diabetic patient in New England to
receive insulin; Miss Mudge, chosen from all my then living
patients as the severest of the severe, whose weight on August
7, 1922, was 69 pounds—just about the weight of her bones
and a human soul, since she had lost 86 pounds in five years—was
in my office this week, a happy woman, filling an important place
in her family, perfectly contented with her diet, and taking 44
units of insulin a day. [And he remarked on the surprising fact]
that after seventeen years the severest of the severe, but a faithful
diabetic (a nurse, by the way), requires only 44 units to live an
active life.

Insulin has transferred the responsibility for the maintenance of the life of a diabetic from the doctor largely to the diabetic himself. Now that the discoverers and manufacturers of insulin have lightened the load on the doctor's back and given the patient a means of completing his life's journey, the world is beginning to take notice of the diabetic and to watch whether he will utilize these means and complete his career in a courageous, cheerful, and productive manner. I firmly believe that diabetics on the whole are brighter than the average individual, but will they live up to this heritage? In our matter-of-fact world the fate, not alone of the present diabetics, but of all diabetics now and hereafter, depends upon each diabetic patient's living an honest diabetic day and contributing something of value to the human family. . . .

I might cite the list of those diabetics who have achieved, but instead I will tell you of my newest reason for considering that my diabetics deserve recognition. Years ago Mr. (we will say) White came to my office because of his diabetes, and with him his attractive young wife. Eventually, I regret to say, he died at about the close of the Psalmist's span of life. Last month another diabetic gentleman—we will call him Mr. Brown—came to the office, and with him his wife, Mrs. Brown, both in high spirits. I watched them both closely, and Mrs. Brown especially, because, of course, we judge of the health of a man by the sorrow or joy depicted on his wife's face. I evidently looked at Mrs. Brown quite intently, for it led her to say, "Dr. Joslin, I see you have a good memory. Yes, I was Mrs. White." Ladies and Gentlemen, do you realize the significance of that? Here is a woman who had lived with one of my diabetic patients until his death, and then, passing over ninety-nine other just men who needed no Benedict tests, deliberately chose one who did—another diabetic. . . . I challenge you to furnish any better example of diabetic optimism.

Once upon a time my diabetics lived 4.8 years; Dr. Allen increased the duration to 6.0 years, and I thought the 25 per cent. gain remarkable. Today, in this year of our Lord 1934, I am convinced from studies of my own cases that the average duration of life of the diabetic contracting the disease this year, and I include the very old and the very young in the average, will be 20 years.[18]

[18]Address delivered at the formal opening of the new Lilly Research Laboratories in Indianapolis, Indiana, in October, 1934.

10

Such were the amazing and gratifying results of the use of insulin. In the meantime, research work continued to enlarge the scope of its usefulness.

The early clinical results (writes Banting again) were obtained from an insulin which we know now contained impurities. Biochemists took up the problem of purifying the product. Abel, of Baltimore, in 1926, was the first to prepare insulin in crystalline form. The medium from which he obtained his crystals contained ammonium acetate, brucine and pyridine. The isolation of the crystals was attributed to the fact that the acidity could be adjusted to the isoelectric point of insulin so slowly and so accurately that a supersaturated solution was obtained. Scott, of Toronto, working with Harrington, of London, obtained crystals from amorphous insulin using a buffer solution of ammonium acetate and saponin. The yield of crystals produced by these methods was irregular.

On searching the literature, Scott found that the pancreas contained considerable quantities of zinc (according to Lutz) and of cobalt and nickel (according to Bertrand). He then found that when traces of zinc were added to a buffered solution of amorphous insulin, crystals were readily obtained. He explained the results of the saponin crystallization by the fact that the saponin contained zinc as an impurity. On examination it was found that Abel's crystals also contained zinc. Scott proceeded to test large numbers of metals and found that cadmium, nickel and cobalt could also be used in the crystallization, but were less satisfactory than zinc.

In the meantime refinements were introduced into the methods of production of the insulin that was being used clinically. With the elimination of impurities the insulin was more rapidly absorbed and the duration of its effect was lessened. This made it necessary to increase the number of doses in order to maintain a patient free from sugar. Since insulin could only be taken by hypodermic injection, the result was an added inconvenience to the patient. [This sometimes resulted in what a recent advertisement for long-acting insulin describes as "hypo phobia." (A diabetic patient is pictured in a state of horror, surrounded by enormous, nightmarish hypodermic syringes, which point their threatening needles at her from all directions.)]

Gilchrist has listed some of the attempts made to overcome this difficulty. "Insulin has been administered subcutaneously in gum acacia, and in glycerine, in an attempt to decrease the rate of absorption. The persistent induration with the former procedure and the large amount of oedema (swelling) with the latter, together with the meagre delay in absorption, caused the abandonment of these modifications. Rectal administration in alcohol and other media was attempted, but with little success. The large dosage and consequently increased cost and the unsatisfactory results rendered this method impracticable."[19] Inunction was also practised for a time in Great Britain, and perlingual application was tried out, but with no better luck. It seemed that the severe diabetic was doomed to multiple daily injections. But ten years after the original work, a way was found to protract the action of the drug.

Hagedorn, of Denmark (resumes Banting) sought to prolong the effect of insulin by adding protamine, which was obtained from sperms of rainbow trout and mackerel. Hagedorn and his colleagues (1933-35) found that the addition of the protamine to their insulin so delayed the action that the day's supply of insulin could be given in one injection. This was the greatest advance in the treatment of diabetes since the discovery of insulin. Scott found that when protamine was added to zinc-free amorphous insulin there was little or no delay in the rate of absorption. If, however, zinc was added, a combination occurred between the insulin and protamine with the characteristic slowing effect of the protamine. It would seem that the Danish insulin contained sufficient zinc or other specific metal to produce this combination.

11

The cause of diabetes was not then, nor is it yet, fully determined. Attempts were made to produce diabetes by injections of streptococci into the pancreas, injections of boiling water into the pancreatic arteries, and X-ray of the exposed pancreas. In

[19]Gilchrist et al., op. cit.

a paper published by Banting and Gairns a series of ingenious experiments was described in the study of factors influencing the production of insulin. These included elaborate transplantation operations, and the effect on the pancreas of local heat applied by irrigating with hot water a thin rubber tubing (and afterwards a glass coil) wound round the pancreas and with both ends protruding through the abdominal wound. The effect of tying off the suprarenals at the same time was also tried. One of their conclusions was a suggestion of a relationship between the blood-sugar-lowering effect of hyperemia (produced by the local application of moderate degrees of heat to the pancreas) and the excess production of insulin on one hand, and the blood-sugar-raising effect of pain and the excess production of adrenalin on the other hand.

(Banting's co-worker in these investigations was Miss Sadie Gairns. Beginning in October, 1922, she assisted him with much of his scientific work, and for many years she was secretary extraordinary, technical assistant, and friend.)

Among his scientific publications will be found a number of cognate researches, which, with various collaborators, he carried out. Following his early papers chronologically, we notice that by and by he strays away from the province of insulin research, gravitating toward other interests. Not that he feared, like Emerson, to "exhaust one vein of thought, much like those Savoyards who, getting their livelihood by carving shepherds, shepherdesses, and smoking Dutchmen for all Europe, went out one day to the mountain to find stock, and discovered that they had whittled up the last of their pine-trees." No, there was little likelihood of that. There was, and there still remains, a great deal to learn of carbohydrate metabolism. The mechanism of the normal state and the manner of its derangement in disease were not so easily made clear. The lighting of a single taper, however brilliant, did not illuminate all the complexities and recesses of the problem, still involved in darkness. No. For he realized, indeed he specifically stated, that he had "only made a start." It was a start long awaited, and now scores, hundreds rather, took up the work. There was a rush to investigate insulin —its method of action, how best to use it, how it might be modified and improved. Experimental and clinical journals published the results (in some cases it were better to say the remains) of these feverish studies. A torrent, an avalanche of "literature" was poured from the press. In 1922, under "pancreas extract," ten articles were listed in the Quarterly Cumulative Index; in 1923, under "insulin," there were seventy-five entries; by 1924 the number had swelled to more than two hundred, and with every passing month the discussion steadily increased in volume and extent.

The original discovery had established a "working cure" for diabetes (not, indeed, a cure, but a practical means of control). How the "working cure" worked, and why, and what else might be deduced from the discovery were now the pre-occupations of medical scientists in every country. Most of these men were honest workers, some of them brilliant and capable of making worth-while contributions, others well-intentioned but unqualified for the work. Not a few, as must always be the case, were merely attempting to "climb on the band wagon," to follow the fashionable trend. At any rate, the genuine investigators had been pointed in a promising way. The main route had been marked; the by-paths and some of the important roads beyond remained to be explored. And at this moment Banting withdrew. How the continuing labourers fared and what they accomplished has been in part related in Banting's own words. He himself, meanwhile, was following other courses.

12

But we anticipate the story. Insulin was still his major concern and still at the centre of his horizon when, the "rush" having reached its full career, he opened offices for consultation at 160 Bloor Street West. What a change from the doldrum days in London! Then, as a half-feathered practitioner, lacking friends and starving for patients, he had whiled away his time as best he could. But now, by the grace of insulin, the diabetic world was at his feet. Diabetics rich and poor thronged eagerly to see him, for had he not been proclaimed far and wide as the prophet of a new hope? As a prophet he was sought by the diabetic faithful, and as a prophet of hope and healing he will be longest remembered.

What the discovery of insulin has meant to the world in conserving lives is indicated in part by tables of statistics. What it has meant in conserving health and energy is beyond all calculation. One striking example has been frequently drawn to our attention. In 1921 a Harvard physician, George R. Minot, developed the symptoms of diabetes. He discovered that his Benedict test was four plus; "As strong a sugar test," he said, "as you'd find in any urine." A strict diet, every particle of food weighed out on scales, was only partially successful in controlling the disease. Then came insulin, and with it a new hold on life for Minot. In 1926, four years after Banting's discovery, Minot and his colleague, William P. Murphy, announced an innovation almost as far-reaching, a somewhat similar "working cure" for another dread disease, pernicious anæmia. They had discovered that the failure of red blood cells to reach maturity in "P.A." was due to the lack of "E.M.F." (erythrocyte maturing factor) and that this deficiency could be made good by liver, in which "E.M.F." is stored. Would Minot have been alive in 1926 without insulin? Supposing he had been able, by means of an heroic diet, to protract an invalid existence for several years, even beyond that time, would his energy in the meantime have been equal to his work? In the answers to these questions all those who suffer pernicious anæmia and are sustained by liver find reason to couple in gratitude the name of Banting with that of their great benefactor, Minot.

An account of famous diabetics, in whose achievements the discoverer of insulin shares a part, could be prolonged for many pages. Let one more example suffice. Mr. H. G. Wells, famed as novelist, historian, sociologist and popular interpreter of science, was a diabetic and a user of insulin. (He was also, incidentally, president of the British Diabetes Association, founded in 1935.) Had not his diabetes been controlled, it is possible that the list of his works might be shorter, and he could hardly have lived, as he did, to be nearly eighty. As it was, he found the disease "an invigorating diathesis," and it is not too much to say that *The Invisible Man* in Wells' later career was none other than Banting.

I very deeply appreciate the honour which you have conferred upon me in awarding the Nobel Prize for 1923 to me and Professor J J R Macleod I am fully aware of the responsibility which rests upon me to deliver an address in which certain aspects of the work on insulin may be placed before you. This I propose to do right and I regret that an earlier opportunity has not been afforded me of satisfying this obligation.

THE FIRST PARAGRAPH FROM THE MANUSCRIPT OF
BANTING'S NOBEL PRIZE ADDRESS

PART VII
The Celebrity

And after all the raskall many ran,
Heaped together in rude rablement,
To see the face of that victorious man,
Whom all admired as from heaven sent
And gazed upon with gaping wonderment. . . .

EDMUND SPENSER.

Fame usually comes to those who are thinking about something else; very rarely to those who say to themselves, "Go to, now, let us be a celebrated individual."

OLIVER WENDELL HOLMES.

1

In June, 1940, at the seventy-first annual meeting of The Canadian Medical Association, in Toronto, Dr. Lillian A. Chase, of Regina, recalled the impression made upon medical students of the period by the initial trials of the new drug.

Eighteen years ago last spring I saw the first child who ever had insulin. The late Professor McPhedran presented to his fifth year medical class of which I was a member a little diabetic boy who, in addition to the usual dietetic treatment had had two doses of "Banting's fluid." I should like to be able to say that we all realized that we were in the presence of a great discovery. On the contrary, with the usual barbarous ignorance of youth, we had our minds more on the time for the Saturday noon bell than on anything that our professor was telling us. It was not until later that we realized that the occasion had been historic.[1]

It was not among medical students only that there was at first a failure to recognize the tremendous importance of the maiden ventures with insulin in the Toronto General Hospital. The sponsor of the new treatment could not complain, however, of a gainsaying generation; by comparison with many another important discovery his work "caught on" almost instantaneously. But there was a lag of a few weeks, of a few months rather, before conviction began to permeate the profession. This was the period during which the evidence was accumulated and presented. Once the facts were clearly set forth there was no demurrer. As Dr. Chase suggests, history very often neglects, when staging her greatest dramas, to announce the programme. But once the implications were made clear, the publicity became tremendous.

Silhouetted against the dramatic dawn of a new era in medicine, Banting achieved a sudden and spectacular fame. Like Byron, he awoke one morning to find himself famous, and as day succeeded day his celebrity grew and extended in dazzling encomiums all round the world. He loomed before the eyes of hitherto doomed diabetics in almost godlike proportions. Scien-

[1]"Diabetes Mellitus: Problems of its Control," by Lillian A. Chase, M.B., *The Canadian Medical Association Journal*, 44; p. 250.

tists hailed him with lavish praise. To the great mass of the public he became the story-book scientist, the laboratory wizard to whom prodigies of achievement were commonplace and from whom further miracles were hourly expected. His glory was trumpeted in the newspapers, clarioned in the magazines. Fantastic stories were invented of the wonders he was soon to accomplish. Nothing was too much to expect. It was rumoured that cancer, heart disease and tuberculosis, as well as a host of minor ailments, would presently yield to his genius.

Sir Henry Dale relates:

It has happened to me on several occasions in London to be rung up on the telephone by inquisitive representatives of the Press, anxious to extract from me information and opinion as to the latest reputed discovery [of Dr. Banting]. Not so long ago a gentleman was very persistent; he would not be put off with a terse expression of opinion. Apparently he had been reading a lecture by Professor Macleod and he wanted to know, in definite terms, whether I thought it likely that Dr. Banting had now discovered a cure for metabolism. It was only the separation imposed by the telephone that prevented me, in a moment of some emotional stress, from trying to find a quick remedy for the metabolism of the inquirer.[2]

Banting himself was of course pursued by reporters. He sometimes received them with good humour but not seldom with marked acerbity. When he returned to London, Ontario, to accept an honorary LL.D. from the University of Western Ontario, his visit was headlined in the now defunct *Advertiser:* "Discoverer of Insulin Retreats Into a Shell at Attempted Interview. Refreshingly Rude." The attempted interview follows:

"In what disease has science made greatest progress towards a cure?" asked *The Advertiser*. "Bah!" replied the great scientist, by this time safely ensconced in the car. The reporter approached. Dr. Banting placed his club bag upon his knees and hid behind it. "Drive on," quoth he to the man at the wheel, and the driver drove. One concluded that the progress of science held little of encouragement.

[2]Address delivered at the formal opening of the new Lilly Research Laboratories in Indianapolis, Indiana, in October, 1934.

This, of course, is an extreme example. Yet " 'Bah!' replied the great scientist" is probably one of the most disconcerting interviews on record. (And "Bah" is probably a euphemism for what he really said.) At other times he was pleasant and informative or smilingly enigmatic.

The first occasion of a public nature in Toronto at which Banting was guest of honour was a luncheon of The Canadian Club at the King Edward Hotel in March, 1923. More than a thousand persons attended the luncheon and as he entered the hall the entire assembly arose to greet him. He was received with cheers and presented with a life membership. He gave a brief sketch of the history of diabetes and then described the pancreatic gland, holding up to the view of his audience the sweetbread of a cow, with the remark that he did not want to interfere with their digestion but that it was important to understand the nature and function of the pancreas. He described the work on insulin and showed two samples of the extract, one made during the earlier stages of the research, and the second a more recent one. The first was light brown in colour, the second crystal clear and much more potent. He concluded with an account of the practical application of the drug, and its results in treatment.

Such events soon multiplied and he was forever in demand to talk about his discovery. This eventually became a wearisome task which he performed with waning patience, repeating the same address, without the demonstrations, a hundred times. It grew more and more difficult for luncheon and dinner committees to secure his services as a speaker: "He reminds one a little," said a newspaper writer, "of a small boy asked to recite something in front of the class when he wants to go swimming." Even scientific societies could seldom get him to talk about insulin. Finally he refused such invitations altogether and in his later years made less than half a dozen exceptions to this rule, and then only when he felt some strong claim upon his gratitude, as at the opening of the new Lilly Research Laboratories in 1934.

He was at first an indifferent speaker. The stumbling delivery of his remarks at New Haven, when he first appeared before a group of scientists in the rôle of a savant and described his investigations, then fresh and startling, was an embarrassment to all who heard him; his ineptitude seemed all the worse when compared with the rounded sentences and polished, if academic, manner of Macleod, who followed him at the rostrum. Gradually, however, smoothed by the wear of practice, his public speaking improved beyond recognition, though never to the point where he could be classed as an accomplished orator. He was more business-like than eloquent. Set speeches, such as the Nobel Prize Address and the Cameron Lecture (the latter repeating some of the best paragraphs of the former—paragraphs which he also employed on several other occasions) were carefully composed and forcefully delivered. Their composition cost him hours of intense effort, and addressing himself to his audience was an ordeal. When the last words were uttered he always felt that a load had slipped from his back. His dislike for speech-making never abated, and the following letter, written to a class-mate many years later than the present phase of our story, sets forth his feeling on the subject.

October 1, 1936.

My dear C——

Your letter of September 28, concerning the guest speaker at your Rotary Club is received.

It is very good of your Club to invite me and I appreciate the invitation. I hope you will extend to them my thanks. I regret very much that it is impossible for me to accept such an invitation. Les King has been after me repeatedly to go to Galt; Bill Tew is anxious that I should go to London; Cornell has invited me to Fort Wayne; and Stevenson pleaded with me to address his nurses. All of these I have been unable to accept. I merely mention them to you so that you will understand how they would jump on me if I accepted your invitation. Some years ago I endeavoured to fulfil my responsibilities and accepted invitations, but I landed up with a duodenal ulcer, as every speech I have ever given has been preceded and followed by hyperacidity, diuresis, diarrhœa and diaphoresis.

Sincerely yours,

F. G. Banting.

In some of the speeches, notably the Cameron Prize Lecture, are to be found examples of apt phrasing, forceful similes and at times real eloquence. There are also occasional awkward expressions and mixed figures of speech. Sometimes his perorations on the subject of work and its rewards pile up in a drift of words

which hardly serve to reinforce his point. Speaking of the ideal
research worker he said: "With self-detachment, self-abandon-
ment and self-abnegation, he must pursue his own idea and
ideal. Above all he must work with intensity, integrity, breadth,
patience, thoughtfulness and faithfulness." This is a profound
saying, expressed in admirably balanced sentences and exhibiting
considerable care and thought. Nevertheless, it reminds us of
the Professor of Worldly Wisdom in *Erewhon,* who plucked a
student for writing an essay on a scientific subject without making free enough use of the words "carefully," "patiently" and
"earnestly"; it is, in short, a little too much. With these slight
detractions, however, it is not to be denied that Banting possessed the gift of direct and pungent English and that he had the
right feeling for words. If it is true that now and again, like
Kipling's Mariners, he "plucked unhandily," it was a fault which
sprang from the direction, rather than the nature, of his talents.
The product of his difficult composition may have shown here
and there a frayed edge or a false colour, but it was stout and
sensible fabric and worthy of its maker. Literary refinements we
do not expect, and those we find are therefore doubly enjoyed.
What he had to say was without exception well worth saying,
and he expressed himself infinitely better, in a formal address,
than do the majority of scientists.

An enduring wish to write, and the consciousness of having
struck off a good paragraph, sometimes led him on into an ill-
contrived "purple passage," in which all taste and discretion
seemed to desert him. One of the worst examples occurs in his
journal of an expedition to the Canadian Northwest, to be quoted
at length in another chapter ("Northwest Saga"). Following
an excellent description, touched with fantasy, of sunrise across
the northern waters, he appears to feel that he is really in his
best form and so launches another paragraph with the freezing
words: "Erstwhile the fingers of the goddess of heaven waved
to us a farewell." Unluckily the farewell continues through
another two hundred words before the author can extricate himself and return to the brisk and amusing narrative which makes
the greater part of this journal good reading.

Of course this was hurried and casual writing, but the same
weakness for strongly perfumed words may be scented here
and there in his speeches, and it was perhaps just as well that in

later years he condescended to accept the help of others in composing an address. Another reason for this was his procrastination in getting down to business on a speech. On one occasion a devoted colleague (call him Brown) fearing that Banting would not be ready in time, composed an important lecture for him, only to find that the Chief had finally, at the last moment, ground out one of his own. When a secretary compared the manuscripts, the latter was found to be not only hurried and incoherent but deeply stained with purple. Banting was wise enough to accept, though perhaps with chagrin, the frankly tactless advice, "For Heaven's sake, use Brown's!"

There are only a very few instances of such "ghost-writing," although the same secretary, asked by Banting for an opinion of the text of a speech already delivered, answered, "Excellent! I don't think you wrote it." To which he responded, striking the arm of a chair with his fist, "Damnation! I can't get away with anything!"

At the right time and in the right mood he could make a good impromptu speech, but he was generally far from nimble and to call upon him unexpectedly when more than a few formal expressions were required was to invite disappointment. At a luncheon meeting of the Royal Society of Canada, he once proved himself capable of the spontaneous exercise of easy banter. It was the year when George Young, the marathon swimmer, first splashed into prominence, and Banting provoked amusement by suggesting that the Royal Society should swell its coffers by arranging a marathon swimming race in the Rideau Canal between Sir John McLennan, the physicist, and General Cruickshank. But his wit was not consistently ready to his call and he was not designed by nature as a fluent, wise-cracking after-dinner speaker.

The part he much preferred to play on such occasions was a passive one. The centenary of Pasteur falling due in September, 1930, a Pasteur dinner was given in Toronto. The *Mail and Empire* report of the proceeding includes these paragraphs:

The great hall at Hart House was crowded with doctors. At the back it was hard to hear. Banting and a reporter moved from the back and sat down on the stone floor in a shadow a few feet from the head table.

And Banting, unobserved, continued to sit on the floor while the Pasteur banquet became a Banting celebration and the leading medical scientists of the continent linked the name of the young doctor with the great Frenchman. Banting's insulin was hailed as the greatest single medical advance since Pasteur, and the serious-faced young doctor still sat on the floor.

2

As a result of the tremendous wave of publicity which lifted Banting to the heights of fame, every diabetic who could afford to come descended upon him in Toronto. From near and distant points in Canada and the United States, from Europe, from the ends of the earth, the sick and weary pilgrims turned their faces toward this new Mecca. They came demanding insulin, and many of them were resolved to be treated by no one other than the Prophet himself. He found it necessary to open an office and for the first time since his London experiment he engaged in practice. Of his previous attempt at practice he had remarked, "I found it too expensive as a pastime so I had to give it up and go into research." But after the discovery of insulin he might easily, had he so desired, have become one of the great fashionable practitioners of his day. His work, however, was strictly limited and was not continued for long. While some patients, making appointments well in advance, came directly to his office, many others were referred for examination, and for a decision as to whether or not they merited a share of the insufficient supply of his wonder drug. When the clinic was established at the General Hospital, patients were sent in rotation as they arrived to Banting, Campbell and Fletcher.[3] This was a curious situation, considering that prior to his discovery Banting had never assumed complete responsibility for the treatment of a single diabetic and had studied at first hand a relatively small number of cases. But what had those of wider experience to offer the diabetic as com-

[3]It is only fair to relate that while Banting was being paid for the care of these cases, Campbell and Fletcher, staff physicians at the hospital, gave their services to the clinic free of charge.

pared with the magic of Banting's hormone? Knowing how many thousands, beginning with Leonard Thompson in Toronto, and Miss Mudge in New England, and growing almost hourly ever since in numbers and in gratitude, owed their rebirth in happiness, vigour and usefulness to the wonderful gift of his insight, a joy comparable only to that "noblest joy" of discovery must have blossomed in his heart. He observed (with what pride and pleasure who can say?) the increasing use of insulin therapy; saw the resurgence of human energies no longer mocked and stultified by disease; saw the light of renewed hope shining in the eyes of the despairing, the resigned, the life-weary; and having prophesied upon the bones, saw that "the breath came into them, and they lived, and stood up upon their feet, an exceeding great army."

"The true doctor," wrote Bernard Shaw (who has little use for doctors in general) "is inspired by a hatred of ill-health and a divine impatience of any waste of vital forces." [4] Banting was a true doctor, and in the years when the miracle of insulin was young he must have been a very happy man. Its results were indeed phenomenal. The comatose roused from their stupor. The lean and hungry were at last able to eat again and to regain their strength. The weary and discouraged brightened visibly following their injections. Little Jack Keightley, rushed from Johannesburg in an advanced stage of the disease, was presently pictured in the papers engaged in a playful bout of fisticuffs with one of his nurses. Another child, a little girl who had been too weak to walk, was shown in bathing dress, ready for a swim.

[4]Preface to *The Doctor's Dilemma*. Dr. Seale Harris of Birmingham, Alabama, who visited Toronto in March, 1923, to learn the new method of treating diabetes, writes as follows: "It was an interesting coincidence that while Banting and his associates were making experiments on animals that resulted in a discovery which literally has saved, or prolonged, the lives of millions of human beings afflicted with diabetes, Bernard Shaw's idiotic protest against vivisection in his drama called *The Doctor's Dilemma* was being played in Toronto by a company of English players. It was with considerable indignation that I sat through a play in which a literary charlatan endeavoured to ridicule and misinterpret the altruistic ideals of the medical profession." (*The Journal of the Florida Medical Association,* July, 1941; also *The Mississippi Doctor,* March, 1943.) *The Doctor's Dilemma,* containing Shaw's usual mixture of whimsical profundity and arrant nonsense, is capital fun; despite the criticisms by Dr. Harris, which are thoroughly justified, the play is not only an attack on vivisection but also a spirited study of the difficulties of a true medical scientist in a world in which there are many medical (as well as literary) charlatans; the type of Sir Ralph Bloomfield-Bonnington was not extinct by 1923, nor by 1943.

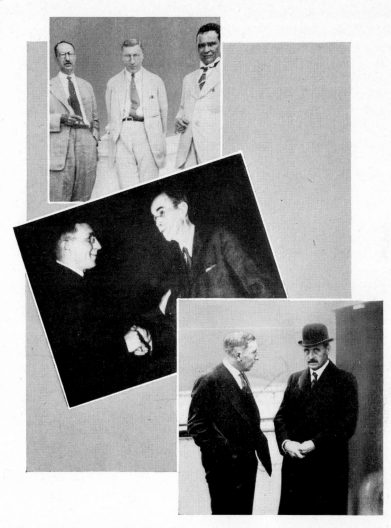

Above (from left to right): Dr. Milton J. Rosenau, Boston, Mass.; Dr. F. G. Banting; Dr. Miguel Arango, Baranquilla, Colombia.

Centre: F. G. Banting and Professor J. J. Abel of Johns Hopkins University.
He and his co-workers isolated insulin in crystalline form.

Below: Dr. F. G. Banting and Lord Dawson of Penn.

Banting was overwhelmed with the gratitude of those he had saved. Gifts of every kind were showered upon him. Pitiful letters, proud letters, joyful letters, letters that were hymns of praise and thankfulness, reached him in ever increasing numbers by every post.

In his speech to The Canadian Club[5] Banting said: "I would like to read you a letter which was received from a child nine years of age. This child has been under treatment at a clinic in the United States. He says: 'Dear Dr. Banting, I am a diabetic and have had the disease for a little over two years. When I went to this particular clinic I had been getting 300 calories'—that is the amount of food that would possibly be contained in one course of one meal that one of us would eat. That amount had to do the child for twenty-four hours—'I don't believe I would have lived a month if I had not received insulin treatment. Now I am getting 1,800 calories. I have gained ten pounds and am still gaining. I am going to start school very soon.' He goes on to say that his father is a doctor and gives him the extract. We have had a number of such letters, especially from children."

And all this while the sensation his work was creating continued to grow in intensity; news produced "the rush," and "the rush" produced more news.

It can hardly be denied that Banting adjusted himself with some difficulty to his enormous fame. To his lasting credit, however, he refused to capitalize upon it. The practice which he undertook was necessitated by the pressure of circumstances and was intended as a means of service rather than a means of gain; he had no intention of deserting research. He might easily have asked, and as easily received, fantastic fees, but his charges were exceptionally modest. Some of his colleagues, unfortunately, were not so fastidiously restrained, and a few were frankly opportunist and quite ready to "scalp" the more well-to-do-visitors. An Atlantic City millionaire came to Toronto with his wife and daughter because the latter was a diabetic. During their stay in the city the millionaire's wife had an attack of acute abdominal pain and her case was diagnosed by a leading Toronto surgeon as

[5]"Addresses delivered before The Canadian Club of Toronto, Season of 1922-23," in *Proceedings of the Canadian Club, Toronto, for the years 1921-22 and 1922-23.* Banting's address is entitled "The Story of Insulin" and is found on p. 231 of Vol. XX.

appendicitis. He accordingly proceeded to remove her appendix —at a cost to the unprotesting millionaire of five thousand dollars. To this was added a bill for two thousand five hundred dollars, submitted by the physician who had first been called to see the case and had referred it to the eminent surgeon. Banting was furiously angry. He felt that the visitors from Atlantic City had come to Toronto on his account, as indeed they had, and that two of his colleagues had taken advantage of them in a manner which he considered shameful. As to the propriety of charging a wealthy patient "whatever the traffic will stand" opinion is divided. There are those who say that the rich must pay for the poor, that huge fees collected from Dives merely help to compensate for the unpaid services rendered to Lazarus. Banting, at any rate, refused to adopt this Robin Hood conception of his place and mission as a doctor. "You must begin with an ideal and end with an ideal," he told a group of medical students. "And if, by the wayside, you falter, and place commercial gain before higher motives, you should stop your studies right now. Medicine is a profession of inspiration, perpetual and eternal." [6]

Among other well-attested visitors to the Prophet's shrine was the diabetic daughter of the vigorous, bearded sage who gave Woodrow Wilson a hard run for the presidency and who afterwards became Chief Justice of the Supreme Court in Washington —Charles Evans Hughes. Miss Hughes was treated by Banting personally and responded to insulin in a most gratifying manner. For this happy result she was always, like other sufferers, profoundly grateful, and the members of the Hughes' family were pleased to number themselves among Banting's friends. Some years later, when visiting the U.S. capital, he decided that he would call to see them and to inquire for the health of his patient. He hailed a taxi cab and asked to be taken to the Hughes' residence.

"Bub," said the unsanctified cabby, wise in the ways of Washington, "do you have an appointment?" Banting, amused, replied that he did not need one. There was nothing in his appearance

[6]The millionaire paid the surgeon without complaint but questioned the justice of the physician's charge. He consulted Banting, who informed him that in a case of appendicitis the diagnosis is frequently more difficult than the operation. Thereupon he paid the physician and sent handsome gifts to the wife of the surgeon. Such is the charm of the knife. . . .—L. S.

to proclaim the world-famed scientist, and to the eyes of the cab
driver he looked like any other Nazarene, with nothing much to
recommend him.

"You're wasting your time, Bub," said the driver judiciously,
"You won't get in." Banting insisted, and the cabby agreed, with
great scepticism, to drive him to the Hughes' home. When he
was paid and dismissed he remarked that he might as well wait.

"You won't be long. You won't get farther than the door."
This dreary prophecy was near to coming true. A liveried servant, seeing an ordinary-looking citizen in a crumpled suit and a
battered, not-quite-large-enough fedora, gained the same impression as had the cab driver, and for a moment disputed his
entrance. While he explained who he was and asked that his
compliments be presented to the family and himself announced,
Miss Hughes chanced to come down the stairs, within earshot of
the front entrance. Hearing a part of the conversation and recog-
nizing the voice of her beloved doctor from Canada, she flew to
greet him and swept him gaily indoors with every expression of
delight and welcome. Before the door closed behind him, he
turned back to wave a cheerful dismissal to the mildly abashed
and slightly puzzled driver. Had Banting given notice by telephone of his intended coming he would have missed the pleasure
of seeing Miss Hughes' surprise.

"Bub," he may have said to himself, "you got in!"

On his way home from the same trip he made an overnight
stop in Rochester, N.Y. There he was interviewed, as usual, for
the newspapers, and the manager of the hotel where he stopped
rejoiced in his presence so much that he refused to allow him to
pay his bill. "I shall be able to tell my visitors," he explained,
"that Dr. Banting slept here." The young doctor must have felt
that he had been suddenly exalted to equal rank with the great
George Washington.

These trifling incidents illustrate both the immense hold
which he had gained on the popular mind as a result of his
achievement and the unimposing demeanour with which he carried his fame.

Albert Einstein, newly arrived in Princeton, was observed as
he strolled down a principal thoroughfare blandly licking an ice
cream cone. Marie Curie "had no time to spend in altering the

hasty simplicity of her life's background." [7]   Banting was equally
unaffected. His manners, his person, his living quarters, remained
untouched and unaltered. As the Autocrat would have it, he was
"thinking of something else."

When he first returned to Toronto after his London interlude,
he stayed briefly with his cousin, Dr. Hipwell. He then obtained
a room on Grenville Street not far away from his work. Of course
his work, at least the paper part of it, went "home" with him.
His room was a litter of books, journals, documents. He piled
books against the wall, and when one row threatened to topple,
he started another one beside it, until eventually they encroached
so far into the limited space that he barely had room to move
around. His desk, transplanted from his London office and with
books and journals shoaled up around it on the floor, was heaped
with papers, with notebooks, with the dusty bound volumes of
scientific periodicals into which he was forever delving. Here
he continued the study of the vast literature of carbohydrate metabolism which he had commenced in London, and here he
obtained that wide familiarity with its complexities to which
Professor Henderson has testified. In the small hours of morning,
"the grandest hours of all," he read and pondered, made notes
and abstracts, conned over the dry mementoes of old and obscure
research, while the cigarette butts accumulated in his ash trays
and fragmentary ideas spiralled ceaselessly in his brain. Then
something struck him as more especially significant, more
especially pertinent to his work, than anything he had found to
date. (What's this? Laguesse discovered more abundant islet
cells in the pancreas of the newborn than the adult pancreas?)
And another spark gap was bridged.

His fame made little difference to this constricted background.
He continued for another year to lead his bachelor existence in a
cluttered room which his landlady hardly dared to invade, taking
haphazard meals wherever he happened to find himself. When
he opened an office at 160 Bloor Street West, he lived in a
similar fashion in an apartment in the top story of the building.

His appearance and his comportment were likewise unpreten-
tious. A newspaper reporter describes the ovation which he
received on one of his public appearances, a formal dinner, in

[7]*Madame Curie*, A Biography by Eve Curie, Doubleday, Doran & Company, Inc., New York, 1939.

1923; the account goes on: "If he appreciates the performance, he gives no evidence that the company can see. There are no acknowledging bows or smiles, nothing at all of finished motions or signs of the public man." There are further remarks on his appearance, and the reporter hardly conceals his surprise at what apparently seems to him to be a certain lack of distinction. "Not even," he says, "a pair of horn-rimmed glasses, nor was there a bit of a beard. . . . A fountain pen and a lead pencil, along with a modest little watch chain—a pair of serviceable-looking spectacles complete the decorations." [8] Once again there is a tribute to his modesty: "The discoverer of insulin almost gives the impression that a number of people were working on the problem and he happened to be around when the result was announced. . . . He is such a generous distributor that he hands away as much of the glory as he can."

This new celebrity, projected abruptly on to the world stage, never posed in the spotlight. He had no desire to inflate his reputation. Jealous as he was of the honours which he knew to be due him (and he made no pretence at a false indifference to the laurels of science) he never strutted, never assumed the airs of an acknowledged "great man." He declined the rôle of a lion, and persisted in the belief that his private affairs were of little concern to newspaper readers. His seriousness seems to have impressed the journalists. He was described as a "grim-faced young doctor from the back blocks," and again as "an earnest young scientist with no frills." The romantic "Kildare" type had not yet been invented and Banting would have made a poor model of the kind. The seriousness the reporters observed was both superficially obvious and deeply inherent in his nature, but on a plane between coursed a joyous zest in living which few of them at first divined. Banting was vitally and vivaciously human when in the midst of kindred souls.

[8]Mr. H. G. Wells wrote of Mr. Bensington and Professor Redwood in *The Food of the Gods*: "They were, of course, quite undistinguished looking men, as indeed all true Scientists are." He adds: "There is more personal distinction about the mildest-mannered actor alive than there is about the entire Royal Society."

3

As month followed month, his publicity grew in volume and vigour and went on unabated so long as the "insulin rush" continued, indeed long after the crowds had commenced to wane and insulin had become more generally available. It continued intermittently for the rest of his life, rising and ebbing and again rising to the headlines. Never again could he be a private citizen like other private citizens. His scientific work and any opinions he cared to release for publication were legitimate news; unhappily the misfortunes which followed him later in his private life were also seized upon by sensation-mongering writers. Meantime, however, he figured in the press as the scientific wizard, the prophet of reanimated bones.

Nor was academic approval very slow in coming.

In the years following the discovery of insulin (writes Professor Best) the whole scientific world joined to honour Banting with a galaxy of awards and medals. It will always be a source of gratification to his colleagues in the University of Toronto that they were among the first to recognize the greatness of the man. In 1922 he received the Starr Gold Medal for his M.D. thesis[9] and the George Armstrong Peters Prize for his important contributions to surgical science. In 1923 he received the Reeve Prize which is awarded for a published report of the best scientific research accomplished in any department of the Faculty of Medicine by a junior member of the staff, and in the same year the Charles Mickle Fellowship which is awarded to that member of the medical profession (anywhere) who is considered by the Council of the Faculty of Medicine of the University of Toronto to have done most during the preceding ten years to advance sound knowledge of a practical kind in medical art or science. The Nobel Prize in Medicine was awarded to Drs. Banting and Macleod in 1923. Banting immediately divided his share equally with the author, and Professor Macleod with Dr. J. B. Collip. . . .

Banting became an honorary member of most of the outstand-

[9]Banting's 1917 degree was the M.B. The bachelor degree was then granted by the University of Toronto on completion of the medical course, while the M.D. was a higher, post-graduate attainment. The course has since been lengthened and the M.D. awarded in place of the M.B.—L. S.

ing scientific and medical societies of the world. Awards followed each other in rapid succession: the Johns Scott Medal (Philadelphia) in 1923, the Rosenberger Gold Medal (Chicago) in 1924, the Cameron Prize (Edinburgh) in 1927, the Flavelle Medal of the Royal Society of Canada in 1931, the Apothecaries Medal (London) in 1934, and the F. N. G. Starr Gold Medal of the Canadian Medical Association in 1936.

In recognition of his great service to science and humanity Dr. Banting was created Knight Commander of the Civil Division of the Order of the British Empire in June, 1934. In the following year he was elected a Fellow of the Royal Society of London.[10]

This, of course, anticipates the present account by many years, but serves to complete, except for the honorary degrees and the honorary memberships in various societies, the roll of distinctions and awards which a grateful world bestowed upon him. Some of the prizes brought cash emoluments as well as honour and the Canadian Government presently rewarded him with a pension. Of that again. But it is clear that had he shown some signs of "swell head," or had he been deterred from his work by the dizzying acclaim of both the multitude and the elect, he could hardly have been censured. He allowed neither of these things to happen. He went his way and kept to his tasks, and though the nature of the latter was somewhat changed with the years, he gave them the same unstinted energy as he had given to the quiet research which first brought him fame.

The award of the Nobel Prize was accompanied, unfortunately, by further disputes and perturbations. It is impossible not to feel, in reading the temperate words in which Banting records the history of insulin, that

> A fever in these pages burns
> Beneath the calm they feign.

For it had not been roses all the way. There had, indeed, been a time when he had been so near discouragement that he had actually thought of dropping the work. Consequently, when the Caroline Institute in Stockholm offered the Nobel Prize to "Macleod and Banting," his first instinct was to refuse it, a Shavian gesture which would have gained him tremendous notoriety but

[10]Obituary, *C.M.A. Journal*, 44: 327.

little credit. Yet, after all, Macleod had spent the stifling summer of 1921 in Europe, while Banting and Best were producing their extract in Toronto, and Banting could never quite forget the anger which had swelled in his heart when it appeared that Macleod would win the major share of the praise which rightfully belonged to him. Now, in 1923, the scales of justice were settling to a proper balance, but the Nobel Prize for "Macleod and Banting" was a strong reminder of the insupportable dominance of the older man which had seemed to threaten Banting's position eighteen months before. The emotions of those fermentative days had never entirely quieted. It needed the persuasions of several of his most trusted friends to bring him to a more judicious state of mind, and even then he insisted that the order of the names must be reversed. He would have much preferred to share the prize with Best, and as soon as the award was announced he made known his intention to divide his own portion of the money (half of the total award of $40,000) with his co-worker.

When Banting was invited by his friend, Dr. Joslin, to attend a medical meeting in Boston in October, 1923, to discuss the use of insulin in diabetes and because of previous commitments was unable to attend, he sent the following telegram (dated Toronto, October 26, 1923):

DR. ELLIOTT P. JOSLIN,
81 BAY STATE ROAD,
BOSTON, MASS., U.S.A.

AT ANY MEETING OR DINNER PLEASE READ FOLLOWING: I ASCRIBE TO BEST EQUAL SHARE IN THE DISCOVERY. HURT THAT HE IS NOT SO ACKNOWLEDGED BY NOBEL TRUSTEES. WILL SHARE WITH HIM.

BANTING.

Macleod, as already mentioned, divided his share with Collip. Despite frayed emotions and a seeming taint of jealousy, the whole affair was thus concluded honourably and generously.

As for Banting, the present writer is forcibly reminded of a comment on his character which was made by the late Sir William Mulock, who afterwards did yeoman service in collecting money for the Banting Research Fund. Trimly clothed in a suit of his habitual shepherd's plaid and seated in an armchair in his bedroom, the old man nodded his famous domed head and patriarchal whiskers and murmured reminiscently: "He would give away his breeches. You didn't have to pick his pocket; he would freely give you the contents." His pale blue eyes, a little rheumy with age and sunken behind old-fashioned spectacles, gleamed with a faint pleasure. "No money sense," he added, "no money sense at all." And somewhere deep in the shepherd's plaid sounded a remote and appreciative chuckle.

4

In 1923, Banting was freed of all financial worries and provided with a modest competence by the Dominion Government. Early in that year the feeling began to grow that the Government should recognize his accomplishment and reward him. Warm words of praise had abounded, but if he were to continue to work in Canada (and to achieve anything better than the smallest fraction of the income he could readily command in the United States) cold cash would be necessary too. Not that there was ever any reason to fear his departure. He was too good a Canadian for that. But here, of course, was only an additional reason for acknowledging and rewarding him and for ensuring him an opportunity to go on with his work.

The first mention of this proposal to be found in *Hansard* is in a speech by Mr. T. L. Church.[11] The irrepressible Mr. Church urged Parliament to lay down a policy like that of the United States, Great Britain and Australia, "of giving financial aid to those Canadians who through their skill, industry and professional ability help medical science. . . . I think something should be provided in the Supplementary Estimates or some substantial financial aid be given to men like Dr. Banting. . . ."

Even earlier than this, however, the movement received a strong stimulus from sources outside the House. Banting's loyal

[11]*Hansard,* 1923; 1: 703.

friend and sometime teacher, Dr. George W. Ross, of Toronto, was one of its chief proponents.

About the middle of March, 1923 (writes Dr. Ross[12]) I sent a memorandum to the Federal Government pointing out Banting's amazing accomplishment in the discovery of Insulin, and took the liberty of suggesting that the Government should recognize it in some material fashion. . . .

In addition to that I asked a number of distinguished American diabetic specialists to write the Government and express their opinion of Banting's work. These letters, without exception, were extremely laudatory and each expressed the opinion that Banting was the discoverer of Insulin. The names of these gentlemen were: Dr. E. P. Joslin of Boston; Woodyatt of Chicago; Wilder of the Mayo Clinic; John R. Williams of Rochester; F. M. Allen of Morristown and Dr. Geyelin.

After about three months of consideration and enquiry, the Government took appropriate action. Rt. Hon. W. L. Mackenzie King (Prime Minister) moved:

That whereas the recent discovery of the insulin treatment for diabetes by Dr. F. G. Banting, of Toronto—as the result of devoted application and research—and the discoverer's disinterested and generous action in placing it at the disposal of the public, have conferred inestimable benefit not only on the Canadian people but on sufferers in all parts of the world, it is expedient that Parliament should give some expression of the nation's gratitude to one who has rendered such distinguished service to science and humanity, and that such recognition should take the form of a vote of an annuity sufficient to permit Dr. Banting to devote his life to medical research.

He said:

Mr. Speaker, I do not think it is necessary for me to supplement the words of the resolution by any comment; they speak for themselves. . . . The Government has felt that some formal expression by the Parliament of Canada . . . would be fitting at this time, and in giving it the form suggested by the resolution we believe we are interpreting the wishes of all Canadians. . . .

[12]Personal communication.

Rt. Hon. Arthur Meighen (Leader of the Opposition):

Mr. Speaker, the resolution, I think, constitutes a beginning, so far as public policy is concerned in this country, of recognition in any substantial way of scientific and humanitarian achievement. . . . I have real pleasure in seconding the resolution.[13]

Other members supplemented these remarks with a variety of comments. Hon. H. S. Beland (Minister of Health) explained the significance of the discovery from a medical viewpoint. Mr. T. L. Church advocated prompt extension of the policy to include other scientists. Hon. R. J. Manion asked permission of the Speaker to point out a factor which had escaped mention, "and that is the fact that as I am informed on very good authority Dr. Banting could have exploited this discovery" and indeed had been offered fabulous sums to do so. Dr. Manion added that commercial exploitation of such a remedy would not have been consonant with the great tradition of medicine, citing the commercialization of Ehrlich's 606 as the only exception to the rule which he could recall. He supported the motion strongly:

I personally am particularly glad, as I am sure is every medical man in the House, to see Canada taking this attitude toward the discoverer of this health-giving remedy, for unfortunately in the history of medicine and surgery too seldom has recognition been given.[14]

The motion was agreed to without a single dissenting voice. To the lasting credit of the Canadian Parliament and the Canadian people, Banting was granted an annuity of $7,500.

The grant came just in time, for Banting was then, so he said, "four thousand dollars worse off than a beggar"; he owed that amount to his father.

"I have never known anything like the relief I felt when that was all paid back, with interest. My father worked hard for it and although what was his was ours, I didn't want to be owing it to him.

[13]Hansard, 1923; V: 4437.
[14]*Ibid.* (It should perhaps be pointed out again that insulin, though certainly "health-giving," is not a "remedy" in the ordinary sense. It does not cure diabetes, and except in very rare cases its use must be continued for life.—L. S.)

"In 1923, I discovered, when I came to make up my income tax, that I had taken in thirty-two thousand dollars altogether, but at the end of the year I had to borrow the money to pay my income tax." What was it Sir William had said?

On the day that Banting was informed of the grant from the Canadian Government he wrote Best a card, postmarked June 30,1923, Southampton, England, in which he said:

"Dear Charlie:

"I have just had a marconigram telling about the Dominion Government. I wish they would give you an equal amount. Surely blessings are falling on us fast enough now. We must keep our heads.

Fred."

No one could say that Banting over-rated his own importance.

5

In 1923, as this card indicates, Banting went to Great Britain, where he was acclaimed both by the profession and by the public and variously honoured. On July 25, while delegates to the British Medical Association Congress at Portsmouth were discussing diabetes, he sat almost unrecognized at the back of the hall. But not for long. Sir Thomas Horder paid a glowing tribute to the discovery and called upon Banting, much to the latter's chagrin it need hardly be said, to make a speech.

In London he ordered a morning suit from a Bond Street tailor because his friends insisted that he would need it. Then one evening at ten minutes to five he was informed that he was commanded to Buckingham Palace for an interview with the King at eleven o'clock the next morning. The suit had not come but was due to arrive in the morning. The Canadian Commissioner took him out and rushed him around to buy hat, gloves and cane.

"Then," said Banting, "I just had to trust to God that the suit would turn up."

Next morning the suit arrived and he was dressed and ready with time to spare.

"I picked out a taxi," he said, "and drove off for Buckingham. I got there fifteen or twenty minutes early and as they were changing guard I drove around to a side entrance. There a big, stately butler met me and ushered me down a long corridor and around a corner to where I would have come in if I had gone through the central court. There were rooms along both sides and I walked slowly, so that I could catch a glimpse through the open doors. They had some very fine pictures.

"He put me in a Chinese room. Presently in came a sloppy individual with the sort of trousers that have pockets on the front. He was some sort of official. He had bad teeth, very bad teeth, and he lounged against the fireplace with his arm on the mantle-piece while he talked to me. 'Lord,' I thought to myself, 'if the King can stand you around him, he'll be able to stand me for a little while. I won't be thrown out inside the first few minutes.' That fellow did more for me than anything else to put me at my ease.

"Then a charming old gentleman came in. He was Lord Something-or-other. He knew Canada well, and liked it and wanted to talk about it. In his youth he had been on one of two warships that lay off Vancouver as part of the British patrol and he had crossed and recrossed Canada afterwards.

"Well, at last they took me into another room to the King and left me alone with him behind closed doors. There was nobody there to watch us, or at least I could see no one. Probably there must have been someone keeping an eye on us to see that I didn't throw anything at His Majesty. We sat talking there as easily as you and I are talking now and I was at home with him after the first minute. He was a very well educated and cultivated gentleman. He talked to me about insulin and asked most intelligent questions about the processes of the work. Then we got to talking about hospitals. I mentioned one in London and by jove he knew in pounds, shillings and pence what it cost to run that hospital! So many pounds in 1900, so many pounds in 1910 and so on. Then he talked for a time about Sir Frederick Treves. . . ."

His Majesty asked Banting about himself, where he had been brought up and educated. He also talked to him about Canada.

Finally he returned to certain aspects of medicine and became so deeply interested in the conversation that the young scientist was permitted to stay on much longer than the allotted time. King George concluded the audience by urging him to direct his talents toward the search for a cancer remedy.

In London he encountered Professor J. W. Crane and they left together for Scotland to attend the Physiological Congress in Edinburgh. Besides attending the meetings of the Congress they found time for a tour through the Perthshire Highlands. Purchasing a ten cent, paper-bound copy of *The Lady of the Lake,* they roamed through the picturesque Trossachs, made famous by Scott's poem,

> And reach'd that torrent's sounding shore,
> Which, daughter of three mighty lakes,
> From Vennachar in silver breaks.

From Scotland, they proceeded to France, and in Paris met Dr. Edwin Seaborn, who was engaged at that time in a research problem in endocrinology. Mrs. Seaborn's diary records that they arrived on July 30. Next day,

July 31.

Dr. Crane, Dr. Banting, Dee[15] and I went to bank. Taxi back to Kardomah for lunch. After looked at pictures, Dr. Banting bought two. I went to opera and for tickets for tomorrow evening. Went to Louvre, then taxi to La Sainte Chapelle. Dr. Banting said the most beautiful thing of the kind he had ever seen. . . . Dr. Banting had a private audience with the King. He told us about it. Dr. Seaborn and Dr. B. have gone to Folies Bergère tonight. . . .

August 1.

. . . Dr. Crane, Dr. Banting, Dr. Seaborn, Dee and I went to L'Opéra. All dancing and very beautiful music also. Had citron preosé at Café after.

August 2.

. . . Dr. Crane and Dr. Banting came up to our room, had chat and had plums and cherries. Dr. S. and Dr. Banting went out to "Freddie's" ("Lapine Agile"—night club).

[15]Dr. Seaborn's daughter.

This was a night club with a rather macabre atmosphere. Lights were few, and dangling skeletons were lowered suddenly in the darkness among the startled dancers.

August 3.

Went out with Dr. Crane and Dr. Banting to do some shopping. Dr. Banting bought picture for me—"Grandpère," taken from sculpture which we saw at "le Salon." Had lunch at Kardomah, when Dr. S. joined us, then went to Petit Palais. . . . After dinner chatted in Lounge for quite a while, then Dr. S., Dr. Crane and Dr. Banting went out to the Moulin Rouge. . . .

In addition to the pictures he bought in Paris, Banting purchased old books from the stalls along the Seine. He also paid a visit to the Pasteur Institute, where he talked with Roux himself (Dr. Seaborn acting as interpreter) and was presented with a number of reprints by the venerable scientist.

August 4.

. . . Dr. Crane and Dr. Banting left about noon. We were sorry to see them go.

In Lille (Dr. Crane recalls) they dined on boiled eggs in a hotel dining-room swarming with flies, and had considerable difficulty with their French. Banting decided that eggs would be the safest food to eat in such a place, but could not remember the French noun he wanted. He made an oval outline with his fingers, he explained and gesticulated, he even clucked like a hen; but the waitress shrugged her shoulders, saying, "Je ne comprends pas" to his finest histrionic efforts. Finally the cashier, overhearing this interchange, barked, "Oeuf," at the waitress, and the problem was solved.

Banting also had some difficulty in cashing a cheque at a Lille bank, but at last succeeded in establishing his identity by means of the medal which he had won in the Great War. Not far from the same city he searched in vain for his old dugout: the field had been ploughed up and the region which he remembered as No Man's Land was a placid expanse of thrifty cultivation.

6

Singled out by fame from among the other sons of Alliston (much to their surprise it must be admitted) Banting made the traditional triumphant return to his home town. Not that he had neglected it in the meantime. But on February 24, 1923, the 11.25 from Toronto brought two celebrated young men, Banting and Best, to the former's birthplace, and to a public reception in the town hall. At one side of the platform sat his parents. Grouped about the guests of honour were the members of the reception committee, the mayor presiding. At the suggestion of the chairman three hearty cheers were given and "the volume of these cheers," states a reporter, "was indicative of the glow of pride in every heart in Alliston." After community singing which helped to relieve the tension of the crowd, Best gave a brief address outlining the discovery. Then Banting was on his feet and after some preliminary remarks about the town of Alliston and reminiscences of the years he had spent there, he turned dramatically toward his parents. He declared that it would have been impossible for him to undertake his research "had it not been for a man who has been right in your midst; and although I have met during the last few years many men and women, I have never yet met any finer or more self-sacrificing than my father and mother." The hall re-echoed with shouts and applause. He then continued to talk about insulin in much his usual vein and concluded with a characteristic message to the boys of Alliston. There were still, he said, profitable fields for research work, but "nothing can be accomplished without hard work."

Following the public meeting a banquet was given to the guests of honour in the Dominion Hotel. Mr. H. Davidson, principal of the Alliston High School, indulged in reminiscences, interspersing his remarks with the repeated question, "Do you remember, Fred?" to the intense delight of the crowd and occasionally to the obvious embarrassment of the guest of honour. Said Banting to a Toronto reporter, "Suppress the personal note and boost the town."

In 1924 he was back again, to open with a golden key the new public library which had been built by the Women's Institute.

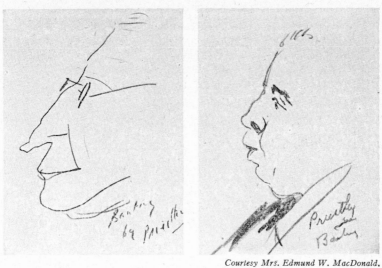

F. G. BANTING AND J. B. PRIESTLEY CARICATURE EACH OTHER

"DR. BANTERING"
BY ARTHUR LISMER, A.R.C.A.

But between these semi-official appearances, he made frequent
flying visits to his old home on the third concession.

"A little while ago, when he was home," his mother is quoted
as saying, "I said to him, 'You, with your name in the paper!
Are you the same little fellow who used to gather eggs on the
farm and go about with your arm around your mother's waist?'
When he was at home he would come into our room, and sitting
on the edge of the bed, tell his parents everything. He still does
that."

His brother, Thompson, has another recollection of his home-
comings. "It's a funny thing," he says, "but Fred could *always*
find a four-leaf clover."

His mother testified to his faithfulness as a correspondent.
"Every Sunday since he left home in 1911 to attend University
he has written to me. All the time he was in school; all the time
he was overseas; all the time since he has been home again. And
while he was suffering from his wound, he wrote too. His right
hand was useless, but he wrote to me every Sunday with his left,
until he recovered."

A visit to the old home was always an occasion. To his mother
it was a great event. If he arrived unexpectedly, Mrs. Banting,
who was always particular about her appearance, who always
wanted a new dress for Christmas, would refuse to see him until
she had "prettied up"—combed her hair and straightened her
dress, or perhaps changed to another one. As long as she retained
her health, and until she was an old woman with snowy hair, her
attitude to her youngest son contained a charming element of
coquetry. She received him as a young girl would receive a beau,
very anxious to look her best.

On less frequent occasions his parents visited him in Toronto.
In 1923, when he opened the Canadian National Exhibition, a
newspaper photographer pictured him with his father and the
managing director of the Exhibition, Mr. John G. Kent. The
caption reads: "A Happy Moment at the Exhibition Opening.
Whatever the joke was it must have been a good one." All
three were apparently enjoying it, particularly the elder Banting,
for the old gentleman is shown with his head thrown back, laughing uproariously. It is a happy picture which persists in the
memory and represents Banting's greatest pleasure in his fame,
that of sharing its privileges with his parents and his friends.

His mother spent a very happy day. To the many who thronged to shake her hand and remark on how proud she must feel, she murmured over and over, "Not proud, but thankful. Not proud, but thankful." She had purchased a new pair of thin black gloves for the occasion; by day's end her right glove was quite worn through.

7

Early in the days of his celebrity Banting became interested in the Arts and Letters Club of Toronto, and after a number of visits as a guest he became a member and continued for years to be an active participant in its affairs. This was coincident with his growing interest in painting and it was among the members of the Club that he encountered many of the artists who became his friends. He was a regular attendant at the Saturday luncheon where a brilliant group of artists and writers invariably gathered. Lawren Harris, A. Y. Jackson, Arthur Lismer and J. E. H. MacDonald (almost forming among themselves the *Who's Who* of Canadian art) were often present, as were also Merrill Dennison, the playwright, Henry Button of J. M. Dent and Sons, F. B. Housser, author of a book on the Group of Seven, called *A Canadian Art Movement,* and Bertram Brooker, skilled in advertising, painting and the writing of plays and fiction; John D. Robins, author of the recent, engaging *The Incomplete Anglers,* and Napier Moore, editor of *MacLean's Magazine,* were also members of the group. It was to this coterie that Banting at once felt himself drawn. He soon introduced another name to the roll of members, that of the widely-travelled mining engineer, MacIntosh Bell (who had married a sister of Katharine Mansfield).

For the remainder of his life Banting continued to frequent the Club, and also the Studio Building in Rosedale where his artist friends were working. Only when he was out of town, or when his work was too pressing, and for an unhappy interval at the time of his divorce, did he fail to make regular appearances. At Christmas, when an hilarious, psuedo-Oxonian dinner was the great event, he clad himself as a monk and paraded in solemnly with the rest of the "brothers," roaring out a song as they followed the "boar's head" to table. He talked, argued, laughed and sang with the greatest gusto and enjoyment. He would have liked to take part in the amateur theatricals but was always lost on a stage and seldom was permitted so much as a "walk on." In one of Bertram Brooker's farcical playlets he was summoned from the audience by a call for a doctor and then had a few lines to deliver when he had reached the stage; this delighted him hugely. (Another of Brooker's skits, produced soon after the return of Jackson and Banting from a trip to the Canadian Arctic, dealt with the "Sevenization of the North Pole and the Groupification of the Eskimos.")

Arthur Lismer writes from Montreal: "When Fred Banting sat in with a bunch of us round the Arts and Letters Club table on a Saturday lunch time, he was a lively sceptic and something of a realist, keeping the artists' flights of fancy with some contact or foothold in scientific truth."[16] And yet the Club represented, at the same time, an escape for Banting from the absolute domination of science, a new vantage point from which the criteria of life were measured with the artist's eye and the exact mensuration of the laboratory was not required; where judgment was tinged with emotion and prosaic facts were coloured with romance, with imagination, with the flowing pattern of dreams.

8

What had become, meantime, of his precious research projects? Having achieved the immortal status of "discoverer of insulin" had he been content to relax his efforts? Far from it. But his life was altered completely by the obligations which accompanied his fame. Not only honours, awards and a pension, but also new duties had fallen to his lot. He had held a lectureship in pharmacology in 1921-22, and had subsequently been appointed senior demonstrator in the Department of Medicine; in 1923 he became a full professor, the first in the University of

[16]Personal communication.

Toronto to be named Professor of Medical Research. How had it come about?

Even before the Federal Government in Ottawa had moved to reward him with a pension, the Provincial Government in Queen's Park had determined to recognize his achievement in some substantial way. Once again we trace the hand of his loyal friend, the invariably helpful and energetic George W. Ross.

"About the middle of January, 1923," writes Dr. Ross,[17] "I made representations to the then Prime Minister of Ontario, the Honourable E. C. Drury, concerning Banting's contribution to medicine. He received them with enthusiasm and after some discussion it was decided to establish a Chair of Medical Research for Banting, of which he should be the first Professor. Banting did not know anything about this move until I told him. He was greatly pleased, but after a short period of meditation he said: 'I want to have Best included.' I wanted to know why, since the plan was devised to honour him as the discoverer of insulin. The only answer I received was 'Well, Best stood by me at a time of difficulty.' That night we saw Mr. Drury and Banting expressed the wish that the Chair should be called the 'Banting and Best Chair of Medical Research.'"

"An Act to provide for an Annual Grant to the University of Toronto for the promotion of Medical Research"[18] was assented to on May 8, and may be found in Chapter 56 of the *Statutes of the Province of Ontario, 1923*. "There is hereby appropriated and there shall be paid out of the Consolidated Revenue Fund of Ontario for the establishment of a Research Fund, to be known as 'The Banting and Best Research Fund,' a sum of $10,000 annually." It was not specifically stated that at least a part of this money was for the purpose of establishing a Chair, but such was the intention.

About the same time another project was afoot. Sir Robert Falconer, President of the University, approached the Chancellor, Chief Justice Sir William Mulock, with the suggestion that the latter should sponsor a campaign to raise funds by public subscription for the purpose of establishing a Banting Research Foundation. Sir William, who had been president of the Toronto

[17]Personal communication.
[18]Short title: "The Banting and Best Medical Research Act, 1923."

and York Patriotic Association which had raised millions of dollars in this way during the first World War, agreed to "sound out public opinion." With this end in view he invited fifty or more prominent citizens, including some of his colleagues of the Patriotic Association, to a dinner at the York Club, which Banting also attended. As a result of this meeting, Mulock decided to undertake the organization of a campaign, and informed Sir Robert Falconer that he might count on the accumulation of a large sum, from $500,000 to $750,000. A committee was formed, with E. R. C. Clarkson as honorary treasurer, and meetings were held at the Toronto Board of Trade. The purposes of the Foundation were stated as follows:

"To provide in the first instance sufficient financial support for the Banting and Best Chair of Medical Research.

"To establish a fund for the adequate financial support of such scientific workers as have proposed definite problems of medical research, and for whom funds are not otherwise available. Such assistance may be given not only to persons working in the University of Toronto but also elsewhere."

The appeal provoked a generous response. Substantial amounts were subscribed by individuals and corporations; many of the contributions were anonymous. A cheque for $50,000, given by a company which withheld its name, was accompanied by the following letter, addressed to Banting:

My dear Dr. Banting,

It was indeed a great joy to me to be able to wire you on Saturday that our corporation would subscribe $50,000 to the Banting Research Foundation.

All of us consider that it is a privilege to be permitted, and quite an honour to be invited, to participate in this substantial effort to memorialize, as it were, your epoch-making discovery of insulin. Our Board of Directors is unanimous in making this subscription, and, speaking for myself, it is one of the most gratifying things that has come to me in my business experience.

A few weeks after the opening of the campaign the *Toronto Saturday Night* published the following editorial:

The campaign to raise $500,000 for the purpose of establishing the Banting Research Foundation which opened on June 29 has so far yielded encouraging results, and the prospects of reaching the objective are excellent. Though the project originated in the University of Toronto and was first promulgated a month ago by its eminent Chancellor, Chief Justice Sir William Mulock, P.C., the fact should be emphasized that the purpose of the Foundation is national and not to be regarded in either a local or provincial sense, and when the organization of the governing body is finally completed its personnel will . . . be representative of all parts of the Dominion; so every Canadian may feel that it is in truth a national institution, no matter if its executive happens to be centred in Toronto. . . .

The necessity of making a start somewhere by the appointment of a provisional board and suitable trustees if research in Canada was to be put on a functioning basis is of course obvious; and the University of Toronto as the birthplace of insulin seemed to be the logical point. But the *University of Toronto Monthly,* organ of the Alumni Association of that institution, is emphatic in pointing out that: "the underlying determination of the Foundation is that the money put at their disposal shall be spent on the solution of definite problems of medical research *anywhere in Canada.*"

In the wording of the second of the formal "purposes" of the Foundation, and in the expression of this "underlying determination," we hear the authentic voice of Banting himself. To devote the money to the financial support "of such scientific workers as have proposed definite problems of medical research" was certainly his idea; to make the Foundation national in its scope was likewise consonant with his wish.

The campaign was successful; the money was collected and invested; the interest from the Fund was used to support research. By the time of Banting's death, Professor Velyien E. Henderson[19] was able to report that nearly two hundred workers had profited by grants made to them by the Foundation.

On June 19, 1925, Banting gave to Mulock a photograph of the Banting portrait painted by Curtis Williamson, thus inscribed: "To Sir William Mulock in sincere appreciation of his inspiration, interest and help." He also presented him with a replica of the Nobel medal. In the Mulock residence on Jarvis

[19]V. E. Henderson and A. W. Ham were honorary secretaries of the Foundation.

Street, crowded with a thousand photographs and presentation pieces and a varied jumble of mementoes, none were more cherished than these.[20]

Nineteen-twenty-three was "the year of the big money." It was in that same munificent year that the Rockefeller Foundation, largely because of the work done in Toronto by Banting, presented a million dollars to the University as an endowment for the maintenance of the Faculty of Medicine. It began to appear that when the University provided Banting with ten dogs, a small laboratory and the services of an unpaid assistant, it had made a good investment.

[20]The oil portrait referred to hangs in the main corridor on the first floor of the Banting Institute, opposite the entrance. It was commissiond by Banting's classmates (IT7) and Banting himself chose the artist. The frontispiece of this book is a photograph of the Williamson portrait.

PART VIII

A Cruise in the Caribbean

I voyage north, I journey south,
I taste the life of many lands,
With ready wonder in my eyes
And strong adventure in my hands.

SIR CHARLES G. D. ROBERTS.

1

BY 1924 Banting was thirty-three years old and unmarried. This was a source of some worry to his old friend, Mrs. O'Neil, who regarded all bachelors as anomalous creatures who sorely needed "looking after." He himself, she noted with relief, was at last inclining toward her view.

Returning from overseas in 1919, he had received his discharge from the Christie Street Hospital (where he afterwards carried out, in association with Gilchrist, the clinical trials of insulin previously described). Miss Marion Robertson, the attractive daughter of Dr. and Mrs. William Robertson of Elora, was at that time occupied in electro-therapeutic work at the military hospital. At a later date, after his return from London, he met Miss Robertson again at the Toronto General Hospital, where she was working in the Radiology Department. Friendship became progressively more deeply coloured with emotion and was transformed into romance. They made plans to be married in the autumn of 1924.

In the spring of that year Banting was invited to be present, and to deliver a paper on his investigations, at the International Conference on Health Problems in Tropical America, to be held in Kingston, Jamaica, from July 22 to August 7, and to be followed by a tournée of all the possessions of the United Fruit Company around the Caribbean Sea. Naturally enough they revised their plans. The Conference was under the auspices of the Medical Department of the Company, and at the end of May the general manager of the Department wrote to him from New York:

Dr. W. E. Deeks to F. G. B., May 29, 1924

I have your letter of May 27, and will be very glad to make reservations as you suggest. I am sure everybody will be very much interested in the title of your paper.

In a previous communication you suggested the possibility of a lady accompanying you, and we replied that we would be glad to give Mrs. Banting complimentary transportation. We do not know if there is a Mrs. Banting, and if she desires to accompany you. If so, please let me know so that I can send a pass for her.

185

This amusing letter must have evoked a prompt answer, for two days later Dr. Deeks wired Banting:

"Will gladly extend complimentary transportation to Mrs. Banting and will discuss itinerary with you any time you are in New York."

And so it was settled: a wedding trip in the Tropics. The wedding date was moved ahead from October to June, and on the afternoon of June 4, in the home of the bride's uncle, Dr. James Caven, they were married. Only the members of the immediate families were present. "The pretty bride and her distinguished groom," reads a newspaper account, "received the full and frank benediction of a summer sun. Even between the closely drawn curtains of the upstairs sunroom, where the ceremony took place, its warm rays filtered." They left on their honeymoon by automobile—not the battered old Ford (which Banting had sold to keep himself in board money during the lean days of the great research) but a shining new roadster.

They sojourned briefly in Preston Springs, and later in the month we find them in Atlantic City, where they stopped for a few days at Haddon Hall as guests of Henry W. Leeds, president of Leeds, Lippincott Company, whose daughter was one of the first insulin users. On June 18 they arrived in New Haven, Conn., where Banting was honoured by Yale University with the degree of Doctor of Science. In conferring the degree, Provost Henry S. Graves said that it was for a service to humanity "beyond all measure."

On July 12 they sailed from New York shortly after noon.

"Leaving here in about ten minutes," Mrs. Banting wrote from Pier 9, "splendid people on board and we're on the boat for nine days straight sail."

Banting wrote in his diary: "Sailed 1.00 p.m. S.S. *Calamaris*, United Fruit Company—beautiful ship and such a comfortable suite has been given us. Box of fruit from the Leeds and a telegram from home and a letter from Sadie. Met all the people in the party and find them all very nice. At our table in the dining-room we have Dr. Nichols, Major Dunham, Colonel Ashford and his son and my wife and I."

Bailey K. Ashford (Colonel, M.C., U.S.A.) was a famous pioneer in tropical medicine. Major-General Merritte W. Ireland

(Surgeon-General, 1918-1931) wrote of Colonel Ashford in his preface to the latter's autobiography:[1]

His work as a scientist has brought him international renown, and has saved the lives of unnumbered thousands. As discoverer of uncinariasis, the hookwork disease, in American territory, and as director of the first mass campaign against its inroads on a stricken agricultural people, Colonel Ashford laid the foundation of all the successful contests which have since been waged against that disease, in our own country and throughout the tropical world.

Ashford's autobiography contains an interesting account of the conference and the tournée. "Of all the friends I made on that trip," he wrote, "none became closer than Banting. We sat together at table all the way to Kingston; and timidly—it was his honeymoon—he made friends with me."

Mrs. Banting to Dr. and Mrs. Robertson

Sunday afternoon, July 13, 1924.

Well, here we are, a day and a half out to sea, and such wonderful weather, and the bluest water I ever saw. I've heard people from the south speak of the blue water, though I never thought much about it, but it's altogether blue—no green at all—and they say it gets to be a perfect sapphire colour . . . as you get farther south.

. . . The people on board are charming. Two ladies in particular—a Mrs. Rosenau from Boston, and a Miss Carter from Washington. The former's husband and the latter's father are very noted doctors. . . . Dr. Carter was the man who helped to conquer yellow fever, and is at present writing the history of yellow fever for the Rockefeller Institute.

Dr. Milton J. Rosenau, famed bacteriologist and public health authority, came to be on intimate terms with Banting during the course of the trip. Dr. H. R. Carter had been associated with General Gorgas in the fight against yellow fever. "He was an old man, then painfully ill, and had made this trip only by a valiant effort. The very soul of honour, with a chivalrous faith

[1]Bailey K. Ashford, *A Soldier in Science*, William Morrow and Company, New York, 1934.

in his brother knights, Dr. Carter opened every door through which the truth might pass, and never once said 'You are wrong,' or 'That is not so.' He always said: 'It may be so, and if it is a question of fact and not interpretation, I'll take your word for it. But I never saw it myself.' He was the beloved old man of this Conference—its 'grand old man.' "[2] He did not live to finish his book on yellow fever, which was completed by his daughter, Laura. The latter was also a graceful lyricist, the author of *Wind and Blue Water,* a copy of which she presented to Mrs. Banting. Banting, too, was pleased to make her acquaintance, as he had much admired a poem of hers called "Neutral," which gained considerable notice in 1914.

Mrs. Banting to Dr. and Mrs. Robertson

Monday.

We have just finished playing games on deck. Dr. Rosenau and I played Mrs. Rosenau and Dr. Parks in golf and quoits. . . . Fred is busy reading a detective story, and this afternoon we're going to work again on his paper. He has to speak in Havana, Cuba, while we're there, which is unexpected, so it means a little work.

. . . Last night there was dancing on the deck, but today it's been raining and the sea is rocky. . . . It's such a fine, roomy big boat, and it rides so steadily, even in this sort of sea. I noticed a few absentees from breakfast today, and one girl up on deck looked a bit greenish, but thus far I haven't felt any qualms at all. It is hot though. I must admit that. I'm wondering how we'll stand Panama.

Tuesday afternoon.

The weather is wonderful again. Last night the moon was full, and we danced on deck and had such a good time. The moon was just huge. Everything down here seems to be so much more concentrated—the sea is bluer, the sun brighter, the sky clearer, and the moon larger. I might say, too, that the heat is hotter. Any fond idea we may have had of a cool ocean trip has been dispelled.

We've been working all morning long, with a secretary, on

[2]Ashford, *op. cit.*

the paper, and now after lunch we're at it again, revising it and adding to it. I'll be jolly glad when it is done. I'm really not of much use, but Fred thinks I'm necessary so I stay around. He's reading something just now, so I can write this.

We get to Cuba tomorrow. This morning at breakfast we passed so close to Palm Beach, Florida, that we could see people on the beach distinctly, and all the hotels and houses.

(Banting wrote in his diary: "Worked on the paper and got it finished—thank Heaven.")

Thursday, July 17, 1924.

My husband having gone sky-larking to gaze at the Cuban hospitals with the rest of the gentlemen, I think this seems an opportune time to get off a note to you again.

It's very hot—unquestionably hot—and we are not allowed to bathe at all here because the water in the harbour is not pure. One has to be so careful in the tropics it seems. One indiscreet move and you get something awful the matter with you. Dr. Deeks tells you exactly what you must do though, and we never eat or drink off the boat.

We docked at Havana yesterday morning about 6.30 and it certainly is a magnificent sight to come into a harbour like this. The sea is very blue and all the buildings are of white stone (coral formation) and they simply shine in the sunlight. There are tall date palms and all sorts of strange trees, and all this together with the two old forts still in use—one on each side of the harbour—makes a most picturesque sight.

About 7.30 a.m. we started off to have a look at the town. We all went separately, and Fred and I went up a queer old street —the narrowest I've seen. The sidewalks are at the most a yard wide, and in some places narrow down to about a foot and a half. People always walk in single file. The buildings are built straight up from the sidewalk, and are mostly two stories high, with a narrow balcony on the second story. The street itself is about as narrow as possible. Along one side there runs a street car track with funny little yellow cars on it and on the other side of the track there's only just room for a car or a mule cart to pass the street car. In places the sidewalk is so narrow there isn't room for a person between the wall and the street car.

The two main shopping streets. . . are both one-way streets and

allow no parking because there isn't room for two big motor cars
to pass. . . . We had a great time trying to shop in Spanish, with
a dictionary and many gestures, but the people are unfailingly
courteous and are all charming. I never saw such pretty girls in
my life. They have eyes like saucers and so soft and dark and
brown they just melt at you.

While we were walking about in the morning we met Dr.
Aristides Agramonte, the leading Cuban doctor, and he called
to us and insisted on our driving with him in his big car. He
has a liveried Spanish chauffeur. We saw Havana and all this
end of the island with him. Then he took us all through one of
the hospitals and then over to his house for some refreshments,
and then gave us his car to go shopping.

In the afternoon, the gentlemen had a meeting and the ladies
shopped, and at night we dressed up and went to a meeting where
Fred spoke on insulin—and spoke splendidly. They had champagne
punch and sandwiches afterward, and then a drive in the moonlight, and then a dance to the most marvellous music on the roof
garden of the "Seville Hotel." It's the one high building in the
city and the view was very fine. The moon. The low, white
buildings. The tropical foliage. The harbour—full of old-
fashioned ships and many lights. A perfect fairyland.

Some of the party couldn't speak English, among them the
hostess (whose name I can't even spell) but those who spoke both
interpreted for us and we managed beautifully.

Banting's record is slanted from a different angle. ". . . Up-
town we met Dr. Aristides Agramonte. He took us to the University and Hospital—1,000 beds. There are a very large number of
medical students. The tuition fee is $15.00 per year. There are
five hundred first year Meds and five thousand medicos all told.
The Hospital, like nearly all buildings, is made of white limestone
which is mined and cut with saws, as it is soft until weathered.
It is of coral formation. The Hospital consists of several buildings, unit system—very large, open, airy rooms, modern in
equipment.

"The Doctor also took us to a monument erected to the eighty
medical students, first year, who were shot November 27, 1871, by
the Spanish Government. The monument consists of the part of
the wall against which they were shot by the Spanish. Students
dissect at the cemetery and it was reported that one of the students

had written or scratched an indecent epigram on the glass front of a grave (people are not buried but laid in a rented plot with glass front; after two or three years their bodies are thrown on the heap). The whole class was arrested and imprisoned and since the guilty man could not be found, eight men were selected by lot, lined up and shot; one man proved that he was absent from his class on the day the epigram was written. Twenty years afterwards it was proven by one of the class that no such epigram had been written. The monument was erected 'To the Innocent' and bears their names.

". . . Anniversary of the Rosenaus' (twenty-fourth) wedding and ours—six weeks—Miss Carter gave us an autographed copy of her book and we sent Mrs. R. twenty-four roses."

Mrs. Banting to Dr. and Mrs. Robertson

S.S. Calamaris, Saturday, July 19, 1924.

Thursday (July 17) the gentlemen had a meeting in the morning to visit hospitals, so we decided to stay home and try to keep cool. I was sorry though that I hadn't gone because some one had sent word that I was interested in X-rays and they had the X-ray department all ready for inspection and asked for me specially. However, the rest was no doubt better for us—it was so hot.

After lunch we all went on a motor trip in the most wonderful cars. You see, in Cuba there are no middle classes—the people are either very, very wealthy or very poor.[3] So all these wealthy people put their cars and chauffeurs at our disposal. We had a big, dark red French car which was very comfortable. We drove through the town and visited the Spanish cemetery, which is very beautiful, but is run in a very unusual way. A funeral here is almost a celebration. The people get dressed up in old Spanish costumes and parade to the cemetery, and the horses are all covered with plumes and bright flowers and ribbons. The

[3]Wrote Banting: "There are only two classes in Cuba—the rich, with their luxurious houses of limestone coral, surrounded by lawns and flowers. They do not work and the women grow fat, both mentally and physically. Their only occupation is to rock themselves in a chair. There are no middle classes and the poor live in congested houses—picturesque in their way—often painted blue or pink. Their children run about naked in the hot sun."

deceased is put in a marble vault and left for five years and then buried. The monuments are very elaborate. One specially fine one is said to have cost $80,000. Fred said, "Enough money to equip a wonderful lab, and do some good."

From there we drove out to a huge brewery where they have the most wonderful gardens—built in a perfect jungle of tropical trees. There are fountains and stairways of coral—and coconuts and dates growing right above you. The fame of this place has spread for years and years all over the island because they give you free of any charge all the ice-cold beer you can drink. We all had a mug of it, and those who are supposed to know said it was fine.

After that we drove out to a reception at Dr. Aristides Agramonte's country house. They are delightful people. His wife is very handsome, with dark eyes and grey hair. She dresses very plainly but never the less stunningly. His daughter is a perfect Spanish type and dresses it. They are very wealthy, of course, and have a great many servants.

The ceiling of the main room went right to the roof, and the floor was of tile—inlaid in a wonderful pattern. They can't use rugs or wooden floors on account of the wood ants, and their furniture is all solid unpolished mahogany, or else wicker for the same reason. Off this big room there was a series of other rooms, opening with swing doors . . . cool and lovely in spite of the heat. The outside of the house has a balcony all around—and all the windows are grated with iron in the Spanish way, and no two of them are the same shape. The gardens are lovely—foliage so brilliant in colour, and droopy mango trees all laden with fruit. The mango is supposed to be the second finest fruit in the world and is not able to be exported on account of its delicacy. It won't keep. It tastes a little like a soft, sweet, juicy pineapple, mixed with malaga grapes. People from the north usually don't like them at first, but we enjoyed them at once. They look like a big peach, with a skin like an orange, only not so yellow or tough.

This is not the whole story of their first acquaintance with mangoes. As they were leaving Agramonte's country house, someone gave them a paper bag of ripe mangoes, which they took with them back to town. There was still a little time before dinner and they went for a stroll in a park. Sitting on a park bench they decided to sample the fruit. Now a mango can only be eaten satisfactorily when it is set in a cup and attacked with an instrument made for the purpose called a mango fork. This was a fact which no one had mentioned to either of them. They expected to eat their mangoes as a Canadian eats an apple. At the first bite, the juice spurted freely. In a ripe mango the juice is very abundant and very sticky. Before they had finished, their faces, their hands and their clothes were liberally smeared. The famous Dr. Banting and his wife, as messy as a pair of children in a jam closet, were observed to enter their hotel by the rear entrance and go up to their room with singular haste. (Readers of Dr. Victor Heiser's autobiography, *An American Doctor's Odyssey*, will remember his account of the perils of mango eating, and of how he established himself as an instructor in this difficult art.)

To return to the letter:

Our whole party was at the reception, besides a number of prominent Cubans. The Secretary of State was there (he used to be Cuban Ambassador to the States) and a number of pretty Spanish girls, and many others. They had a splendid orchestra in the great room for dancing, and the refreshments were salads and sandwiches and champagne punch and ice-cream made from the frozen milk of a grated fresh coconut, mixed with a little ordinary milk; it was the most delicate and delicious thing I ever ate. Our appetites for dinner at the hotel were very indifferent.

That night we stayed in and rested, and yesterday (Friday) morning, Miss Carter and Mrs. Deeks and Dr. Vincent of New York and Fred and I went out with a Mr. Daniels, manager of the United Fruit Co., for a long drive through rural Cuba. Saw all the small towns around and the banana farms and drove to the top of Mont Jesu, the highest point of land, for a view of the island. In the rural part of Cuba almost all the houses have tiled roofs, and are painted either a vivid pink or a bright blue, and sometimes both.

When we got back to town we had their famous pineapple drink. It's made just by crushing a ripe pineapple and adding a very slight amount of water to the juice. One would never recognize the pineapple here by the ones we get up north. These are so sweet and mellow and soft and no fibre in them at all.

So much for Cuba. We sailed last night at 5.00 p.m. and are

still within sight of it, as we are going the long way around—the eastern end of the island.

The S.S. *Calamaris,* steaming softly onward through the lazy tropical seas, brought them to their ultimate destination, Jamaica, where the Conference was scheduled to begin on July 22, in the Myrtle Bank Hotel in Kingston. To this point was gathering an impressive assemblage of medical savants: Sir Leonard Rogers, Sir William Arbuthnot Lane, Sir Arthur Newsholme, Sir James Kingston Fowler, Prof. J. W. W. Stephens, of Liverpool; Dr. Pierre Lepine, of Lyons; Dr. Geo. E. Vincent, of the Rockefeller Foundation, New York City; diminutive Dr. Hideyo Noguchi, the famous Japanese bacteriologist, and Sir Aldo Castellani, with his heroic moustaches, whose compilation on Tropical Medicine had become a standard textbook. Also gathering for the Conference, or for the concurrent entertainments, was an assemblage of the savants' ladies—young and old and in-between—gracefully dominated by Lady Newsolme ("a perfectly delightful old lady," wrote Ashford, "with a fair complexion, few wrinkles, and pleasant pink-ruddy cheek, with a half-luminous, half-motherly expression in the eyes") and by charming, redoubtable Lady Lane, with her beflowered and befeathered hats, gallantly succeeding one another atop her astonishing wig. It was a gay time, but in some respects a difficult one: the weather was oppressively hot and the activities, both scientific and social, were almost too numerous; the entertainment, though varied and delightful, was unremitting.

The Conference was concerned with the whole vast field of health problems in tropical America, and there were also papers by several of the more distinguished participants, including the one read by Banting, which had been called for out of compliment to the speakers and because of the general interest of their subject matter, rather than because of its direct application to tropical medicine. The Conference continued for seventeen days. On Banting's copy of the programme he made check marks opposite the titles of papers in which he was particularly interested (e.g., "The Causation of Cancer," by Sir William Arbuthnot Lane); he also made caricatures of Sir Leonard Rogers, Dr. F. L. Hoffman, Sir Arthur Newsholme and a number of others.

Mrs. Banting to Dr. and Mrs. Robertson

Kingston, Wednesday, July 23, 1924.

Well, this is the first minute I have had since arriving here on Sunday night to write to you. Every minute of the time has been filled up for us. The conference started this morning—although the reception was last night.

We arrived about 9.30 on Sunday night and all the officials and their wives came down to the boat to meet us and had motors ready to drive us up to the hotel. It's a fine hotel, built for hot weather. Right on the sea shore—with huge verandahs all around and lots of shade. . . . They don't even have screens on it—just in the bedrooms. The doors in the bedrooms are made like a wooden screen so that the air can get right through. . . .

Monday morning the English crowd arrived and later on in the day another boat from the Southern States. The English people are delightful—and we've become excellent friends already. Lady Lane has been sweet to me and so have they all. Lady Newsholme is rather older but sent for me and was most gracious. Sir Thomas Oliver is fat and round and pink-cheeked and jolly and Lord Fowler is so nice. He's taken a great shine to Fred. They've all been just wonderful to us. Sir Leonard Rogers—the man who has charge of the Leprosy work for the British nation and who has done such marvellous work—is here and we had a long talk to him yesterday before we visited the Leper colony here. They are certaintly doing magnificent work. He says that in children and in the early stages it can be cured and that in twenty years if the precautions can be taken—like in these leper colonies—there won't be any leprosy.

Monday afternoon there was a reception and dance at 4.30, then a meeting at night. . . .

Tuesday (July 22) we motored all over this end of the island. Drove up through the mountains and saw the really native life—women working on the roads with pipes in their mouths and others carrying huge baskets of fruit on their heads. They are all so straight and walk so well. Tuesday afternoon we had a bathing party . . . then at night the formal opening by the Governor-General, and a dance. Fred sent me a huge armful of American beauty shaded roses and I wore my white dress and had a beautiful time. Wonderful floor—good music—everything.

Today the conference is in full swing and tonight there's a song recital by Mrs. Deeks—every minute of the time is filled for all of us from 8.30 a.m. till 11.00 at night. Strenuous life. Just now we're planning a Ladies' Night for next Friday. Mrs. Deeks to sing a song or two—on the conference—Miss Carter to read a poem on it and they want me to give the paper of the evening on a new microbe called "Feminensis Amorita." Major Harris, of the New York *Times* and *The Century Magazine,* is here reporting and writing up the conference and he's going to write the thing and wants me to read it. It's to be a take off on the medical papers given before. Can't say whether I'll do it or not yet. One of the English party has to contribute something silly and Mrs. Rosenau is to be chairman.

She added a postscript:

I'm enclosing some clippings from a Havana paper which although they're in Spanish I wish you'd keep for us for Fred's mother's scrapbook.

Kingston, Jamaica, July 25, 1924.

The boat with mail leaves tomorrow so I must try to get off a note. Laura Carter and I begged off a 150-mile motor trip today so we could get a rest and write a letter or two. We just haven't a minute left to us—they have entertained us so lavishly. One would have to be cast iron to stand the rush and not melt away.

I wrote you—can't just remember what day but nevertheless I think it was the day before yesterday. Well, that afternoon we had a swimming party at 4.00 p.m.,[4] Dr. Muller of New York and Laura and Fred and I, and then we had tea on the lawn— then dressed for dinner and went on to a lecture by Dr. Vincent of New York—who is a world-famed orator and is President of the Rockefeller Foundation and has control of all their funds. Sir Leonard Rogers told me he'd heard him speak in London last year and that he just made Winston Churchill look foolish. He's really wonderful and so nice. Then after that Mrs. Deeks gave a song recital and then we all went out on the lawn and had the picture taken which I'm enclosing. The flash went off too soon though and no one was ready. Laura is talking to Lady Newsholme and half of the people aren't set at all. It was too bad.

Yesterday we went on a motor trip to one of Mr. Keefer's plantations and went on a little "gathering up" train through the sugar cane fields and banana fields and cocoanut groves.[5] Got

---

[4]Banting's entry for the same day reads: "Convention opened by a paper by Dr. Bass on Malaria. Papers all day. . . ."

[5]Banting's diary: "Yellow Fever day at the Conference—Agramonte and Noguchi on opposite sides concerning origin. . . ."

home at 7.00 p.m. and dressed for dinner and went to hear Dr. Noguchi's paper in the evening on his serum for yellow fever. . . .

Then the Governor of the Island is "At Home" for us on Thursday next. That's the same as Lord Byng at home.

The English people are perfectly lovely and Lady Lane and Lady Rogers and Lady Newholme have each asked me to visit them when we go abroad. . . .

The British fleet comes tomorrow and although we've been asked to somebody's country house up in the Blue Mountains for the week-end—just try and get me out of here. . . .

We had thought of putting on a ladies' night but the heat has submerged our enthusiasm and it's all off, thank heaven.

This afternoon there's a bathing party on again. . . . The swimming pool is a netted-off field of ocean strongly wired and netted for keeping out the sharks which seem to abound. It's perfectly safe though, and the water is so warm and salty and nice. Fred and I are both as burned and brown as can be.

Kingston, Tuesday, July 29, 1924.

. . . The fleet arrived on Saturday and the town has been *en fête* for them ever since. The *Hood* is the largest warship in the world. She weighs 49,000 tons and can travel forty-eight miles an hour.

The officers were all here for a dinner and dance on Saturday night and we met them—some of them, for there seems to be so many—and we had a splendid time. The gardens were a picture —all Japanese lights through the palm trees, and the whole air perfumed with jasmine. . . . The Admiral and the Governor were both here and everyone wore their very bestest best.[6]

Sunday we went on an all-day motor trip, through the mountains and up to St. Anne's. . . . Lady Lane says she's travelled all over the world and has never seen such magnificent scenery anywhere. The roads just wind and wind and wind—back and forth and climbing all the time. Sir Leonard Rogers and Lady Rogers had asked us to go with them so we did so and had a lovely day. He is supposed to be the biggest man at the Conference—scientifically—and he's a peach. I had him autograph my fan—and it has become quite a treasure now—several other famous people have signed their names to it.

[6]Banting's diary: ". . . Very gay party. . . ."

Monday we were rather specially honoured by being asked to a luncheon on board the *Repulse*. The doctor on board had known Fred in London, England, and they had met again at the Polo Match at the Commandant's tea on Saturday afternoon. They sent over for us—the boats are so big they have to stay away outside the harbour place and it takes quite a while to go out. However they sent for us—and Miss Simpson (Sir Wm. Simpson's daughter) and we two and the daughter of the Commandant went over. We had lunch on the quarter deck and then saw all over the ship—in a way that visitors ordinarily aren't allowed to see. They showed us the inside workings of the huge guns, which weigh 760 tons and shoot a shell weighing 1,925 pounds—and 425 pounds of cordite—for twenty-two miles. It was fascinating and we spent the whole afternoon and had tea there, but in so doing I got so hot and so frightfully sunburned that I had blistered shoulders and couldn't go to the dance last night. . . .[7]

Today the ladies of the Convention entertained the ladies of the Committee to a very swish luncheon. . . . Fred made his speech today at three, so that hurried up the end of the luncheon and as soon as that was finished we all went over to an At Home on the H.M.S. *Hood*.

Fred's speech was just splendid. Sir Thos. Oliver spoke so nicely after—about his directness and his simple modest manner and his sincerity and his genius. . . . All the others too spoke of it and of what a splendid paper it was.

Dr. Seale Harris of Birmingham, Alabama, who also attended the Conference, being invited to discuss pellagra and to study the food conditions and nutritional diseases on the banana plantations, was favourably impressed.

"Banting's address on 'Insulin in the Treatment of Diabetes,' delivered in Jamaica, was," so he writes, "one of the best of the many which I heard him deliver. I have read it since his death; and, in my opinion, it is the simplest, clearest, most concise discussion of the underlying causes of diabetes and the use of insulin in its treatment that has ever been written. While Banting was not in any sense an orator, he was an impressive talker, who expressed his ideas in plain and forceful language."[8]

[7]Banting's diary: "Saw all over boat and it makes one proud to be British."

[8]Harris, *op. cit.*

Banting himself had been greatly worried over this paper. "One night at the Myrtle Bank Hotel," writes Colonel Ashford, "at at a ball given in honour of the Delegates, he touched me on the shoulder and said:

" 'I see you do not care to dance, and my Marian is dancing. Let us run off to some quiet place and read each other the papers we are going to present tomorrow, and—and advise each other.'

"We had to sneak down the lawn to the shore. And there under a swaying electric light beneath the palms he read me the wonderful story of his work, the light that has flooded the dark corners of a hitherto incurable disease, a genuine conquest of Medical Science. He read it just like a boy who had been told to write a composition and is afraid it isn't good enough. I interjected a few phrases simply for clarity of expression. He was so grateful that I felt guilty, and exclaimed:

" 'Good God, man!—it's the substance, not the words!'

"He told me that he knew now what had drawn the two of us together. It was that opportunity which we both had had of directly applying our own remedy, curing our patient, and getting immediately therefrom the powerful stimulus to ambition in research which a successful case brings. . . .

" 'But,' said he with charming naïveté—"after all, you know, I am only a laboratory man. I know next to nothing of the art of medicine. I'm the greenest man here. All this is new to me.' " [9]

From such humility and trepidation came the performance of the following day which was afterwards so highly praised. Nothing of all this appears in the diary. There is no record of the laudatory comments. He noted only: "Gave my paper on Insulin," and turned to something else. He was simply relieved to have it over.

Mrs. Banting's letter of July 29 continues:

The At Home today was very fine and we had the honour of being presented to the Admiral, Sir Frederick L. Field, in his private suite. . . . The ship is magnificent and the mascot is a tame kangaroo—the dearest little thing you ever saw. Perfectly tame and he drinks tea and everything.

[9]Ashford, *op. cit.*

Tonight there's a meeting and Fred is there and there's a dance later on—and then a swimming party. . . .

Ashford sums up the Jamaican Conference in the following paragraph:

This was one of the most illuminating international conferences that I have ever attended, first, because men had taken the trouble to boil down their information and present it in an interesting form, and second, because these men who were receiving the hospitality of the United Fruit Company felt a certain moral obligation to give the best they had in them to such an educational expedition. It is true, however, that Professor Fulleborn was left with his mouth standing open at Sir Aldo Castellani's classification of microbes into little germs and big Germans; that one of the delegates made the mistake of taking an extra magnum of planter's punch before his turn came to speak; and that Dr. Agramonte made a violent onslaught upon the mild-mannered little Japanese Noguchi, and by his mere personality introduced a serious doubt in the minds of his hearers as to whether or not Noguchi's corkscrew-looking spirillum was the cause of yellow fever.

(Agramonte, who had been associated with Reed, Carroll and Lazear on the famous United States Army Yellow Fever Board which established that the stegomyia was the vector of yellow fever, was right in his contention. Noguchi's spirochete has been exculpated and a filtrable virus is generally accepted as the cause of the disease. Noguchi himself died of yellow fever in 1928 while investigating it on the west coast of Africa.)

Mrs. Banting to Dr. and Mrs. Robertson

Caribbean Sea, S.S. Yacapa,

Saturday, August 2, 1924.

Well, we arrive sometime tomorrow at Puerto Castillia, Honduras, and although we don't move our things we're going ashore to see the city and the country around—so I believe—and I'll be able to post this. We left Kingston yesterday (Friday) at 2.00 p.m. after a delightful stay. Honestly we did have a wonderful time. The hotel we stayed at cost over $20 a day each if we'd had to pay—but we had a splendid room and bath and wonderful meals and it didn't cost us a cent. I might have said a penny. We've been using English money and my mind has become a chaos of mental arithmetic. . . .

I don't know when I wrote you last—but Thursday night we had our official dinner—the ladies separately but we joined the men for the speeches. . . . Thursday afternoon was the Governor's reception—a delightful lawn party—and Wednesday was a day of important lectures for the men—which I also attended—and drives for the ladies. After the papers we had tea and a swim so it was more fun than a drive in the heat. . . .

At the dinner the other night Fred made a speech representing Canada and spoke *very* well. . . . Castellani—one of the world's great scientists—got up and spoke of "Banting—one of the greatest men in the world" and the whole crowd applauded.[10]

Tela, Honduras, Central America, August 5, 1924.

We are now in port at Tela, Honduras (Spanish Honduras) and are sailing this afternoon at two for Puerto Barrios and from there we go by train to Guatemala city. It's a twelve-hour trip on the train up into the mountains—but I'll write more of that later.

We have "done" two tours since I wrote you last. Puerto Castello on Sunday and Tela yesterday and today. Puerto Castello is a small place—built entirely by the fruit company— on a place which had been a marsh and is now filled in with sand dredged up and covered with thick rich sand from inland. They have spent hundreds of thousands of dollars on it. Fine big buildings and a huge wharf, and working men's houses and electric lights and sanitation. It is a very lovely place situated at the foot of a mountain—with all the tropical foliage. From there we went by train over to Tryillo, a little Carab town across the bay where Columbus is said to have landed in America.[11] It's very old as you may imagine. We saw over the place all day and at night they had a dance on board and all the people came down and we had a great old time. You'd be surprised at the people here. All young married people—charming girls who dress so well and live so nicely in spite of their isolation. There are a great number of young college men here too who are so glad to see people again from home.

[10]Banting's diary: "Final dinner to close conference. I had to make a speech."
[11]Founded in 1524 by Columbus on his fourth voyage.—L. S.

We sailed at 10.30 p.m. and got to Tela at 6.00 a.m.—and yesterday we saw miles and miles and miles of bananas and pineapples.[12] We went by train for 150 miles through the jungle from one plantation to another. You see the only method of transportation here in these countries is by rail. There are no roads and one either has to trail alongside the railway track on a mule or go by these queer narrow little trains. Even what few motors there are run on iron wheels on the tracks. The jungle is even more jungly than I thought. Just a dense mass of undergrowth and vines and big trees. One can't possibly get through it without cutting one's way.[13] Besides there are so many wild things it isn't safe to try. You can hear the baboons at night and see heaps of monkeys and parrots. . . . I haven't seen a monkey yet but I have seen some flocks of magnificent parrots. Some with tails more than two feet long of droopy gorgeously-coloured feathers. There are snakes too and the train we were on had the day before run over a fifteen or twenty-foot-long boa constrictor that was almost as big around as a stove pipe. I saw the hide of it, and that's no exaggeration of its size.

There was a dance last night but I was too tired to go. A great many felt the same way so we begged off. This climate is too hot to dance in.

Well, I must go. Fred's at the hospital just now and we're going to meet them in a few minutes for some surf bathing. There's a peach of a beach here—right on the open sea, and it's one way to keep cool.

It is curious that neither in Banting's diary nor in Mrs. Banting's letters do we find any mention of the fact that Honduras was in the throes of a revolution. Colonel Ashford, having described the U.S. colony and the establishments of the United Fruit Company, including a modern, well-equipped hospital, observes that:

It was odd, on returning to the port, to see the other side of the page: dishevelled and ungracefully-clothed patriots ripping and tearing up and down the streets and calling upon this national figure to live—*Viva!*—and that other national figure to die—*Muera!* But each was to be done dramatically, not peaceably. All this was

[12]Banting's diary: "Left for train ride to see bananas and saw them."
[13]Banting's diary: "It is impossible to gain a conception of it without seeing the conglomerate vegetation."

accompanied by a considerable whooping, and a banging of pistols which never seemed to hurt anyone. It might have been, as they say in Kentucky, that they were "jist fixin' t' git ready." But it was diverting enough. We enjoyed it, and so did they.[14]

From Banting's diary:

August 5.

Visited Tela Hospital. Sailed to Cortez. Sea a little "rolly" but pleasant. Arrived Cortez at night.

August 6.

Visited old Spanish Fort. Sailed for Puerto Barrios at 2.00, arrived at 6.00 p.m.—danced to Marimba music. The Spanish Fort failed to be captured by Drake, but was later taken by an unknown Englishman. The walks are about twenty-five feet thick—solid stone, and the cannons and old cannon balls still remain. Below the Fort are still to be found bottles of quick-silver, with which the Spanish extracted gold.

August 7.

Twelve-hour ride to Guatemala, having luncheon at Quirigua at Dr. MacPhail's Hospital, from where we visited, on mule-back, the Obelisks of the ancient Maya village, supposed to have been built in A.D. 400. Arrived in Guatemala at 10.00 p.m.—went direct to Palace Hotel.

Mrs. Banting to Dr. and Mrs. Robertson

Palace Hotel, Guatemala, C.A.,

Saturday night, August 9, 1924.

Saturday night is not the very best in the world to write letters, especially when the musicians are gathering already to dance, but nevertheless I do want to write from this city and this will be my only opportunity. It's a beautiful place. Quite the loveliest I've ever seen. It is situated in a beautiful valley at a height of 4,800 feet above the sea and the climate is a joy. Cool at night and gloriously fresh and warm all day. Seven years ago it was destroyed by an earthquake but it has been rebuilt again and is a city of exquisite old bits of stonework built into more or less modern one-story Spanish houses. All white of course. It is surrounded

14Ashford, *op. cit.*

on all sides by mountains and the trip up from the sea takes
twelve hours, circling around and around mountains that are
simply beautiful. We arrived on Thursday night and were met
by a delegation of all the important people, among them the
President's chief of staff. This city is the largest in Central
America and is the capital of this country.

The first thing we did on Friday morning was to make our
official call on the President and we arrived in much state and he
received us most graciously with his cabinet. After we had sat
around and heard some speeches of welcome, etc. (a whole mob
of people were there) some fat man in a frock coat offered me his
arm and took me up to His Excellency again and I'm darned if
he hadn't chosen me to lead the parade with him. I was simply
scared stiff at first—when he offered me his arm and the guards
came to attention and we strolled off and the rest of the people
lined up in twos and twos and walked behind us. We walked all
around the grounds and over to the Embassy and around the street
to see a monument and all the time movies were winding us up.
It was really too exciting for words. After a while it began to get
a bit funny to me . . . it was such a disadvantage not to be able
to speak Spanish when my President didn't know a word of English. We finally sent for an interpreter and got on much better.
He's a delightful person—so handsome and such a soldier and so
respected by everyone. I never was so thrilled in my life. I still
don't know why he honoured me.[15]

In the afternoon there was a big reception here. His Excellency was here, too, and this time he took in Lady Newsholme
and I went in with the Minister of Foreign Affairs—the next to
the President. After the supper, when we sat opposite Lady Newsholme and His Excellency, we danced on the roof to the
"Marimba Band"—the national music of Guatemala and my beau
the Minister (I can't even say his name) and I led off the dance, as
Lady Newsholme didn't dance. More excitement. Fred thinks
this is a fool of a country. They separate us at all the
functions. . . .

[15]It is just possible that the interpreter was one of the most famous of
the delegates, Colonel Ashford. The Colonel writes: "Guatemala reminded
me considerably of those little principalities of the Middle Ages where the
duke, until he was killed to make room for another one, was nearly an absolute monarch. The President at the time of our visit was a full-blooded
Indian, and I was his interpreter, to which office I elected myself by invitation."—A Soldier in Science.

From Banting's diary:

August 9.

Arose at 6.00 a.m.—Left in car No. 7 of the party of about ten cars. Our party consisted of Sir Arthur and Lady Newsholme, Dr. and Mrs. Rosenau and our two selves. After passing through the avenue of trees on the outskirts of the city and past the old Spanish aqueduct of brick construction, we visited the zoo. A tame monkey became great friends with my wife, and was the chief notable of the inmates. The road was fairly good, but wind-ing, narrow and sharply curved in places. Instead of the cactus fences of Jamaica, many of the fences were made of bamboo, lashed side by side, with cactus fibre. As we drove out of the city, we met innumerable numbers of women with round, straw market baskets on their heads; many also carried children on their back slung in a gaily coloured shawl. Little children, also with their burdens, trotted after the women. They all appeared to be in a great hurry and it was remarkable to see them half running with their big heavy basket balanced on their head, gay red, yellow and blue shawls, loose skirts and bare feet. We saw but few men and they were usually driving oxen, hitched to a covered cart. All the natives seemed friendly and returned a wave by flexion of the hand or a smile. In the baskets might be found needlework, corn, beans, all sorts of fruit and vegetables, live chickens.

The natives are almost pure Indian in type—they are cleanly, industrious and hard working—each man for himself on his own plot of ground. The women have slim, straight, athletic figures, in contra-distinction to the Cuban and Jamaican types, who are fat and flabby. Dr. MacPhail says their home life is simple and quiet and very fine. . . .

Antigua is situated at the base of Mount Fuego, seven thou-sand feet above the sea. The mountain top (volcanic, though supposedly extinct) is fourteen thousand feet above the sea. The city was the first centre of civilization . . . and was built in 1530. In 1541 it was destroyed by earthquake and volcanic eruption and the capital was then moved down to Guatemala city.

Although the city bears the marks of its ruin by the 'quake and the eruption it still retains much of its ancient grandeur in the form of the ruins of old cathedrals and the university. The first place we visited was a subterranean crypt in the cathedral. The figure of Christ was beautifully carved in wood surrounded by offerings and the candles were kept burning in front of it. There were old tombs alongside. The pillars that remain standing are beautifully carved. . . .

Leaving about 2.30 p.m. we drove out to the Indian village of San Juan del Absepo to visit an old church. . . . From San Juan . . . we drove through the valley of Alinolonga. This is the earliest seat of Spanish influence—being built in 1527. It was almost totally destroyed by inundation (volcanic) in 1541 (at which time the Government was removed to Ponchoy). At Alinolonga were held tournaments and from here Don Pedro made his explorations to find Japan. In his wandering he was killed by Indians. His wife caused the palace to be painted black in mourning and appointed herself Governess. Her reign, however, was short, because on September 8, 1541, eight days after her inauguration, an earthquake and volcanic eruption occurred and she and her eleven ladies-in-waiting and her child were submerged in the avalanche of lava which flooded the lower two stories of the chapel. The walls of the upper story still remain and bear a tablet in commemoration of the 'Woman without Virtue' (meaning, without luck).

In Antigua we visited also the old hospital—a one-story expansive building of thick stone walls and beautiful tiled floors —fairly modern operating room and the wards surrounding the usual tropical patios. There are about five hundred beds, and nuns with large white head-dresses in charge.

On the way home we noted the geological formation and found it to be of volcanic origin. Cuttings from the side of the hills show the strata of ashy stone laid down by volcanic eruptions at different periods. Clouds hang about the hills, which are tree-clad even to their tops—there being very little solid rock. . . . On the mountain sides there are patches of cleared places where corn is grown. In places it is so steep one wonders how it is ever cultivated.

The tourist looked at historic monuments; the physician looked at the hospital; the Canadian (friend of Canadian geologists and engineers) looked at the geological formations; the farmer's son looked at the fields: with his usual multiplicity of interests, Banting looked at everything. The only essential difference between this and later journals is that he was not yet commenting on the suitability of the landscape to be sketched in oils. Later on, according to his likes and methods, a landscape was "paintable" or "not paintable." From how many different angles he looked at the world!

To return to Mrs. Banting's letter:

Tomorrow at 6.00 a.m. we go on (we certainly make early starts) and I hate to leave this place. It's a perfect climate and the people are delightful. It's the loveliest spot on the whole trip.[16]

Saturday night, S.S. Taloa, August 16, 1924.

. . . Well, we're at sea again after "doing" the country of Costa Rica. We arrived in Christobel (the Atlantic port of the Panama canal) on the thirteenth—Wednesday—and saw all over the locks and the town and had lunch ashore and looked in the shops at Colon. You see the port is like this:

	Canal	x Panama
Colon x		x Christobel

and Christobel, the American Colony, is right across the street from the native town of Colon.

The canal is simply amazing—one can only see it to appreciate the tremendous construction of it. . . .

We changed ships at Christobel and came on the Taloa to Port Limon in Costa Rica. . . .

The Government of Costa Rica entertained us all the time while we were there at the Hotel Française, and as well put on a big banquet for us—about twelve courses and many wines, and yesterday morning the faculty of medicine took us driving and had a breakfast party before the train left. Today we've spent in Port Limon and tomorrow after calling at Christobel again we go to Almirante. . . .

The visit to Panama was recalled by Banting in January of the following year in the Apha Omega Alpha Address delivered at Ann Arbor, Michigan. He said:

Last summer it was the privilege of those of us who attended the International Health Conference to visit the Canal Zone.

[16]Banting's diary, August 10: "Guatemala is a lovely old place and we would like to have lingered on."

Driving from Christobel to the Gatum Locks, the western end of the Canal, we passed the ruins of the old French Canal which de Lesseps was forced to abandon because it was impossible for European engineers to live and work in a country infested with yellow fever and malaria. Today the Panama Canal is a monument not only to the advancement of scientific engineering but also to the advancement of medical science, for its accomplishment by the American Government was made possible by splendid organization and work of their Public Health and Sanitation Commission. Between the time of operation of the French and Americans in the Canal Zone, Sir Ronald Ross had proved that the mosquito transmitted malaria. Similar proof was provided in the case of yellow fever by Reed, Carroll, and Lazear and Agramonte and with the eradication of the mosquito the Canal Zone was made habitable for American workers.

In Costa Rica we passed over approximately one hundred and twenty miles of railway which, it is said, cost one man per tie as a toll of human life from disease, during its construction. . . .

In the Cameron Lecture we find another reference to the same journey. Discussing the etiology of diabetes, he considered the rôle which had been assigned to diet and added these reflections:

In 1924 while visiting Panama, I was told by Dr. Clarke, pathologist of the Ancon Hospital, that on examining five thousand men who were applying for work on the construction of the Panama Canal, he had only found reducing material in the urine of two cases. Neither of these cases proved to be diabetic. This is more remarkable because a large percentage of the labourers were natives of Dominico, where the main article of diet is sugar-cane. From the time the children are weaned till they die they eat the raw sugar-cane. There are also wealthy Spaniards living in Panama who eat large quantities of refined cane sugar. Even much of their food is cooked in syrup. The incidence of diabetes among this class is surprisingly high.[17] The effect of the ingestion of refined cane sugar is even more startling in India, where, I am told, there is no diabetes amongst the poor class but that about forty per cent. of the wealthy class over fifty years are diabetic. The climate, racial heredity and environment are the same but the wealthy people can afford to purchase large quantities of

[17]Banting's diary (August 15, Costa Rica): "I saw a number of cases of diabetes which were all among the over-fed carbohydrate-eating wealthy class. . . ."

refined cane sugar. In the United States the incidence of diabetes has increased proportionately with the consumption per capita of cane sugar. One cannot help but conclude that in the heating and recrystallization of the natural sugar-cane something is altered which leaves the refined product a dangerous food-stuff.

Picked at random from speeches on medical subjects ("Medical Research" and "The History of Insulin" respectively) these quotations clearly indicate how Banting kept his eyes and ears open, kept his interest keen, and kept his curiosity from being muffled or blunted by honours and entertainments, by the constant round of parties, receptions, "At Homes," banquets and teas. His travels were profitable as well as pleasant. His mementoes included the usual trivia, but there were other mementoes, like those above, redeemable in the coin of thought. The question of diet, as a causative factor in diabetes, for instance, a question which often recurred in his thinking, was first focused in his attention during this visit to Central America.

Banting's observations regarding the relatively low incidence of diabetes among the indigent and labouring classes in the tropics and its relatively high incidence in the same localities among the upper classes, who can afford to buy refined cane sugar products, is of more than passing interest (comments Seale Harris.)[18] It should be added that Deeks had preached for years that the high carbohydrate diets, particularly of refined cane sugar products, which all classes consume, is the cause of many diseases, including diabetes and pellagara which occur in the tropics.

From Banting's diary:

August 21 *(Panama).*

Saw the sun rise—out of the Pacific Ocean—from our windows at the Tivoli and left by 7.00 a.m. train for Colon. Panama is only nine degrees north of the equator, but in spite of this it is much cooler than many of the other ports, so much so that the gentlemen were comfortable in northern dinner coats and the ladies wore wraps.

Left — very regretfully — the English party — Newsholmes, Thompsons, Castellanis and Patterson, and sailed on the *Metapan* for South America (Capt. Barratt).

[18]Harris, *op. cit.*

August 22.

Arrived in Cartagena, Colombia—most picturesque old city. Drove around the city; called and had luncheon with Governor Martini and sailed at 5.00 p.m. from Porto Colombia. Martini's son is a graduate of Woodstock College in Canada and a number of other young Cartagenians have been sent to Canada by the Governor for their education.

Having read *Four Bells* we were prepared to find romance and interest in Cartagena and were not disappointed. Old Mount Popa is very prominent with the ruins of the ancient monastery on its crest, where it is said the Spanish nuns and priests threw themselves from the windows down the precipice at the approach of Drake. The old cathedral still stands—with much elaborate frescoing and huge old dilapidated wooden doors, and even the ancient secret passageway tunnelled under the river and through the rocks up to the monastery on Mount Popa is still to be seen (three miles of tunnels).

The houses of the city are all Spanish in type—narrow streets and patios behind—and although the reds, blues and yellows in their day must have been a fearful muddle of colour—now softened by time and weather they are very beautiful against the white of the newer buildings and the green background of the mountains.

We sailed at sunset up the long harbour and the last we saw of Cartagena was a row of royal palms in silhouette against a most magnificent sky of vivid sunset colours.

August 23.

Arrived in Puerto Colombia, and although we planned on a quiet morning, Dr. Urieta from Barranquilla came down and insisted on the whole party going up there for a luncheon. Puerto Colombia is very primitive—mud huts and streets, mud everywhere, and the kiddies just never wear any clothes at all. Barranquilla, on the contrary, is more modern, although the streets are very narrow and muddy; the houses of the better classes are of fine Spanish architecture and the A.B.C. Club (Aristocracy, Beauty and Culture) where we had lunch is a beautiful building—which cost over one hundred and fifty thousand dollars to build. . . . The famous Colombian emeralds are very difficult to get as they are all shipped to France, but we were fortunate in being presented with one by Dr. Roderigues. We motored in the afternoon all around the town and got home to the ship for dinner.

August 24.

Party left at 7.00 a.m. by special car (motor on rails) for Barranquilla, thence by river boat up the Magdalene River and across country through a series of rivers and lakes to Sebulla, a small town, and then by train to Santa Marta to join the *Metapan*. The water course thus taken is one of the secondary outlets of the Magdalene River, which is one of the largest rivers in the world. . . .

August 25.

Santa Marta—such a picture from the harbour—surrounded on three sides by a ragged ridge of mountains and in the distance the snow-capped peaks of the Sierra Nevada range (fourteen thousand feet in height). The houses of the town all glitter white and the cathedral towers stand out prominently. There is a wonderful sand beach round the circle of the harbour and from the boat it is one of the loveliest places we have seen. At close range it is not so picturesque. The streets are narrow and muddy and the houses not specially attractive. The usual Plaza Central, as in all the other Spanish towns, was rather small.

In the afternoon we motored out to see the monument . . . of Simon Bolivar—the liberator of Colombia. The house where he died in 1830 is still standing and we were shown the room he died in and the table on which the autopsy was done. . . .

August 26.

On board *Metapan*—at sea—having sailed last night at midnight.

August 29.

Rolly sea—a good number of the passengers sick. Wonderful sunny clear day, and the bluest blue of the Caribbean. Laura Carter says it is deeply, darkly, beautifully blue.

September 4.

Arrived New York City. . . .

Courtesy the Artist and The Imperial Oil Review.

CARICATURE BY J. W. McLAREN

PART IX
Home and Abroad

For peregrinations charmes our senses with such unspeakable and sweet variety, that some count him unhappy that never travelled.

BURTON.

1

RETURNING from their Caribbean honeymoon, the newlyweds planned their home. Since Banting plunged immediately into his work and became occupied with other problems, the details of the construction of the house were worked out by his wife in conjunction with the architect and the contractor; Banting nevertheless took an eager interest in the plans and some of the stones which were used for trim were secured by his direction from the farm at Alliston. An attractive home was built for them on Bedford Road and was furnished almost overnight to be ready for the reception of Lord Dawson of Penn, Physician to the King, who was visiting Canada and was their first house-guest. It was considered to be a model of tasteful design and beautiful interior decoration and it inspired an almost lyrical description by Katherine Hale in a popular magazine. But more and more perceptibly as the years went by, a darkness grew in the house, a cold mist crept softly from room to room, and unhappiness came to dwell there.

Banting's new home was only a short distance from his laboratory in the Pathology Building (now the Dunlap Building) on University Avenue. Home and laboratory at first encompassed his chief interests, marked the ambit of nearly all his activities; his restless life seemed to be conforming at last to a definite pattern. At the same time his interest in painting and in the painters and writers whom he met at the Arts and Letters Club was growing apace.

Of all the members of the Club, Banting had closest affinity for A. Y. Jackson, whose forthright character was in some respects much like his own, and to whom he paid the tribute of imitating his style as a painter. Some of the others, although he admired their work and enjoyed their friendship, were a trifle too "high brow," too metaphysical, for the realist in him fully to appreciate. Brooker, for instance, was at that time deeply engrossed in a study of the prophetic books of William Blake. Lawren Harris and F. B. Housser were much interested in theosophy. Speculative mysticism seemed to be in the air.

215

As he listened to talk of "cosmic justice," "pantheism" and "reincarnation," Banting suddenly conceived what seemed to him to be a most phenomenal idea. He was soon involved in a dark conspiracy with MacIntosh Bell and, presently, with Bertram Brooker. In the course of his far-ranging travels Bell had spent some time in India, spoke Hindustani fluently and possessed a collection of Oriental costumes; Brooker was a playwright, an actor, and a producer and director of amateur theatricals: these were the elements which went to the formation of an elaborate plot. Banting permitted it to become known that the Emir of Baluchistan (let us say), a severe diabetic, would soon be arriving in Toronto for special treatment. It also appeared that the Emir was a profound philosopher and a leader of theosophical teaching; that he was not only a great ruler but a great prophet as well. It was natural enough that certain members of the club should express their anxiety to be presented to the Emir and to hear his revelation from his own lips. Banting demurred a little. The prophet, he explained, was averse to publicity, had refused to see reporters, and disliked having his meditations interrupted by any sort of visitors; besides, he spoke no English. It was just possible—of course he could not promise, but it was certainly possible—that the Emir might consent to meet quietly with a small number whose tenets were like his own, and converse with them through an interpreter. Banting would certainly do his best to arrange it.

With unexpected graciousness, the Emir acquiesced. Harris, Jackson, Button and Housser, not all of whom, strangely, had the philosophical bent, were invited to attend at the Bedford Road house about eight o'clock of a momentous evening. Earlier on the scene, to discuss their plan while dining, were the Bells, the Brookers and the Bantings. Immediately after dinner they adjourned to the kitchen, where Bell and Brooker were "made up" as swarthy Orientals and attired in suitable costumes from Bell's collection. Bell was to play the Emir, while Brooker assumed the rôle of his interpreter. When the door bell rang and the other guests arrived, a conspiratorial hush possessed the kitchen, and the Irish maid-servant, who had been helpless with laughter during the preparations, was forced to stifle her mirth. After waiting for a decent interval, the Prince and his attendant vanished softly through the back door and as softly appeared, in all the splendour of the mysterious East, at the front entrance. They were gravely announced by Banting, who played his minor part with the greatest decorum. To judge from his reputation, the Emir was more loquacious than was his usual wont; he spouted Hindustani in a rapid torrent of inexplicable words, and his deep eyes flashed with the fervour of his message. Solemnly, in broken, heavily accented English, his interpreter translated the wise words of the sage. The listeners were silently attentive, deeply impressed. Then, suddenly, just as the hoax seemed assured of full success, Button straightened in his chair, looked sharply at the interpreter, and exclaimed in a tone of surprised delight: "It's Bert! Hello, Bert!" Banting was much chagrined and made an attempt to quell the interruption; for a few minutes longer the farce was continued, but every word the "Indians" uttered provoked hilarious laughter, and more laughter, until the Hindustani was drowned in merriment and Emir Bell re-discovered his English.

2

In 1925, Dr. and Mrs. Banting went to Europe, their ultimate goal being Stockholm; the Nobel Prize had been awarded two years previously but this was the laureate's first opportunity to visit the Swedish capital and deliver the required address.

They sailed from Quebec on the *Empress of Scotland*, Wednesday, August 5, 1925, bound for Cherbourg.

Mrs. Banting to Dr. and Mrs. Robertson

S.S. Empress of Scotland, Friday.

It is a glorious morning but very cold. My hands are still stiff from being outside, and it's hard to write. We have just come through the Strait of Belle Isle, between Labrador and Newfoundland, and are out in the open sea. The weather is clear and sunny and we've just passed a field of seven icebergs—one a huge thing which Fred is now trying to paint from memory.

There is a small but very interesting passenger list. Mostly English—with several titles among them. Last night there was a "ball" on board—fine orchestra and a beautiful ballroom. The ship was built by the Germans and is simply huge; there are eleven decks—with an elevator—and it's absolutely impossible to find anyone on it. I've walked miles looking for Fred—and he for me—so now we always leave a message in the stateroom where we'll be.

Our accommodation is very grand—much nicer than we expected. They changed it when we got here. . . . I suppose the courtesy was made possible by the small sailing list. Anyway, we're spoiled to death. The maid draws my bath and calls me, and brings tea before we get up, and our dinner things are all laid out ready, and dear me we'll forget how to eat if it keeps up. The valet who looks after Fred is a wonder—a real old English valet who never says a word and you never have to ask for anything.

We're both feeling fine and rested . . . catching up with some sleep.

These English sculptors, "March Bros.," are charming people. They did the Champlain monument at Orillia you know.

The "March Bros.," Sydney and Vernon, were returning to England after installing the Champlain monument at Orillia and the War Memorial at Victoria. During the course of the voyage they struck up a warm friendship with Banting.

Tuesday, August 11, 1925.

It is Tuesday afternoon and in a moment or two we'll have tea and after that I must pack up because we leave the ship tomorrow at 8.00 a.m. Very regretfully too. It has been such a beautiful trip. So many charming people and such food. Honestly we're all past caring what comes next. The chief steward of the ship has diabetes and when he heard Fred was on board we've been simply snowed under with kindness. We've had special menus for our own group every night—special desserts, special everything. . . . I'll bet Fred has gained five pounds. He's the only one who has stood up against it. Everybody else has gone flat.

Yesterday was spent sketching. Mr. Sydney March sketched both Fred and me and it is very cleverly done. We're hoping to be able to get out for a day to their studio out of London. Charming people—so clever, and very attractive. Fred has had a beautiful time with them, and they've given him a lot of pointers on his work. They've had great times together.

They were travelling in the congenial company of Dr. and Mrs. Fitzgerald. Fitzgerald was Director of the Connaught Laboratories in Toronto. His contribution toward solving the early production problem of insulin has been mentioned in another place.

Restaurant Jeanne d'Arc,

Place du Martroi, Orléans.

Sunday, August 16, 1925.

I must make the most of this paper—it's all I've got and at that I swiped it from the place we had dinner to get a note off to you from here. . . .

We left the boat on Wednesday a.m. about eight, and very regretfully. She was a wonderful boat and we did make some pleasant friends. The motor met us at Cherbourg, and we motored off at once through Normandy. . . . We had lunch at Caen and saw the things of interest there, chiefly two old cathedrals built in 1066 by William the Conqueror on his way to England—one for his Queen Matilda, whose tomb is there, and one for himself. The country all through is rolling and beautiful and dotted with little villages. Groups of old stone houses with flowers around, and all the women wear little white lace caps and wooden shoes, and drive donkeys in two-wheeled carts. I haven't seen a four-wheeled carriage in France.

We stayed the first night in the Normandy Alps in a place called [illegible]—it is a type of hotel like D'eauville or some of those. Gloriously situated in the mountains, and such cooking and music and quiet service. Thursday we left early for Le Marne—lunch there—and came to the Chateau country—the valley of the Loire River. Stayed all night and the next day at Tours. Came on to Blois yesterday and on account of a national holiday had no accommodation at a hotel so were put up by a nice French family for the night in a house over two hundred years old.

Came on here today and finished seeing the Chateaux. Went through 11 (eleven) all together—and this amount of paper is inadequate to describe them. Simply fascinating. Full of the romance of French history for hundreds of years. This is the town of Joan of Arc, and we had dinner tonight at this restaurant facing on the Square where we could see the monument erected to her on the place where she was burned to death.[1] The place is full of her. She certainly is an inspiring figure. But the whole country is full of inspiring legends and heroes. It will take the next two years hard reading to piece together all these impressions.

This is a charming hotel—*baths* and everything—and tomorrow we go on to Paris.

Hotel Westminster, Paris,
Wednesday, August 19, 1925.

Please excuse the pencil, but Fred has gone to Geneva with his fountain pen. . . .

We got here last Monday. Wonderful trip and perfect weather. We have a suite at this hotel—three bedrooms, two baths and a sitting room and it's much too grand. You see they made a mistake, but it was all we could get, so here we are. . . .

Today we did the shops in the morning, the Luxembourg Art Gallery this afternoon, and the boys left for Geneva at nine to-night. Too much of a hurried, tiresome trip for us, so we decided to stay here. . . .

We leave on Saturday for Belgium.

The side trip to Geneva was for the purpose of attending a medical convention. From the Hotel Westminster, in the Rue de la Paix, they transferred to the Inter-Allied Union Club, 33 Faubourg St. Honoré, formerly the residence of Henri de Rothschild. This was one of the most exclusive clubs in Paris, designed for the use of distinguished visitors of all nations: a far cry from the modest surroundings to which the Nobel laureate had been accustomed from boyhood, and even a sufficient variant from the circumstances of his previous visit to Paris (Hotel d'Orleans). The whole atmosphere of these various journeys during the early years of his celebrity—the palatial liners, the luxury hotels, the elaborate foods and costly wines—was in notable contrast with the homely backdrop of the opening scenes of his career. It took him some time to become accustomed to the ministrations of a valet. The flunkeys who attended him made him vaguely uneasy. And even in the palace of the Rothschilds, only extreme deprivation of sleep could make him lie abed in the morning. Given half a chance, he still kept farmer's hours.

---

[1]Saint Joan actually was burnt at the stake in the market-place of Rouen, not in Orleans (May 30, 1431). Other minor inaccuracies in these hurried letters must be overlooked.—L. S.

Actually, of course, this atmosphere of wealth was transient and accidental. He was still—and in spite of later additions to his income, he always remained—in a middle class position with respect to money. The European tour may have an air of opulence, but in point of fact it was not conducted on the grand scale, and many of the places where the party chose to stay were not pretentious. It is amusing to think of a possible comparison between the wealth of any of the grandees who fêted this Canadian doctor and the huge sums he might have acquired, had he wished, from the commercial exploitation of insulin.

Characteristically, however, he escaped with relief from the glitter of the *haut monde* to the quiet attentiveness of an art gallery, to the quickening interest of the wards and laboratories of a hospital, or to the grassy seclusion of the countryside, where he could set up his easel and play with his paints. His interest in tea-time conversation was slight. He used to tell the story of how Pasteur, when a guest in the palace of Napoleon the Third, vanished from a tea-party given by the Empress and was presently found in his room, engrossed in the microscopic study of a drop of the royal wine. Banting was not *farouche*, but neither was he debonair. He was never quite at home in high society.

Mrs. Banting to Dr. and Mrs. Robertson

Royal Hotel, Lille,
August 22, 1925.

Today we came up to Arras by train from Paris, then motored up here. This was all German territory through the war, and Dr. Fitzgerald came here right after Armistice with the army of occupation. We crossed over some famous Canadian battlefields on the way up—Vimy Ridge, St. Eloi, Arras, Hill 70, etc., and went through some cemeteries—beautifully kept, with lovely flowers. . . . We're staying here until Monday—then going to a Belgium seaside place for a few days—then Brussels and Amsterdam.

Victoria Hotel, Amsterdam,
Friday, August 28, 1925.

We came to Holland on Wednesday night after spending Monday and Tuesday at Knocke, Belgium. It is a small summer place on the sea—just a short way from the famous "Zeebrugge" where the big naval battle of the war was won. We went all over the place and it was so interesting. Also went to Ostend and Brugge and Blankenbourg—a small town famous for its laces—and Professor and Mrs. Fitzgerald bought us a wonderful luncheon set of hand-made Brettonne lace for a wedding present. It was such a nice idea. Wednesday morning we caught a train by an eighth of an inch (after walking miles) for Brussels—the capital—and we spent the day there. . . . We came on to Amsterdam Wednesday night and came to this hotel—so comfortable and such pleasant people. The city is full of canals and little boats, and it's so picturesque. Fred is thrilled to death. He was out at 6.00 a.m. this morning and is gone again now for the day. . . . We'll be here for a few days —maybe until Tuesday or Wednesday of next week, and from here visit the Hague and Haarlem and the other places about. The Dutch are such friendly people and so cheery. I suppose we feel at home with them because they are more like Canadians than the French or Belgians.

The climate is soft and misty most of the time, but today it is sunny, though there isn't the snap to the air that we have. It feels so moist and soft, and they say it is always like that. The peasants still wear their native costumes, so colourful and pretty, with high hats and wooden shoes, and there are flowers every-where. Fred brought me in a bunch of two dozen wonderful roses yesterday. Sold on the little street flower markets for the sum of one gilder (which is forty cents). The flower markets are all over and they look so lovely against the grey walls and they all reflect in the water in the canals. You see there is a canal right up the middle of the street. The place is full of picture museums too.

Amsterdam, Tuesday, September 1, 1925.

We have just come in from the Hague and had some tea and now Fred has gone off with Dr. Fitzgerald to see about our reservations to Copenhagen on Thursday. It is pouring rain and very unpleasant out—but weather means nothing here. They have so much rain and dull weather no one pays any heed to it. The Hague is about an hour on the train from here (express trains) and is the capital of Holland and a very nice city. We spent most of our day at the Art Gallery but it is not in it with the "National Gallery," which is here at the Rychs Museum. Satur-day we went to Haarlem, the home of Frans Hals (our pet artist) and Sunday we spent the day at the Gallery here. Monday Fred

FREDERICK BANTING AND HIDEYO NOGUCHI, 1924

and I went off by boat up the canals to Volendam, Marken Island and Monnikendam, and had a wonderful day.[2] Tomorrow we are going to shop and loaf about and leave on Thursday. Yesterday was the Queen's birthday and honestly I never saw such celebrations. We went up the street after dinner last night and the whole city was out, from the baby to grandmother. You could hardly move, and the people would catch arms in a line in the centre of the street and parade, dancing and singing. It was the gayest sight, with all their bright costumes.

Apart from the costumes, the Holland people are much more like our own people than any we've met yet. You can even get tea here that *is* tea, and we had bread the other day for the first time. I was so glad to see it I nearly embraced the waiter. In France you just *can't* get bread. Always those awful hard rolls and no butter, except for breakfast, and then it is fresh and unsalted. Even here we get unsalted butter, but it is sweet and fresh and nice. The French breakfast nearly finished us—but it sounds so like the Americans to kick, so we just wished for tea and toast in silence, after several vain efforts. . . .

You asked me to tell you whom we met, etc. Well, that's difficult, because purposely we have tried not to meet anyone. Except in Paris when the Rockefeller Foundation entertained us at luncheon. It has been wonderful to do as we wanted and not be rushed about. It's been a great rest for Fred. He's even forgotten he's got a Lab. at all. Yesterday on the way to Volendam some American from New York spotted him and came up and spoke, but he was very nice. . . . Our packing has been very simple. Baggage is such a bother on this side. We have found the convenience of a little of it. . . .

I guess after all we're in our hearts like the Californians. Old Ontario is good enough for me. You get a chance to dry out once in a while.

Wednesday.

. . . Fred went off for the day painting. I made up a lunch for him off the breakfast tray. They always send cheese for breakfast although we never eat it—it is a custom and you can't change them—so today it was useful and I made cheese sandwiches and he left at ten o'clock and got home at five-thirty. An

[2]This trip was advertised as "starting from Amsterdam by the magnificent steam yacht *Havenstoombootdienst,* through the canals of Monnikendam via Broek in Waterland (called 'The Dead Cities' of Holland) to Volendam and the Island of Marken, returning via the Zuiderzee."—L. S.

old Dutchman saw him sketching and sent his daughter out with some lovely hot coffee for him. Wasn't that nice? So typical of the people here.

Professor and Mrs. Fitzgerald went on to Copenhagen, leaving the Bantings in Amsterdam. Their trip consumed two days, while the more venturesome younger couple completed it in four hours, and so, with the help of the Royal Dutch Air Service, overtook them. The flight from Amsterdam to Hamburg, however, was more of an adventure than they had bargained for. The plane ran into a severe storm, and was heavily buffeted by swirling winds. This experience so terrified the passengers bound for Copenhagen that all but the two Canadians cut short their journey at Hamburg. Dr. and Mrs. Banting would gladly have followed the example of these prudent Dutchmen, but were anxious to keep their appointments in Denmark.

F. G. B. to Dr. and Mrs. Robertson

September 6.

Just a note to say that we are both well, and though travelling is a little strenuous at times, especially by aeroplane, things have gone fine.

The porter has taken our bags. We are off to Oslo. . . .

From Oslo they proceeded to Opdal, and from there to Trondhjem. At Trondhjem Banting stopped to sketch, and one of the finest of his pictures was painted from sketches he made at this time. But the ceremonies in Sweden awaited them, and they hurried on to Stockholm, where they were at once caught up in a busy round of meetings and receptions.

Mrs. Banting to Dr. and Mrs. Robertson

Stockholm, September 15, 1925.

Excuse the rush. We've been so gay here we haven't had time to write, and now we're leaving in a few minutes and I have only a little time—I can't tell you all about it. The dinner and reception was last night, and lunch today, and tonight the lecture. Fred is likely going strong now and Mrs. Fitzgerald and I are holding hands nervously at home. Ladies don't go it seems. . . .

The King of Sweden, who always gives a dinner to the Nobel laureates, is out of town unfortunately, but I'm sure we've met everyone else of importance and I've never met nicer people. . . .

We're both very tired today. It has been so busy here. Really they have been wonderful. Tonight a huge bunch of roses came, with the loveliest letter from a lady in the north part of Sweden whose child has been saved by insulin. . . .

Had a parcel today registered from Budapest from Dr. Karxcag—of a group of wonderful etchings, and good wishes for the lecture.

Banting afterwards made a point of paying a call on the Swedish lady who had sent the roses. A hearty child and a happy, grateful mother welcomed him with joyful enthusiasm. In Scandinavia, as elsewhere, his achievement was his passport to every circle, every heart. His name, and the name of his wonderful extract, insulin, were hilt and blade of a magic sword, an Excalibur, which cut through barriers of language, nationality and social custom.

3

In 1926 there was a journey to the Canadian West for the purpose of attending the annual meeting of the Canadian Medical Association, which convened that year in Victoria. As usual there were side-trips and excursions and many other meetings and banquets in addition to the main conclave; the itinerary was also extended to include a visit to Alaska.

Two or three letters will suffice to give the flavour of the time. On a post card picturing Mount Edith Cavell, in the Jasper National Park, Mrs. Banting wrote to her parents:

Jasper, May 2 [1926].

Isn't this a lovely place? Really an inspiration. I can't hold Fred and his paint brushes. He was off fifteen minutes after we arrived.

Letters followed:

Atlin, B.C., Friday, June 11, 1926.

. . . Well, we got to Skagway on Wednesday morning and left at once for White Horse—in the Yukon. It's a twelve-hour train trip over the most magnificent route. One wonders how they ever were able to construct the railway. It literally clings to the edge of the sheerest precipices and twists and turns until you're dizzy. Part of the way runs along the old trail of '98. "Summit," the high point of the Pass, is the international boundary and on one side of an imaginary line flies the Stars and Stripes with a guard of Alaskan soldiers or police and on the other side is the Union Jack for the Yukon with a group of N.W. Mounted Police in their scarlet coats. . . .

"White Horse" is the end of the line, and is the place where Service wrote *The Songs of a Sourdough,* etc., and the headquarters of the trail of '98. It's a queer little rough town, full of beautiful husky dogs. The whole country is full of them—they're the only means of transportation in the winter. White Horse is pretty primitive. The town water is delivered in a wagon and one pays six cents a pail for it. All their food except chickens and eggs and moose meat is imported—nothing grows at all in the sandy, rocky soil except rhubarb and a few shrubs and millions of blue wild flowers with a sweet perfume and wild roses. . . . One uses canned milk of course. I guess we don't know we're alive in Toronto.

This country is undoubtedly interesting and it's rugged and beautiful, but heavens it makes one glad one lives in Ontario. I love the dogs and the mountains and the blue lakes with their lovely shadows but Toronto and Elora are good enough for me any old time. We leave for Skagway on Tuesday and then on to Victoria.

S.S. Princess Charlotte
en route from Alaska to Victoria,
Sunday, June 20, 1926.

It is Sunday afternoon—just after lunch—and tomorrow at 6.30 a.m. we get to Vancouver—and leave again on this same boat for Victoria at 9 a.m., arriving at four o'clock. . . .

Yesterday we stopped off for an hour in Prince Rupert. . . .

It has been a fine trip down. Really remarkable weather but I must say I'm glad to get back to a land where it gets dark at night. I don't like going to bed in the middle of daylight.

There is a much nicer crowd on board this trip. We've been with a young couple from San Francisco. . . . They are rather nice and not so actively American as a good many we've seen. There is a certain type of travelling American—loud-voiced, braggy and ignorant, who really would turn the rest of the world dead against the U.S.A. if one didn't remember that there are lots of nice ones. . . .

Victoria, June 22, 1926.

We're being entertained to death and it's very gay. Had tea with Lady Barnard today—glorious gardens! and she's so sweet herself.

We're both feeling fine but we'd need to be with this rush. Will be here all week and will try to write from Vancouver. Fred has been deluged with telegrams to speak at all the stops but has refused them all.

Sicamous, British Columbia,
Thursday afternoon, July 1, 1926.

I'm perfectly ashamed not to have written but honestly we haven't had one free moment from the day we got to Victoria until now. Of course now it is too far away to write you details of the meetings. It was a wonderful success and we all came away like rags. They nearly entertained us to death. However, we got over to Vancouver hoping for a rest, and if anything I think the pace there was worse than ever. Fred had caught a bad cold at the reception at Government House and we were both tired out and got into Vancouver at 6.30 Saturday night to find that we had to be guests of honour at a reunion of the 13th Field Ambulance (Fred was with them in France). It was a lovely party and they sent me flowers. Fred did enjoy seeing all the boys again. . . .

Two days were spent in Penticton.

It was so hot and the Doctors all seemed to stop work and drive us about and feed us till we couldn't move. Real Western hospitality.

We have just come into this place and we're hot and tired and hungry. . . . We're going on to Calgary on Sunday but meanwhile I hope to get off all my polite letters to Victoria and get a few hours' lost sleep caught up. There's nothing here but a dear little hotel and a station and a lake and I pray to heaven there's no doctor within fifteen miles. . . .

The paper which Banting read to the Association in Victoria was on "Medical Research." His remarks at that time, as well as other speeches on the same subject (which taken together constitute the best expression of his research credo) will be discussed in another place.

There are other stories of the western trip. Of how he was summoned from his train in the small hours of the morning for a consultation at the bedside of an aged prospector, dying of diabetes. (This was the sort of thing he was always willing to do; had the patient been mayor of the town, governor of the province or wealthiest man on the coast, Banting might not have been accessible; but since he was an impecunious old man, out of luck and dying, and since, moreover, he represented a part of the romance of the old West, Banting hastened to his aid. There was little that could be done; at the next stop a telegram was received announcing his death.) Of how a young girl was brought into a hotel unconscious, where Banting recognized her as one of his early patients and discovered that she had missed her lunch, gone riding, and developed insulin shock. (He was able to restore her with glucose, although her nurse protested vigorously that she was a diabetic and must on no account be given sugar.)

Much as they had enjoyed their trip, they were very glad when the last stop was called and their train delivered them safely to the Union Station in Toronto. Banting thankfully gave up for a time his strenuous rôle as "guest of honour" and returned to the quieter employments of a research scientist and to shorter, leisurely, incognito journeys in search of "paintable" landscapes, safe from requests to make speeches.

PART X

Landscape with Figures

A man who has only one object in life, only one line of rails, who exercises only one set of faculties, and these only in one way, will wear himself out much sooner than a man who shunts himself every now and then, and who has trains coming as well as going; who takes in as well as gives out.

My hobby has always been pictures, and all we call art. . . . I am convinced . . . that to enjoy art thoroughly, every man must have in him the possibility of doing it as well as liking it. He must feel it in his fingers, as well as in his head and at his eyes; and it must find its way from all the three to his heart, and be emotive.

DR. JOHN BROWN.

To have reached the age of forty without ever handling a brush or fiddling with a pencil, and then suddenly to find oneself plunged in the middle of a new and intense form of interest and action with paints and palettes and canvases, and not to be discouraged by results, is an astonishing and enriching experience. I hope it may be shared by others.

WINSTON CHURCHILL.

1

To CONCEIVE a rounded semblance of the true Banting, a fully matured and richly civilized being, we must turn from the study of the scientist and world traveller, and consider him now as an artist. An amateur artist, true. But the adjective carries an implication of clumsy enthusiasm, of maladroit or casual or sporadic effort, which in this instance is wide of the mark.

The amateur and the self-taught form no small group among the artists of the country (writes William Colgate).[1] They are to be found everywhere and in almost every occupation. Their leisure hours they devote to drawing or etching or sketching or to the more formidable task of putting their impressions of the countryside on canvas. Without thought of pecuniary gain or recompense other than their own pleasure, they are content, as someone wittily phrased it, "to paint for their own amazement." It is by no means an uncommon experience for the non-professional to have his work hung at exhibitions of the various established art societies beside the work of men of wide reputation. Indeed, nothing has contributed more to the development of a sound and just appreciation and taste in art throughout the Dominion than "the growth of that happy company the unincorporated and undaunted" and usually unorganized "society of amateurs."

As we have already seen, Banting dabbled in paints at an early age and made creditable pictures as a schoolboy. Then he busied himself with other things and the talent was apparently buried and forgotten. During the rueful year in London he resumed his boyhood's hobby and improved the long intervals of waiting with fresh excursions into the delectable realms of art. Obtaining a lithograph of some fishermen pulling their boat up on shore, he copied and re-copied it many times, learning how to mix his paints and apply them. (At first he mixed too much, dabbed too often.) He battled ennui with palette and brush. He forgot his dashed hopes and his hobbling practice as he squeezed blobs of colour from his paint-tubes.

And then, at the most unlikely moment, the whimsical fates,

[1]*Canadian Art, Its Origin and Development,* by William Colgate; Toronto, The Ryerson Press, 1943.

231

who appeared to have forgotten his existence, decided to take a hand in his affairs. Their emissary, Dr. Moses Barron, brought him the inspirational message, and Banting, suddenly galvanized, started off in pursuit of that *Fata Morgana* so many had followed in vain, that "hypothetic hormone," insulin. This most engrossing chase left him little time for side-issues, and once he had successfully cornered the phantom hormone he was captivated, rapt, consumed in himself with elation and anxiety.

The splendid years which followed were filled with duties, with honours, with a thousand preoccupations. And yet he had not altogether forgotten his brushes. "By thronging duties pressed," he nevertheless found time for an occasional hike to the countryside with palette and paints. Professor C. C. Macklin recalls how Banting once slipped away from a medical convention in Montreal and escaped to the mountain for half a day of indulgence in the quiet luxury of painting; this was not an isolated instance of his guilty truancy. In the academic atmosphere of conventions and formal dinners, he was often to be observed making surreptitious caricatures on the back of the programme, or the menu, or a scrap of paper from his pocket. When conventions continued for several days, with the endless reading of learned papers, his seat was often seen to be empty of a fine afternoon, and those who knew him understood that the scientist had for the time been overcome by the uneasy soul of the artist, restless for the out-of-doors.

In January, 1925, two of his oil sketches were displayed in the exhibition of the Hart House Sketch Club. A Toronto newspaper congratulated him on his "pictorial début," but expressed surprise that he did not choose to paint dogs, "like Landseer." The reporter described one of his sketches, representing a dilapidated house with a tumble-down lean-to attached, as a "bilobular study in house decomposition." "He depicts," said the writer, "not only the pathology but the pathos of his subject." "His northern landscape [the other sketch] is a bold, conical, pine-topped bluff, around the base of which curves a torrent of cobalt blue over snags and rocks and under a heavily-clouded sky." The first of his paintings to be exhibited in public were thus typical of the themes he fixed upon habitually in his subsequent work.

Other exhibitors in the same show were Professor C. T. Currelly, the Egyptologist, Professor C. P. Coleman, the geologist, and Professor C. K. C. Wright of the School of Practical Science. It would therefore appear that artistic talent, or at least artistic enterprise, was a common commodity among Toronto professors in the nineteen-twenties, and this may have had some effect in stimulating the efforts of Banting. A much more potent influence came to him from a half-dozen professional painters, who soon were numbered among his friends. In Europe he haunted the galleries and exhibits and made the acquaintance of a number of artists. On board ship he encountered the March Brothers and enrolled himself briefly as their pupil. In Toronto his portrait (now hanging in the entrance hall of the Banting Institute) was commissioned to Curtis Williamson, an old-school perfectionist who enforced him to undergo endless sittings, but from whom he extracted much information and amusement during the course of them. Banting himself commissioned "The Beaver Dam" from Gordon Payne, O.S.A., as well as other pictures from a number of artists. Wherever he went he sought out artists. While others strove to force themselves on his attention, and were therefore avoided, a competent painter was the object of his sincere and cordial interest. (This, by the way, was a distinction shared by painters with destitute veterans of the first world war.)

2

His most enthusiastic and lasting attachment was for the famous "Group of Seven," and the only distinct influence to be seen in his own work derives from this source. As a newspaper writer once remarked, Banting's pictures had always "a soupçon of the Seven"; perhaps rather more. Of these, Lawren Harris and A. Y. Jackson became intimate friends.

Over a period of many years no other man was privileged to associate more closely with Banting than was "Alex" Jackson, the dean of Canadian landscape painters. A stocky, baldish man, with a small-boy grin and at the same time an unobtrusive dignity, he had an infinite capacity for the friendship and instruction which Banting desired. He has said that he never regarded the scientist as a pupil. Nevertheless, the constant association on many country excursions, the casual comments at day's end on the sketches the day produced, and more especially the cogent stimulus of example, were so strong a force in combination that Banting's finest pictures have been mistaken for the work of his præceptor.

At St. Tite des Caps, on one of the Quebec excursions, Banting did a winter street scene which, with a friendly inscription on the back, he afterwards presented to Percy Ghent. When Ghent took the sketch to be framed he covered the signature and asked the framer—who had an enviable knowledge of Canadian art—whose work it was. "A. Y. Jackson," he answered with not a moment's hesitation. A few days later Ghent saw Sir Frederick and told him his sketch had been identified as the work of Jackson by an art expert. He threw back his head and laughed; "Just wait until I tell A. Y. that one."

Ghent later reminded Jackson of the incident. "But I had my revenge," the artist chuckled. "Fred did a number of sketches of the north country that were used to illustrate a magazine article. All were good, but one of them especially so, and knowing his habit of giving away his work, I scrawled my name on the back of it to denote possession by first claim. When the article appeared, Banting was credited with all the sketches save the one with my name on the back. 'I wouldn't have cared a scrap,' Fred told me, 'but they stuck your name on the only decent sketch in the lot.' "

In a beautiful booklet of thirty-seven pages Jackson has recorded the story of this remarkable friendship.[2] It was when Banting knocked at the door of the artist's studio to purchase a war sketch that the two first met. "He was nervous. He looked over the sketches, picked one out, asked if it was for sale, pulled out the money and went away with the sketch." That was all.

Yet this was the beginning of an association which brings no exact parallel to mind. A distinguished scientist, far-famed for learning and imagination, turned to another type of work as a recreation and apprenticed himself with an almost naïve humility to a painter. But Jackson was as simple and ingenuous as he.

[2]*Banting as an Artist,* by A. Y. Jackson, with a memoir by Frederick W. W. Hipwell. The Ryerson Press, 1943.

Few other masters could have offered him an example of a manner and a method so completely native to his own heart. Jackson's painting has none of the perverse waywardness which seems to spell superior ability for the dilettantes on the fringe of modern art. It is bold, straightforward and as clear as day. It is also brilliantly designed, both in composition and colour, and painted with masterly assurance. Such work is the expression of a personality closely akin to Banting's. They met on the common ground of humanity, simplicity and the love of nature.

The commonest fault of the amateur painter, according to Jackson (who ought to know since he has been approached by scores of them seeking advice) is to make a half-dozen niggling dabs where a single confident brush stroke is required.

> A line for the shore,
> A stroke for the main.
> The will to do more,
> But the skill to refrain.[3]

One of these amateurs of painting, a lady, once came to Jackson for an opinion of her work. Finding that it suffered from the aforementioned fault and knowing that another of the lady's hobbies was the making of tea-cosies and similar articles from felt, Jackson gave her a singular piece of advice. He told her to lay aside her brushes and paint and take out a lot of pieces of coloured felt when she went sketching. This was to impress upon her mind the desirability of simple design, of mass, of the adequate use of clear, unmixed colour. Banting, likewise, was guilty of dabbing too often at his canvas, but in his case the fault was soon cured. He knew that a skilful surgeon seldom makes several strokes with his scalpel when one suffices.

It was about this time that he came across a picture which disturbed him mightily. It was a large canvas of Lake Superior by Lawren Harris and was so daring and unorthodox that it made him angry. Those knobby, rounded hillocks in regular series, like the tread on a heavy-duty tire—were there really excrescences like that on the north shore? Of course not. He was both attracted and repelled. He could not understand how it was that paint on canvas should move him so strongly. Why was he filled with

<hr>

[3]Written by a Chinese student of art at Columbia.

annoyance and yet so deeply interested that he returned to the Art Gallery six times to see it? On one of these occasions he viewed it in the company of Dr. James MacCallum, friend and supporter of Canadian artists and beneficent patron of Tom Thomson.

"How do you like it?" asked Dr. MacCallum.

"Like it?" retorted Banting. "Like it? I think it's the damndest painting ever hung on a wall!"

MacCallum laughed. "Let's go to see Harris in his studio," he said, "maybe he will be able to tell you what it's all about."

Accordingly they went to the Harris studio and Banting was introduced. "We've been admiring one of your pictures," said MacCallum, not quite truthfully, and he added with a gleam of mischief, "Tell him what you thought of it, Fred."

Banting reddened. He murmured something non-committal, did his best to side-step the question. But Harris pressed him for an answer. Finally, he blurted again that he thought it was the damndest picture ever hung on a wall.

Harris laughed good-humouredly. "Why?" he queried. "If it's really as bad as that I ought to know about it. What do you think is wrong?" So Banting confessed. He said that it irritated him that anyone should pretend to see in Nature what obviously was not there; that anyone should so distort a landscape that it became a sort of caricature of the actual scene. He was perfectly certain that there was not a spot on the north shore of Lake Superior that bore more than the faintest resemblance to the picture in question.

Harris then explained, very seriously and with strong conviction, that he had made no attempt to hold a mirror up to Nature, that he had used the elements of the landscape as the *materials* for his design, suppressing some, rearranging the others, simplifying the whole; that he had tried to paint an artist's-eye view rather than a camera-eye view of the scene he had studied.

And so Banting learned, although not all at once, that painting is more, much more, than a laborious method of competing with colour photography. There is more than one way to paint a cat as there is more than one way to skin it. The effects that a painter may produce are manifold and the means of producing them are varied. No mode of painting, however unlike the models previously admired, can be denied to the experimental painter. It suddenly occurred to him that artists, like scientists, might engage in research. The scientist, in physics and physiology, searches for the truth of Nature's being. The artist, working with paint or clay or stone, declares the result of his personal quest for the truth of Nature's aspect.

New practices introduced by the experimentalist in art may initiate new schools of painting and sculpture. But the scientist is expected, nay required, to produce new things: that is the whole reason for his existence. Contrariwise, the artist is too often expected, too often required, to follow closely the methods of his predecessors, to manufacture pictures of pictures. It was once fashionable among landscape painters to include somewhere in every picture a brown tree, in imitation of the mighty Claude. The bold spirits who first abandoned this tradition were regarded by many as iconoclasts.

A scientific theory, subjected to satisfactory proof, can be established over night, as Banting's own experience served to show, while changes in art are often not accepted in a lifetime except by a handful who understand and by a somewhat larger handful who wish to *appear* to understand.

"He realized," writes Jackson, "that success in art mostly went to painters who were akin to the fashionable practitioners in medicine rather than to the research workers."

The style and subject matter of Canadian painting had undergone a radical change. Examples of Canadian painters who painted with fidelity the Canadian scene had not been lacking, but the majority of them had painted it in a derivative style, somehow contriving to make the landscape of their native concessions assume an odd likeness to the English meadows of Constable and Gainsborough. Others disavowed their birthright altogether, and such distinguished expatriates as Paul Peel can be said to be Canadian only by the accident of their birth. Canadian culture emerged slowly from the colonial phase in which everyone looked to Europe for precedent. But painters of the younger generation avoided the prosperous glitter of the salons and tramped the woods with the true spirit of adventure and the true inspiration of art. Tom Thomson, several of whose paintings Banting owned, was so impoverished as a result of this pioneer attitude that he was forced to use both sides of many of his panels, but he refused to bow to the dictates of artistic fashion. Fashion, as her custom is, eventually about-faced and the struggles of the truly native artists grew somewhat less hard. Yet originality, now as then, is a rather dubious qualification if the aim be worldly success.

Jackson asserts that Banting soon acquired a general idea of the range and direction of Canadian art. "He knew many of the artists. He was very welcome in art circles. He became a very popular member of the Arts and Letters Club and was a good friend to the young people in the Art Students' League. He was generous in his admiration and never allowed his eminence in science to give weight to his opinions on questions of art."

He never played the dilettante with an artistic hobby. He worked at it. He became one of the rugged, far-roaming, out-door painters. Apart from a few canvases painted at home, most of his work was painted on small birch panels out-of-doors, in good weather and bad. In open fields on sunny days, in the lee of wind-swept hills on chilly autumn afternoons, anywhere and everywhere that gave promise of good hunting for an artist, Banting set to work. And for long hours he painted, even in mid-winter, until the bright snowfields were dimmed in subsiding light. He waited upon the whims of the Canadian landscape, now stern, now genial, as though it had some command upon him that required to be interpreted and obeyed. Pine trees, stalwart or niggardly according to their kind; maple trees, quietly green or glowing with vivid colours according to the season; birch, beech, oak, elm and willow—crowded with their various shapes and tints his imagination and his pictures. Lakes and rivers gleamed beneath his brush. A foreboding sky with a storm hiding behind the hills elated him. All of Nature seemed bent on suborning the fancy of a great scientist to other and merrier uses.

The happy and proficient painter he became, at the prompting of his own wish and under the influence of Jackson, took time to grow. The first sketching expedition they made together was to St. Jean Port Joli on the south shore of the St. Lawrence in March, 1927. This was an old story, though fresh with every year, to Jackson; to his companion it was something new, and the painter was not unamused by the reactions of his protégé:

There was no sign of spring. It was cold and windy and very exposed country. We would crouch behind barns and rail fences to sketch. He was almost frozen stiff every day, but he

Courtesy of Dr. C. A. Rae.

ST. TITE DES CAPS

Courtesy of C. A. G. Matthews.

STE. IRENÉE

struggled with frozen paint and fingers. His only comment on one bitterly cold day was, "And I thought this was a sissy game." We moved on to Bic and then to Tobin, a little dead sawmill village. We got off the train and found there was no place to stay. A kindly insurance agent, Mr. Berubé, put us up. The sun shone. The snow melted. When Berubé found Banting drove the same make of car as he did, we were treated as members of the family.

3

In the same year they went to the Arctic. Various members of the Banting family possess mementoes of the adventurous journey. One received a post card with a picture of a forlorn little boat, a weather-worn relic of the last expedition of Sir John Franklin. Others cherish examples of Indian and Eskimo handicraft; others sketches. His nephew Edward, in Alliston, an ardent collector of birds' eggs, was delighted by the gift of an auk egg from somewhere in the dim whiteness of the North where his famous and far-wandering uncle was having the time of his life.

Jackson had been given permission by the Minister of the Interior to go on the *Beothic,* which was calling at all the Royal Canadian Mounted Police posts in the North. Banting was jealous of such a wonderful artistic opportunity. The thought of such a trip excited him immensely and he tried to get permission to go along too. With no success. He was crestfallen. But O. S. Finnie, the Deputy Minister in Ottawa, saw a chance to gratify Banting's wish and at the same time to make use of his services for the Department.

The R.C.M.P. posts co-existed with the posts of a great fur-trading company which at that time virtually administered the North, since the Eskimos depended on their trade with the Company for their livelihood. In earlier times they had followed the caribou in their wanderings, obtaining fresh meat from the herds. But the merchandise obtainable from the Company in exchange for furs had induced them to remain in the vicinity of the posts and devote themselves to trapping. Much of their food was purchased by barter in the Company's stores, and the Department desired to know what effect, if any, abandonment of the nomad life, with the change in diet and living conditions which settling down involved, might have had upon the well-being of the Eskimo tribes. Who could better decide this question than an on-the-spot medical expert whose report would be weighted with the prestige of a great scientific reputation? The Deputy Minister was well aware that if Banting accepted this task he would carry it out with conscientious thoroughness. Consequently, a few days before the boat left, he received a wire from Mr. Finnie, saying that if he could put up with very rough accommodation they would find room for him. He was offered the job, though not the title, of minister of health to the Eskimos. This was a welcome change from laboratory duties, and best of all he was travelling with Jackson through territory which, though it was desolate in the main, was often dramatically beautiful.

From Banting's diary we catch some glimpses of the North:

July 16.

. . . All loading completed about 2.00 p.m. and after a few pictures of the expedition were taken we set sail. When we cleared the wharf I ripped off my white collar and threw it over-board—went to cabin and put on my old army breeches and grey shirt, leggings, boots and sweater—good-bye to civilization for two months at least. . . .

July 18.

The fog whistle woke us at about 4.00 a.m., got up at 5.00, speed slackened, fog whistle blowing intermittently—entering the straits of Belle Isle. Saw our first icebergs after breakfast—fog lifted about ten, numerous icebergs. Alex and I did pencil drawing of many of the larger ones. The sun came out for a few minutes and showed us the marvellous colour close bergs may have. . . .

July 19.

Warmer, then fog, clear sea. Spent most of morning sizing canvas. . . .

I still feel very lazy and not inclined to think about research work. We got several drawings of icebergs which I have done over in ink.

July 22.

Friday, 11.30 a.m.—We have just crossed the *Arctic Circle*. We gathered in the dining-room—toasts to the ship, the expedition and the Mounted Police. . . .

"We shared a small cabin with Dr. Malte, the Government Botanist," writes Jackson. "It was a cheerful company with G. P. Mackenzie in charge, Captain Falke, Inspector Wilcox, Dr. Stringer and a number of husky R.C.M.P. boys. We did a lot of sketching from the deck of the steamer, making rapid notes in pencil and working them up in the little cabin. Malte was soon at work, classifying specimens in the dining saloon next door. Every little while he would come in to celebrate the hundred and thirtieth specimen or the furthest north for some particular variety. The wealth of material made the celebration almost continuous. I ran into him at 1.00 a.m., lying on his stomach on a patch of moss, a large magnifying glass in one hand and a note-book in the other. Banting and I in our rambles would pick up specimens for him. One of these, a trailing saxafrage from Somerset Island, was such a rare find that we had to join in the celebration. . . ."

From Banting's diary:

July 23.

. . . About 7.00 a.m. anchor was cast [in Godhaven harbour] and immediately Eskimo natives paddled out in their kayaks. The whistle was blown and the flag unfurled. The Danish flags were hoisted and the Governor of the Island, the local governor and Marconi man came abroad. They stayed for breakfast. We got a few drawings of the kayaks in the water. The natives handle them with remarkable skill. . . . The Governor showed us some primitive Eskimo artist paintings and we bought four ($1.50 each).

Alex and I started out to paint. . . . Unfortunately I only had one board and had to stop after both sides were covered. It was wonderful to gaze about at this little northland village with the bay and its icebergs beyond. Dogs everywhere, . . . natives smiling at us. Alex would chuckle and about a dozen times he said, "I just want to laugh. It hardly seems possible that we are here." It was difficult to realize that it was not a dream.

There are two or three hundred natives at Godhaven. . . .
Some of the girls would be accepted by Ziegfield for his Follies,
while others are typical wide-faced, low-browed, semi-mon-
golian. . . .

July 24.

About 3.30 p.m. went through field ice for about an hour.
Did a lot of sketching; wrote to Mother and Father.

July 29.

[Near Craig Harbour, Ellesmere Island].

. . . Alex and I stayed on the ship but as the ice sheets were
floating about so much, it was very difficult to paint.   I got a very
good sketch of Jones Island off the mouth of Craig Harbour. . . .

July 30.

Landed at Etah, Greenland. . . .

July 31.

. . . Made about a record trip across the strait to Bache. . . .
Went ashore and for a walk.   During the course of the walk I
was possibly closer to the Pole than any one on the continent. . . .
Provisions and coal were landed in a hurry (writes Jackson),
and we got out just before a large ice-pack crowded in on us.   The
R.C.M.P. boys who had come with us were left in ones and twos
at the various posts, and those they were relieving, who had been
there a year or two, came back with us.   We steamed up Lancaster
Sound, landed at Beechey Island, picked up the record the last
visitor, Captain Bernier, had left in a whiskey bottle.   There was
still lots of debris about of Franklin's camp where he spent the
miserable winter of 1845-46.   We made sketches of Cornwallis
Island, quite a distance away, but ice conditions were bad and the
magnetic pole was bedevilling navigation.   Captain Falke said he
wished the Russians owned it and kept it in the middle of Siberia.
We turned eastward, through fog, rain, wind and ice, into Arctic
Bay, then Pond Inlet, which seemed like a summer resort with its
fine sweep of sand beach, Hudson Bay Post, Police Post and happy
Eskimos.   A couple of the R.C.M.P. boys we picked up were
peeved because they were being sent "down south" to Hudson
Strait.   We accumulated a lot of material.   Studies of icebergs,
glaciers, floe-ice and the rugged coastline, and more intimate stuff
we got ashore.   Sometimes we would find ourselves working at

one or two o'clock in the morning. The twenty-four hours of daylight was demoralizing. As we went south there seemed to be more variety to the light and cloud forms and it was good to have night again.

Banting afterwards wrote an introduction to *The Far North*, a book of drawings published by Jackson in 1928, in which he gives his own account of their experience and a vivid picture of his companion:

Sketching was done under considerable difficulty; cold and wind would have chilled the enthusiasm of a less-ardent worker. Jackson cherishes an illusion that the finest colour is generally to be found on the most exposed spots. A restless desire to find what lies beyond the distant hills makes it hard to keep up with him. The barren waste proved to be rich in form and colour, strange rhythms and unexpected vistas. During our all too brief and exciting scrambles ashore, he would be chuckling and laughing all day—a mood I found contagious.

This was the longest single period which Banting had ever devoted to sketching and his comrade felt that his work showed great promise. The oil sketches are vivid and well-designed and many vigorous pen-and-ink drawings came back with him from the North.

But he was not the man to neglect the assignment given him by the government. At every stop he visited the Eskimos near by and conducted a painstaking investigation of the changed conditions of Eskimo life. What he found was disquieting. The preserved foods to be had at the Company posts, which formed the staples of their diet, offered insufficient variety for a properly balanced regimen, and he observed the signs of physical degeneration. Medical aid was almost entirely lacking and, as is often the case where primitive peoples live in contact with the fringe of civilization, the tribes were actually worse off than in their aboriginal innocence. The things he obtained for his furs were "by no means as good for the native," wrote Banting in his diary, "as his former life without these things."

Neglecting the natural sources of their fathers' livelihood to spend their days in the quest of furs, these simple people had declined in vigour and had fallen easy prey to recurrent epidemics of disease, to the extent that whole settlements had been wiped out, others decimated. It was obvious that the report which Banting must return to Ottawa would be "dynamite," pointing as it would to negligence and indifference in high places. Luxurious coats, rich stoles, lustrous scarves of fur were being brought from the Eskimo country at a deplorable cost in human health and human life. The Department had done well in sending Banting to investigate. A determination grew within him that something constructive must be done without delay to remedy the situation. And as it is by now abundantly clear, any such resolve on his part was a force most difficult to deflect. His feeling was one of dismay rather than anger, but that abated not a jot from the strength of his purpose.

On returning to Montreal Banting and Jackson had an unfortunate encounter with the world of journalism. Jackson was queried by a reporter as to his reasons for living in Toronto and was asked if he did not find it a more narrow-minded, more bigoted city than Montreal. He replied that on the contrary he considered it more liberal, or words to that effect. Now Jackson had been much acclaimed in Montreal and treated with generous hospitality and he was therefore much embarrassed to see the printed account of this interview headlined in a Montreal newspaper thus: "Jackson Says Montreal Most Bigoted City." This, however, appeared later. In the meantime, the same reporter, who also wrote for a Toronto paper, accompanied Banting on his train journey to the latter city. At Port Hope they were joined by Mr. Vincent Massey, afterwards Canadian High Commissioner in London. Their Pullman became the scene of an animated discussion of the Eskimo situation. The reporter, who was present during the conversation and who asked questions of the other participants, was given clearly to understand that everything said was strictly "off the record." According to the long-established etiquette of journalism he was thereby obligated to keep such revelations out of the press until specifically authorized to publish them. Banting, of course, like any other agent of a government, was required to make his report directly to the Minister or Deputy Minister of the Department which he served. An account of his report would then be released, if the Ministry wished its release, through "official channels." It is sometimes permissible for a public servant in these circumstances to give out information to the press with the knowledge and approval of his superiors, and in certain cases without that approval if he feels that something they are entitled to know is being withheld from the people. But it is contrary to all respectable usage to divulge the information to the newspapers before it has been reported to the Ministry. Imagine then the anger and disgust which possessed so choleric a man as Banting to read a full and blatant version of what he had committed in confidence to the ears of the reporter in the headlines of the next edition of a stirring Toronto newssheet.

Precisely what he said, and what he thought, on reading those headlines is not recorded but may readily be conceived. His telephone conversation with the editor was hot and profane, and to say that reporters of this particular newspaper (the "Daily Blat" he called it) were afterwards treated by him with scant courtesy is to understate the case. Banting on his high ropes had full command of "thoughts that breathe and words that burn." (It may be added parenthetically that his subsequent experience with the "Daily Blat" at the time of his divorce confirmed his opinion of its perfidy and that he grimly refused to have any further dealings with it.)

High words were not enough to get him out of his present difficulty. He communicated at once with Mr. Finnie, the Deputy Minister, and gave him a full explanation of what had occurred. Premature publication of the substance of his report, made worse by the garbled form in which it appeared, was all the more unfortunate because he had entertained the hope that the Eskimo troubles would find their solution in amicable discussion between the Government and the Company. This happy consummation would be prejudiced, if not entirely precluded, by the manner in which his findings had been so rudely set forth. He had been made to appear as accusing the Company of wilful neglect, even downright fraud. He seemed to hear the faint preliminary rumble of an imminent storm, and he at once took alarm. Somewhat disgruntled with the Company, angry with the newspaper, and annoyed with himself, he was still more deeply perturbed at the possible consequences of the hue and cry in the press and feared immediate legal action on the part of those he had offended. His position would be difficult to defend. Laying aside all other business, he hurried at once to Ottawa for an interview with the

Deputy Minister. He then proceeded to hunt out the records of previous commissions to the Eskimo tribes, seeking confirmatory evidence of the situation as he had been bold to present it. He was preparing a brief for the lawsuit which he felt sure was impending.

But he had scented from afar a storm which never broke. The governor of the Company, indeed, invited him to his office for a discussion, and he agreed to go, feeling that the lightning was now about to strike. He presented his case at considerable length and urged it with many persuasive instances. The governor, who was certainly capable of appreciating this great defect in the Company's methods, gave no sign. He was polite but guarded, and Banting went away nonplussed. He was afterwards visited by agents of the Company and further discussions took place.

No legal action was ever taken and his next communication from the governor was a Christmas greeting. The outcome was satisfactory, for a series of adjustments in the administration of the North followed close upon his investigation, and the injustice which he had perceived was in some degree remedied. The clouds passed over and Banting turned again to his work. Once again he beguiled his leisure with the pleasant avocation of art. But the tempest which never broke, which he anticipated in vain, had reverberations later on.

There was still another *sequela* to the Arctic journey. In Volume I. No. 1 (May, 1930) of the *Canadian Geographical Journal,* Banting published an account of it. (This article was illustrated by a number of drawings, the best of which, as mentioned before, was erroneously attributed to Jackson.) The observations there set forth attracted the indignant attention of no less an authority than the famous Arctic explorer, Vilhjalmur Stefansson. In his delightful, iconoclastic book, *Adventures in Error,*[4] in which the wolf-pack, the ubiquitous snow house and other "standardized errors" are thoroughly disposed of, Stefansson devoted more than five pages to a discussion of Banting's paper. He made use of twelve brief quotations, accompanied by twelve blistering commentaries.

Banting had written, for example, that "in protected spots the

[4]Vilhjalmur Stefansson, *Adventures in Error.* Robert M. McBride and Company, New York, 1936.

flowering mosses of various colours . . . reminded us of a summer day at home." To which Stefansson rejoined: "Either Banting here made some startling discoveries or he was a bit confused as to the nature of mosses. Not a few works of reference divide plants into flowering and non-flowering, putting the mosses on the non-flowering side of the fence."

Again, Stefansson quoted the remark that ". . . the native has *no* natural immunity," and he added chillingly: "The only necessary comment is to say that the italicization in this quotation is ours."

But the body blow came when Banting committed mistake number eleven. "In a country where there is no sunshine for three months of the year," so he wrote, "the people are dependent on their food for their vitamins."

Reading this, the master explorer rubbed his hands together gleefully, dipped his pen in vitriol and indited the following *critique:*

The inference seems to be that if there were more sunshine these remarkable people would not have to depend on food for any of their vitamins. The recipient of one Nobel Prize for endocrine studies may then well be candidate for another in comparative racial physiology and in deficiency diseases.

(In another place in the same chapter Stefansson observes: "I like to contrast my benevolence with the misanthropy of the satirists. . . .")

The explorer confesses, however, that the impressions and conclusions of his own first *year* in the Arctic were "mostly wrong," and he adds a saving paragraph at the end:

To guard against misunderstanding I close this discussion of the Banting paper by reminding you, and insisting upon it, that I am on the whole one of his great admirers. It appears to me that his career and character are both of a high order. That is my point. We get from eminent and deservedly respected men substantial contributions of misinformation useful in maintaining the general unreality (or shall we say poetic quality, imaginative charm?) of our world outlook.

Banting could take comfort from the company in which he found himself. Having finished with him, Stefansson turned his devastating attention to an unguarded statement by Sir James H. Jeans with respect to icebergs, a statement quoted "with implied approval" by Robert A. Millikan. Jeans and Millikan went down together before a whirlwind onslaught.

4

Banting loved to draw caricatures.[5] For many years his "doodling" took this form; faces looked up at him from menus and blotters.

For serious portraiture he had little talent, although he did attempt it. (Was there anything he did not try?) The Irish maid-servant (who had helped to attire the "Emir") sat for him several times, very stiffly but also very patiently, while her employer laboured with manful earnestness to commit her likeness to canvas. After many efforts he at last became so completely exasperated that he threw down his brushes and gave it up.

But the urge was too strong to let him rest and if the Celtic features of the maid were too much for him perhaps those of another sitter would prove less intractable. Mrs. Banting went on a trip with Mrs. Mackintosh Bell and was to be away for about six weeks; Banting thereupon invited Bertram Brooker to join him in portrait painting, each doing a picture of the other. Brooker, who had little taste for it, somewhat reluctantly agreed. Every Sunday morning he appeared at the Bedford Road house about ten o'clock. This was the hour appointed and Banting, who rose early *every* day was a little put out if his friend failed to appear on the minute. One of them was painter for the first hour while the other was sitter; then the rôles were reversed for the second hour; after lunch they painted for two hours more. Banting assaulted his canvas with grim gusto, resolved to achieve a likeness or be damned; with knotted brow and determined hand he fought the refractory paints and his frustration exploded in strings of fire-cracker expletives. It would *not* come right. Seiz-

[5]He had often seen the lightning sketches which Arthur Lismer dashed off at the Arts and Letters Club, many of them of Banting himself.—*Note contributed by A. Y. Jackson.*

ing a palette knife he scraped away the paint and began again. He angrily wiped his brushes on the front of his smock (it soon became stiff with paint from waist to knee). At the end of an hour Brooker would call time and Banting was always surprised to find that his stint was done so soon; he probably would have gone on painting until dark. As a sitter he was restless and impatient. He always propped his own picture where he could look at it and the more he looked at it the less it looked like Brooker. His fingers itched to correct the faults he saw in it.

According to Brooker's own account of the results attained, his portrait of Banting resembled an Arrow collar advertisement in its precision and neatness, for he was an expert technician, but unfortunately it was not recognizable; Banting's portrait of him, though bearing a faint resemblance to the subject, was a very muddy canvas, painted and repainted and painted over until it looked as if it had been used for cleaning brushes. When Mrs. Banting returned she laughed at them both so heartily that the disgruntled painters abandoned their work and decided to leave the domain of portraiture to Wyly Grier and Kenneth Forbes. The pictures were never finished. Banting returned with relief to his landscapes.

5

In 1928 there was a trip to the North-West, a trip which Banting recorded in a detailed journal. Here we may read the story of an adventure in the wilderness closely akin to the tales of the great expeditions into the interior when the pathfinders of earlier times explored the country. These were tales which Banting loved to read. When he began to collect Canadiana the journals and memoirs of explorers were particular favourites among his books. When he himself ventured out beyond the frontiers he felt the blood of pioneer forbears leap warmly in his veins and looked about him at the rugged country with a new freshness and delight. Thompson, Mackenzie, Charlevoix, the gallant Jesuits —he was one of a glorious company!

Something of this spirit permeates the journal. It shows,

besides, his deep affection for the land, his love for depicting it in paint, and the breadth and intelligence of his interests: there was hardly an aspect of Canadian life which did not appear to him a matter of intimate concern. For these reasons the "North-west Saga" is reserved for a separate chapter.

In 1930, Jackson and Banting made one of their numerous trips to Quebec. They reached Mal Baie, a narrow village stretching upward along the road from the mouth of Murray River, on March 4.

"It was too cold to paint," Banting notes in his diary, "not on account of the paint, for with the heater it was soft and manageable, but ten degrees below zero is too cold to be sitting cramped up in one position for an hour or two." Apparently he is referring here to a little device which he "dreamed up" himself; it consisted of a sort of inverted cone, specially made for him at the Institute, with a spirit lamp inside, and was designed to be placed under a paint box for the purpose of keeping the paints warm and soft. It was not quite such a complete success as this entry might indicate. Jackson reports that it worked beautifully in the studio and sometimes, on a perfectly windless day, it even worked out-of-doors; but where it was really needed—out on the cold, windy hills—the spirit lamp invariably blew out.

Banting fills several pages in his entry for Ash Wednesday with a description of the community and reflections on the character of the French Canadian and the influence of the Roman Catholic Church. Next morning they were up early and left for St. Fidele, another little village below Murray Bay.

Thursday, March 6, 1930.

. . . Tonight, while doing some pen-and-ink drawings, I heard the cry of a new-born baby. Alex came up and told me that a baby had arrived while we were eating our supper. We then remembered that they closed the door into the kitchen while we were at the dessert. . . .

This is a wonderful village for sketching. We are well housed, warm and (so far) good food. It is a great life. The more I see of the country the more I wonder why people in general and myself in particular live in the city. . . .

March 7.

'Today is cold, raw and grey, with a fair breeze. It was cold sketching. . . .

These frame houses do not hold the heat. It was hot when we went to bed last night but before morning it was cold as the Arctic—without the fur. I got up and put all my clothes (including my tie) on top of the bed clothes. . . .

It is a week tonight since I left—one-quarter of the time gone and only five sketches on the wall to dry. If we can only get a little decent weather this would be a wonderful place. There is a composition everywhere one looks.

March 8, 1930.

. . . It has been snowing all day. . . . It was blowing a real Western blizzard and it made me think of those days of long ago when it was necessary to leave the old farm house on such a winter's night. . . .

Monday, March 10, 1930.

It has been a great day. Blue sky, bright sunshine, snow banks from the storm, warm enough to work (but cold enough in the wind). Did four sketches—two fair, one very poor and one doubtful. . . . I have been amusing myself in the evenings by pen and ink drawing. It is good sport and helps one's draughtsmanship. Tonight I did an old doorway. . . .

Tuesday, March 11.

. . . There is plenty of hard work to painting. It is often very cold and I have even lit matches to warm my hands. The light may change half way through a sketch and then it is a terrible job to finish it. When one stands up for a sketch one gets tired and when one sits the snow melts and finally wets the seat of one's trousers and it is mighty cold and uncomfortable. Then again, if one sits on a stone, tailor fashion, one's legs go to sleep. . . . Alex is a terrible fellow to walk and I trail along behind. It is tiring and makes one's back ache at times, but after a day's sketching one eats, sleeps and feels satisfied—even if the sketches are poor. . . .

March 12.

It stormed all morning, so we stayed in and repaired the light sketches of the last two days. This afternoon it cleared up and we hastened to avail ourselves of the snow on the roofs. The sun came out and for a little while it was most exciting. As clouds passed it became dark and light and one had to work fast and furious. I got one fairly decent sketch. To sketch, one must be able to draw, get tone, get colour, get relations, get design and get simplification. That is all there is to it. It is strange that Alex and I can do the same scene and when the sketches are finished he has an improvement on the original, while I have a poor imitation. Such is art.

There seems to be an almost inexhaustible supply of painting material in this village. The houses group well. There are hills to the north and the river to the south. The latter has not been much use to us, as it has not been clear enough. The material is here but I fear that I will never become an artist.

Downstairs they are at prayers. They are steaming through at 90 miles per hour. I cannot see that they can make out what the reader is saying, and I bet they do not think of the words. It is a ritual, but they are good people. . . .

We had to shoo the cat down from our room twice today. She is the most pregnant looking cat I have ever seen and I fear that she has designs on my bed for a nursery.

He sketched continually in all sorts of weather (writes Jackson, in the memoir already quoted) and was pleased with a word of approval. But his usual question, when he showed me a sketch, was "Now what's wrong with it?"

To return to the diary.

Friday, March 14, 1930.

This morning it must have been below zero and a 30-mile wind. I did a drawing, but thought my fingers were frozen, so came home. I tried again this afternoon, with the same result. Alex gave me a lesson in pen and ink tonight. He is a funny fellow. He lets you struggle along and when it is hopeless he shows you how it is done.

We were right about the cat. . . .

March 15, 1930.

Last night there was a windstorm. This old house cringed and creaked like the *Beothic* in a high sea. It was cold. I slept all huddled up, for to move meant a cold chill. When the position caused a cramp and an ache I turned over. Today was just about too cold to paint. The paint caked [despite the "heater"] and fingers became too stiff to guide the brush. There was very bright sunshine. So bright was it, in fact, that all the middle tones were absent. . . .

Sunday, March 16, 1930.

. . . I have resolved to keep on working and by the law of probabilities I am bound to do a decent sketch sometime. I have 26 boards dirtied on one side and 14 clean boards and my holiday's half gone. I will soon start to use both side of the boards.

One can get used to the cold. I find that I can stand it much better than at first. I am getting fat, for my sweater feels better outside my vest. The wind and sun have accounted for the upper layers of the skin of my face, and I am beginning to look like a sailor. It is a great country. The more I think of the city the more I want to live in the country, and the more I think of being a Professor of Research the more I want to be an artist, or something else, with more work and less responsibility.

March 20, 1930.

. . . Oh, for a warm day when one can take one's time and work out the colour relations and detail in a sketch and when the paint will not gum up. I now have my hand in despite the weather and I think I could make a decent sketch if conditions were anything like right. There is a tremendous waste of paint to be considered. I have used nearly five large tubes of flake white and have only two and a half tubes left. My motto now is fewer and better sketches. But how is one to know weather and sketching materials before one starts on a trip? Part of the joy of a holiday is not knowing where one will be next day or next week. One has enough of travelling on schedule at home. I always did hate having to be at a certain place at a certain time.

Later they transferred their headquarters to St. Simeon, but found it less satisfactory than St. Fidele ("This town is sort of commercialized and feels touristy"). The weather turned from bad to worse—blizzards and continuous cold, "neither good colourful grey days, nor old colourful snow; fresh snow does not reflect light and colour as well as old weather-beaten, semi-honeycombed snow."

Finally they struggled back through deep snowdrifts to St. Fidele.

Between the two towns (Banting wrote on March 27) one goes down to sea level twice and up to 900 or 1,000 feet again. Our second dip is about two and a half miles from St. Fidele and there is one terrible hill up this side. It is the longest and steepest hill I have ever climbed, except the night Alex and I climbed up the rock at Craig Harbour, Ellesmere Island. . . .

It is rather nice to be back in old St. Fidele. I suppose Mrs. Trembley still licks the knife on the way to the stove to cut off one's portion of meat. . . .

Banting dressed like an old farmer (writes Jackson). No one knew who he was, which pleased him. He did not want to be known as a doctor in places where there was almost no medical service. On the first trip to Quebec he called himself Frederick Grant.

Their time was growing short. Banting wrote in his diary:

March 29, 1930.

Packed up. Tried a sketch, but it was mostly a dud, so did some drawing. After an early supper we left for La Malbaie by horse and cutter. . . . Before we left St. Fidele, when we were returning from the last sketch, we met the Curé and his brother. The latter is a veterinary and lived in Toronto for five years. He asked if I was any relation to Dr. Banting, for he had met the doctor at the Connaught Laboratories and I looked very much like him. The cat was out, and within an hour I had a patient in the person of the lady of the house with the baby. From the description in French, as closely as I could ascertain she has a little infection of the perineum. When we arrived at La Malbaie I sent out gauze and boracic acid for a compress and through Alex gave her directions for diet, laxatives, etc. They do not have doctors much in those small, isolated places for it is very expensive.

March 30, 1930.

. . . Today was only the third day in the whole month when one could paint in comfort without being cold and the paint sticky. . . .

April 1, 1930.

Left for Toronto at 8.30 a.m. I hate to leave this country. There are so many fine things about the people. Life is less complicated. They have simple faith, large families, little of this

Courtesy of Miss Sadie Gairns.

GRANADA, SPAIN

Courtesy of The Art Gallery of Toronto.

ELLESMERE ISLAND

world's goods, and happiness. They work long hours and steadily, but not too hard. They are never in a hurry. They pay very little taxes—no income tax. . . .

On the whole it was a good trip. Despite the most unfavourable weather we got a number of fairly good sketches. Alex was well pleased with the result.

In March of the following year there was a similar expedition and Banting filled thirty pages of his diary with an account of their adventures, interspersed with numerous complaints of the weather and frequent comments on French Canadian character and customs. All the sketching diaries are permeated also with a warmth of admiration for Jackson.

On March 17, 1931, he wrote:

Alex says, Sometimes one can make something beautiful out of the commonplace, or one can make something commonplace out of the beautiful. There are those supreme moments in sketching as in everything else. At times all goes well and one feels that one can get something out of the view—and again there is the grand view, but work as hard as you like and the sketch is rotten. . . .

Again on March 18:

Alex invariably wants to know what is over the hill. Today he walked me for miles—we took a luncheon, built a fire and made cocoa with melted snow in our fifteen-cent dipper. . . .

This trip was much like the previous one. He recorded good days and bad, good sketches and "buckeyes." On April 3 he wrote:

It has been delightful here up to the present, for we have been out and trying, every day but one or two; some days we did not attempt anything, but now I begin to feel that I want to be back at a different kind of work. Tonight after packing up—for we leave tomorrow—I began for the first time in three and a half weeks to think of the laboratory and research. I am beginning to feel physically fit and anxious to be on the move. . . .

6

Jackson again takes up the story:

There were sketching trips to the Georgian Bay in the early spring and the autumn, studying the forms and colour of rocks and the wind-blown pines and the play of light on the water. From the mere amateur, Banting was developing into a vigorous painter . . . he was learning to simplify and to keep his colours fresh. Apart from that he was not concerned with theory or the philosophy of art.

He was a good companion, ready to go anywhere, patient, persistent and energetic. . . .

[Later on] we worked in the La Cloche Hills, south-west of Sudbury. From the top of them you could see the big smoke-stacks of the nickel mines. We had arranged for a boy from a mine near by to make a camp for us. He wanted to do a swell job. He built a wall of logs four feet high and a frame to put the tent on top of it. It was ten feet high inside and the coldest tent I ever slept in, but on the rocky hills there was plenty of dead wood and we could make great bonfires when we were sketching and that rather compensated for the cold nights in the tent. Going out by canoe we had to buck our way through the ice for several miles.

The last trip we made together, with Donald McLeod[6] another amateur with us, was to St. Tite des Caps, a little village on the Cap Tourmente Plateau. It snuggles in a valley, and while it is not very old or far away it has a sense of remoteness from the world, and artists, perhaps because "le vicaire" used to drop in to see us, were regarded as good fellows by the natives. Banting always had a crowd of kids about him. He liked them. I

[6]"McLeod relates with amusement stories illustrative of the way the layman regards the initial efforts of the raw but ambitious amateur. One of these is said to have amused Sir Frederick Banting greatly. Shortly before Christmas one year, McLeod took a number of sketches to a local framer, a first-rate artisan incidentally, disposed to be rather outspoken in his views concerning Canadian art and artists. He was asked which, if any, of the dozen sketches were worthy of frames. For several minutes he surveyed them critically as he puffed his pipe. Then he said with grave deliberation: 'You have no reason to be discouraged; when Doctor Banting first took up sketching, he came to me with some sketches to be framed, and some of them were even worse than these.' "—William Colgate, *op cit.*

remember his saying that when he went to Spain he tried to sketch with a swarm of ragged, unruly urchins around him and thought of these nice, well-mannered little kiddies who used to watch him in Quebec.

Banting visited Spain in 1933 to attend a medical convention. But as Jackson intimates the trip had its artistic by-products. Most of the Canadian paintings, especially those done in Quebec, envisage a landscape not altogether primitive, nor yet entirely cultivated: They lack the man-made quality of populous, old-world scenes, but the houses and barns of the habitants, in a rugged setting, were always favourite subjects. The Spanish work shows the same delight in simple architectural forms. The pale stuccos and brilliant tiles, pictured in florid sunshine, were well suited to his talents.

Except for a few marine studies done in Gloucester, Mass., panels done in Spain and Norway, and in other European countries which he visited briefly and where he had little time to paint, are the only ones which do not represent his native land. The great majority of his work is Canadian in subject and Canadian in spirit. In 1935, as already mentioned, he went to Russia to the International Physiological Congress. Although he saw a good deal of the country he had almost no time to sketch. A set of ten pen-and-ink drawings made along the Georgian Highway were pronounced admirable by Jackson and are as well-designed as his best. Some account of other journeys, during which he spared a little time for sketching, has been given previously.

There is one picture of peculiar interest in which the scientist and the artist meet. It is a painting, now in the possession of Miss Sadie Gairns, of the laboratory in which he worked. An array of test tubes and flasks; a small autoclave in the corner; on a shelf by the window a series of bottles that trail tubing downwards like pendant vines; the paraphernalia and the atmosphere of research. But he saw in this laboratory something that few scientists see. He saw colour and design. And the result is a picture somehow faintly reminiscent of Van Gogh, and utterly different from Banting's other compositions. It was an early piece of work but a good one and he used a photograph of it on his bookplate.

In February, 1943, in the art gallery of Hart House, Toronto, a collection of some two hundred of Banting's sketches and paintings was displayed to the public. These were loaned for the purpose by more than one hundred individuals and associations to whom he had presented them. The exhibition was the result of a suggestion by Professor Barker Fairley and was arranged by a special committee consisting of Lady Banting, Surgeon Commander C. H. Best, Professor Fairley, Dr. F. W. W. Hipwell, Dr. A. Y. Jackson and Professor Hardolph Wasteneys in co-operation with the art committee of Hart House. Through the brightly lit room, radiant with colour and breathing forth memories to the artist's friends, trooped schoolboys and sages, artists and critics, and a motley host of the admiring and the curious.

"Sir Frederick Banting," wrote Pearl McCarthy, "had written his autobiography. But not in a book, or in words. He left it to be discerned in the things he created."

To Jackson the room was poignant with vivid reflections of the past. Viewing the collection detachedly, however, he paid it the tribute of sincere praise. "Some of these paintings," he said with a twinkle, "we should never have hung but for fear of offending those who very kindly sent them to us; nevertheless, take seventy-five or eighty of the best, and you have an exhibition of which any professional painter in Canada might be proud."

A second and related hobby, less ardently practised, was woodcarving. Jackson thinks the Loring-Wyle studio was probably the cause of these efforts. Banting spent many hours there while Frances Loring modelled in heroic size the thoughtful features of a masterly portrait head. The essential spirit of the scientist confronts us in the pondering gaze of this massive work. The great "prone brow oppressive with its mind" surmounts a serious, contemplative face, and the firm lips and strong chin complete an air of resolve. While this portrait was in the making its subject evinced a lively interest in the technique of sculpture, with the result that might have been expected—he tried it himself. The Hart House exhibition included wood-carvings as well as paintings. A walnut chest with a landscape in *bas relief* on the front and, on the inside of the lid, motifs representing the North American Indian's practice of medicine, was the most ambitious of these. There were also another walnut box, a walnut humidor, a pipe rack, and a pair of book-ends.

Wood-carving was never a strong enough attraction to lure him from the service of his first love, painting in oils. Paint was his favourite medium, and his best.

His sketches are scattered far and wide. "He took a sincere pleasure," wrote Jackson, "in showing them to his friends and if he thought they liked them he would give them away. He sent a few paintings to public exhibitions but only when he was urged to do so. The pleasure was in making them, in mixing up a lot of colours in a sketch box and all the adventures that led up to it, the freedom from responsibility, scrambling over unknown country, getting burned by the March sun, smoking a pipe before the camp-fire or the welcome at the little hotel and the good meals and looking over the day's work."

The best of the paintings are boldly and cleverly composed. They are never blurred, misty, or wanly tinted; all is well-defined and glowingly coloured. Swinging white clouds against an ardent blue sky. Flaming trees. Thick yellow sunshine. Dazzling snow.

Immortal in the Canadian landscape, in the broad counties of Quebec and Ontario, roam these companionable figures of the artist and the amateur, the painter and the scientist, the happy truants from a workaday world who yet work hard at their play, the protagonists of a pastoral poem of friendship and enduring beauty, of country faith and peace.

PART XI
North-west Saga

The stars awaken a certain reverence, because though always present, they are inaccessible; but all natural objects make a kindred impression, when the mind is open to their influence. Nature never wears a mean appearance. Neither does the wisest man extort her secret, and lose his curiosity by finding out all her perfection. Nature never became a toy to a wise spirit. The flowers, the animals, the mountains, reflected the wisdom of his best hour, as much as they had delighted the simplicity of his childhood.

RALPH WALDO EMERSON.

1

I N 1928 Banting went on a long and difficult expedition into the
Canadian North-West with his old friends, Jackson and Bell.
Perhaps the finest of all his journals is the one which records his
experience in the wilderness.[1]

June 27, 1928.

Got my Last Will and Testimony written up to date, railway
tickets, etc., etc. Had a conference with Professor Burton, Dr.
Hendrick, Cameron and Brebner concerning Hendrick's work on
mice tumour with colloidal arsenic.

"See Canada first" is my motto at present. The only places
that I am particularly anxious to see—apart from trips in Canada
—are Australia, New Zealand and India. I can't understand . . .
people who are not compelled by family or finance, going each
summer to the same place—in Muskoka or a lake or town—always
the same place, people and things. [Some] go for recreation and
on account of high life are "wreck-created," while others who go
for recreation are re-created. A change is the main element in
the latter process. A man or woman cannot get much rest unless
he gets free of the ties that bind him to others forty-five or fifty
weeks of the year. I somehow seldom want to see a place more than
once. Atlin, Summit and the Rocky Mountains are notable
exceptions to this rule. I must get a map of Canada and draw on
it the trips and places I have been.

I have certainly got some work ahead of me next fall—besides
the Lab. work and the Cameron Lecture in Edinburgh, I must:
(1) get out and go over all those early papers relating to Insulin;
(2) write a sketch of Dr. Helmcken; (3) articles on Indian medicine; (4) Eskimo medicine; (5) Early settlers in Canada; (6) The
history of the Town of Alliston—get my Canadiana book-plated
and catalogued; (7) Do some 21 x 26 canvases.

June 28.

Left Toronto at 9.05 p.m.

[1]The experiences recounted in this journal antedate some of the incidents already described, but for reasons given previously it has been thought
to deserve a separate chapter; it treats of a wider range of subjects than the
Quebec journals, which are primarily "sketching diaries."

June 29.

Got up at 5.00 a.m.—Passing through rocky bush country. One wonders what it is good for, but values change. Pulpwood, mines and tourists have made this northern part of the Province an asset. There is great work to be done in developing this great country.

June 30.

Up 6.00 a.m.—Had long talk with Alex and Mack in p.m. We are all agreed that Canada should shut down on immigration. It is not quantity but quality that we want—workers not shirkers, farmers not strikers. It is all right to fill up our vast territories with people who come determined to make it go and who are mentally inclined to like us and like Canada, but most English of the class that come out here have a superiority complex and an inferiority content. . . .

July 1.

Cool, rain in places—passed through mile upon mile of fine rank green wheat. Mack's cousin, Percy Bell, late O.C. of the 12th Field Ambulance, got on at Winnipeg. . . . The hills approaching Edmonton are beautiful, but too green to paint. I have been reading a book called *The Fall of the Russian Empire,* by Edmund A. Walsh. It is wonderfully well written. I should judge that Walsh has a classical background upon which is superimposed a thorough training in modern history.

July 3.

At 9.30 a.m. we take off to the land where summer is summer and winter is winter—to the land where mosquitoes are mosquitoes, black flies black, and bulldogs—no bull. However, the latter are said to be gentlemen, since they go to bed at night.

I hope we have time at Fort Smith to visit the salt wells. There are huge deposits of salt which are the result of the precipitation at the surface of the salt from super-saturated springs. . . .

All day we have been slowly travelling north by east. The train is made up of freight and coaches—about a mile long. Stop and shunt about at all stations. There are four carloads of yearling buffalo—250 in the shipment—from Wainwright—to be turned loose up north—they have already taken up 6,663—about equal number of bulls and heifers.

The country for the most part has been flat, covered with

poplar, some muskeg, myriads of flowers—tiger lily, paint-brush, anemone, wild strawberries, etc. At Lac la Biche we stopped for about two hours. The sun set a little after nine and gave wonderful mauve tints on the lake. There are many Indians at this place—a little out from the town they were congregating from all sides for their midsummer festival. . . . It is a good settlement, surrounded by fine farm lands. The lake abounds in fish—fine seven-pound white fish are taken. . . . This immense area could be farmed and will, some day. Too much education takes the boys from the farm. What will Canada do for a peasant class? Foreign farmers prosper, educate their children, who then leave the farm. The school system demands the English language be taught and in due course the foreigner will be Canadianized.

In discussion with Mack we agreed that we should be nationalists—it is the best way of being Imperialists. The greatest way we can help the Empire is by developing a true Canadian spirit, promote our own resources, timber, power, mines, fisheries, agriculture, ranching, oil, salt, clays, etc.

July 4.

Arrived at Waterways about noon. The most remarkable and surprising thing is the amount of vegetation. Each side of the railway is a veritable jungle—tall, straight tamarack and spruce two feet in diameter, a thick tangled undergrowth. . . .

Got our rooms on the Hudson Bay steamer, the *Athabasca River*—a flat-bottom, rear-splash propeller—got luncheon, sorted luggage for old duds and the three of us started to walk to Fort McMurray—three miles—on the junction of the Athabasca and Clearwater rivers. This is a famous quarter as the old trails—Indian and white—for centuries and centuries have been up the Clearwater from Athabasca—portage to the head waters of the N. Saskatchewan—down which they went to Lake Winnipeg—out the Red to Lake of the Woods or out the Nelson to Hudson Bay. This was the route of many early explorers including Mackenzie, Franklin, Richardson, Dease, Simpson, Warburton Pike, Tyrrell.

At McMurray we visited the old Hudson Bay post, but did not stay, owing to the fact that millions of mosquitoes rose all of a sudden with war whoop and poison arrows and flew upon us as the Indians did of old. Had dinner at Fort McMurray at the hotel kept by a fine French lady. Mosquitoes pestered us all the way home, but the cool of the evening took them away. A wash and a cold drink refreshed us. After combing the dead bodies out of my hair I went out to watch the sunset which was gorgeous.

Mr. Christie, of the Department of Interior, North-West and Yukon branch, is here in charge of the buffalo transportation. . . .

In transporting buffalo they darken the corral with tar paper so that the animals see daylight at the far end and they run through like sheep.

July 5.

After breakfast Mack took me for a canoe lesson—two hours steady paddling—up the Clearwater about two miles. I sat in the stern on the return trip. The scenery was magnificent. Did a little sketch in Waterways.

We moved out about 8.30 p.m. Stopped for about three hours off McMurray and at 11.00 pulled into the Athabasca. . . .

July 6.

All morning we steamed down the Athabasca, going from side to side, in order to avoid shoals. New channels are constantly being formed; shoals and islands are very numerous. The clay banks are being continually worn away. Tall spruce and gum-wood trees line the river, and at places the banks are quite high. . . . The river is very murky, so is all water used on the ship. The boilers have to be cleaned every trip. It seems that everyone drinks the river water. It is a wonder that they have all not got goitre. If drinking muddy water will cause goitre every man, woman, child and Indian should have it.[2] There was about one-half inch of mud in the bottom of my wash pitcher this morning. There are millions of "bullfrogs" here at the wood pile but they do not seem to bother anyone.

This wide, curving river with low tree-covered banks is not bad to look at but no good for painting. The sun sets about 10.00 or 11.00 p.m. and rises about 2.00 a.m. here and it never gets very dark. The Northern sky is the same green as I have seen in Norway, Labrador and the Yukon.

This morning we apparently saw the last of the tar sands. They stretch for at least sixty miles. There are only six passengers

[2]McCarrison believes that bacterial infection of water plays a part in causing simple goitre. (McCarrison, *The Simple Goitres*, London, 1928.) The only proven relationship between drinking water and goitre is thus expressed by Boyd: "The soil of high countries is denuded of iodine, so that the drinking water is poor in that element." (*A Text-Book of Pathology, An Introduction to Medicine*, by William Boyd, Lea & Febiger, Philadelphia, 1938.)—L. S.

on this trip—Mrs. G., Montreal, going to visit her son a N.W.M. Police; Inspector M. of the B.C. Provincial Police (has a daughter twelve years old with diabetes); a half-breed boy going home, and we three.

The factors that determine hydro power in the cold north are the depth of the stream and reserve water at a given place. If a river be shallow it freezes to the bottom. At Edmonton the N. Saskatchewan is broad, shallow, with clay banks. Almost any dam would be undermined, making hydro-electric power not feasible. . . .

As we approached Athabasca Lake the river divides into many channels, the land is low and marshy, covered with rank green grass; many wild ducks were swimming about. The Captain told us that it used to abound in muskrats but since the price of the skins went higher they had all been trapped and now there was not one to be seen. Great quantities of ice come down with the spring floods. We saw trees that had been half ground off by the ice, so that one saw a complete cross-section of the lower three or four feet of trunk and the whole root system.

July 7.

About midnight last night we landed at Chipewyan. Alex and I got off the boat at Fraser Dock and walked around the bay through the village and re-embarked at the second call (three or four miles). There is a large three-story R.C. Mission, an R.C. Church, a Protestant Church, H.B. Co. store-house and a number of very good houses—all painted white. The whole bay is rocky, and tree-covered hills encircle the bay. In daytime it would make good sketching, but there was scarcely enough light at 1.00 a.m.

Arose at 6.30 this morning and had a hot bath. The steamer is wooding. We entered the Great Slave River at 8.05. It is muddy, broad, winding, and flows between low banks. The trees are not so tall as at McMurray. The *Northland Echo* with its convoy of buffalo passed us on her way to the buffalo dump about twenty miles south of Fitzgerald.

There are two sick Indians aboard. They have headache, cough, constipation, tightness in chest. It looks like the flu that is in its summer course. Mrs. Bebuque, who has been at Chipewyan while the Judge was north, told me that the Sisters there have to look after great numbers. It is treaty money time and the Indians from far and wide congregate. At the Chipewyan Mission they have about 250 Indian children. The younger ones are taught French, English, singing games. The older ones are taught housework. Last week a little girl of sixteen got married and left the convent to live in a tepee and raise children and die of T.B.

When the Indian gets sick he fears pain, is liable to become despondent. On the last trip of the *Athabasca Lake* an Indian complained of being sick one day; he did not work or speak the next day and jumped off the steamer into the river . . . they could not save him. One can readily understand how when the small-pox epidemic was on they "jumped into the river and drowned." Indian workmen on the steamers here receive $40 per month. They seem to be quite happy and play at their work, but each one is subject to fits of sulkiness. Some seem very slow and stupid, while others are smart and intelligent and work hard. When I was half through asking questions of the Indian patients, which they answered for the most part in grunts, they turned their backs on me and would answer no more.

Mosquitoes and bulldogs are the curse of this country. Landed and said farewells at Fitzgerald about 2.00 p.m. Met Mr. and Mrs. M. . . . She is a full blood squaw, but educated, refined, clean, tidy, fine looking and the best moccasin maker of the north (according to Mack). Met Tom Riley, an old Alliston boy. His family left Alliston 1901. Crossed the portage—seventeen miles—in H.B. Co. Ford. Crossed into North-West Territories just out-side of Fort Smith. The driver took us to Mountain Portage for a view of the rapids. We visited Government House, designed and built by "Lockie" Burwash. . . .

Sailed about 10.00 a.m. on a little tiny turbine pushing three scows, loaded with freight. We unrolled our beds on the foremost scow and tried to go to sleep, but the mosquitoes were too much for us. If we got down into our rolls we melted; if we presented so much as a finger or the tip of our nose it was immediately seized upon by mosquitoes. As the cook says of the variety in the Amazon "they are large, savage and bold. They take a hunk out of one shoulder and light on the other to eat it."

Sunday, July 8.

. . . I told Alex and Mack the Sheldon story. They both think I should write it. Mack has just finished an Indian mystery story of Wanderlust Island. It would be remarkable to find an island on which there was no rain, no storm, no cold, no snow, no heat, but just sunshine; no mosquitoes, no sand flies, no bulldog flies or howling huskies, no snakes.

July 9.

Arrived at Fort Resolution about 6.00 a.m.—had breakfast and went ashore. Unfortunately, Alex and I went down to the swamp to the south of the town and a cloud of mosquitoes enveloped us and did not leave until we had been driven back to the boat. Did a couple of poor drawings. Fort Resolution is the most paintable place yet—Indian tepees, tents, drying racks for fish, old log buildings, whitewashed, various coloured boats drawn up on the shore.

Five people died of the flu yesterday. As we walked past the tents the sound of coughing came from almost everyone. People were just stirring and building their fires in front of their tents to cook breakfast. One young Indian sat by a fire holding a hot towel to his face. He told me he had earache very bad. I wonder if the mosquito carries it? Both pests are universal in the village. It is difficult to know what should be done about the Indian poverty, which is almost universal. They have a wretched life, but cannot seem to rise above it, even if given an opportunity. . . .

[There followed an extended account of a side trip to visit mining claims.]

July 12.

The hottest day I have ever experienced north of Havana (94 degrees in the shade at Resolution), and added to the heat there were mosquitoes in the shade and bulldogs in the sun. There was supposed to be a boat for us at nine, but it did not arrive. . . .

Did a sketch in the p.m. and after supper the motor launch arrived to take us to Resolution. On leaving the hot shore, flies and mosquitoes, we put on our overcoats. It is scarcely conceivable that there could be such a change in temperature in such a few minutes. The lake was quite rough when we got about halfway across. Great Slave Lake is notorious for its sudden squalls. Canoeing is thus very dangerous any distance from shore. Early in the p.m. Alex and I went out about a mile to a shoal to get a sketch of the mainland but it was no good. There was an off-shore wind and it took good stiff paddling to get home. Just after supper—about 8.30 the boat arrived and at 11.00 we arrived at Fort Resolution. We all spent the night at M's (Northland Trading Co.) house—in bed rolls on the floor.

July 13.

The forenoon was spent getting ready for the trip. We also visited the Mission and met Father Manzoa. It is astonishing to see such a fine church and mission in this otherwise purely commercial country. The Roman Catholic Church has certainly done and is doing most creditable work here—teaching and raising orphans, nursing and looking after the sick. The R.C. surpasses all other churches in Indian missions and their good work cannot be too highly praised. The priest, brothers and nuns are all of the finest type and by their example in living, in their dealings and in their teaching exert the highest influence for good among the Indians.

We also visited Dr. B——. He is Doctor, Post Master, Government Agent, etc., in the town. He tells us that there have been sixteen deaths from flu in the past two weeks. All deaths have been among the Indians and mostly among the old people. The usual thing is that they get flu, take no care of themselves, get up and out too soon, get pneumonia and since they have no resistance, die. The Indian is very subject to lung trouble. In the big epidemics of 1918-19 the flu did not extend north past Chipewyan, and this is the first outbreak in this area. It is said also to be very prevalent at Fort Rae and Yellowknife. They had an outbreak of scarlet fever here in 1919, with very heavy casualties. In the height of fever the Indians frequently rolled in the snow. Smallpox has also visited here. I shall have further conversation with Dr. B—— on my return to Resolution.

After lunch we set out for Goulet Island in a little scow fitted up with a thirty-five-horse-power gas engine—Mr. Grier, Gus, Mack, Dawson, Alex and myself. The lake was fairly smooth and it was warm and free from mosquitoes. Arrived at Isle du Goulet about 7.30, supper, did a sketch (finished about 11.00 p.m.)—went to bed.

July 14.

Lake very rough. This Island is pre-cambrian in formation, but though there are beautiful quartz veins there are apparently no minerals. . . .
Did two sketches in the p.m.—still too rough to venture over to the next island.

Sunday, July 15.

Still pretty rough, so we pulled in to a small island—rock, a few blades of grass, cranberries, and four large and two small

Photograph by Maurice Haycock.

ON *THE BOETHIC*, 1927

seagulls. The island is about the size of a public school boys'
baseball diamond—no trees, very little driftwood, which is usually
so plentiful—cold and windy. Pulled out our bed rolls and spread
them in the lee of a rock and crawled in clothes and all (except
boots—it is against my scruples to go to bed with boots on).
After having a bath and washing my underwear early in the day,
I neglected to apply a clean suit, so I stripped by the dying embers
of the supper fire and put on the heaviest I had.

Monday, July 16.

It is still cold, windy and a heavy sea, with overcast sky. Did a
sketch. About 4.00 p.m. it was sufficiently calm to proceed. The
course was almost due north. About one hour, during which time
we had gone about four or five miles, we landed on the north-
westerly of a horseshoe group of islands. Mack was first ashore
and before we had all landed he gave a shout and called us all
to him. We had hit the island of our search. He had found the
iron deposit which he had seen twenty-five years ago. Without
waiting for supper, we all started out and made a survey of the
deposit—going over to the adjacent island—everywhere it seemed
could be found iron ore. Down came a heavy rain—tramping
through the bush and grass with which the intervals between outcrops are covered, we were soaked. About 9.00 we had hot supper, turned in—well satisfied. I did a hasty sketch.

July 17.

Got up early—the morning was spent in mapping, taking
observations, sampling and "staking." Four claims were staked
—MacIntosh, Dawson, Jackson and Banting. The iron is in the
form Fe_2O_3. In places where there are quartz veins the iron has
crystallized with the quartz in the form called speclerite. We got
some very fine specimens of this. The great deposits are in out-
crop of metallic rock in appearance like the freshly broken surface of sheet iron. It has a reddish-brown streak, is fairly soft
and crumbles at the edge. One of the largest outcrops was 353
yards long and about 50 yards at the widest place. We have no
idea of the depth of ore.

At 2.10 p.m.—after lunch—we pulled out, turning north for
the mainland at Gros Cap. The lakes in this area are studded
with islands, some very small, others seven to ten acres in extent.
There are said to be wonderful fish of several varieties—white-
fish, trout and pike. Let us hope that the Government will not
allow them to be fished out. . . .

7.00 p.m.—We are having all the full experiences that Great Slave has to offer. About three hours ago, while leaving an island about half a mile out, suddenly a bump and the scow stopped. We were fast on a rock. The fore part had missed it but the rear stuck firm. All the weight was put in the two canoes or shifted to the fore and with poles the ship was free. The engine, propeller and steering gear were tested and examination for a leak—everything was O.K. The canoes were recalled and the journey resumed. . . .

The water as we approached Gros Cap was much cleaner. It was very cold. There is reported to be ice in the east end of the lake yet. The lake is full of shoals and rocks and before shipping can be established the distance between the top surface and bottom will have to be measured in a few places. Alex has been trolling all afternoon but no luck yet. Before this time the water was too dirty for the fish to see the spoon if they happened to be more than three or four inches away and even at that distance they would scarcely be certain enough to follow. It may be that they are too fat and lazy to pursue the sportive spoon. At any rate, Alex is having rotten luck, but knowing his persistence, some poor fish is certainly going to get caught by head or tail or in some fashion.

Encamped at Gros Cap for the night. The Cap consists of a high level plateau divided by fjords which was very beautiful. After supper Mack, Alex and I went for a walk on the plateau, which is almost perfectly level with not more than two feet of surface soil in any place and mostly smooth flat rock. The soil is covered with moss and irrigated by tiny ditches. We found a number of caribou horns. To the west side of the plateau there are scraggly spruce. The varying coloured moss, interspersed with grey green rock for a foreground and the scraggy trees against the richly coloured sunset sky made a very fine picture, but the effect was too transitory to paint.

July 18.

Sailed early on a calm lake, warm but not hot. Landed at the mouth of Yellowknife Bay for luncheon. Two Indians (Dog Ribs) came to camp. They sat by our campfire spitting promiscuously. They said that twelve of their band had died of flu. About 2.00 p.m. we met the Police boat from Resolution. They were looking for the launch *Fort Rae*, which had been missing eight days. They told us that they had called at the Yellowknife Indian village and that there was not a living soul in the place.

They wanted a rifle to shoot the dogs which were prowling around the village (to save them from starving), as the Indians had abandoned their village and left dogs and everything. (Mr. Grier says he knows of Indians who left their dogs to starve in the spring when moving camp and in the fall pay as much as $100 for this essential animal.) After snowfall the dog is the only means of transport. . . .

Mr. Dawson says that the death of the Indians is a big loss to the fur trader, because they always owe the trader for a year's supply. They are always a year behind. Sometimes they owe as much as $400.

About 6.00 p.m. we ascended a narrow portion of Yellow-knife Bay and entered the river—beautiful scenery. About two miles up the river we landed at the portage. Taking all our belongings we crossed amid terrific clouds of mosquitoes, the weather being hot and sultry. Arriving at the other end of portage we crossed the lake to the camp. . . .

Alex and I went trolling and Alex got a two-foot pike to within a foot of the canoe, but it got away. We landed and Alex made a sketch while I watched him. Very windy all night, the lake quite rough.

July 19.

For the past five or six days I have been having a lot of hyper-acidity, likely due to the fat bacon and once boiled beans. My nose is still stiff and sore from sunburn, behind my ears is nearly raw from mosquito bites—but I can walk twenty-five miles, paddle or carry a pack—apart from these minor ailments I feel fine.

July 20.

Alex and I had a day's sketching. He did two good ones and I did three of a sort. We paddled to the portage landing and walked to the river; getting the large canoe from the scow we paddled down the Yellowknife about two or three miles. . . . Got home to camp about 6.30—after supper Alex and I went out to sketch, but as the smoke of a large bush fire (which had been burning about three weeks) fogged the sunlight, Alex trolled while I paddled. We got three large deep-water pike.

These bush fires not only destroy the forests, which are of but little value here, but they destroy the game and fur—both of which are becoming more scarce.

There are loons on this lake and for three nights now they

have been whistling, screaming, crying and howling. It is good they cannot bark, but they do well at imitating the stray Indian dog which prowls about camp stealing anything he can get.

Tonight I feel tired after paddling about twelve or thirteen miles, walking the portage, climbing the rocky hills and doing three sketches. . . .

Sunday, July 22.

. . . While passing through a group of islands we came upon an Indian encampment. Tents scattered among the islands, fish-nets stretched here and there—dozens of dogs and ragged children; sober, coughing, slow, slovenly looking Indian men came down to the rock when we pulled in to inquire the way. Alex remarked how different they were from the smiling, active Eskimos. The Indians strolled down casually, one by one, and only the men and a few boys came, whereas under similar circumstances, every Eskimo would be down waiting with a smile and greeting.

Monday morning, July 23.

. . . Had a fine run, passed Gros Cap, but though we would have liked to sketch it was too fair and fine so they slowed down for fifteen minutes. The sea became quite rough as we approached Wilson Island and it was necessary to put into a small island which consisted of a peculiar conglomerate rock. Had supper, camped. When nicely asleep at 12.00 midnight, Dawson roused the camp with word that the wind was down and the sea calm. He had coffee ready and we started out about 1.00 a.m.

July 24.

It was cold but the sea was becoming more calm. . . . Words cannot describe the sensations, impressions and mental exuberance of such an experience. The beauty of the sky with its purple, blue, yellow and red and its continued play of colour as the afterglow gave place to sunrise. At one time there was a grey cloud to the north that looked like a fruit basket full of luscious fruit of all kinds and then as if to suggest the next course it changed to resemble a frying pan over a grill with steam rising from it. This same cloud then flattened across the sky and sil-houetted elephants, trees, dogs, houses, horses, tents and almost any shape one could think of. One lone star—the much storied star of the east—seemed to invite a play of fancy in astrology, and wonderment into what really guides the destiny of man. Astronomers of old had used this same star to clothe their secret desires in the guiding of kings and warriors; philosophers and alchemists had plied their trade in the grey dawn when this star is queen. . . .

5.00 a.m.—Breakfast at Stoney Island. Two fresh graves mark the spot where two new victims of the flu forever rest.

Reached Resolution about 11.00 a.m.—visited the Hudson Bay post. . . . [We heard] about a priest who was at Resolution when Mack was here twenty years ago. This priest was very fond of liquor, so as it is difficult to obtain it in a quantity sufficient for daily consumption, he provided himself with a small still. With this apparatus, he was able to obtain at times even an excess to which he helped himself. Complaints of his demeanour reached the Bishop, who came and demanded that the still and all the liquor be thrown into the lake. The Bishop and many of the natives watched the priest paddle out to deep water—three hundred yards—and saw the real invention of the devil splash into and be swallowed up by the sea. They did not see a second splash, however, as a stick of wood on a rope followed the still. After the Bishop had gone the priest was seen searching for his float and finally re-loading his precious still into the canoe.

[We were told] that the Indians of the Mackenzie valley were becoming very degenerate. They had lost the art of making their own toboggans, snowshoes, sleds, clothing or canoes, dugouts, arrows (except moccasins). They did not store food but depended for their subsistence on the supplies of the companies. These tribes are inherently savage and cruel. They were at first more friendly to the white man because they did not think that there were so many whites in the world, but now they realize that they are a failing race and that they are rapidly going down before advancing civilization. Their own art and mode of life has gone and civilization has brought insidious subordination. Their natural laziness has increased, since they feel there is no use trying to rise with the tide of new ideas and new things. Their daughters mix with the white and their race is no longer pure. Game and fur is very, very rapidly disappearing. Fish are scarce in this lake and hence they have to work for dog-feed. White-man epidemics are periodically introduced and each takes a terrible toll of human life. The deaths from flu at Resolution have now amounted to twenty-four—all Indians. . . .

July 25.

. . . Alex and I were put up at Mr. M——'s. Sketched all day—did one good one and two indifferent sketches. We had breakfast and supper here and luncheon at the city restaurant. (My hyperacidity has been a constant source of annoyance for the past two weeks. Soda about three hours after meals keeps me all right, but I hate taking so much of it). . . .

July 26.

Smith, engineer of the *Speed,* just in from the Hay River, says that there have been twelve deaths from flu there and it is one of the smallest settlements on the river. Godsell said yesterday—on being asked how the flu came in—that one of their men brought it to Smith and gave it to the helpers on the *Distributor*—these Hudson Bay boats are big flat-bottomed, rear-paddle-wheeled steamboats that burn wood. They take about ten Indians to carry on the wood from the wood piles which they have scattered along the river banks. These Indians got it and distributed it the full length of the trip. On the return journey there were places where whole communities were down with the disease and not a soul about to meet the boat or do anything.

July 27.

Alex and I sketched all day. We have noonday meal at the restaurant and get breakfast and supper here at M——'s. . . .

. . . The other evening he told us some of the inner workings of the post—for example, mink from the south were selling at 10-15, while local mink were selling at 20-25. They import and mix them in with fur from here. October rats were selling at $1.00 and March rats at $2.00. They hold them over—a summer-killed mink is only worth a dollar or so. The skin under the fur is black while winter-killed mink have white skin. They soap the skin then try to pass it off. Arctic hare is almost like white fox—they sew tails, clips the ears and crop the whiskers of the hare and try to pass them.

A Mr. MacFarlane,[3] a trapper from Rocky River, says that the country there is rocky, water is blue, not muddy, river rapid with numerous falls, fish abundant. He says the Indians are not honest and that they steal—e.g., he put up 2,500 dried fish for dog-feed and while he and his partner were away to the post the Indians stole them. The Government has given the Indian game reserves where white men cannot go, but where only Indians can trap. The Indian does not trap in his own reserve but sets his trap lines in among the white trappers and no doubt watches both traps when possible. The white trapper is thus handicapped

[3]Not the same trapper who is elsewhere referred to as Mr. M——.—L. S.

both in regard to territory and neighbours. If he decides to make a permanent camp and especially if he makes any improvements the Indians come and camp around him.

As to morals, the Indians here are not too strict. They do not in any way look down on illegitimate children or girls who have them. They usually arrange a marriage after pregnancy is established, but not always. Grace Norn, a famous character of this town, has never been married but has two daughters and a son (there were eleven people living in a house twelve by sixteen feet —Grace's father and mother, her brother, her son and his wife, herself, her two daughters and their one baby). One of her daughters is almost white and would pass well on Broadway or Piccadilly. The other is decidedly Indian; this latter lived with a Negro two years but he left her and she had a baby that died. Recently she had another baby by an Indian chap here. . . .

Mr. M—— told of his intention of establishing an outpost up the Hay River a few years ago and some Indians were very anxious that he go himself and live among them. As an inducement the Indian said he had three daughters and he could have his pick for a housekeeper. The Indian girls either go to convent and get educated until they are about fourteen or fifteen or they stay home. It does not seem to matter in either case as they are right after a man at the age of sixteen years. If they are not married they are sneaking out at night and the boy will wait (even at thirty below zero) till they come out. It does not take them long.

There are in all four traders at Resolution. . . . M—— has them all going, if I am any judge. They continually try to put something over on the other fellow—for example—Mr. D—— at Hay River always kept his "Permit" until Christmas—he then sent a couple of bottles to another trader as a present whereupon the latter got drunk for three or four days and D—— remaining sober got the pick of all the fur.

M——follows fur prices on the 'Peg market and he found last April that muskrat skins had dropped to $1.50. Now there were about 5,000 skins up the Slave River. A trader up the river came to the post here for two or three days. Very casually M—— expressed the view that rats would be very high this year and said that since the trader was in from the river he thought that he would go up that night and buy them all in at $5.00 per. M—— knew that this fellow swore that he would not tell [his employers] and that he would run home and tell. Sure enough, the river trader's visit was cut short, he returned to the river that night and furiously bought in the 5,000 skins at $5.00 each or $3.50 above the outside price.

From the scarcity of game and life in the surrounding country, I should judge that it would be very difficult to live off the country —berries and fish are plentiful in most places, however. Mac-Farlane says that the Indians shoot the caribou whether they want them or not. He says that he has seen twenty or thirty dead caribou untouched. They shoot until ammunition runs out, just for the sake of killing. . . .

July 31.

. . . Alex and I went over and called on Dr. B—— and while there had a talk about the present state of the neighbouring Indians. The people of the Slave River are about the lowest in culture and intellect of any tribe of Canada. It is questionable whether or not the Government is doing the best thing in giving them so much. The poor old red-man is doomed. Even here, where civilization has scarcely permeated, they cannot stand up under the strain. They have little pride these slaves; if a Cree is given a calling down his dignity is wounded, he is nevermore a friend; if a slave is called down they respect the speaker all the more.

Epidemics play havoc with them but T.B. is the constant reaper. In the recent flu epidemic Dr. B—— visited a number of families in their homes. "Some of their stews were not fit for a dog," he says, and further, "The Indian can digest anything"; "If it were not for his lungs he would live forever." Infant mortality is high. They have large families or rather large numbers of children, nine or ten being common. Of these, two or three gain adult life. The mothers nurse the children two or three years—possibly because they think they will not become pregnant again as long as they nurse the child. Dr. B——has seen a child nursing at its mother's breast one minute and smoking a pipe the next. One old squaw was keeping herself a physical wreck by long nursing of her family and applied to the doctor for help as her husband was out of work and the doctor told her "now is your chance to nurse him too." They are fond of smoking—women and children all smoke if they can get tobacco. Even a two-year-old child can smoke a cigarette.

Despite the fact that they live near or on the water nearly all the time, they are very dirty. They are afraid to get wet lest they take cold. Three months after a diphtheria epidemic an old lady came to ask the doctor if it was safe to wash her hands yet. Few of them can swim. Their clothes, too, are sometimes very dirty, but I notice washings out on the line. They tell me they are white men's clothes—some of them. They often buy a new dress and put it on over the old one—finally the old one rots and drops off. However, running is their long suit. They can be around all summer and without preliminary training lead a dog team over the snow for long distances. Summer heat causes them extreme lassitude and laziness, but they stand the winter cold remarkably well. Without fuss or warm clothes they will run before the dogs all day and with a single blanket roll up for the cold night possibly with their feet sticking out.

They still stick to some of the old superstitions. There is yet a smooth rock at Yellowknife covered with knives, pipes and every kind of stuff—enough to start a store—these are gifts to the gods for luck on the hunt. There are certain superstitions that are decidedly man-made, for the women are out of luck—for example, certain fine parts of the moose—nose, tongue and heart—cannot be touched or eaten by a woman without bringing very bad luck. A house where a husband dies is often deserted by the family as they never like to touch the dead or anything that has belonged to him. They are equally superstitious about the mysteries pertaining to the origin of life. A woman when menstruating is unclean, and they have special holes beside the fireplace for them to hide in during this period, or if they are travelling by water she is not allowed in the canoe but must sit on a pole between two canoes, with her feet in the water; or, if travelling in winter, she must not walk on the beaten trail but make a trail of her own. She must never give birth to a child in the dwelling-house. She must either build a separate tepee or go into the bush. Labour is a much less difficult procedure than with white women; they frequently have no assistance whatever.

When the Mission here opened the Indians were all badly scared. Several times when the sermon was going on, one of them would hear some noise and give the alarm and all would run from the church. For years they all seemed to be afraid of an unknown enemy. During this epidemic a white man went to Yellowknife to feed the Indians and their dogs. He delivered 250-300 fish per day and did a great deal to keep humans and dogs alive— without him likely all would have died. Unfortunately, one day he took a dead Indian in his canoe to burial and the people, sick and helpless as they were, objected to eating fish that were brought in from the nets in the same canoe.

Bobby says the Indians are always trying to put something over. They want an article that costs $5.00 when all the money they have is only $4.50. If once they get an article for $4.50 they think they should always get it for the same. I have been keeping the odd eye on an Indian boy who is supposed to be digging out a cellar under the house. He has a couple of little kids to play with —I could do as much in half an hour as he does in a day, but he gets his fifty cents per hour.

The Indians here are terrible gamblers—particularly at Christmas, in the spring when they come to sell their winter catch, treaty time and, in fact, whenever they come together. They gamble large sums if they have not small sums to use—dollar bills, beaver, white fox, muskrat, rifle, canoe, tepee, and finally clothing goes into the pot. A hunter may come to the post with two or three thousand dollars' worth of fur and he usually sets aside a portion with his wife to pay his debts. One man started a game with eight hundred rat skins; he lost all these, then he lost his $75.00 rifle, his dog team, six dogs ($600), two canoes, his tepee, blankets, stove; in the morning he had only his wife, whom he would have gambled too. One of his winners gave him a small canoe in which he went away. In due course, he came back with eighteen beaver and lost them also.

They draw wonderful hands. A white man (who is forbidden by law to gamble with the Indian) would lose everything in a game with them. They do not know how to shuffle the cards but turn them over and over, with the result that the high cards get together. A pair is discarded and four are drawn in the hope of getting the four of a kind or a run.

M—— has his sailboat fitted up and took us for a sail. He certainly knows how to run a sailboat. C——, one of M——'s traders from Hay River, came in for a few days. He has not been out for fifteen years, and though only thirty-six or thirty-seven years old, is quite an old-timer. He is an excellent hunter, expert trader, has unbounded love and admiration for M——. He told many instances that illustrate Indian character—for example, he went shooting with an Indian and his two sons. He shot seven deer and for the help of getting them in he gave the Indian and each son a deer. A few weeks after, the Indian brought him a quarter of moose and threw it down in the store and next day demanded $5.00 for it. On another occasion a young Indian having left his rifle at his

winter hunting ground, borrowed rifle and ammunition from
C——. He returned with a couple of moose. C—— asked for a roast
of fresh meat and the Indian wanted pay, but C—— refused.

The Police have been busy putting out fires recently. Yesterday an Indian came in with two moose from an island off the
south-east coast and today three white men had to go with engines
and put out the fire he started. A large fire is raging around
Little Buffalo River and another west of the Yellowknife. Some
say that Indians purposely start them, for they believe there will
be moose there next year after the fire. Others say that the
Indians set fire or are at least careless because of their secret hatred
for the white man.

Before leaving Resolution, a word of the village. Most of the
houses are made of logs, some of them whitewashed and others
plastered with grey, yellow mud. There are only two modern
houses in town—the Doctor's and M——'s—and neither of these fit
into the scheme of things. There is one blue house; drying
scaffolds for fish, piles of drift-wood, upturned canoes and boats
of all descriptions make a jumble of the water-front. The first
time we passed through Resolution there were dozens of tepees,
but owing to the flu epidemic the Indians nearly all left. There
were only two tepees that could be used in sketching, and one of
these was placed in an impossible position. The whole population drink the lake water, which is so muddy that a layer two
inches thick is opaque. Typhoid germs would have a wonderful
time if ever introduced here.

August 1.

Mack and Dawson finally landed from the claims. The aeroplane landed for a fill of gas and took off for Fort Simpson.
Evelyn of the Lake left for Smith; the *Aphrodyte* left for Hay
River and the *Speed 11* left for Smith. This rapidity of action
must have left Resolution paralyzed. . . . Twenty-eight hours
brought us to Fort Smith. Several fires were burning on the
banks of the Slave.

August 2.

. . . The bootlegger is a gentleman compared with most of
the traders—at least they sell to people who know what and from
whom they are buying. The poor Indian or Huskie cannot
count. He brings in a number of different kinds of skins and
puts them on the counter. He watches the trader value them.
They come to, say, $2,000. The Indian then buys a blanket and

spreads it out; he then buys a box of tobacco, sack of flour, some ammunition, etc. When he has named a number of things he asks how much that comes to. It comes to, say, $200. He then buys a rifle, ammunition and a tepee. They are added up and amount to, say, $200. By this time the Indian is lost in figures—he should have $1,600 left, but he may be told that he has $800 or $1,000. He makes a few more small purchases and his fur is all spent. Thus the dishonest trader with a knowledge of mathematics puts it over the hard-working, trusting native. As education advances this procedure becomes impossible. The Indian takes his skins one or two at a time, or he calculates their value and knows what he should get for them. . . .

Did a sketch at Chipewyan.   *August* 6.

Arrived at Waterways.   *August* 8.

                                                    August 9.
Did two sketches and bought four bear-skins at McMurray.

                                                    August 10.
Arrived at Edmonton—Mr. Collins, Assistant General Manager of Alberta Railways, gave us the hospitality of his private car.

PART XII

"The Biggest Experiment"

Scientific truth is the remotest of mistresses; she hides in strange places, she is attained by tortuous and laborious roads, but *she is always there!* Win to her and she will not fail you; she is yours and mankind's for ever. . . . You cannot change her by advertisement or clamour, nor stifle her in vulgarities. Things grow under your hands when you serve her, things that are permanent as nothing else is permanent in the whole life of man. That, I think, is the peculiar satisfaction of science and its enduring reward.

H. G. WELLS.

1

BANTING commenced his scientific work in Toronto in the Department of Physiology under Professor Macleod. In 1921-1922 he was Lecturer in the Department of Pharmacology under the late Professor Henderson. In October, 1922, he was joined by Miss Gairns; a "lab. boy" made the third of a trio for whom a one-room laboratory was hardly sufficient space. Headquarters were soon transferred to the Pathology Building (now the Dunlap Building) on University Avenue, but although three rooms were now available overcrowding was still a problem, since the number of workers under Banting's direction had been tripled in the meantime. One room was a combined office and laboratory in which Banting and Miss Gairns did their work; one was an animal room and workshop; the single room remaining was set aside for the two Fellows, Dr. William Brebner and Dr. A. W. White, and later provided a working place for G. W. Ross, Gordon Cameron, E. J. King, W. R. Franks and G. E. Hall. Needless to say the whole group never worked simultaneously; several of them, in any case, were engaged in research only for part time, and several were away at intervals for post-graduate work of varying duration. Nevertheless, three rooms were not enough.

Banting was appointed Professor of Medical Research in 1923 and this was his Department. A meagre "set-up." But other Departments of the Medical Faculty were also ready to expand. The Banting Institute became inevitable. It was planned and erected to house the Departments of Pathology and Pathological Chemistry and Bacteriology, all the clinical laboratories and the Department of Medical Research.

The money came from various sources, listed at the time of the formal opening by the then Chairman of the Board of Governors, the Hon. and Rev. H. J. Cody:

The Provincial Government purchased from the University for a very generous sum properties at the entrance to the Park. The University made that contribution to the general medical effort. The Provincial Government, in addition, fulfilled its promise to give $200,000 to the clinical laboratories and $100,000 for the Banting Research laboratories. So that we had available a sum of $800,000 towards the purchase of the houses on our grounds and the erection of the building. When tenders came in we found that the total cost would be about $935,000. We had $800,000 available. We took $100,000 from a series of accumulated balances, with full knowledge and consent, I may say, of the Government, and we spread the additional $35,000 over a period of three years in our general University budget. In that way we have covered the cost of ground and buildings.[1]

Work was begun on November 21, 1928, and a six-story Georgian building was erected, made of reinforced steel and concrete, the exterior of red brick with stone trim. On September 16, 1930, it was formally opened, in the presence of representatives from thirty British, American and Canadian Universities, by Lord Moynihan of Leeds, President of the Royal College of Surgeons.

Said Lord Moynihan:

The inauguration of the Banting Institute of the University of Toronto is for me one of the happiest duties of my whole life. This is a moment of high romance in a "Land of dreams come true." Dr. F. G. Banting reading for the Primary Examination for the Fellowship of my College and still keeping his mind on problems of General Medicine became possessed of the idea of extracting the hidden virtues of the Islands of Langerhans, and of using them in the treatment of Diabetes. As will so often happen with the dreamer of dreams he surrendered every other object to this quest. He came to Toronto, was allowed the use of the physiological laboratories, was helped by an assistant, Best, whose name is forever linked with his own. The result of his labours, announced ten years ago, is now the common possession and the equal pride of the Nations of the World.

> One man with a dream, at pleasure,
> Shall go forth and conquer a crown.

Banting has conquered, and today, as a gift from all mankind, he wears with so becoming humility, the crown of immortality. In his honour we raise today this temple of science.

Memorials are of many kinds. Some are graven in stone, some are cast in bronze, some are written in letters of gold upon the roll

[1]"A Record of Proceedings at the opening of the Banting Institute, University of Toronto, 1930," University of Toronto Press, 1931.

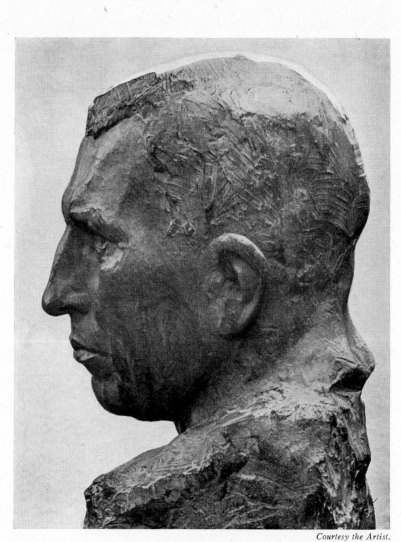

HEROIC HEAD
BY FRANCES LORING, A.R.C.A.

of honour which enshrines the names of the saviours of their Country. There is yet another memorial, born in the hearts of those from whom a heavy load of suffering and of sorrow has been lifted, and dedicated by them as an act of homage to a great deliverer. Take the journey of Autolycus and gaze down into the multitude of homes in which live the men and women and children of every nation, of every race, of every creed, from whom the cold hand of death has been turned aside by the skill of him whose services to humanity we commemorate today. Consider, too, that this is not the work of a moment nor even of one age but that it will continue forever. In the grateful hearts of those rescued from death and of those who spend their lives in the sacred ministry of healing the true memorial to Banting will be found. Is not his indeed a crown of immortality?[2]

Said Mrs. O'Neil, when she had read the newspaper accounts of the glittering ceremony: "I am proud to know the young man the Banting Institute is named for."

To which Banting returned a prompt and felicitous reply. "My father's name," he said, "would grace any building."

In spite of his monumental silences, the newspapermen, at the time of the opening of the Institute, regarded him with an affection that made itself evident in their stories. There was a heart-warming atmosphere, a more or less protective and humorous relationship. It stripped the affair of anything bordering on the pompous. One man described the chief figure in the ceremony as looking "like a small boy who has been caught stealing jam." Another told his story in the form of a dream. How he had gone to Olympus to interview the gods and what they had said to him. Eventually he came upon a bearded old man, bending over a retort. He asked him how he liked Olympus. The old man smiled—silently.

"Dr. Banting all right," concluded the reporter.

But there was a real life drama behind the scenes. Several days before the official opening, Banting began to suffer from abdominal pain. Dr. G. W. Ross, happening to drop in at his office, heard his complaint and examined him at once. Diagnosis: acute appendicitis.

[2]*Ibid.* Lord Moynihan's brilliant address was entitled, "The Science of Medicine."

Here was a pretty state of things! The formal opening only a few days off, Lord Moynihan journeying across the ocean for the ceremony, and the principal figure in the whole show developing an acute abdomen! What should he do? Be admitted to hospital, undergo an operation and accept his honours *in absentia?* Knowing how small was his liking for ceremony, we may safely assume that this side of the question did not greatly trouble him. But it was to be a great day for the University, for the Department. And Lord Moynihan was coming so far! Banting's absence would dampen every spirit. He *had* to be there.

It was decided that it would be safe to defer operation. Luckily the attack passed off. He felt better. But on the gala day he again experienced twinges of pain. He walked about gingerly, wondering what that appendix looked like, and his bemused manner, on which the reporters commented, may have been more appendiceal than Olympian.

Again the symptoms subsided. There was no second severe attack but about a week later he was admitted to the Toronto General Hospital and Dr. D. E. Robertson relieved him of his appendix. Banting and the Institute, said a hospital wit, were opened together.

While he was convalescing, his friend, A. Y. Jackson, returned from a second trip to the Arctic. Banting at once suggested that he should accompany Jackson on a sketching trip by way of recuperation. Dr. Ross offered them the use of his cottage at the mouth of the French River and they left Toronto on October 12, remaining away until the twenty-ninth. It was their seventh sketching trip together.

The Institute was a building which had cost nearly a million dollars and which contained $90,000 worth of equipment. The possibilities seemed limitless.

The Department of Medical Research occupied a part of the fifth floor and at first there was ample space. Later it expanded until it took in almost the entire floor. Eventually it began once more to be cramped. But how spacious and luxurious it seemed after the three-room quarters in the Pathology Building!

It was a far cry from his beginning. "The one thing I dread," he remarked to a friend, "is affluence. I have a lovely office now, with pictures on the wall and a swivel chair, and I can't do anything." [3]

Did he mean that he had run out of ideas? According to the testimony of his colleagues he was never short of ideas, but one of them offers the opinion that his best work, scientifically, was done in the Pathology Building. He himself confessed to the ironical sensation that once he had all the equipment and all the assistance he could use he felt suddenly arid, suddenly a little bit lost. This was a passing phase. But the nature of his duties was changing; he was weaned away from the laboratory bench by the requirements of desk work and the complaint that he could not do anything was often reiterated in this sense.

There was another factor, too. Why had he given up the work on insulin? Largely because he felt that further advance must be biochemical in nature and he lacked the training to undertake it. There were other instances. He once conceived the brilliant idea that a good way to investigate the possibilities of the synthesis of proteins would be to study the sequence of chemical events in the oviduct, where protein is being manufactured. He made a beginning at the problem, using gross methods inadequate for the purpose; then he realized that he was out of his depth and laid the work aside. Microchemical techniques would be necessary. He procured the equipment and turned over the job to others. But we can hardly doubt that somewhere deep in his mind a seed of frustration was sown.

What effect had all the public and academic commotion on his future prospects and career?

He had shown early in life, says Sir Henry Dale,[4]

... what he could do by natural insight in alliance with an iron determination and without any normal apprenticeship in research. The best reward, from his point of view, would probably have been an opportunity to make good such defects of equipment by some years of quiet and disciplined study in the world's most productive centres of research, and then to return to researches chosen for himself in the light of the wider experience.

[3]"Marble desks, cushioned chairs, suites of rooms, in buildings of fine architecture are not the essentials of research. I sometimes think they detract from its true spirit, Pasteur and Bernard worked in a cellar. . . ."—Banting, The Alpha Omega Alpha Address, Ann Arbour, 1925.

[4]*British Medical Journal*, I: 383-384, March 8, 1941.

Conditions, in any case, conspired to make such an arrangement difficult, or impossible. No other medical discovery in living memory has so caught the public interest as the discovery of insulin; and Banting, in particular, soon found himself, to his embarrassment, a mark for popular enthusiasm and excited expectation, in Canada first, and later in the world at large. Money was freely forthcoming, and it would have been difficult for those in authority to avoid founding a Banting Institute for Medical Research, with a Research Chair for himself as its director, or for Banting to refuse such a flattering opportunity.[5] The whole atmosphere of haste and exaltation, however, could not fail to be detrimental. In spite of all pleas for patience and caution from those who were soberly concerned for Banting's future and for his further value to medical research, he had become a public figure; everything concerning him was "news," and the world at large had been taught what to expect. Every few months a new rumour was set afloat in the popular press, attributing some fresh discovery to Banting. . . . His comings and goings were chronicled like those of any film-star.

Even a research worker of long experience and established repute would have found himself inhibited by such an atmosphere. When half the world is agape for a miracle it takes unusual courage to offer it the results of some sound and necessary but unexciting piece of spadework. The matter for surprise is, not that Banting should have seemed for a time to be somewhat embarrassed but that he should, in the end, have been so little deflected from the proper use of the opportunity which had been given to him. For a few years, indeed, he seemed to feel a constraint towards problems of the kind which popular rumour expected him to solve. Before long, however, he had settled down to a good and varied programme of important but relatively long-range researches, gathering round him a group of collaborators whose training could supplement at different points what was lacking in his own. There was no further discovery like that of insulin, but he and his group did work of substantial and permanent value. . . .

These observations are profound, but some of them at least are not entirely closed to question. Was Banting best suited to

[5]The Banting Institute, as already indicated, was by no means devoted entirely to medical research; it housed several Departments, of which Banting's was one. He was not appointed "Director" of the Institute nor even of the Department. He was Professor of Medical Research.—L. S.

be a research worker himself or had he a greater talent for "drawing out" younger scientists?

Banting had a good deal to say about medical research. The pre-eminent position and great prestige which resulted from his personal triumph and from his vast experience in directing and advising others entitled him to a most attentive hearing. His views on the subject may be encountered *passim* in many of the lectures on insulin as well as in the papers specifically devoted to the theme.

The earliest of these was delivered on Thursday, March 6, 1924, at the dedicatory exercises of a new group of medical and research buildings of the Department of Public Welfare of the State of Illinois and the University of Illinois, in Chicago. Banting's address was printed in *The Institution Quarterly,* official organ of the Public Welfare Service of Illinois, and reappeared, with slight alterations, in the May issue of *Hygeia.* Its author apparently shared with Claude Bernard and other famous experimenters a distaste for the labour of composition, since on several later occasions, when pressed for an address or an article, he was to resurrect the paragraphs which had served him in Chicago, trim them up with a little fresh material and use them again.

But as the years passed and his experience grew, his ideas crystallized. Although fresh conceptions are seldom introduced in the later speeches, the exposition of the old ones is more spirited and explicit. In the twenties, except when using historical examples or when talking about insulin, he generalized, sometimes rather prosily; in the thirties his masterly narratives of particular research projects enabled him to develop his points more cogently. The speech delivered in Boston on September 26, 1939, at the one-hundred-twenty-seventh annual meeting of the Supreme Council 33°, Scottish Rite Masons, in which he discussed the work on dementia præcox subsidized by that fraternity, is probably the finest example of this illustrative method. It contains his mature reflections on the work of a lifetime. It is the final expression of his creed and his last major effort in public speech.

There are several reasons for the progressive improvement. Obviously his experience both in the laboratory and on the platform had taught him much. But to one reader at least there would appear to be another factor of almost equal importance.

When discussing the work of other members of his group ("I am merely their emissary," he declared in Boston) he was able to let himself go with greater enthusiasm and greater ease than when discussing his own. If he lost something in immediate knowledge and personal appeal this was compensated by lessening of constraint. It should also be frankly admitted that he occasionally sought assistance from others in preparing these lectures, but to those who knew him and to those acquainted with the early speeches, it is a familiar voice which speaks.

General Observations on Research

"At this moment it is revealed to us that medicine has come to a new birth," wrote Sir Clifford Allbutt in 1919, describing this new birth as "nothing more nor less than the enlargement from an art of observation and empiricism to an applied science founded upon research."

Beginning his Chicago address with this quotation Banting went on to say:

Through all time the men in medicine who have stood above the ordinary have been those men, who, with minds of high order, starting from the proved facts of science, extended the domain of knowledge into the unknown, through patient, discriminating and skilful pursuit of research. . . .

He then reviewed some of the highlights of medical history, stressing the continuity of the quest for knowledge.

The physician and patient of today accept this accumulation of knowledge without question, but we must remember with Sir Michael Foster: "What we are is in part only of our making; the greater part of ourselves has come down to us from the past. What we know and what we think is not a fountain gushing forth from the barren rock of the unknown at the stroke of the rod of our intellect; it is a stream that flows by us and through us, fed by the far-off rivulets of long ago. What we think and say today will mingle with and shape the thoughts of men in the years to come, so, in the opinion and view that we are proud to hold today, we may, by looking back, trace the influence of those who have gone before."

Research (said Banting) is built on research. Roux was led to his investigation of diphtheria antitoxin by the work of Pasteur.

Von Behring, following researches of Roux and Yersin, produced the first diphtheria antitoxin. Roux applied the antitoxin treatment and not only decreased mortality from this disease by seventy-five per cent., but also by a study of its infectivity abolished the ravaging epidemics previously so common.

In another speech, delivered before a meeting of the Canadian Medical Association at Victoria in June, 1926, he added the following remarks:

A few generations ago epidemics of diphtheria were common and considered almost inevitable. One of the treatments frequently used consisted in placing a thick slice of fat pork sprinkled with cayenne pepper on the throat. As a child I remember a small cemetery, long since disused, on the outskirts of my home town. This cemetery was the result of an epidemic of diphtheria. Previous to this epidemic there had been no need of a cemetery but the large number of deaths in a short space of time necessitated hasty burial.

Medical research (he said in another place) is the most truly international commodity we possess. It knows no protective tariff, no embargo, no boundary line to prevent its free dissemination for the good of all. At present it is the common language and common spirit among the nations.

A true knowledge of God's creation (he declared) dispels superstition, fear and disease . . . and leads to that humility with which the informed intelligence recognizes the omnipotence of the Creator.

THE RESEARCH WORKER

A lecture[6] devoted to this theme was delivered by Banting at the sixty-seventh convocation of the University of the State of New York, at Albany, N.Y., on October 15, 1931:

Research men are born, not made. The research man is fundamentally inquisitive—not about things that everybody knows, but about things which nobody knows. The child starts out in life with an inquisitive mind but the average child is satisfied and contented by the answer given by an adult. The child soon loses that inquisitive quality if he is suppressed. As a child grows older

[6]Frederick G. Banting, M.D., "Medical Research," *New York State Journal of Medicine*, March 15, 1932.

it is not always in his best interests to answer his questions, but he should be encouraged to answer them himself as far as possible. In 1923 I visited the City of Washington and had the pleasure of meeting an eminent physician of that city. He told me that every Saturday morning he took his two boys, of six and eight years, for a walk. On one occasion the two boys plied their Daddy with questions until he became displeased and told them that they must think before asking. When they arrived at the zoo they went to see the lions and after some time the older boy asked, "Which is the daddy lion?" His father told him that it was the one with the mane. On thinking it over the child said, "I don't think you are quite right about that, Daddy, Mother's hair is longer than yours." I would like to follow the career of that child, for he has the making of a research man. His answer also involved a fundamental principle in Research—the challenge of authority. He did not accept without due consideration the explanation given to him.

In an address delivered at Ann Arbor in January, 1925, and quoted in an earlier chapter, he said of the research worker:

He must have initiative for though he may at times have to obey authority, if he is to be a success he must, if necessary, depart from tradition and follow his own scheme of campaign. . . . Some men think too little and work too much.

There is no doubt (the Albany speech resumes) that many children who have natural research minds lose the gift by improper training or lack of cultivation. Our modern school system with the large number of children placed under the care of one teacher, and the standardized course of training does not permit of encouraging originality, but great care should be taken not to suppress it.[7] . . .

Research workers must have imaginative minds and natural powers of observation. The essential qualities to be looked for in a Research man are honesty, common sense, balanced enthusiasm, self-confidence, tenacity, system and method in keeping notes and in planning and carrying out experiments, and unreserved devotion to the problem in hand. If a man is not honest he may deceive himself and be led to draw conclusions from false results which will not stand repetition by other workers. If a man lacks

[7]Compare the paragraph of similar import by Madama Curie, quoted in the first chapter.

common sense he is liable to be easily side-tracked, and is led to do foolish things in the name of Research. If a man does not possess enthusiasm, he very soon becomes lazy and gambles away his time, but if he becomes over-enthusiastic, he may become carried away and arrive at conclusions too hastily. If he lacks self-confidence, he can never convince himself or others of the value of his work. The young worker must not become discouraged even if the trend of experiment goes against theory. If he has not the tenacity to continue he will often miss out and, because of incompleteness, his work will fail. The Research man who lacks method and system is like a ship without a rudder. The young worker who has not an unreserved devotion for his work is not likely to succeed. . . .

A man's worth in Research should not depend on his personality but it does become a very important factor, because co-operation with other workers is essential in most research problems. The young worker who is adaptable has a great deal in his favour for he will get more assistance from other workers and they in turn will come to him for advice.

How pertinent to his own experience! Was the young worker of 1922 as adaptable to work with others as this ideal young worker he postulates? Certainly the Banting who delivered this address had come a long way from the Banting who discovered insulin; he had become an easily approachable and very sympathetic department chief who not only worked well with others, but had the happy faculty of making others work well together. The additional attributes here specified for the research man were also to be found in the speaker, for "when a tinker talks of tinkers he really talks of himself." This picture of the research man is a half-conscious self-portrait.

Elsewhere he stressed the importance of "a facility in the constructive association of ideas," and he regarded this ability to "bridge spark gaps" with a sudden discharge of mental energy as the peculiar and characteristic talent of the born research man. His tribute to the significance of the initial idea as the starting point of all research will be remembered from an earlier page. It was not to be considered, however, as the be-all and the end-all. A pithy sentence from the Boston address sets forth his ultimate view. "It is better to gamble five thousand dollars on a questionable idea proposed by an earnest, well-trained worker than it is to give one thousand dollars for research on a good idea proposed by an incompetent and mentally lazy investigator."

As between the idea and the man, he preferred to wager on the man.

THE TYPES OF RESEARCH

The Devil found that curiosity
Was a most potent goad for human pride.
What is the colour of a worm's inside?
How many eyelids has the female flea?
What is the shape and weight of a man's soul?
Faustus was much intrigued and he pursued
His studies lost in stately solitude.
Delving far deeper than the patient mole.[8]

Faustus, that is to say, was a devotee of "pure science." What of Banting?

Medical colleges of Canada (he told his Victoria audience) are all engaged in research. Much of this research seeks to throw some light upon fundamental problems and because of its very nature may not appear to have immediate practical importance. But it is always valuable. An example of this is the research on the different types of diphtheria bacilli by the late Dr. Westbrook, who was at one time President of the University of British Columbia. His classical descriptions of types are standard for bacteriological laboratories throughout the world. The numerous workers on the morphology of red blood cells, and the chemical workers on the estimation of salts in small quantities of the blood, could not see any practical application of their researches, yet the knowledge that they acquired now forms the groundwork for the clinical investigation on pernicious anæmia in progress at Winnipeg under the auspices of the Gordon Bell Memorial.

Faustus is justified; "pure science" is vindicated. On the other hand, he recalled in the same address (it was a favourite example) how Roux and Yersin digressed into academic bypaths, while von Behring, a man of more practical bent, seized the main point of their theory, produced the antitoxin, and won well-deserved

[8]From "The Repentance of Doctor Faustus," by Wilfred Rowland Childe, in *The Golden Thurible*.

acclaim for a vital service to medicine. Banting must have recognized in this Teutonic genius for the practical a kinship with his own nature. He had the same alertness for possible clinical uses of whatever he brought to light; he was *toujours en vedette*—always on the lookout. Laboratory discoveries of the type which engrossed him were those which received their testing, their sanction and their application in the clinic. "The laboratory," he roundly declared, "is secondary to the bedside." His admired Sir James Mackenzie had hailed the partnership of physiologist and clinician as a promising development, and had warned that joint investigation should not be limited to the advanced stages of the disease;[9] the salute and the warning were both echoed by Banting.

His laboratory, then, while it was the centre of all his own activity, he recognized as a side room, an adjunct to the sick chamber, a place where the problems of the sick were to be solved. The intellectual's absorption in a puzzle for the puzzle's sake he no doubt understood and shared, but although he was certainly not sentimental and was a truly "scientific" scientist, the impulse behind his work was his warm and deep humanity.

Writes Dr. George Hunter, Department of Biochemistry, University of Alberta:

His interpretation of "medical research" was generous because he realized that all scientific research moves on one front. Yet he knew what he was about. His great motivation in life was to relieve human suffering, and although always sympathetic with so-called "pure science," he got visibly more enthusiastic as the problem approached the medical and human level.

In the Boston address Banting explains the three-fold nature of research—"clinical research, experimental or medical research and pure fundamental research." The latter is "pure science."

The people working in fundamental research are working in problems of chemistry, physics, engineering, electricity, physiology, bacteriology, etc., purely for the purpose of advancing our knowledge in these sciences. Their work is exacting, their terminology is specific, their training is highly specialized and they are usually not interested or concerned about the practical application

[9]*The Future of Medicine*, by Sir James Mackenzie; Henry Frowde, Hodder & Stoughton, London, 1919. pp. 49-50.

of their findings. Quite a difficult matter, therefore, for the ordinary clinician . . . to . . . understand what these scientists are doing, let alone attempt to apply any of their results.

Clinical research consists largely in trying out new remedies, determining how best to use them, as Campbell and Fletcher had done when insulin was new and mysterious. It also involves the practice of acute observation and the evolution of fresh ideas from watching the uncontrived "experiments" of nature. It is obvious from what has been said, however, that there is a wide gap between fundamental research and clinical work.

We are left, then, with experimental Medical Research, which is the liaison department between pure fundamental research and clinical research. The people engaged in experimental Medical Research must first of all appreciate the problems which confront not only the general practitioner but the specialists in all phases of medicine. It is necessary, then, that some of these workers be graduates in medicine and have some clinical experience. On the other hand, the people in experimental Medical Research must also be able to interpret and understand the work and the results of projects in the various spheres of fundamental research. Thus it is necessary that some of their staff be specialists in the field of chemistry, biochemistry, physiology, electrical engineering, biology, physics, etc. Their final requisite is that they must be capable, either independently or under supervision, to apply their special knowledge and the results of fundamental research to an experimental project which has a definite and specific clinical purpose. It is usually from such sources that the tools for final clinical research are made available.

This thesis is brilliantly illustrated by an account of the work on silicosis and the preparations for investigating schizophrenia. (Both of these projects will be mentioned later.) It also serves to indicate the nature of the personnel in Banting's department.

RESEARCH AND TEACHING

Aspiring devotees at the shrine of Research he divided into two classes: those who came to be assigned a task, at which they worked diligently and meekly, and those who came with minds alight and hearts afire, eager to try out an idea. The plodding efforts of the former he would not dignify with the proud name "research"; better he said, to use the word "technology." For "to be a great scientist one must also," as Professor Wechsler has expressed it, "be very much of a poet or, at least, have much ingenuity and wide imagination"; and "while there are innumerable people who do scientific work, many are not great scientists because they do not possess ingenuity and imagination, because they lack wings."[10]

In the Albany lecture Banting outlined what he felt to be necessary for drawing out and enhancing the natural vocation inherent in the second group:

Towards the final year the undergraduate who has the Research mind usually selects subjects which are of most interest to him. Very often this interest has been stimulated by his admiration for the professor as much as by the subject itself. In my own case it was a teacher on the Surgical Staff of the University of Toronto who instilled in me the desire for post-graduate work in Surgery. It is in post-graduate work that the real training for the Research man is obtained. The student who remains for a year as a junior in any department of the university is usually given a small amount of teaching but his major work in such departments as Physiology, Pathology or Biochemistry is a Research problem. It naturally follows, therefore, that the manner in which the student is treated in his first actual taste of Research will be important all through his life. The professor who allots a day's work to his post-graduate students and comes around the following morning to collect the results is doing great harm to his student. I have in mind an eminent professor who has had from four to eight undergraduates under him every year for twenty years and who never produced an outstanding Research man. On the other hand, he has produced routine technicians.

I believe that the student should be allowed to work on his own problem if he has one, or if a problem is given to him he should make it his own. He should be given every assistance in the working out of the problem, but he should be made to plan his own experiments, draw his own conclusions and consult the professor for suggestions or advice. The reading of the literature

[10]"Sigmund Freud: a Critical Appreciation," in *The Neurologist's Point of View,* by I. S. Wechsler, M.D., L. B. Fischer, New York, 1945.

on the subject should be left in the student's hands but he should be warned to read all scientific articles in the most critical and analytical fashion. Too much reading of the literature is not to be advocated. Too thorough a review of the literature, before beginning work, is inadvisable for there is scarcely a subject in medicine on which there is not a wide diversity of opinion and confusion of thought.[11]   After completing the Research work the student will be able to evaluate the experimental results that are related to the problem. When the work is completed the young Research student should write his own report, giving his results and any conclusions that may be drawn. If the paper is published, it should be published in the name of the worker, or if it is reported at scientific meetings the paper should be given by the worker. In this way the student learns that he will get out of his work advantages in direct proportion to the energy which he puts into it.

At Ann Arbor, after describing his ideal Research worker, he had said:

. . . The problem of the Research institution today is to provide for such men. They are difficult to deal with. To them their idea is everything and unfortunately even today there are places and people who sap the man of his idea, dissuade him of work and turn him out.

In his best-selling novel, *The Citadel*, A. J. Cronin, himself a doctor, has given a vivid fictional representation of how a brilliant young man, inflamed with an idea, was frustrated of his purpose by the authorities of an English institution which was avowedly given over to Research, and how the effort was made to reduce him to the common level of the hack "scientists" among whom he was forced to work. This incident, like much of the rest of the book, is probably autobiographical; certainly it has a

[11]The Chicago address contains the same idea: "In the medical literature of today we have textbooks, scientific treatises, journals and magazines. One wonders if there is an end of knowledge. I fancy the pages that are covered with cancer literature, if spread out, would cover the state of Illinois. Yet its solution is not at hand. I sometimes wonder if we are helped by too full a knowledge of medical literature. I must frankly confess that, had I read all that was written on diabetes and known all of the conflicting views and theories I would probably never have tackled the problem."

real basis in fact and it embodies in living character and emotion the unfortunate situation which Banting described.

The German system of attributing everything from a laboratory to the chief of the department (continued Banting, turning to a favourite theme) is not for the betterment of Research. Fortunately it has not met with general approval in these democratic countries of ours. The head of a Research institution is rapidly becoming a counsellor, advisor, constructive critic and a director, rather than a participant in Research. He may have come through the experiences of having some of his best ideas and work published by, and attributed to, some eminent authority under whom he has worked and now he feels for the youthful enthusiast. This factor has done more to raise the United States to the foremost country of the world in Medical Research than any other factor. The reason is that it makes Research men. It stimulates the individuality and develops personality. Our religion, our moral fabric, our very basis of life are centred around the idea of reward. It is not abnormal therefore that the Research man should desire the kudos of his own work and his own idea. If this is taken away from him the greatest stimulant for work is withdrawn.

With what firm faith Banting upheld this democratic doctrine, and how, as a Research director, he not only adhered to it but went beyond it, exceeding himself in fairness and practising in place of simple justice a larger generosity, will appear in subsequent pages. It was always the first of his cares that every young man or young woman who laboured under his direction should receive the proper credit.

We turn once more to the Albany lecture:

At the present time there is a vogue for obtaining postgraduate degrees. In every laboratory there are M.A. and Ph.D. students engaged in Research. The student believes that the Ph.D. degree gives him a rank and standing which will enable him to better his position. Since almost all universities prescribe Research work in their Ph.D. degree these students present themselves to the laboratory. Many of this type of student have not the qualities to make them Research men. Much time is wasted in the effort to try to make them something that they are not.

Possibly one of the worst features of the post-graduate degree is the thesis which is frequently published.[12]

The young Research man can be assisted by training him in observation, in the careful and accurate recording of his results, and a careful supervision of the methods in his work. He should be encouraged to put down his ideas in a notebook so that he can refer to them and think about them before trying experiments. The young worker should be given as much latitude as possible in his work, but he should feel that he can discuss his problem with the professor at all times. He should not be laughed at and his ideas should be treated seriously, however foolish they may be, and as far as possible, he should be made to answer his own questions. The young Research worker will greatly be helped by discussing his problem in perfect confidence with some person in whom he has absolute trust. The mere telling about it often clarifies the idea itself.

This was my own experience as a post-graduate student under the late Professor C. L. Starr. It is impossible to describe in words what he gave to me, but I know of no man of whom it may be more truly said, "What you are speaks so loudly that I cannot hear what you say." I always got encouragement and inspiration from Dr. Starr and never left his presence without feeling stronger and better able to carry on. He was an idealist and unconsciously imparted this idealism to those who were associated with him. I recall at least a dozen outstanding surgeons who owe much of their success, both in practice and Research, to the influence of the late Dr. Starr. I can give no better advice to the ambitious Research man than that he should seek out such unselfish leadership.

The teaching departments of a medical school may be equipped with good teachers who are not necessarily good Research men. It is unfortunate that these two qualifications are not always combined. We still have with us teachers who have a mind like an encyclopedia, and who have the idea that knowledge is power. These men demand that the student memorize facts and place a premium on memory rather than on originality. The

[12]A post-graduate degree of a different kind, the F.R.C.S., had always been one of Banting's dearest ambitions. It was finally granted to him on the recommendation of Lord Moynihan, but since he had dreamed of winning it by his personal knowledge and proficiency as a surgeon, rather than because of indirect influences on surgery, his ambition was only half realized. Other degrees, purely academic, held little interest for him.—L. S.

THE BANTING INSTITUTE, TORONTO

head of a department who is not interested in Research should not have contact with students. . . .

If Banting spoke slightingly of the post-graduate degree as an end in itself he constantly encouraged his students and fellows to pursue post-graduate studies; whenever he visited a Research centre he considered its possibilities for the further training of some of his own group. What he had missed the others should have; but let them have no regard for the "prestige value" of advanced education. The aim was a practical one—to better their minds and their working capacities.

In speaking to the Boston Masons about the work on schizophrenia he illustrated his own methods of securing trained personnel:

A neurohistologist is a rare individual but for the experimental approach to this problem he may be a necessity. We think so and have made it possible for one of our graduate students, who has shown real brilliance in both experimental neurology and in his hobby of histology, to complete his Medical Course. This training takes time, but I venture to say that this chap accomplishes as much work in the four summer months as the average graduate student does in a year.

We went far afield to bring back to Canada a brilliant young neurophysiologist—excellently trained in the principles and technique of nerve and ganglion work. . . . We began to train another of our own young men as a neurophysiologist, to study the more minute aspects of brain and nerve physiology. It will take several years before this chap—soon to be a graduate in medicine—will likewise be a neurophysiologist—but a year in Philadelphia, Boston or New York will give him the assurance he needs to strike off on his own towards the conquest of schizophrenia.

. . . With few exceptions the best thing to do is to pick the man you think is possessed of ideas and initiative and capable of doing the work, train him yourself or send him away for a year or more, then bring him back, give him the responsibility of his problem and guide rather than direct him. He will usually make good.

. . . We have never hired a person to do experimental work but we do hire people who want to do experimental work. They, and they alone, are the research workers who will eventually pay dividends.

Having set forth his doctrine and examined it, let us again consider his practice. From the platform we return to the laboratory and from the verbal creed to the sermon of good works and
material examples.

As a scientific leader, he was a paradox, for he was really not a
scientist; at any rate he was not one of those scrupulously well-
trained and deeply-learned scientists who add to their gifts of
imagination and patience the many special techniques of thought
and of method which they have learned through long apprenticeship. As Sir Henry Dale has pointed out, Banting never served
a normal apprenticeship to science. He did his work, therefore,
without the benefit of such acquired techniques and with a
limited range of knowledge. Like a boy who goes fishing along
a famous stream equipped with a stick, a line, a bent pin and a
worm, he was almost pathetic as compared with the other fishermen, who carried handsome rods and reels and used cunning
and elegant trout flies. He began by catching an enormous fish
and was thereupon acknowledged as something of an angler. But
he was never really one of the brotherhood. He continued to
fish with the bent pin and the worm. And yet, though he never
caught another fish of comparable size (who else could boast of
such a giant?) he seemed to know which pools to try and how to
land his catch. What might he not have done with the proper
equipment?

Sir Henry Dale has deplored this lack of equipment, this lack
of training, and there can be little doubt that had he had it
Banting would have gained in penetration and scope; he would
have gained also in inner assurance, for he was sometimes painfully conscious of his shortcomings. On the other hand, one of
his intimate and trusted colleagues, a man well qualified to form
an opinion, has expressed the view that Banting really was little
the worse, for his special purposes, to be without the usual, intensive scientific discipline. "Banting wasn't designed for a detail
man," so his friend avers, "but found his peculiar forte in just
the sort of work he was doing."

Another instance of a similar kind, full of instructive parallels,
is the career of Francis Galton, who was intellectually more brilliant than Banting but whose efforts were more diffuse, less
effectual.

From the standpoint of the ordinary professional scientific man (writes Havelock Ellis)[13] he was probably an amateur. He was not even, as some have been, a learned amateur. I doubt whether he had really mastered the literature of any subject, though I do not doubt that that mattered little. When he heard of some famous worker in a field he was exploring, he would look up that man's work; so it was with Weismann in the field of heredity. . . . His attitude in science might be said to be pioneering much like that of the pioneers of museums in the later seventeenth and earlier eighteenth centuries, men like Tradescant and Ashmole and Evelyn and Sloane: an insatiable curiosity in things that were only just beginning, or had not yet begun, to arouse curiosity. . . . But, on this basis, Galton's curiosity was not the mere inquisitiveness of the child, it was co-ordinated with an almost uniquely organized brain, as keen as it was well balanced. And he knew how to preserve that exquisite balance without any solemnity or tension or self-assertion, but playfully and graciously, with the most unfailing modesty. It was this rare combination of qualities—one may see it all in his "Inquiries into Human Faculty"—which made him the very type of the man of genius, operating, not by profession or by deliberate training but by natural function, throwing light on the dark places of the world and creating science in out-of-the-way fields of human experience which before had been left to caprice or not even perceived at all.

Banting was less brilliant than Galton, but so far as his scientific work was concerned he was less of a dilettante. He founded no new branch of science but he perceived scientific problems where no one else could see them. To his scientific friends the other analogies will be obvious: the semi-professional, semi-amateur status; the insatiable curiosity in things only just beginning (such as aviation medicine); the keen, well-balanced intelligence; the common sense; the lack of solemnity or pretension. This is what Ellis regards as "the very type of the man of genius, operating, not by profession or by deliberate training, but by natural function."

One of the many youthful investigators who came under Banting's influence and profited from his direction was Dr. Jean McNamara, an Australian physician who did interesting work on

13"The Art of Thinking" in *The Dance of Life*, Houghton Mifflin Company, Boston and New York, 1923, pp. 126-128.

poliomyelitis. Dr. McNamara was fresh from her experience in several Research centres in the United States when she arrived in Toronto to work in the Connaught Laboratories. She had been disappointed, on the whole, with her studies in the States, but after a short period in Toronto she paid a well-deserved tribute to her new adviser. "I thank heaven," she is quoted as saying, "that there is one place in the world where complicated things are made simple instead of simple things being made complicated!"

This faculty, the gift for simplification, is the single trait that has won more plaudits than any other from those who worked with Banting. He had the ability to reduce a problem to its elements, stripping away the petty encumbrances which tend to confuse beginners. (And sometimes those who are no longer beginners.) A flurry of inconsequences was blown away as if by a strong wind, revealing in simple outline the basic contours of the work; revealing, too, the misconceptions so often ranged beside it.

A conference in the office. A problem to discuss. An assorted group of scientific experts stating their assorted views. Talking, talking. Arguing technicalities. Talking. Sometimes quite losing themselves in their own astonishing words—the polysyllabic Greek and Latin words which litter text books and confound the minds of students; the horrible chemical terms which join segment to segment, after the German pattern, endlessly, like monstrous tapeworms.

Banting, humped in his chair, sucks thoughtfully at his pipe, or smokes one Buckingham cigarette after another, saying little.

Finally he speaks up. "Wait a minute," he says, "Just what are you talking about?" He looks mystified. "Or do you know?" he asks.

"Remember, I don't know much about the problem," he says again. (For his mystification is genuine.) "This is really out of my line. Just what did you mean by the statement that the so-and-so co-efficient can be easily determined by such-and-such a procedure? And what is the significance of determining it? Is it something we really have to know?"

He listens intently to the answer. "Do you think," he says, "that you could put that in something more like English?"

Eventually he gets what he wants in ten or twenty words, mostly Anglo-Saxon.

"My God, man!" he says at last, "why didn't you say that in the first place? Now just what is it you want to do? Am I right in supposing that such-and-such is the general idea and that you propose to try it out by doing so-and-so? Correct me if I'm wrong. This is something I'm not familiar with. Is that the gist?"

"That's it," says the expert. Or "Not quite," says the expert. And either way the air is getting clearer, and everyone present, perhaps including the expert witness, understands the problem a little better, sees what is essential in it and what is not, is better able to take part in the discussion which continues.

Again, let us say, a colleague comes to his office to ask a question.

"This is silly," says Banting, filling his pipe, "this is just plain silly. You aren't supposed to be asking me questions. I'm supposed to be asking you. That's what you're paid for." He grins, tamps the pipe. "What do you want to know?"

The colleague puts his question. "No," Banting replies abruptly, "You don't want to know that. Tell me how much you know about so-and-so."

"Next to nothing," says the expert. "Very little, as a matter of fact, is known about it. There's nothing in the literature."

"All right, then," says Banting. "See what I mean? I can't possibly answer your question, nobody can answer your question, until somebody answers mine. Mine comes first. It's a fundamental problem, and if no one has done any work on it, that's where you have to start."

Suppose, on the other hand, that the expert replies: "There have been two papers on the subject, one by Jones and one by Robinson. Jones says yes to the question; Robinson says no. Their results are directly opposed."

"What was the difference in their methods?" asks Banting.

"No difference."

"There *must* have been a difference. If Jones did precisely the same thing that Robinson did, then Jones would have reached the same result. There was certainly some difference, however small, in their method of approach. Find out what that difference was, and in all likelihood you will have the key to the problem."

In some such manner, in some such words, Banting counselled his fellow workers. Junior members of the department, at first unused to these habits of thought, were sometimes astonished at his ignorance, sometimes believed his percipience greater than it was; even practised research workers, however, acknowledged the profit they derived from his direct, common-sense appraisals, tinged as they were with scepticism and always straight to the point.

It is said that Winston Churchill, when discussing with other Allied leaders in Washington the many complex problems of the conduct of the War, won for himself the sobriquet of the "axe-man" because of the way he hewed staunchly through all distractions to the main theme at issue. So with Banting. An incisive, practical mind in conjunction with a vigorous and free-wheeling imagination made his advice worth seeking.

Above all, he was distinguished by uncommon "horse sense." There is a story told of the argument which developed when a truck driver misjudged the clearance and jammed his truck under a covered bridge so that it stuck fast and could not be moved forward or back. The driver wished to tear away a part of the wooden superstructure of the bridge; the keeper of the bridge wished to dismantle the upper part of the truck. Finally a passing urchin made the obvious suggestion that if the air were let out of the tires the truck would be freed, and this very simple expedient settled the dispute. Banting repeatedly played the rôle of this long-headed urchin. His natural acumen was never confined in academic ruts. His common sense was most uncommonly good.

His questions were revealing. They showed, first of all, how little he cared about making an impression. He himself referred to some of them as "damn fool questions," and assuredly he was never afraid of betraying ignorance. They might be "fool questions" and again they might not; he was willing to take the chance. Questions that no one else would ask, for fear of seeming stupid, were often the very ones that needed to be brought to notice; they often pointed to the little problems that had been overlooked as being much too easy and obvious, while actually they were neither.

What was known, he inquired, about carbon monoxide in the exhaust fumes of an aeroplane? The experts opened their mouths to answer. They paused. Just what *was* known? Come to think of it, less was known than should be. And so began a fruitful series of investigations.

At other times a question might prove to be a calculated trifle; it was not as simple as it seemed. With Socratic innocence he would drop a harmless little query into the midst of a warm discussion, follow it immediately with another, and develop by means of additional questions the trend of some deeper problem, until it was impossible to say if he were really thinking aloud or expressing in this oblique and provocative fashion an idea which he had been mulling over in his mind for some time in advance. What was he driving at? It was never safe to be lulled into complacence.

When Banting found himself ill-informed about the work of one of the others of his group he was seldom content to remain so.

"I happened to be reading," he would say some morning, "that paper of Wallingham's you referred to, and it occurred to me that you might be well advised to follow up his suggestion about so-and-so."

A young man who had done work in the Department on a rather esoteric problem was asked how much Banting knew about it.

Nothing much to begin with (he answered) but he was intensely interested. He asked me a thousand and one questions and he did some reading in the literature and before I had finished he was very well grounded in the whole business. I have never known anyone who would pick up something new so rapidly and so excitedly. I remember, too, that he stopped me from trying to do a piece of work that had already been done successfully. He was full of odd scraps of information. Once he showed me a little trick he had picked up in England years before which saved me a day or two in the lab. In my opinion he was an ideal chief. Mainly, I think, because he was always interested in my work and interested in me.

Perhaps the case has been overstated with regard to Banting's reading habits. He acquired a good deal of his information at second hand from others who were more omnivorous readers; in later years, particularly when he had to go to Ottawa to argue the merits of various wartime research projects, he greatly valued the assistance of a colleague who could summarize the necessary information for him and put a concise memorandum on his desk. It would be very unfair to think, however, that he had to be "primed" for a show; the work was of such wide range and such great complexity that no one person could grasp all the details, especially since they changed from day to day as the studies progressed. As for the literature, it was of course immense. And Banting, like Francis Galton, read what he needed to read.

In this way Banting amassed a wide variety of information in a score of different fields. His knowledge was splintery and disjunctive, except along the lines where his own work had been done. But he fitted together whatever pieces came to hand and went in search of whatever was missing. And since no one can know it all, the difference between Banting and the most learned savant was not so great as he himself appeared to think. They all have lacunæ of some sort, and many are able to hide their deficiencies from a cursory glance by the solemn devices of silence and bluff which he did not deign, or did not bother, to employ. Writes Dr. Earl J. King:[14]

For seven years it was my privilege to be associated with Banting and to see his department of medical research grow up from its small beginnings in three indifferent rooms in the old Pathology Building of the University of Toronto to the present highly efficient organization in the Banting Institute. . . . A more kindly and sympathetic director could not be desired. The young, and often timid, worker could always go to him with the confident expectation of having his ideas listened to patiently and with interest, of having flaws in his reasoning pointed out, and of obtaining wise and unbiased advice as to whether a project was worth embarking upon. Banting showed a fine critical capacity in assessing research possibilities. He realized that there could be a bad question as well as a bad answer, and that nature can only be expected to give a clear reply to a properly formulated query.

[14]"The Late Sir Frederick Banting" (Letter to the Editor), *The Lancet*, April 26, 1941. p. 551.

His mechanical sense was excellent. He had a flair for working out apparatus. As might be supposed, he believed in keeping it as simple as possible. If one of the others devised an elaborate mechanism which would require to construct it the services of three glass-blowers and two machinists for a period of a week, costing the Department several hundred dollars, Banting might offer as a substitute an awkward-looking assemblage of odd flasks and bottles, bits of rubber hose, anything and everything that could be made to serve.

"It isn't that I begrudge you the money," he would explain, apologizing for the home-made alternative, "but if this will accomplish the same purpose, and I rather think it will, it would be foolish to spend two hundred dollars to buy what you can get for ten. One hundred and ninety dollars will buy a lot of animals for your experiments, will maybe buy some other things you need. What do you think of it?"

At the same time, if convinced that an intricate apparatus was needed to do the work, Banting could be very helpful in figuring out the details. If he distrusted complexity it was only when he thought it unnecessary; he preferred a direct route to a circuitous one. And complexity had its dangers. Too much thought, so he said, was lavished on equipment, too little at times on the basic idea of the investigation.

Examining a mazy and tortuous contrivance, rigged like a man-o'-war and bristling with fancy accoutrements, he turned to the technician at his elbow and said, "What do you think of the set-up, Walter?"

"Seems to me," said the technician, "that it may be a little too complicated. Too many things to go wrong with it."

"My thought exactly," said Banting. And with a growl that was hardly apologetic, he added, "Of course, I'm just a damn farmer. All this is out of my line."

But ideas, rather than appliances, won his deepest, most constant interest. He loved the processes of logic, the Holmesian deductions, the daring speculations and the sudden perception of analogies. He loved to get hold of an exciting idea and to clear away incomprehensions, his own and others, to make it plain.

He loved the interplay and the conflict of accomplished, resolute minds when all were off soundings and the varied skills of his crew of experts might all be required to sail the ship. These conferences were important. These ideas were important. Periodically all sections of the Department were gathered together for their common aid and benefit, "chewing the fat" and consulting with each other; and every idea put forward, every sort of contribution, was carefully recorded in the minutes.

Banting was very scrupulous in apportioning credit. There were only two who deserved it: the man who conceived the idea and the man who did the work; more often than not they were one and the same, and one man only was ace and king. Let the rest stand back. In other cases collaboration was essential and should be properly recognized. He himself, as we shall see, was the least obtrusive, the least self-seeking of all; he was never what General Eisenhower has referred to as a "glory hopper," and this was one reason for the hold he maintained on his group.

When insulin faded from the centre of Banting's interest and he turned to other work, his new themes were varied and he was as busily engaged as ever. His bibliography, nevertheless, is small. The total number of papers published in scientific journals is only sixty-two. Of these, thirty-six deal with insulin, many of them being simply the published texts of more or less routine speeches in which nothing new is added or announced; one of them, "Medical Research and the Discovery of Insulin," is the Chicago address extensively quoted above, and has been considered as dealing primarily with research and only incidentally with insulin; still another, which marks his only return to experimental work with insulin in his later years, is a paper published in 1938 in the *American Journal of Psychiatry* in conjunction with Dr. G. E. Hall on "Physiological Studies in Experimental Insulin and Metrazol Shock," and so is far afield from his earlier investigations. There are four other publications on medical research, not counting the address to the Boston Masons. This leaves a remainder of twenty-two; when it is remembered that a number of these are general surveys or reviews and that there are a few (such as the article he wrote on Pavlov in 1936) which are literary efforts rather than scientific treatises, it will be seen that the number of original papers on scientific work apart from insulin is very small indeed—fewer than twenty in twenty years.

There were two years, 1927 and 1928, when he published nothing of this nature at all. Again, in 1940, he was too busy to oblige the editors.

How was it that over all the long, rich period of his prime he wrote so little? He was not the type of worker to rest on his laurels. One answer, of course, is that he was too busy with his directoral and other duties, and certainly he was able to spend much less time in his own laboratory than he would have liked. Another reason was his general attitude to medical "literature," some idea of which has already been gleaned from his speeches. He deplored hasty publication and he was more interested in *doing* the work than in writing the paper.

It has been found to be a poor policy, and it is a fallacious standard (says Dr. Charles F. Code, of the Mayo Clinic) to measure a man's research worth by the number of his publications. If there is any field in which quality and not quantity really counts, it is the field of research. We in North America have, in the past few decades, been caught in a whirl of publications in which the number of reports by a single investigator may reach four or five hundred or more. This has been partly due to the tendency of those who hire and fire to place excessive emphasis on the quantity and not the quality of publication. In England the medical scientific group on the whole has a sounder view. It is well illustrated by a conversation I heard while working in England some years ago. One of the young men in the laboratory remarked one day, "You know, I have not published a paper for a year, and I am a bit worried about it."

Our chief, Professor C. Lovatt Evans, turned to him and remarked, "You have been working, haven't you?"

"Yes," replied the young man.

"Then don't worry; it is not the size of your bibliography which counts. Always remember this: Hopkins, one of the best biochemists in England, has a bibliography of only twelve or fourteen papers. Each is a classic."

Dr. Code goes on to relate that of the 483 scientific communications published by the physicists and chemists of the Institute of Radium, Madame Curie had only thirty-one to her credit! A book she had written was published posthumously, bringing her total bibliography to thirty-two publications. "Thus," concluded Dr.

Code, "when the standard of quality is high, quantity fades into insignificance." [15]

Banting's papers were few in number. It is not desired to imply that each of them was a classic. Apart from the papers on insulin it is improbable that any of them will take a prominent place in the history of medicine. But they represent sound, careful and imaginative work and a few have real importance. The time has not come, nor is this the place, to evaluate such importance as they possess in the perspective of developing science; this task awaits a later time and a better qualified appraiser. But it will be worth while to glance at them briefly, if only to determine what subjects engaged their author's interest.

A valuable investigation of suprarenal insufficiency[16] was carried out with the assistance of Miss Gairns in the laboratory of the old Pathology Building. Those who are familiar with subsequent research in this field will recognize on reading the paper how close the authors came to anticipating results of the first significance. Purely as a demonstration of Research method it is an admirable achievement.

The years 1930 and 1931 saw the publication of worth-while papers on the antitryptic properties of blood serum and on the enzymes of stools in intestinal intoxication.

But in 1933 appeared the first of a series of publications on a subject to which Banting devoted more time and thought than to any other.[17] The very name of cancer strikes the average person like a frightful malediction, a whispered horror of something obscene and terrible. Fear is seconded and increased by ignorance and it is the popular opinion that all forms of cancer are incurable. It is for this reason and because the unsolved problem of malignancy remains perhaps the greatest challenge to medical science, that any intimation about cancer research is always "news." When it was presently noised abroad that the great Sir

[15]"The Rôle of Medical Research in a Medical Centre," by Charles F. Code, M.D. Address before the Manitoba Institute for the Advancement of Medical Education and Research, Winnipeg, October, 1943. *The Canadian Medical Association Journal*, 50: 308-313, April, 1944.

[16]Banting, F. G. and Gairns, S., "Suprarenal Insufficiency," *Am. I. Physiol*, 1926, 77: 100-113.

[17]Banting, F. G. and Gairns, S., "Immunity to Rous Sarcoma," *Transactions of the Royal Society of Canada*, 1933, 27 App. B, CLXVI.

Frederick Banting was studying cancer, he began to be hounded by the press; during his later years he was repeatedly annoyed by unauthorized, inaccurate and over-optimistic reports of his work.

"In 1925 I visited the laboratory of Dr. W. E. Gye, and since that time my main interest in medical research has centred in the cancer problem." [18] Dr. Gye, Director of the Imperial Cancer Research Institute, is thus credited with starting him on a new trail. Six papers, including a summation in the Walter Ernest Dixon Memorial Lecture, embody the effort of years. The tremendous amount of work, much of it unpublished, which sprang from his interest in Rous sarcoma and related tumours may be glimpsed in the following paragraph:

During the past ten years we have used approximately 6,000 fowls for experimental work on Rous tumour and of these 118, or approximately one bird in fifty has shown some degree of resistance. Of the 118 birds there were forty-four birds which received more than five direct transplants and remained negative following regression of the first tumour. Some of this group were kept in the laboratory as long as five years, during which time they received upwards of forty transplants. . . .[19]

Many significant facts were unearthed. For instance it was early found (June, 1930) that the plasma of Rous-resistant birds neutralized the cell-free active filtrate of a Rous tumour, a filtrate capable of causing the disease unless so treated but perfectly harmless following neutralization. Over forty experiments of this nature were carried out. A seemingly endless number of ingenious experiments in the transplantation of malignant cells and the use of variously modified tumour extracts is recorded. There were numerous attempts to produce resistance to Rous sarcoma. Following the principle of the toxin-antitoxin mixture used so extensively, Banting and his co-workers (Gairns and Irwin[20]) gave birds repeated injections of neutralized or partially neutralized

[18]Banting, F. G., "Walter Ernest Dixon Memorial Lecture: Resistance to Experimental Cancer," *Proc. Ray. Soc. Med.*, 1939, 32: 245-254.
[19]"Walter Ernest Dixon Memorial Lecture."
[20]W. R. Franks was also working on cancer at this time but was approaching the problem from a different angle; although there was reciprocation of ideas, his work was independent of Banting's.

serum-tumour extract mixtures. "The procedure was modified and many experiments were carried out, but the difficulties could not be overcome. If too much serum was added there did not appear to be any immunity produced; if too little serum was added the injection resulted in a tumour which killed the bird. It was impossible to predict the potency of a tumour extract, consequently the amount of serum necessary to neutralize it could not be calculated."[21]   A number of chemicals were also tried as modifying agents but with similar negative or equivocal results. The object was to kill the tumour cell by physiological means so that the hypothetical antigenic properties might remain. However no resistant birds were produced by any of these procedures. Subsequently, with the use of other methods, there were hopeful exceptions to this depressing rule, but the results seemed consistently inconsistent. Many of the experiments which were carried out with chickens in an endeavour to produce resistance were modified and repeated with mice, using Balogh tumour. During a two-and-a-half-year period 1,489 mice were transplanted with Balogh cells and 13 became resistant, or 1 in 114 mice.

All the work on experimental tumour (wrote Banting)[22] requires a large number of animals and a great deal of time. It is essential that control animals be used in all experiments, but, even with this precaution, there is such a great variation in the individual bird or animal that results are often difficult to interpret. . . .

The work to date does not appear to contribute much toward a specific treatment for cancer. I believe, however, that a better understanding of the factors which produce immunity and resistance will ultimately lead to such a treatment.

To this better understanding Banting made a material contribution. In discovering insulin he capitalized on the researches of a hundred predecessors who prepared the way for him. In experimental cancer research he himself may well be numbered among "the lone grey company before the pioneers." Perhaps only those who are actively participating in scientific research can fully appreciate the value to science of the negative results of

[21]Banting, *Ibid.*
[22]*Ibid.*

those who try and fail. Dr. W. E. Gye has been warm in his praise of Banting's work and the fact that he was selected to deliver the Walter Ernest Dixon Memorial Lecture on this theme is in itself sufficient tribute.

Four of the most engrossing papers in his list are concerned with the experimental production of coronary thrombosis and myocardial failure. Two were written in collaboration with Hall and Ettinger, one with Hall alone and one with Manning and Hall. The methods used were the repeated intravenous injection of the stimulating substance in the blood which simulates parasympathetic activity, namely, acetylcholine, and later the repeated and prolonged stimulation of the vagus nerve in dogs. How they came to try these methods and how they attempted to overcome the many technical difficulties make a tale of genuine adventure, though patently the labours required were tedious. Certainly the results aroused widespread interest and were considered sufficiently important by Professor Boyd to deserve mention in the next edition of his *Textbook of Pathology.* Whether or not the pathogenesis of an important group of cardiac diseases will be traced to excessive parasympathetic activity waits upon time and further research to decide; Professor Ettinger's recent studies seem to be less positive than the early work (which was cautious enough in its conclusions) but the putative relation between vagotonia and coronary disease remains a wakeful idea with much evidence to support it. Chronic stimulation of the vagus results in ulcers of the stomach and duodenum as well as in infarcts of the heart, so that a neurogenic basis for a variety of affections, including gall bladder disease, seems more than a possibility. It is interesting to note that Lucas, Hall and Ettinger published a paper[23] at this time in which it was shown that acetylcholine does not alter the activity or concentration of esterase in the blood of a dog. The Department had varied resources and problems were frequently attacked from several directions.

This brief summary does not exhaust the catalogue of Banting's specific contributions to science. It touches only the summits and judgment even of these must be deferred to experts.

[23]Lucas, C. C., Hall, G. E. and Ettinger, G. H.: *J. Pharm. and Exp. Therap.* (*Proc.*), 1935, 54: 151. The other papers mentioned will be found in the bibliography.

Despite the acknowledged value of his later work, it is probable that Banting achieved most in the end by his "influence," which was pervasive and yet specific.   A shadowy figure in the wings when many a scientific drama was on display, he had made his contribution earlier—in the conception of the "plot" or in helping to "whip the act into shape." Hall, Franks, Irwin, King, Ettinger, Lucas, Black, Mendel and the rest composed a brilliant cast. ("Each of them," said Banting, "knows more than I do.") But each of them has vied with his colleagues in paying tribute to the producer and director of the show. It is difficult to say, in general terms, how this influence was exerted, although an attempt has already been made to do so. Yet instances spring readily to mind.

Dr. G. E. Hall first approached Banting some years before attaining to a degree in medicine. A graduate of the Ontario Agricultural College at Guelph, he came to see his future chief with no idea of applying for a job. He had a question which he hoped that Banting would be able to answer. A number of the chicks he was studying had died mysteriously of a disease which caused swelling of their tissues, a sort of dropsy. Why? As it turned out the chicks had died of malnutrition (the unlooked-for result of certain feeding experiments) and the swelling they exhibited was malnutrition œdema.

But Banting, too, had questions. He was working with Miss Gairns and others on the problem of intestinal intoxication. Hall volunteered the information that a rapid fall in temperature was capable of producing diarrhœa in chicks and that when this was allowed to occur a number of them would be found dead in their incubators. Had temperature been considered as a factor in the incidence of acute intestinal disease in young humans?

Banting cocked an eye at this "farmer" from O.A.C. The suggestion had the ring of sound coin. Agriculture, as taught at O.A.C., appeared to be an excellent scentific proving ground. But the ideas! They were essential in the man.

When Banting discovered that there was a statistical relationship between temperature and the incidence of acute intestinal disease (from a comparative study of weather records and the records of the Sick Children's Hospital) he was confirmed in his opinion. Here was a man he needed. Here was a man whose

BANTING AT HIS DESK IN THE BANTING INSTITUTE

talents must be nurtured. He promptly communicated with the authorities in Guelph and arranged to have Hall come to Toronto to work with him.

Nor was Hall the last to be imported from O.A.C. Banting had tapped a new source of talent and thereafter he maintained liaison with the Guelph College, particularly with W. R. Graham, Professor of Poultry Husbandry, and secured for his department in Toronto a succession of promising young workers. It was also from Professor Graham, who became a close friend and associate, that he obtained the pure-bred fowl which were used in his cancer research.

A process now began of which Hall was at first hardly conscious. A course in bacteriology, Banting suggested, would be useful for his work. Then a course in something else. Summer courses, spare-time studies, the departmental work itself seemed all to be tending in the same direction. Gradually he was being impelled, or rather "edged over," toward medicine. Not that he was unwilling. His work was meantime progressing well and Banting was more and more resolved that he should receive every opportunity. He registered in the medical course, his chief acting as sponsor with the University authorities, and completed it in record time. It is not now permitted to assume so heavy a load of credits; Dr. Hall is himself of the opinion that a shortened and very intensive course, with the forced effort which it entails, is not desirable. At any rate he gulped down the curriculum, swept through the examinations and qualified as a physician.

But this was not enough. For a good research man there must be special training in basic science. In the years which followed he alternated between his work in the Department and post-graduate study, part of it abroad; always in the background stood Banting, ever ready to assist. He wrote letters, made arrangements, counselled and encouraged. Dr. Hall gratefully acknowledges his unfailing kindness. His thoughtfulness and generosity seemed hardly to recognize a limit.

But Banting, although never disingenuous, had something at the back of his mind. He had recognized research talent in Hall; he had worked with him on the pathogenesis of coronary thrombosis, on schizophrenia and other problems and had constantly watched over the jobs he had done with other workers or alone.

He had also recognized a marked ability for administration. The "plot" began to shape. For many years Banting had planned to drop the reins, to shift his administrative duties to someone else and to ease himself out. He wanted to escape from the desk and get back to the laboratory. A small room and a big idea. Fewer committees and less correspondence. There was also a cherished plan to buy a farm, to rusticate in the country and potter about in a garden, to raise walnut trees and to meditate in peace. Also to paint, to write, to pursue his hobbies. With this in view he had requested his brother, Thompson, to price a number of farms in the vicinity of Alliston. (The sum named to Thompson and the sum named to "Sir Frederick" would probably differ.) And with this future in view he had groomed a successor in the Department.

Gradually he began to turn over administrative work to Hall. When he had to be out of town Hall substituted for him. When he went to England, Hall took his place. Innumerable letters winged back and forth between them.

Franks, King and several of the others studied abroad at Banting's instigation. Much of this advanced work was made possible through arrangements he contrived. But if he sent them to England or to the United States to study he was loath to see them remain.

Writes Dr. King:[24]

By securing endowments he hoped to make it possible to keep the most gifted talent at home. "Too many of our best men go to the States and we lose them," was one of his complaints. At the same time, he was a firm believer in a broadened outlook. He encouraged men to come to England, to go to the United States, to Germany—"to get another slant on things." And he made it possible for several to come, who otherwise would not have so benefited; to his beneficence I owe myself two years of valuable experience in this country [England] and Germany. His feelings for the Imperial ties were strong. He particularly liked his students to come to England. He welcomed British researchers, and hoped that Canadians would show themselves worthy of the welcome accorded them in the old country. His gratification with any recognition they might gain was great.

[24]E. J. King, *op. cit.*

It was thus that Banting picked his "team," prepared and inspired them. He was proud to be associated with their work; he watched their success with selfless delight. Like Robert Frost, he "went to school to youth to learn the future," but in youthful zeal and ebullience, he was the youngest of them all. He called his corps of research scientists "my biggest experiment."

How large a part did he take in their actual endeavours? Perhaps the best example in pre-war years of his participation from the sidelines is the story of silicosis research. As he explained to the Boston Masons:

Silicosis is a disease of the lungs contracted by people working particularly in gold mines, where there is a considerable amount of quartz dust in the air as a result of blasting, drilling, crushing, etc. The miners, after a few years, find that they are no longer able to work as long without getting short of breath, their breathing is interfered with and perhaps a chronic cough develops. The individual has developed silicosis—a gradually increasing fibrosis of the lung, which has decreased the aerating surfaces to such an extent that he can no longer work. This man and his family must now be looked after by the compensation boards. Such compensation has amounted to millions of dollars each year in the Province of Ontario alone and the toll of human life has been equally significant.

The rest of the story may best be told in the words of the chief participant in the work, Dr. D. A. Irwin:[25]

Some medical discoveries, such as insulin, follow quickly the flash of genius that creates them. Other advances come only after a decade or more of slow laborious experimentation and require the unselfish leadership which has faith in ultimate success and is capable of infectious enthusiasm and constructive criticism in the various aspects of the problem. Silicosis was such a problem and Sir Frederick Banting was the leader who made possible the success that has been achieved.

In reviewing the progress of silicosis research in his department, to frequent visitors, Banting always acknowledged that the Professor of Mining Engineering in this University,

[25]Irwin, D. A., "The Contribution of Sir Frederick Banting to Silicosis Research," *The Canadian Medical Association Journal*, 47: 403-405, Nov., 1942.

Professor H. E. T. Haultain, was responsible for his early interest in the problem. In 1927 Banting and Professor Haultain were associated, for the first time, while engaged in the construction of a high speed centrifuge of new design. As Banting always possessed an insatiable curiosity concerning developments in fields other than his own, and especially so if they were taking place in Canada, many discussions of the achievements and problems of the Ontario mining industry must have taken place at odd moments during that year.

The problem of silicosis undoubtedly was a frequent topic of discussion, standing as it does midway between the mining industry and the medical profession. Those familiar with Banting can readily imagine the flood of questions. Why should the presence of rock dust in the lung produce a nodular fibrosis? Which mineral or minerals are responsible? Is the fibrosis due to the cutting action of the sharp edges of the mineral particles in the constantly moving lung? If so, why should a chicken's crop show no fibrosis, as it contains mineral grit and does considerable contracting and relaxing? Can silicosis be produced in experimental animals? What about the lungs of mine ponies? What measures can be used to prevent silicosis or treat the silicotic?

During that year Banting's interest in silicosis must have been considerable, because, engrossed as he was with his experiments on cancer, he began some experiments on silicosis. From his reading he knew that silicious dust particles were practically insoluble in acid but slightly soluble in alkali. This suggested the possibility that a slight alkalosis might enable the lung to rid itself of silicious dust by the process of solution. His first experiments were designed to ascertain if the feeding of alkali would increase the excretion of silicious material from the body, by way of the kidney. The experiments failed to give the desired information, as the best chemical methods known at that time were not sufficiently sensitive or accurate to permit even the measurement of comparatively high concentrations of silica in body tissues and fluids. On his instigation such a method was later developed in his department, and has been probably the most valuable tool of silicosis research.

In 1928, Banting decided that silicosis research should continue and expand as a departmental problem. As he did not wish to divide his efforts between cancer and silicosis he encouraged an associate to take on the latter while he continued with his work on cancer. For the next four years the research continued along two lines. It was approached as a pathological problem, in which attempts were made to produce the disease in experimental animals and follow the pathogenesis of the lesions. A study of the mechanism of dust elimination from the lung was also carried out. The second approach to the problem was biochemical in nature. During this period, industries in which silicosis was a problem became acquainted with this research work and learned of Banting's interest in silicosis. The next phase in the development of the research work was a direct outcome of this acquaintanceship and the increased facilities for experimental work afforded by the new quarters in the Banting Institute to which the department was moved in 1930.

The year 1933 saw the beginning of Banting's greatest contribution to silicosis research. Until that year the research work on the problem was carried out in Ontario, by the Banting and Best Department of Medical Research, the mining industry, and the provincial Department of Industrial Hygiene. Each group worked independently and there was little or no co-operation between groups. That year both the McIntyre Porcupine Mines and the Ontario Mining Association sent representatives to discuss the general aspects of the problem with Banting. On these occasions the departmental members, engaged in silicosis research, were gathered to meet the representatives from the mines in his office. He made an excellent chairman, saying little himself but provoking discussion by encouraging each person present to voice his opinions and theories on the varied aspects of the problem. In those days opinions varied greatly and these differences when discussed at length stimulated further thought and experimentation. A meeting would last all day and the following day the members would meet in smaller groups to continue the discussions, go over experimental results, and plan for the future. These early meetings gave a pattern for those ahead which provided a clearing-house for the interchange of ideas and experimental results, and paved the way for the hearty and friendly competitive spirit that since that time has existed between the various experimental and clinical groups.

The first two meetings produced immediate results. A suggestion made from the McIntyre Mine that certain gases present in mine air might accelerate the progress of silicosis was investigated experimentally as a joint effort. Three members of the department were then sent to visit the McIntyre Mine, with instructions from Banting to "feel, taste and smell the dust that produces silicosis." Liberal financial assistance, to support the increased tempo of departmental research, came from the mining industry at that time and continues to the present. This liaison stimulated silicosis research to the mutual benefit of both the department and the mining industry. The facilities of the laboratory were made available to the industry and the practical experience of those in the industry guided and moderated the theories that were formed in the department.

Banting had subdivided his department into groups capable of exploring new approaches to medical problems through the basic channels of chemistry, pathology, physiology and physics. Such an arrangement aided in solving many problems in silicosis research that overlapped from one basic channel to another. At least seventy-five persons would necessarily be mentioned if the names of those contributing to the different aspects of the problem during the next few years were given. Space does not permit such enumeration but the main problems can be given brief mention. New light was thrown on the mechanisms by which the lung retained and eliminated dust. Considerable attention was paid to the dust present in mine air. Improved methods were developed to measure the concentration and identify the components of dust. New knowledge was gained from a study of the tissue reaction produced by minerals known to be in mine air dust when present as individual minerals and in combination with each other. The various stages of silicotic fibrosis were studied in human and animal lungs. The distribution and metabolism of silica and silicates in experimental animals and silicotic and non-silicotic individuals added fresh knowledge to the subject. Joint researches were carried out with other university departments, especially Physics and Mineralogy.[26] In all these facets of the problem Banting counselled and stimulated the workers and facilitated their research in every way possible.

By 1936 it had become evident that of all the many minerals known to be present in Ontario mine dusts, silica alone was capable of producing fibrosis in the lung. The fibrosis was not the result of the physical action of the sharp silica particles, but was caused by silicic acid formed when the silica particles dissolved in the tissue fluid. Obviously, the disease could be

[26]Close co-operation with other Departments was a part of Banting's creed. He actually paid, from the resources of his own Department, the salary of a research worker engaged in the development of the electron microscope under the direction of Professor E. F. Burton of the Department of Physics. He recognized no narrow departmental limitations.—L. S.

prevented either by preventing silica dust from entering the lung or, if present, preventing the formation of silicic acid. Although the mining industry had made great strides in diminishing the amount of silica dust in the mine air, it was thought that the irreducible minimal concentration, present under practical working conditions, still presented an industrial hazard. On this account special attention was paid to an investigation of antidotal dusts that might be deposited in the lung with the silica and in some way prevent the formation of silicic acid.

The search for an antidotal dust was carried out as a joint effort between the department and the McIntyre Mine. After several failures it was discovered at the mine that, *in vitro,* metallic aluminum powder prevented silica from passing into solution as silicic acid. Animal experiments carried out by the same investigators showed that aluminum dust in all probability acted in a similar manner in the lung. These startling findings led to extensive elaboration of this work in the department. The experiments not only confirmed the work done at the mine but showed that in animals aluminum dust was an effective treatment in established silicosis. The mechanism by which aluminum exerts its antidotal action was also revealed.

Banting was one of the first to urge the immediate clinical trial of aluminum dust as a prophylactic and therapeutic measure in silicosis. A clinical trial of the effectiveness of aluminum therapy was soon under way at the McIntyre Mine. This was facilitated by the development, in the department, of a mill to produce and disperse the finely particulate metallic aluminum dust necessary for such a clinical application. Banting followed with great interest the frequent reports of the favourable results that surpassed even those anticipated from the animal experiments. One regret that he carried on his last journey was his inability to be present at a conference to be held in Timmins during his absence to discuss advances in the clinical application of aluminum in silicosis.

Although thoroughly conversant with all the details of the experiments under way in the department, he conducted little silicosis research himself. He compared his rôle, in this problem, to that of "a catalyst which accelerates a reaction without taking part in it." On this account he rarely mentioned silicosis in a public address or scientific paper for fear that people might assume he had carried out the work with "his own two hands." Any reference he made to the work of others was only made after he had consulted them and their names were always associated with the work mentioned. When the first report on the prevention of silicosis by metallic aluminum was ready for presentation to a special meeting of the Toronto Academy of Medicine the authors requested Banting to honour them by presenting the paper. He was adamant in his refusal, explaining his stand on the grounds that he had never in the past, nor would in the future, report for the first time the original findings of others.

[When requested by long distance telephone from a centre in the United States to make a speech about silicosis he firmly refused—he had already refused by telegram and was being approached the second time. His solicitor was persistent. Banting offered to ask someone more closely involved in the work to take his place, but this offer was rejected; he alone was wanted. Finally he waxed angry. "What you want," he growled into the telephone, "is not a speech on silicosis but an exhibition of Sir Frederick Banting. I'm not on exhibit!"—L. S.]

Those closely associated with Banting know that he appreciated and enjoyed being able to offer leadership in the silicosis research and that he secretly felt honoured by the unanimous acceptance of his leadership. He was approachable, to a fault, by all who wished to discuss silicosis research or suggest a new idea on the subject. He especially enjoyed meeting the members of the mining industry and on several occasions visited the mines. One of his most valued possessions was a souvenir of a visit to the Hollinger Mine in the form of a piece of quartz containing a heavy deposit of gold. He felt he was not justified in retaining the entire sample, so he had it cut and presented one half to the Royal Ontario Museum. Dr. Banting was honoured by Fellowship in the Royal Society of London and his leadership in silicosis research played an important part in this award.

Here, in the silicosis work, was a sequence of research which he was able to use in his Boston speech to demonstrate the interrelation of fundamental, medical and clinical methods. It is obvious, however, that the work on silicosis appealed to him largely because of its practical importance. Was this always the case?

At the other end of the scale is a job in fundamental research ("pure science") which he initiated from intellectual curiosity.

It serves to show the wide range of his interests and the all-inclusiveness of his investigative approach.

Writes Dr. Colin C. Lucas:[27]

The nature of "royal jelly" had for many years interested and tantalized the late Sir Frederick Banting. It was in 1930 that the writer was first treated to an enthusiastic account in Dr. Banting's provocative and stimulating manner of some established facts and some of his fancies concerning the life history of the honey bee. While the social organization in the hive excited his wonder and admiration, it was the peculiar nutritional properties of the food given by the nurse bees to the developing queen bee which particularly intrigued him.

My own interest was aroused as he recounted the pertinent facts. . . .

All female larvæ are fed on "royal jelly"—a thick, milky material, generally believed to be a secretion of the pharyngeal glands of the nurse bees (young workers) for the first two or three days after hatching, and during this period their anatomical development is similar. Only the queen continues to receive this special diet. Any larva from a fertile egg, if given royal jelly throughout its larval period, develops sexually so that it becomes a perfect or true female bee, or what is called a queen; otherwise, the larva develops into a sexually immature worker. Although the queen is considerably larger she is structurally much the same as the workers but with these important differences: the pollen-gathering apparatus remains undeveloped, while the spermotheca and ovaries are highly developed and the mouth parts and sting are modified. The fact that this remarkable anatomical and physiological differentiation of the female larva is dependent upon diet indicates the importance of royal jelly as a nutriment.

Dr. Banting spoke of his intention to initiate studies on the chemical nature of royal jelly, its enzymes, vitamins and any other physiologically active principles, and to see whether it would affect other insects and how it would influence young mammals. An invitation was extended to the writer to collaborate in such an investigation, but acceptance of this tempting offer was impossible at the time. Royal jelly was again discussed when in 1934 I accepted a full-time appointment under Dr. Banting at the University of Toronto, but chemical problems related to other

[27]Colin C. Lucas, "Chemical Examination of Royal Jelly," *The Canadian Medical Association Journal*, 47: 406-409, Nov., 1942.

departmental projects always seemed to obtrude themselves and force postponement of the royal jelly study. In 1938, however, an actual start on this work was finally made as the result of a visit from Mr. Gordon F. Townsend, then a recent graduate from the Ontario Agricultural College, now Provincial Apiarist for Ontario. Mr. Townsend expressed a desire to investigate royal jelly. Sir Frederick at once offered him a Fellowship to work on this problem under the writer. Collection of royal jelly commenced immediately and in September the chemical examination was begun. Banting was by this time too occupied with the organization of the Associate Committees of Medical Research and of Aviation Medical Research of the National Research Council to take any active part in the study, but his continued interest and enthusiasm in the problem proved most stimulating and his occasional pungent criticism was an invaluable corrective. The bulk of the actual work was done by Mr. Townsend.

Dr. Lucas then details the results of chemical examination and of a few preliminary nutritional studies. It was found that adding fresh royal jelly to the diet of fruit fly larvæ caused them "to reach sexual maturity earlier than did the control flies and increased notably (up to 60 per cent.) the number of eggs laid by the females."

Changing world conditions "so altered the research programme in the Department that the work had to be temporarily discontinued, but before his untimely death Banting had at least some knowledge of the composition of this peculiar 'food' which had for so long aroused his interest."

Was anything in the realm of science beyond the reach of his omnivorous curiosity?

Another important job in which he took a somewhat similar part was the work on schizophrenia. Accounts of it may be found in his much-quoted Boston speech and also in a comprehensive paper, "Physiological Studies in Experimental Insulin and Metrazol Shock," presented by Dr. Hall at the ninety-fourth annual meeting of The American Psychiatric Association, San Francisco, June 6-10, 1938. Concerned in this work were R. C. Sniffen, D. A. Irwin, Bruno Mendel, B. Leibel, G. E. Hall, J. E. Goodwin, D. P. C. Lloyd, W. R. Franks, A. E. Byrnes, S. Gairns and Banting himself. The aspect which Banting studied, in collaboration with W. R. Franks and Miss Gairns, was the "anti-insulin activity of serum of an insulin-treated patient." Dr. N. L. Easton, who was in charge of research in the Ontario Hospitals, drew their attention to a schizophrenic patient who developed a resistance to insulin to such a degree that successful shock could not be obtained, even when she was given 1,000 units in a single dose. This phenomenon intrigued Banting so much that for months after her discharge, uncured, from his immediate surveillance, he had samples of her blood sent to him at regular intervals from a distant hospital. His further contribution to the general problem may be gleaned from the papers cited.

Banting's success in the administration of his Department was largely a triumph of personality. In September, 1938, when he was leaving Toronto on one of his many fact-finding expeditions, the members of the Department arranged a party for him, which occasioned the following letter:

> R.M.S. *Duchess of Athol*,
> *September* 23, 1938.

MY DEAR HALL:

Please express to the Department my deep appreciation of their spontaneous and entirely unexpected "send-off." I want to tell you that it touched me deeply. As time advances, values in life tend to change, and with this change—truth, friendship, loyalty, and all those things that make life worth living—become more deeply cherished.

In the past I have given much of myself to the building of the Department. In this Miss Gairns has been my guide and anchor. Now my greatest joy in life is the pride I feel at the accomplishments of all those who constitute our group.

I have tried to help people on their way of life. Few of those I have helped have ever expressed any appreciation—but I am almost overcome when I think of you fellows having the kindly thought to come to my house to say good-bye.

This act helps to bind still further those strong ties and inspires within me a desire to be of greater service to all of you.

> Sincerely,
> BANTING.

BANTING IN HIS LABORATORY

Drawing by Charles Comfort, R.C.A.

PART XIII
Full Measure

He who has put forth his total strength in fit actions has the richest return of wisdom. I will not shut myself out of this globe of action, and transplant an oak into a flower-pot, there to hunger and pine; nor trust the revenue of some single faculty and exhaust one vein of thought. . . .

RALPH WALDO EMERSON.

1

BANTING's only child, William Robertson Banting, was born on the third day of April, 1929. Two years later his celebrated father, by then forty years of age, missed being home for the second birthday but was not forgetful of the occasion. He was sketching in Quebec at the time with A. Y. Jackson and he wrote down his meditations on his son in one of his voluminous, catch-all diaries:

April 3.

Bill's birthday started out by fog, then sunshine, then clouds and rain, then intermittent sunshine and cloud. How like life itself! The wind was in the west and it was colourful. I hope his young life will be sunshine, but he will have clouds and storms and mists. Above all, I hope his life will be useful. I do not wish for him the flowery beds of ease and if he is any use he will have his bad times and the good times will be short. I have just been thinking how unsatisfactory a thing life is. After working hard and finding something new, or working hard and gaining wealth, or working hard and accomplishing some end, when the work is done that is the end of it. After all, work is the only thing in life that brings happiness.

This philosophical strain was brightened by good spirits and cheerful comradeship in his relations with Bill. As the boy grew up his father was the best of companions. It is true that he related so many stories of his wartime experiences that Bill's imagination became crowded with pictures of battlefields, and his first drawings at school, where he was allowed to draw what he pleased, consisted of endless rows of crosses, which at first were very puzzling to his teachers. But this dubious psychology was an accidental side effect of a story-telling bent which was a source of much pleasure to both father and son. There was a long series of tales concerning a hyperactive "little nigger boy," who bounced about from country to country and continent to continent with wonderful resilience, gathering a candy-coated knowledge of geography and observing with fresh enjoyment the wonders of South America and Europe and all the other fascinating places

333

which Banting senior had visited. The nigger boy had astonishing adventures, he met astonishing people, he saw astonishing sights. Whenever his feet touched the earth he trod on enchanted ground. Emily Dickinson was not quite right when she wrote:

> There is no frigate like a book
> To take us lands away.

Sometimes the spoken word can weave a spell more potent, a spell, besides, which may take its effect when books are as yet beyond reach. The letters which Banting wrote to his son in later years are simple, spontaneous and delightful. Just what they should be. But his natural gift for story-telling was somehow inhibited by paper and pen and his few attempts to commit his tales to writing are sombrely flat. It was one of his many abortive plans to make a book of them. Perhaps it is just as well that the butterflies of his imagination were never caught and pinned.

Other children shared the same pleasure. When he visited the homes of his friends he would frequently vanish up the stair and be discovered some time later spinning bedtime yarns to wide-awake little listeners. His services were always in demand.

Wherever he went children seemed to congregate around him. A friend reports seeing him on a Toronto street-car with a dirty little urchin on his knee who was listening intently to the tick of his watch. When he went to Quebec with Jackson, children flocked to watch them paint. From Banting's diary we may cull an entry almost at random:

When we sketch near the village or within reach of them there is always a crowd looking over one's shoulder. They always think it is "très beau." Even children recognize Alex as the painter, for he always draws and holds a larger crowd. If we are close they run from one to the other but always prefer his work. However, there is one little girl—a round-faced kiddie of ten—who likes my painting and thinks I'm wonderful for I drew her little brother and gave it to her. It did resemble him.

In another place he wrote:

We had assistance at lunch time, for four small boys (there being no school today) followed us down to the swamp where we usually camp. They gathered wood and birch-bark and we gave them chocolate bars and oranges.

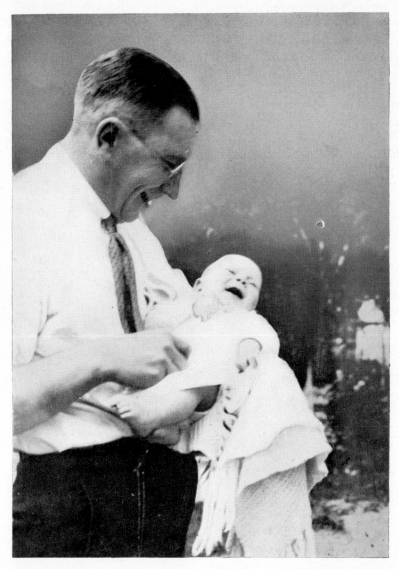

ONE OF THE EARLIEST PICTURES WITH W. R. ("BILL") BANTING

Again we find this, when Banting was visiting Quebec city alone:

Got up early and started out with sketch book. Did a drawing of the roofs of a house from the cliff near Laval's monument, then went down to the old market place and did Notre Dame des Victoires—the oldest church in Canada. Had some lunch and then did the oldest house in Quebec—where the Ursuline nuns first lived. I was then "taken in" by a couple of young ladies. They had been watching the drawing and as they both talked English and French and talked a great deal in both languages, they complimented me on the drawing and wanted to know where I came from—was I from the U.S.? They both lived in Quebec. One girl's father was Irish and mother French. Also the other girl's father was Irish and mother French, but her father died and she calls her present father "Monsieur," since he is not her father and is French. They invited me to go and see the narrowest street in the city—"Sous le Cap." They chattered away and told me that hundreds of tourists came in the summer-time and that the bus used to take the tourists down this narrow street, but that one day a child was run over and killed and then they would not let them go down any more. They warned me not to give the kids pennies, for if I did, unless I had hundreds of pennies, there would not be enough and the kids would "mob" me. The kids were very rude and spit on ladies who didn't give them pennies and even snatched the purses of ladies or kicked their shins. They "often showed tourists about" and sometimes they got twenty-five or fifty cents, and one day some kids begged of a lady they were showing around and one of the girls pushed the kid over but the kid kicked her on the shin and she had a great big lump on her leg and it turned blue. I asked them what they did with their money. They both saved it to buy clothes. One of them had a bank account of $1.40. They used to buy candy but it made their teeth rotten—and they both displayed rotten teeth—so they never bought candy any more. I suggested that oranges might be good for their teeth or any raw vegetables would be better than candy. By this time we had arrived at the street, so I gave each a dime. I was supposed to go up the street, but I happened to go back to the market place to do another sketch and I saw my two young ladies eating ice-cream. They hid in a doorway. . . .

On the whole he found the children of the province very mannerly, a fact on which he frequently commented. Later on when he went to Spain, he remarked on the contrast between the little Canadiens, who were neatly and brightly dressed and well-behaved, and the dirty, ragged, disorderly Spanish "imps."

The Santa Claus parade at Christmas time customarily passed down University Avenue under the windows of the Department when it was situated in the old Pathology Building. Banting made a habit of inviting his friends' children and Bill's friends to enjoy the spectacle with him. There must be "something for the kids" and, oh yes, the windows must be washed! At other times he preferred to let them be dirty rather than to tolerate a disturbance of his peace by window cleaners, but when the glorious parade was scheduled nothing must obstruct the view.

He had a general weakness for the young. Although his reception of adult reporters might be variable, boys and girls in their 'teens who once or twice requested interviews for their high school papers were welcomed with warmth and kindness. Four of them one day filed into his office and sat down in a stiff row on his couch.

"Well?" said Banting, waiting for the questions. But no questions came. The "journalists" looked at one another uneasily. Who should be the first to speak? Banting suppressed his amusement, remarked that it was the strangest interview he had ever given and began to ask questions himself. Was this young man going to college? Had he chosen a vocation? What did the young lady plan to do once she had finished high school? The ice being broken the youngsters began to talk and the interview proceeded easily and well.

If "the great man is he who never loses his child's heart" (Mencius) then Banting was great in this. He was a child with children.

2

None the less he was undoubtedly a "difficult" person. Even in the mellower years of his greatness, when the hyperbolic early nineteen-twenties had passed, he was sometimes unaccountably stiff, strangely unsympathetic. A colleague entering the Professor's office in the Department would realize that he had brought composition," each part conformable with the whole, is not to be expected. Banting is not the right subject for neat and elegant portrayal. He resists all efforts toward a formula.

His friends are themselves a part of the picture. It may safely be said that the majority of them, whether scientists, artists, farmers or physicians, are plain-spoken persons with the qualities of daylight and moderation. A subtle, elusive or unsettled character seemed seldom to attract him. He preferred sunny and decisive personalities, people who knew what they wanted and did not constantly perplex themselves and him with "wordy nothings." Imaginative they might well be; he preferred them so. But he seemed to choose even the insensitive in preference to the complex or tortuous. His liking was for "people" rather than "personalities."

A biographer who sets out to talk to Banting's friends will find scientists of every stripe, and will be struck by the fact that pretension, or "side," occurs in almost directly inverse proportion to the degree of intimacy of the friendship (as judged by the obtainable information and assuming a willingness to impart it.[1]) This applies almost equally to those who are not of the scientific fraternity. It would seem that the surest barrier against Banting's friendship, given honesty and good will as prerequisites, was affectation or an air of egotism. Farmers, miners, working men and craftsmen were frequently on better terms with him than Exalted Sir Knights.

The roaming investigator will talk, too, with artists, musicians, brokers, doctors, politicians, writers, bibliophiles, educators and sportsmen. The multifariousness of Banting's interests and amusements will be reflected in this catholic choice. There will be a noteworthy number of stout, bluff, pipe-smoking citizens, trenchant in their speech and engagingly earthy. But there will be sensitive and exclusive souls as well, with whom he was capable of ready sympathy. And finally the searcher cannot fail to observe that although Banting was true to his own generation, to old friends and classmates, a surprising number of those who knew him well are younger men, vital, energetic, ambitious, in whom (is it too much to imagine?) he recognized certain of the

[1]The only unwillingness to talk encountered by the present writer among the many friends who were interviewed arose from a reasonable and creditable doubt as to the propriety of certain revelations.

traits and many of the circumstances of the Banting of thirty years before.

Society in the narrow sense he shunned. A Toronto hostess of much experience in the entertainment of celebrities insists that he was "a perfect boor," by which she appears to mean that he would not exert himself to be pleasant to her tame lions and beribboned tabbies. People he did not like he simply did not like; when forced to mingle with them his manner could be not only cool but positively forbidding.

"No one," so he said, "has ever had an idea in a dress suit." His boredom was only too apparent at dressed-up dinners and receptions, unless he could find a kindred soul or two with whom to beguile his time. He had little time to spare for Rosencrantz and Guildenstern.

In 1930 he told a friend: "I am still wearing the dress suit I bought in 1919—my first. I bought it second hand then for twenty-five dollars. It was made five years before that. My wife hates it but it is still a good suit—fine old pre-war cloth." And this sums up his attitude exactly.

Among friends and acquaintances of his own choice he was a different man. The stiffness was replaced by relaxing cordiality, the coolness changed to warmth. Those who encountered him at such times found him extremely winning, an easy talker, a brisk raconteur.

There was nothing he liked better than a sing-song, and to gather a group around a piano while someone played familiar melodies and everyone joined in the choruses was better than a royal levee. His own contribution was a very respectable baritone part and all the enthusiasm of a Y.M.C.A. secretary.

Long discussions of old times and old themes, new work and new problems, politics and fishing, art and science, detective stories and poetry, were among his greatest pleasures. He once spent most of the night in reciting verses, particularly Kipling and Robert Service, at the summer cottage of a Toronto friend. Of the Rubaiyat, too, he had many stanzas by heart and there was always that favourite line, the last,

"Where I made one, turn down an empty glass."

His activity in the Arts and Letter Club has been mentioned previously. He was also a regular attendant at the meetings of the Caduceus Club, of which he was elected president and to which he presented an elaborate book, with illuminated pages and a silver plaque on the cover, for the roll of members. He was usually present at the Saturday luncheon of the Arts and Letters; sometimes also on Thursday. On Wednesday he frequently lunched at the Military Institute with Leech, Hipwell, Barraclough, McKay and Rae. Although meetings of the Faculty had generally to get on without him, the Faculty Club brought him a wider association among his colleagues of the University.

Many holidays and week-ends were spent in the Muskoka region. He eventually had a cottage of his own but he was also oftentimes the guest of G. W. Ross, C. A. ("Archie") Wells or J. W. ("Jack") McLaren. His summer house on the island at French River was given to him by Dr. Ross.

Banting loved to fish. In comfortable old clothes and with a soothing pipe between his teeth, he spent numerous happy hours on lake or river. He had many fishing companions and sometimes he was after more than fish; his "catch" on several occasions was a contribution of money for research. "I would fish with the Devil himself," he used to say, grinning, "if I thought I could get a dollar out of him for the cause." But more often he was intent on the bass, and with "Fred" Hipwell and Herbert I. Kurtz, the stockbroker and promoter, or with some other of his cronies, he would disappear from the city on a fishing trip, forgetting the cares of the Department and "roughing it" royally.

Yet even then he was still a research man. Kurtz recalls that once when they were plagued by mosquitoes Banting propounded a novel idea for repelling them. He had noticed, he said, on many occasions ever since his boyhood, that frogs seemed immune to mosquitoes; a bullfrog might be sitting on a log where mosquitoes swarmed about, yet the mosquitoes never lit on the frog. Was there something in the frog's skin, or something on it, that the pestiferous insects disliked? Why not investigate? Banting's companions laughed; was he really serious or was his tongue in his cheek?

It was Herbert Kurtz, incidentally, who was Banting's principal guide on the stock market. There had previously been rash and unlucky ventures with New York promoters, but his later experiences were profitable. He was genuinely interested in the promotion and development of Canadian mines and visited a number of them when the opportunity presented. His association with the work on silicosis brought him into contact with mining interests and with typical curiosity he probed his way about with questions. He was one of the original purchasers of the Crowshore Patricia property and had shares in other gold-mining properties as well.

On his return from one of these journeys he wrote the following letter to his son who was then at the Onandaga Camp.

Toronto, Tuesday, August 9 [1939].

DEAR BILL:

I have been wondering how you are getting along? I guess there are so many things to do that you have not had time to write. How about writing me the first day that it rains?

I was up to a camp at Marmora (140 miles to the north-east of Toronto) for the week-end and caught some fish. When there I visited a smelter and got another specimen for our museum—a sample of pure Cobalt metal, and also a piece of stellite, which is a mixture of metals.

The garden is fine but requires a lot of water these hot days.

Love,

DAD.

The reference to gardening points to another hobby. His third and final home in Toronto, at Rosedale Heights, had a hill-side garden on which he lavished the greatest care, competing with his friends in the culture of dahlias. When Hall laid some long-stemmed tulips of an uncommon variety on his desk at the Institute he was seized with a true horticulturist's excitement. Where had the bulbs been procured? He must have some at once. Was there any particular secret to raising tulips? Dr. Hall likewise taught him the art of grafting roses and he was nonplussed by his initial failures. Was this a special gift? Or did you have to go to O.A.C.? He tried it again. And again. And then again. For several weeks he devoted his spare moments to the art and eventually, after many trials and disappointments, achieved a fair degree of success. This simple accomplishment gave him greater pleasure than a new medal or a learned degree. The floral beauty that grew under his hands was a source of lasting satisfaction, annually renewed.

4

One of Bantings pastimes was reading detective stories. Perhaps it was more than a pastime. In the Alpha Omega Alpha Address, delivered at the University of Michigan, Ann Arbor, in January, 1925, he said: "I would recommend you to read Sherlock Holmes. He observed details, asked why, made deductions, solved mysteries." Was not this precisely what was required of a research scientist? It is not necessary, however, to pretend that he read stories of mystery and adventure because of their utility or because they gave him a mental work-out; he read them for fun, read them in enormous numbers, but was always best pleased by the most logical, most closely reasoned solutions.

In his 1931 diary of a sketching trip in Quebec we come across this:

Last night I finished reading *White Face,* a detective story by Edgar Wallace. It is a marvel the way that man turns out interesting, consistent, connected and fairly plausible stories. They are not works of great literary value, but are amusing and thrilling, and pass the time.

Again he wrote:

I read until late and half finished *The Crying Pig* murder by Victor MacClure. It is an English detective story, has considerable atmosphere, and is very well written throughout.

(Meanwhile, "Alex is reading *San Michele.* He never reads a useless book and even makes fun of me for reading detective stories.")

He took a lively interest also in "real detective" stories, the records of actual crime. In 1928, while visiting the Canadian west coast, he went several miles out of his way to obtain at first hand, from the persons involved, a story of murder and summary justice during the gold-rush era. The old man and his wife who were the narrators of the tale had been invited many years before, so they said, to accompany two prospectors to a distant point in almost inaccessible terrain where one of them claimed to have discovered a gold-bearing stream of unmatched richness. Mr. A——, the discoverer of the stream, had decided that he could not pan all the gold alone and transport it to civilization. He had, therefore, asked the others, first another prospector, Mr. B——, and then Mr. and Mrs. C——, the narrators, to enter into partnership with him, Mrs. C—— acting as cook for the party. This they had agreed to do. After several days' journey over difficult country they reached the fabulous stream and found it even richer than they had hoped. They pitched camp and began to pan for gold. They panned gold and still more gold until at last they decided that they had obtained all they could carry, an immense fortune in nuggets.

They started back. But at their first camp on the return journey Mrs. C—— awoke in the night to observe Mr. A—— in the very act of murdering with an axe their comrade, B——. It was undoubtedly his plan to dispose of the C——'s as well and to keep all the gold for himself. She screamed and roused her husband, who sprang to his feet and valiantly grappled with the murderous prospector. A terrible struggle ensued, in which Mrs. C—— also took part, and the wretch was overpowered and bound hand and foot with ropes.

Next day, having buried the unfortunate Mr. B——, they resumed their journey, guarding Mr. A——, his hands and arms still bound, at the point of a gun. To transport all the gold it was necessary to carry a part of it for a mile or so, then double back for the rest, and repeat this laborious process endlessly, covering the same ground three times. Supplies were running low. They were in constant dread of the murderer; one or other had always to be awake to guard against him. Ultimately they decided that the risk was too great.

Their solution was amazing. Instead of hiding the gold, to return for it later, and delivering the villain to the authorities, they determined to try him on the spot. Mr. C—— was the judge and his wife the prosecutor, defence attorney, court stenographer and jury. Mr. A—— was found guilty of murder and was sentenced to be hanged by the neck. The traditions of British justice, as interpreted by Mr. C——, called for a rope rather than bullets; Mr. A—— must be disposed of properly and decorously. So hanged he was, though with the greatest difficulty.

The C——'s then officiated at the burial service, their second such performance in a week, and returned triumphantly to town, where they presented to a thunderstruck constable of the North-West Mounted Police, a detailed, written account of the "trial" and execution. This incredible case was examined over and over in a series of courts and the incredible Mr. and Mrs. C—— were finally given their liberty.

Such, at least, is the tale which Banting heard from their lips. And such is the tale which he repeated, with a wealth of picturesque details and great vividness, to many of his friends.

Another diary (spring of 1930) has further examples picked up from Jackson. There is a story of the murder of a young provincial police constable, which was solved in true Sherlock Holmes fashion by a study of the tracks left by the murderers' automobile; another in which important details of the evidence for the conviction of a criminal included the type of sawdust found on a pair of overalls, the observation that the left-hand pocket of the overalls was more worn than the right and the detection of three types of hair on a towel. Such stories Banting re-told with relish. He was a gifted raconteur and could keep a circle of listeners enthralled.

But why not write the tales he could tell? His imagination was quite equal to rounding them out with convincing particulars. No doubt of that. Or altering them to taste. Or even devising new stories of his own. He was by no means loath to try, and several of his friends egged him on. In conversation with Mr. Napier Moore, editor of *Maclean's Magazine*, he outlined some of his plots. Would *Maclean's* be interested?

"Write them down," said Moore. "Send me the manuscripts."

But the manuscripts never came. Whether from lack of time or because he could not satisfy himself with the written versions of his yarns, Banting never submitted one for publication. In his case the tongue was mightier than the pen; he could not quite recapture in ink the prodigal colour and ingenuity of his verbal triumphs. No matter how hard he might try, the vigour and spontaneity were lost. He was always a little apprehensive, too, lest his stories be printed and read, not because of their merits but because of his name. He had no wish to impose in this way on editors and readers. Nothing doing. The very thought of it was enough to frighten him off.

His interest in thrillers, however, was perdurable. He carried them when he travelled. He read them on trains. He read them in bed at night. And the "daddy of them all," Sherlock Holmes, remained a favourite.

"It is a capital mistake," he would say, quoting from *The Second Stain*, "to theorize in advance of the facts." Also (from *The Blanched Soldier*):

When you have eliminated all which is impossible, then whatever remains, however improbable, must be the truth. It may well be that several explanations remain, in which case one tries test after test until one or other of them has a convincing amount of support.

These selections may be said to illustrate why a research scientist was devoted to thrillers; it is probable, however, that they illustrate nothing more than a sharp eye for a good quotation. He might have found his examples in psychological novels or philosophical treatises. But not he: give him a good, sensational murder mystery and he and the author would match wits. Dorothy Sayers, Agatha Christie, Edgar Wallace, Rex Stout, Ellery Queen—he knew them all.

"Murder," he explained to a friend, "is so relaxing." Tobacco and a murder mystery composed a rounded evening.

Banting was an inveterate smoker, alternating between cigarettes and a pipe. The cigarettes were invariably Buckinghams. A Toronto newspaper observed with some truth: "He is extremely bashful, particularly if he is in a place where he cannot smoke a cigarette." The pipes were sturdy briars with capacious bowls; he sometimes carved his initials and a date on the lower surface of bowl and stem.

Deciding that the cigarette habit was bad for his ulcer, he several times resolved to ration himself severely. He fixed on one cigarette per hour as a reasonable quota and for a time he marked his cigarettes in red, 9, 10, 11, etc., to indicate the hour at which

each was due. This device soon failed of its object and he continued as before, almost, if not quite, a chain smoker.

While on sketching trips with A. Y. Jackson in Quebec he
experimented with some of the French Canadian tobacco. Two
brands, particularly Rose Quesnel, are mentioned with approval
in a diary written in the spring of 1930.

I think they are good, unadulterated tobacco leaves with
"body" to their smoke. [One brand] is a strong, vigorous
daughter of Lady Nicotine, while Rosy is much more gentle
and I think I can get along with her much better.

Again he writes:

I am out of Buckingham cigarettes and they have none in
town, so I am smoking mostly Rose Quesnel (French Canadian)
mixed with Edgeworth. It goes very well. . . . There is "atmosphere" in this Rose Quesnel, and I am expecting to paint better
and be able to express the country better by its use.

Of another French Canadian brand he reports:

I must say that I like the taste of this Canadian as well as
any I have ever burned, though it requires open air or a wind
while smoking, and I am still a little doubtful of the effect on
my tongue.

He once reached the conclusion that the profit on all brands
of tobacco was excessive and he therefore decided to cure and blend
his own. Large jars packed with tobacco leaves, together with
honey and other curing agents, adorned his shelves at the
Institute. He also blended several varieties of tobacco (spreading a newspaper on a table with little heaps of "Hudson Bay,"
"Latakia," etc.) to suit his own taste.

"It really wasn't bad," says a pipe-smoking friend who tried
it, but others have made wry faces at the recollection of these
home-made mixtures. "Anyway," says one, "he appeared to like
the stuff himself. It was never wasted."

Two of the most characteristic photographs show Banting at
his desk with a pipe in his mouth and a glass caddie of tobacco
close by. In one of them he is concentrating deeply, pen in hand,
on a document. ("What are you going to do, then?" said Watson
to Sherlock Holmes in The Red-Headed League. "To smoke,"

answered Sherlock. "This is quite a three-pipe problem and I beg you not to speak to me for fifty minutes.") In the other he is looking up from the desk with a grin of welcome, the pipe jutting up jauntily to one side. Neither of these photographs was approved for release to the many school children who wrote to ask for a picture. He felt that the pipe made them both unsuitable. The children always received small copies of a formal camera portrait instead. The Lady Nicotine must not appear.

His reading apart from detective stories and scientific literature was varied. In one of the Quebec diaries there is the following entry:

We got a whole roll of papers tonight—*Police Gazette, Miner, Hush,* and the *Daily Star.* I hope the sender will sometime know that it was a decided come-down for us. . . . Alex was interrupted in *San Michele,* while I was reading Plato in the *History of Philosophy.*

His excursions into philosophy went neither far nor deep. He concluded that the work of the great philosophers should be made more generally available in popular form. Beyond the assertion that philosophy was a "good thing," there was little further comment. He strove toward a wider appreciation of every aspect of life, but although his taste was comprehensive it had definite limits.

History he found more sympathetic to his mind. Particularly the history of his own country. The seventy-two volumes of the *Jesuit Relations* he pondered over pleasurably for years. Charlevoix, Mackenzie, Thompson—the early explorers and adventurers—he read with avid interest. Local history was another pursuit and he knew many of the details of the settlement of Simcoe County. A history of the town of Alliston was one of the many self assignments projected for his retirement. Still another was a history of Indian medicine.

His collection of Canadiana was one of his proudest possessions. From Eaton's book department, Britnell's bookshop and Mrs. Dora Hood's bookroom he purchased the greater number of his books. Wherever he could lay hands on a rare volume relating to Canadian history he was definitely in the market. Fifty dollars was the largest sum he ever expended for a book, but fifty dollars seemed a large amount. Although he could be grandly generous when he chose, he was cautious in smaller matters, ever mindful of his father's dictum, "A penny in the bank for every penny spent." When another copy of the same book was offered to him later for twice the price, he was delighted to think that he had got a bargain.

Miss Blodwen Davies, to whom Jackson had introduced him, helped to sort out his collection and sometimes advised him on purchases. Her admirable biography of the Canadian painter, Tom Thomson, shows the influence of Banting in its final chapter. Reading the coroner's report on Thomson, he saw reason to doubt that the artist had met his death by drowning, which was the official verdict. A suspicion of foul play was never fully confirmed, but Miss Davies succeeded in marshalling a body of evidence which is most suggestive. Banting sought in vain to obtain permission for re-opening the grave. Forensic medicine and criminology held a fascination he could not resist.

His work, his play, his changing and ever-enlarging interests, his public duties and arduous journeys imposed a considerable strain on his health. On the whole it was excellent. Mention has twice been made of a gastric ulcer. In the early years of his fame he suffered acutely from dyspepsia and although the diagnosis was made and treatment instituted he seemed to benefit relatively little. An intolerance for fatty foods also directed suspicion toward his gall bladder but it could never be shown guilty. Later on, when his personal affairs had become more stabilized and when his appendix (was this coincidence?) had been removed, the severity of the attacks definitely lessened. He continued to be careful about his diet, but it is worthy of remark that when fishing or sketching or roughing it in the wilds he seemed capable of eating anything.

We turn again to the diaries:

March 1, 1930.

Arrived in Ottawa—had breakfast. It seemed a little odd to have breakfast, for it is now six weeks since I ceased the practice or habit of breakfasting. When travelling, one must eat. . . .

[St. Fidele] Tuesday, March 11, 1930.

. . . It is strange but since coming on this trip I have not had the least trouble with hyperacidity, and yet I often have to eat fried food.

Thursday, March 13, 1930.

. . . When we got home tonight, cold, tired and hungry, the big plate of hot soup went right to the solar plexus. I am afraid I am going to get fat again if this keeps up.

March 18, 1930.

. . . We got home by six and had a huge hot dinner of (1) soup, (2) hash, (3) omelette, (4) wild strawberries and fresh cake, (5) strawberry pie—but we could not eat any pie. . . .

He took considerable pride in his stamina. That he was sturdy and robust and young for his years was convincingly demonstrated later in some of the experiments to which he submitted in Aviation Medicine Research. The North-West journey had been rugged, too, and in rural Quebec he struggled valiantly over the hills in the face of bitter weather. After one such excursion, in deep snow and across difficult country, he wrote in his diary:

"It is a satisfaction to know that I can walk ten miles under such conditions and still have a little left over."

Perhaps the perturbations of his personal life told more markedly than all his exertions. We turn with regret to consider them.

5

The April day which "started out by fog, then sunshine, then clouds and rain, then intermittent sunshine and cloud" seemed to the diarist who described it to be a microcosm of life. The inner weather of his own personality was undeniably changeable; the outer weather of extrinsic events affecting him had seemed to display from the first an April whimsicality, one moment bright and glancing, the next moment bleak and chill, then all at once tumultuous.

The domestic storm which broke suddenly in 1932 had long been preparing; his friends had required no special divination to see it coming. There are times when the taut and lowering atmosphere which precedes the onset is more unbearable than the actual throes of the storm, and this was such a time. It broke, none the less, with benumbing abruptness.

The nature of the circumstances which led to Banting's divorce will be sought for in vain in the present narrative. Suffice it to say that the events precipitating an action in court were in some sense incidental; they were part of a longer, more involved, subjacent sequence which it would be profitless and unkind to attempt to trace. The elements of a deep-seated incompatibility may already have been noted by a percipient reader. The rest of the story belongs to the realm of "old, unhappy, far-off things" which dwindle and fade into the past but leave unmistakable traces behind. Unfortunately such traces are proof against total erasure. The marriage had lasted eight years.

In an undefended divorce action Mr. Justice Logie granted a decree *nisi* to Banting on April 25, 1932. Also granted to the plaintiff was the custody of his three-year-old son, although he was not required to enforce this part of the judgment unless he so desired. The final decree followed in due course.

A prior agreement had been reached with the newspapers that the divorce proceedings would not be flagrantly dealt with in the press. Coverage would be limited, it was promised, to a brief announcement. But one of the more sensational dailies broke faith; the others thereupon followed suit. A few details of the evidence were printed by one paper, more by another, still more by a third; the whole unfortunate affair was soon blackened with printer's ink. Banting, already distraught and sick at heart, had just grounds for indignation and a human excuse for fury. The general belief in his violent dislike of reporters derives in considerable degree from his bitterness at this time. The belief that he was indiscriminately rude to the fourth estate is a slanderous myth; he received reporters well whenever they treated him fairly, but in the spring of 1932 he was made to suffer, though not for the first time nor the last, at unscrupulous hands.

Although he had desired a divorce, the final break affected

him deeply. He became seclusive and distrait. His usual haunts
he temporarily deserted. He prowled about in his laboratory or
his apartment, smoking incessantly and wrapped in gloom. A few
"get-togethers" with the "old gang" were for a time his only
diversion.

Gradually his horizon brightened. He resumed his normal
occupations. The clouds were dispelled. In his apartment in the
Athelma block, crowded with books and journals and the
mementoes of his travels, he was tended by a loyal and efficient
housekeeper, Mrs. Elizabeth Proctor. Here he entertained his
friends and his modest parties gained a reputation for spontaneity
and spirit. He threw himself energetically into his work. The
broken threads were mended.

6

There were two important additions to the group of workers
at the Institute during the middle nineteen thirties—Drs. Bruno
Mendel and Herman Fischer, refugee scientists. Growing uneasiness in Europe drove many scholars across the Atlantic during the
early years of the Hitler régime, for although two-thirds of the
world might be indifferent or complacent, the finest intellects who
were caught up by the terrible force of this atavistic movement
were not long in perceiving which way the "wave of the future"
was bearing them. Einstein is the most familiar example, but
there were scores of others. Mendel and Fischer were among the
most important of the group which came to Canada.

Dr. Mendel, an accomplished German Jew, well known to the
world of science for his researches on the metabolism of cancer
cells, read the signs of the times in 1933 and fled with his family
from their home in Berlin to take up residence in Holland. But
even in Holland, although they liked the country and the people,
they felt unsafe. To the Jewish community it seemed incon-
ceivable that Germany, traditionally the second home of the
Hebrew race, should be the centre of the most virulent anti-
Semitism, still less that the contagion of a barbaric creed, coupled
with Germany's military might, should extend beyond the borders

of the Reich. They remained in Holland to rue their optimism, but in August, 1936, three years before the outbreak of war, Mendel, his wife and his three children fled once again, this time to Canada.

Mendel had never met Banting but was acquainted with his work and knew that he was engaged in cancer research. He called at the Institute.

"All right," said Banting, "tell me all about it. Tell me about the Nazis. What they have done and how much you hate them. Get it off your chest. In Canada you are free to talk. Say anything you please. I want to hear the whole story. Go ahead."

Mendel explained that he had had three years to "get it off his chest," since he had lived for that length of time in Holland. But he told the story of Nazi aims and Nazi methods as he and his friends had seen them and Banting listened thoughtfully.

"He knew a lot about it already," says Mendel, "and later on, at the time of Munich, he was one of the very few of my acquaintance here (President Cody was another) who saw the folly of 'peace in our time' on Nazi terms. He told me that he was deeply ashamed of the Munich agreement."

The conversation turned to research. Dr. Franks, who was also studying cancer, joined them.

"What are your plans?" Banting asked his visitor.

"I should like to come to work here," was the answer.

Banting could give no immediate decision, he said, but would see what arrangements could be made; the Board of Governors would be meeting in about a month.

The talk went on. Years before, in 1929, Mendel had made the interesting discovery that the "normal" metabolism of malignant cells was inhibited by the presence of a certain tricarbon sugar, glyceraldehyde. In the work which was then in progress at the Institute it had been desired to make use of this discovery, but advance was hindered by their inability to obtain the sugar; they had sent for it far and wide, without result.

"How much do you need?" said Mendel. They told him that a gram or two might be enough for the time. He smiled. Among his effects he had brought some of this precious glyceraldehyde—two kilograms—at least a thousand times more than they had hoped to obtain. It was manna from heaven.

Sir Frederick treated the new arrivals with characteristic kindness. Before her husband had had time to get back to the hotel after his first interview at the Institute, Mrs. Mendel received a telephone call.

"This is Dr. Banting," said the voice on the wire. "I know you must be lonely in a strange land and a strange city. You must certainly have dinner with me this evening. Yes, yes, I insist. Bring the children. I shall call for you all about seven. Seven o'clock in the lobby of the hotel."

Sharp at seven they found him waiting. He had brought a friend, a Jewish financier. It was all naïve, delightful, transparently kind. Says Mrs. Mendel, reminiscing:

He wanted so much to make us feel at home. It was wonderful. He was quite enchanting. He took us to dinner at the Old Mill and I remember he said, "You have lost your home, but so"—with a rather wry expression—"so have I." We had dinner and we danced and we talked. We talked and talked. It was a very memorable evening.

Although his appointment could not be officially confirmed by the Board of Governors for about a month, Dr. Mendel began his work at the Institute almost at once. He had brought his own technician with him and also his equipment; all that he actually needed was a laboratory in which to work.

Banting called frequently at the new Mendel home on Bedford Road, where he would sit in a great armchair before the fireplace and delight the children with stories of his travels. There, in 1937, he met Brüning, former Chancellor of the Weimar Republic, and plied him with searching questions about the last days of German democracy and the beginning of Nazism. If Brüning had done this or done that, would it have made any difference? Would it have been possible in any way to stave off the coming of Hitler? Why had the Republic crumbled?

When the Mendels went abroad and Mrs. Mendel's mother remained in Toronto with the children, Banting used to call her on the telephone to make sure that everything was all right. He paid her a visit to keep her from being lonely. Was there anything she needed? She must not hesitate to call him if there were anything he could do.

He entertained the family in his apartment. He gave them one of his pictures, a winter landscape from Quebec. Little wonder that they should all remember him with great warmth of affection and great pride in the association.

"He was so vital a presence," says Mrs. Mendel, "that simply to think of him seems almost to bring him back. He sits down again in his armchair by the fire and tells us so vividly and charmingly of the places he visited, the people he knew and the causes dear to his heart."

Dr. Fischer had a similar experience of Banting's kindness. Many Canadians, viewing pictures of the German horror camps, Belsen and Buchenwald and the others, have felt that they have cause to reproach themselves for Canada's narrow and parochial attitude to the reception of refugees in the years immediately preceding the war; they were not without examples of a more liberal and intelligent reaction.

During the Spanish Civil War Banting was an outspoken supporter of the loyalist cause. In August, 1938, he stood sponsor for the relief ship which was sent to aid the loyalists and he wrote to Dr. Cannon, of Harvard, who was active in the work of the Committee to Aid Spanish Democracy, that his sympathies were with the democratic group in the Spanish conflict, adding "if my name would be of any value to you, you may use it as you would your own." The policy of legalistic non-intervention stirred his impatience; the more realistic attitude of the Russian government won his approval. He was consistently and clear-sightedly anti-Fascist throughout all the sorry period of democratic temporizing.

7

The background and basis for his international views was provided by his later journeys abroad.

It was in 1933 that he went to Spain.

After spending about ten days in London (he wrote to a friend on his return) I found it was impossible for me to be present at the meeting of the Norway Medical Society, since the airplane transportation was discontinued for the winter months.

My purpose in going to Norway was to receive an honorary fellowship in their Medical Society, but I was not able to take in that part of the trip.   From London I went by ship to Viego, in the north-west corner of Spain, where I remained four days and got my first sight of Spain and a view of the Spanish customs.

From Viego he went to Madrid, where he attended the International Cancer Congress and dispatched a series of letters to friends in Toronto:

> *Palace Hotel, Madrid.*
> *October* 24, 1933.

I arrived in Madrid on Monday, October 22, but got a less pretentious hotel until this morning.   I went to the Congress rooms here and got a portfolio full of reprints, directions, cards of introduction and tickets to the theatres.

I cannot begin to give you my impression of Spain but it is more magnificent, more grand, and has more imposing buildings than any place I have ever been.   Paris is no greater than Madrid in historical, grandiose buildings.   Palaces, galleries and churches rival France and surpass England.   I have written over eighty pages of diary so you can have more in detail when I get home. If I only knew Spanish and French I could get along much better. The official language of the Conference is French.

I have done no painting as yet.   Palaces are not paintable.

> *Madrid, November* 1.

I am still in Madrid and have been painting on the outskirts of the city all day.   It is the best day I have had since I left home, but oh I'm tired!   I have walked miles.   Did three sketches, none of them up to much for it is new stuff for me.

Tomorrow I go to Toledo, the oldest city in Spain, and the day after I go to Seville in the south, then Granada and Barcelona.

The Conference as an educational institution was a wash-out, but I met the English and American groups of Cancer research workers. . . .

To a medical correspondent he confided further details after his return.   Of the Congress he wrote:

I found it disappointing from the scientific standpoint, since the papers were nearly all given in French and were given with a view to obtaining a head-line and publicity in European papers. The real value of the Congress was in the meeting of the English and American groups in the more friendly and inspiring atmosphere of the private bar of the Savoy Hotel. Every afternoon at four o'clock a dozen or so of us would meet to discuss not only cancer but Spanish customs, bull fights and the eminent cancer authorities of Europe. At these informal meetings there were Cramer, of the Imperial Cancer Research and his group; Cook of the Cancer Hospital, London; Ewing, of New York, and his group; as well as representatives from Edinburgh, Glasgow and several American cities.

To return to the on-the-spot letter of November first:

I was at a bull fight on Sunday and must say it was more spectacular and less gory than I thought it would be.

Granada, November 9.

I just arrived here last night and it rained today, which cramped my style a little but I covered a lot of ground. There are so many kids in Spain that I have not been able to make a single sketch on the spot. I simply make a drawing and by the time I am finished they are about fifteen deep and crawling all over me. They smell of garlic and I shake them off when their heads get too close to mine for fear there will be a crawling-over. However, it is a fine country for painting—but not what I expected—everything is close up.

The Professor of Medicine of the Granada Medical School called on me and wants to take me out for the day tomorrow. He does not speak a word of English but had a young doctor from Mexico to interpret for him.

I have not done any thinking since I left Madrid and do not know when I will feel called upon to do any again. I would like to be able to travel on and on. It is interesting to watch people and the Spaniards take a lot of watching. They are very kindly and friendly. Twice this morning men brought out chairs for me to sit on while I sketched. On the train you simply must take some of their food. They have plenty and eat plenty and often.

Barcelona, November 19.

I leave Spain on Tuesday for Marseilles, Geneva, Rome, Florence, Venice, Milan, Paris and Le Havre.

I have not time to go farther north this trip. Spain and Italy will be enough at present. I will have an excuse to come again for Germany, Poland and Russia—and the Balkans. When I retire I am going to travel.

One more day in Spain. I hate to leave. I would like to go back to Granada and stay at the little villages and towns between Granada and Alecante. It was the finest and most paintable of all Spain and I passed through it on the train.

Barcelona is large, modern and unSpanish. Today everyone voted. There were lines of people waiting at the voting booths every couple of blocks. There are 1,300,000 people in Barcelona and all live in six-story apartment houses on fine wide streets. Art and civilization do not go well together. I am not sorry to leave this city.

I have had plenty of time to think and have a new theory for cancer research. I am making notes in my little black notebook. You see I can never get entirely away from the lab. I have kept all the English reprints from the Conference to read on the boat. I hope there won't be too much other work to be done when I get back for I have a lot of things I want to do in the lab. This is the first time in years that I have been dissociated far enough from work to get a look at it. It pays.

Rome, November 27.

Except for Granada I am entirely unknown in this part of the world. I am not even going to visit the University here.

This is the best trip except the Arctic that I have ever had, but you will read it all in my diary which is over two hundred pages and going strong. It will likely slowly die from now on as I am facing home.

While in Rome he received letters telling him that the British and Canadian newspapers were crediting him with a new development in the silicosis work. It annoyed him so much that he cut short his trip and booked an earlier sailing.

He had spoken about the silicosis work in England, giving credit to Dr. Franks, Dr. King and Dr. Irwin, who were working on the problem, but as usual the reporters had twisted the story for news value.

He hurried home to set the record straight and to prevent misunderstandings.

8

In 1935 came the visit to Russia. This was for Banting a most stirring experience. Although the prime object of his journey was to attend the International Physiological Congress, meeting in Leningrad and Moscow under the presidency of the world-famous, eighty-six-year-old patriach of physiologists, Ivan Petrovitch Pavlov, he eagerly seized the opportunity to see as much as possible of the Soviet Union and to study the enormous experiment of state socialism. The breadth of the revolutionary changes, the immense scale of the national upheaval, the bold and multifarious plans staggered his imagination. Typically his enthusiasm boiled up at once. Such reverence for science! Such enormous sums devoted to research! Such tremendous strides in education! Where was there anything like it? The laboratories were magnificent. The investigative spirit was the leaven of their daily bread; it was the national diet of the Muscovite.

The striking juxtaposition of the New Russia with relics of the Old constantly allured him. To a friend in Toronto he wrote:

Rostov-Don, July 11, 1935.

. . . I have just completed the famous Volga boat trip from Gorki to Leningrad. It was a most interesting and delightful trip. We had four or five hours ashore each day to see the old cities—Kazan, Samara, Saratof. They are a strange combination of very old and very new. Factory units— (factory, workers' houses, recreation and culture building, schools, hospital, first aid clinics, maternal care clinic and huge apartments for the workers)—and next door to all this the old houses of the former days, old churches now put to various uses. Many of the summer palaces of the former rich are now rest homes for workers. Everyone is enthusiastic, happy and working. Thousands and thousands of workers are attending schools and universities. Science and art flourish everywhere. The cities of the Volga were storm centres in the revolution and now they are proud. Travel in Russia is much easier and more pleasant than in Spain, Italy or France because of the guides.

Banting began his travels in Russia first class, later decided that this was a poor way to see the country and its people. Despite official protests he travelled thereafter in second-class coaches. Like every distinguished visitor to the U.S.S.R. he was taken on a conducted tour and it was afterwards alleged that he saw only those things which his hosts wished him to see. He himself asserted that he sometimes slipped away on his own to avoid too much "guidance." What had he expected to see before setting out? Are there preconceptions to reckon with? We know from an earlier diary that he had read with interest and admiration a history of the revolution written by a Roman Catholic priest, who was far from being favourably disposed to the Bolsheviks. So that whatever else he may have heard or read he was not uninformed of the darker aspects of the new régime in Russia.

One of his diaries, written five years before the Russian journey, contains this paragraph:

Capitalism in its narrower sense is doomed, for even if the Russian Five-Year-Plan does not succeed one hundred per cent. it will sufficiently succeed to show the world what can be done. No country wants to go through the bloodshed and terror that has purged Russia of her traditions, her religion, her ancient civilization and her system of living, and all countries should be studying the situation to find wherein the good points of the system can be applied to their own country.

From Russia he wrote again:

July 19, 1935.

The Volga boat trip was fine—Stalingrad power trucks, Rostov collective farms, farm implements, factories. Every town has its old tree with new roots.[2] Old houses, new apartments, old palaces of wealthy merchants, new palaces of administration, old private gardens and new parks of rest and culture.

The U.S.A. in its days of boom was not so busy or active as all Russia is now. This activity is all the more difficult to understand in a people that are naturally slow, undecided and hesitant about almost everything. Nothing is done in a hurry and only trains and boats ever do anything on time.

The Georgian Highway motor trip was very fine. Better than Switzerland, but less rocky and larger in scale than the

[2]New tree with old roots?—L. S.

Rocky Mountains. It has always existed as a mountain pass and its history antedates the earliest record.

Tiflis is a most interesting city, old and new. It has been captured and changed hands twenty-nine times. It is the centre of Georgian civilization but the most mixed people I have ever seen. There are two universities, including medical faculties, one in Russia and one in Georgia. The people in the street have characteristic costumes of Georgian, Russian, Persian, Greek, Jew, Mongol, Tartar and Kurd. It is sub-tropical with fruits, flowering trees and palms.

Batum is smaller, only sixty-five thousand, but over forty dialects and languages are to be heard. It is a seaport town and is more mixed in people. Everything is interesting.

Tomorrow we land at Yalta. The ship is skirting the north shore of the Black Sea, calling for passengers and cargo every few hours. Sometimes we go ashore. Language is a great handicap. There are only two others on board who speak English. Every foot of the ship is occupied with people. The peasants sleep all over the decks, passages, among the machinery and in the lifeboats. Their food bundles and babies are an interesting mass object. There is a high wind and the sea has a surface wave, but no deep roll fortunately. This south Russia is entirely different from the north.

Kiev, July 29, 1935.

. . . Kiev is in many ways the finest city I have yet visited. It is the centre of Ukraine culture and all signs, books, etc., and the language are Ukranian. Possibly . . . the wide, clean streets . . . appeal most. The buildings are fine and there are good museums and old churches. It was a former capital of Russia.

I leave for Moscow in the morning and will be there about three weeks and will cover the Physiological Congress in Leningrad.

I have now seen the country as far as Eastern Russia goes and want to go to headquarters and get something of the constitution, laws and statistics.

He got his wish. In the article[3] which he wrote for *Canadian Business* on his return he seemed to have caught the prevailing

[3]Sir Frederick Banting, K.B.E., "Science and the Soviet Union," *Canadian Business,* February, 1936.

Russian passion for comparative figures, as it is heavily larded
with statistics of "before" and "after."

To return to the letter:

I have never been any place that is so interesting, where travel
is so easy and where one is so well looked after.   One can go where
one likes and do as one likes within the scope of one who does
not know the language.   The people are most kindly.   In fact
it is a great country.

Everyone works and people seem thirsty for knowledge.   They
read and study on the trains, in the parks and while waiting.
Most people carry books or magazines.   I would like to come
here for a year to work.

With the same thought in mind he dashed off a post card to
Hall:

Leningrad, August 10.

I think that you should consider coming to the U.S.S.R. for
your post-graduate work.   The Congress is under way.

BANTING.

"Wherever he went," says Dr. Hall, "wherever he visited the
centres of research and post-graduate study, he kept one object
in view: 'Would this be a good place for someone in the Department?'   He studied foreign labs. with this idea: 'What can we
learn from them here?' "

He concluded that there was much to be learned.   Not only
medicine, but every branch of science seemed to be gathering
speed and increasing power.   Science applied to agriculture.
Science applied to industry.   With all the zest of a junior com-
missar he amassed the statistics of the sweeping transformation.

On his return he wrote:[4]

The greatest experiment that the world has ever known has
just been carried out within the Soviet Union.   This experiment
involved the lives of 170,000,000 people who use 189 languages
or dialects and who occupy nearly one-sixth of the land surface of
the globe.   It was an experiment of government.   In the successful carrying out of this experiment science was a major factor.
Science and the fruit of science had been almost denied these

[4]"Science and the Soviet Union."

people from the beginning of their history until 1917. The Bolsheviks suffered privation, fought and if necessary died for those far-sighted leaders who promised the people education and science.

In order to understand the situation in the Soviet Union today it is necessary to realize that before the revolution only about ten people out of every hundred could read and write. The country was one of the least industrialized in the world. The vast majority of the people were backward, down-trodden peasants who lived on farms or in small villages. Of the 170,000 doctors (at the rate of one doctor per thousand population) required for the medical care of the people, there were but 19,000 and these were for the most part located in the cities of the west and in the army and navy. The country was about one hundred years behind the rest of civilization. The problem that faced the new government in 1917-18 was gigantic; nor could the task be commenced until the bloody revolution was accomplished. During the past ten years progress has been stupendous.

Education was one of the first aims of the new régime. As early as 1919 a society was formed to liquidate illiteracy. The idea was to help one another. The membership rose to over 3,000,000; for example, during 1931 over 19,000,000 adult people learned to read and write. The schools were crowded to capacity, there being morning, afternoon and evening classes. Thousands of new schools were built. At present every child must attend school until fifteen years of age. During the first Five-Year-Plan 15,500,000,000 rubles were spent on education. By the commencement of 1933 there were 485,000 students in universities, 913,000 in technical schools, 435,000 in workers' faculties, 1,500,000 in the apprenticeship and crafts schools, more than 4,350,000 in secondary schools and more than 19,000,000 in elementary schools. The Soviet school taught children in seventy different national languages.

The education of medical students has been carried out in the same increasing scale. The number of doctors has now increased from 19,000 to about 60,000, and they are adding about 10,000 per year. Because of almost universal hospitalization of all sick people, they will not require as many doctors as other countries, since a doctor can attend more patients in a hospital ward than in scattered homes.

Not only have they made great advancement in the teaching of medicine and the application of public health measures, but they have laid the foundations for the advancement of medical science through research.

The government of the Soviet Union gave 15,698,398 rubles in 1933, 31,517,418 rubles in 1934, and 35,780,748 rubles in 1935 to the All-Union Institute of Experimental Medicine for the purpose of Medical Research. "Appropriations for the construction and equipment of the buildings will exceed 100,000,000 rubles."

The training of engineers of all kinds has received particular attention. The foreign engineer is being rapidly replaced by the young graduates of the Soviet Universities. . . .

Following this barrage of statistics Banting turned to the theme which pleased him best when discussing Russia—the universality of its science. A medical scientist himself, he was not confined within narrow limits. He wrote:

In most countries the science professor of a university takes little heed of the application of scientific principles to industry. Germany was the first country to utilize scientists in industry, and for this reason she became the leader in the manufacturing of chemicals, dyes and precision instruments. The United States followed Germany's example. In the Soviet Union there is a two-hundred-year-old "Academy of Science," consisting of ninety-three Academicians. This body represented the trained minds in the various branches of science—Biology, Mineralogy, Physics, Chemistry and Botany, as well as in the cultural subjects, and had museums, botanical gardens and a library of 3,500,000 volumes. In 1929 the Academy of Science, imbued with the new spirit, volunteered "to study the country's productive forces and contribute to the utilization and to elaborate the methods of applying the scientific theories and the results of scientific experiments and observations to the task of socialist construction in the U.S.S.R." This group of scientists devoted themselves assiduously to the problems of the state. Their scientific knowledge was applied to the development of electric power, mining, industry of all kinds and particularly to agriculture. The government backed them with adequate financial support. . . . These investments in research have yielded dividends in thousand-fold results.

Today, scientific research and the application of science to industry and agriculture is the most impressive activity in the Soviet Union. There is no country in the world that is progressing so rapidly in this regard. . . .

In the new experimental stations that are springing up all over Russia, scientific research is being applied to the study of all sorts of diseases of grains, plants and animals. Experiments are being carried out for the control of weeds, since nothing will decrease the yield of grain per acre like weeds. From the world's stock of grains the U.S.S.R. has obtained five hundred varieties of wheat, two hundred and forty-six samples of barley, as well as numerous kinds of oats, buckwheat, beans, peas, flax, cotton, etc. These grains and plants are being experimented with in all sorts of ways with the view of obtaining the best yields in the various districts and under the varied conditions that exist in the Soviet Union. Whole plantations of citrus fruits are being set out in the southern part of Russia. One may drive for hours through the new tea plantation around Batum or the new tobacco plantation about Yalta. By the cultivation of the rubber plant the Soviet Union will be ultimately independent of the rest of the world for her rubber supply.

At the recent conference in November, 1935, thirty-two academicians and five hundred scientific research workers were gathered together in a conference on livestock and wheat problems. It was formerly thought that wheat could only be grown on the black earth belt of central Russia, but the research on soil, fertilizers and varieties of wheat has now made it possible for Babelov to state that potential wheat land in the Soviet Union amounts to 812,000,000 acres, as compared with 910,000,000 acres suitable for wheat in the United States and Canada combined. Of the 400,000,000 acres of wheat now sown throughout the world the Soviet Union has about 92,000,000 acres.

. . . In one of the southern cities I had a long conversation with a very intelligent "member of the party." I asked him if the Soviet Union was going to flood the world market with wheat. He explained that this was not the case, since the southern wheat lands were now being planted with citrus fruits, tea and tobacco. Furthermore, they were not interested in world markets except in so far as they could sell their products for the purpose of raising foreign credit. These foreign credits would be used to buy in those foreign countries the needed commodities which could not be obtained or produced within the Soviet Union. . . .

. . . All of these huge enterprises require men of executive capacity, intelligence, foresight and judgment. These qualities are to be found in the men who rise to office within the Soviet Union. The life and activities of their great commercial and industrial men do not greatly differ from the life and activities of industrial men in our country—nor does the financial man—banker and organizer of industry differ so much from those that perform this service in other countries. There are privileges and luxuries that our financial leaders buy. In the Soviet Union these privileges and luxuries are given to him by the people. They honour service. Honour, appreciation, and trust of comrades spur and inspire men to plan and work for the common good of all. Man cannot exploit his fellow man. There is no unemployment in the Soviet Union. Conditions are improving very rapidly. Everyone is tremendously enthusiastic. The health of all is cared for by the state. All people have the opportunity to rise as high as their talents and industry will permit in whatever field of endeavour they may select. Every person's future is invested in the state. The state in turn provides for the education of children and an old-age pension. This sense of security brings happiness and peace of mind and permits true culture.

Pasteur, the great French scientist, said: "The future belongs to science and woe to the nations that close their eyes to this fact." The Soviet Government is building a gigantic structure on the solid rock of science and research. For this reason there now remains not a vestige of doubt as to the future success of the Soviet Union. *Her future is doubly secure because no people in the world so fully realize that the science of today is the research of yesterday, and the research of today is the science of tomorrow.*

The most fanatical and exacting of party members could hardly have asked for higher approbation of the Communist régime. It must be remembered that the widespread acclaim of the U.S.S.R. to which we became accustomed after June, 1941, was not a universal fashion in 1936, and that many influential persons spoke then of the "menace of Bolshevism" in terms very similar to those used by Hitler; in fact there were many who regarded Hitler's Germany as a bulwark against the Reds and this attitude may well have been a determining factor in the foreign policies of Britain and France. It therefore required stronger conviction to praise the Soviet Union in 1936 than in 1945, and that a man like Banting, basically conservative and Imperialist, should so far forget his prejudices as to indulge in unmixed praise of the Russians is evidence that he was both courageous and perceptive. He was not a convert, however, to

AT THE ACTON FISHING CLUB

the doctrine of Marx and Lenin, and he once expressed the opinion that Pavlov, who had been a Czarist, was a truer prophet of the New Order than were many avowed Communists. Indeed, although he praised the social reforms and the improvement of economic conditions which followed the revolution, what chiefly endeared the Soviet Union to Banting was its profound faith in science.

So great is the regard for science in the Soviet Union (he observed[5]) that in recent years they have built for Pavlov immense laboratories at the cost of 8,000,000 rubles. They provided him with abundant facilities and assistants to carry on research work. . . . He was a national hero. His four books were widely read and their substance interpreted to the people. . . .

Acknowledging the exceptional services Pavlov rendered to the people of the Soviet Union, the Council of People's Commissars of the U.S.S.R. decided to perpetuate his memory by establishing a monument to him on one of the central squares of Leningrad; to rename the first Leningrad Medical Institute the Pavlov Institute; to instruct the Academy of Sciences of the U.S.S.R. to publish his complete works in Russian, English, French and German; to preserve his brain in the Brain Institute in Moscow; to preserve as a museum his Leningrad study and laboratory in the All-Union Institute of Experimental Medicine; and to grant his widow a personal pension of one thousand rubles a month. All expenses incurred were to be charged to the state.

Was not this warrant enough for any admirer of the Russians? Pavlov, despite a misguided loyalty to Alexander, had not been molested during the most terrible days of the revolution. (Banting relates that when his experiments were disturbed by a noisy group of soldiers he rushed to the steps of the building, sent for the leader, commanded that the troops be taken away and kept away—and was obeyed!) Subsequently, because he was a great scientist he became a national hero. Could anything be seriously wrong with a nation like that?

The early thirties had witnessed the Great Depression. Hundreds of Torontonians were still "on relief." In Russia there

[5]"In Memoriam: Ivan Petrovich Pavlov, 1849-1936," by F. G. Banting, *The American Journal of Psychiatry*, May, 1936.

was "no unemployment." Could Banting be censured for his enthusiasm? But when someone pointed out that the same claim was then being made for Nazi Germany, he could see the aptness of the remark, although he rejoined that the apparent improvement in Germany was in no real sense comparable, and that social justice was maintained on a higher level in the U.S.S.R.

Not a Communist. Not quite a Red. But he was certainly a stalwart friend of all that was best in the proletarian dictatorship.

For Pavlov himself, still very active in the year before his death, Banting's admiration was boundless:

He was a great lecturer because he had a clear conception of things and was able to impart a clear picture to his students. He had a great memory for things in which he was interested. He had a one-track mind. He handed over the care of his home to his wife and totally abandoned himself to his problems. He did not even read newspapers or periodicals, but relied on his wife to keep him informed of the outside world. He loved art like all research men and loved music like all Russians. He was passionately fond of flowers. He played "Gorodki" with his assistants almost to the time of his death. During conversation he flourished his arms and his face became animated. He was vivacious and demonstrative. He had great vigour and vitality and was filled with energy and enthusiasm.

How like, and again how unlike, were the Russian and the Canadian!

. . . All who knew Academician Pavlov were charmed by his kindly personality. His long life was crowded with scientific achievement for the benefit of mankind. He was indeed a citizen of the world. Advancing years did not dampen his enthusiasm or decrease his productiveness. . . .

When Banting's passport expired he had still not seen enough. He wanted to renew it for another two weeks, but encountered some difficulty in making his arrangements; the official to whom he applied apparently raised objections. According to the story which he used to relate when he came back, the barrier dissolved at once as soon as he produced from his pocket a photograph of himself in animated conversation with Professor Pavlov.

Pavlov was recognized anywhere and Banting's own picture was a likeness. Before he could say "Tovarisch" the passport was renewed. Any friend of Pavlov's was a friend of Russia.

After his return to Canada Banting gave enthusiastic interviews about his journey and was disappointed that Toronto newspapers gave them less space than was usually devoted to the rumour of a new "discovery." Fred Hodgson did a full-length interview for *Soviet Russia Today*, where it was featured as the leading article in the October number.[6] Banting seemed for once to have found a theme about which he was willing to make speeches. The Caduceus Club permitted his encomiums to run overtime. The following summer he went to Newmarket to open the summer school of the Workers' Educational Association. He even jestingly addressed his friends as "Comrade."

Some day, he said, he would return.

9

Chairmanship of the Medical Research Committee of the National Research Council was a duty which seemed to devolve upon Banting with the enthusiastic assent of everyone but himself. His most important work in this capacity was accomplished during the war and will be sketched in outline in the chapter which follows. But even before the war he was busy with the affairs of the Committee.

In the early autumn of 1938 he set out on a fact-finding tour of the Dominion. His aim was to investigate Canada's facilities for Medical Research in the universities and colleges of every province. His survey embraced the smaller as well as the larger schools. Indeed it was in the former that his hopes chiefly centred, for the facilities of Toronto and McGill were familiar to the Committee and funds were not unavailable, while the smaller laboratories with more limited budgets were less well known and their potential capacities less developed. But all the Canadian universities, large and small, needed money for research. It was,

[6]"Sir Frederick Banting Tells About Soviet Science." *Soviet Russia Today*, Oct., 1935.

after all, not the size of the centre that counted, but the size of the men—the scope of their abilities and the range and daring of their ideas.

If research were in active progress in all parts of the country and if professors and laboratory directors with the basic material necessities for such work already at hand could turn to a central source for funds to promote specific research studies, few of the nation's original scientific minds, its future explorers and dis- coverers in science, would be unprovided with the things immedi- ately necessary to carry on their investigations. Ten dogs, some simple instruments and apparatus and a few ordinary chemical reagents had been all that Banting himself had needed for a start. So small an investment, so rich a return! Lest Canada miss the chance to make similar investments in the ingenuity, skill and persistence of young Canadians, Banting was now setting up a sort of brokerage of ideas, where limited financial support was available and where, of course, no absolute guarantee of dividends was demanded.

Banting was accompanied on this trip by Dr. (later Wing Commander) C. B. Stewart, the secretary of the Committee and a brilliant young graduate of Dalhousie University. Journeying with Sir Frederick from one end of Canada to the other, staying with him in hotels and travelling with him on trains, listening to his off-guard conversation and being present at his interviews with scientists and politicians and the press, Stewart had an unequalled opportunity to observe the features of his mind.

In the Maritimes, Quebec, Ontario and the prairie provinces west to the sea, Banting and Stewart visited every institution of every sort where medical research might conceivably be carried out. Sir Frederick met the regional members of the Committee and talked over the possibilities. He talked to professors, to research assistants, to medical students. He toured the labora- tories, showing an alert and well-informed interest in the prob- lems of medical and other workers. He attended formal dinners and receptions where he met and talked with the nation's leading experts in academic and practical medicine. Everywhere he went he encountered old friends—specialists in metabolic diseases he had come to know well in the insulin days (Dr. I. M. Rabinowitch welcomed him in Montreal); doctors who had at some time engaged in research in Toronto (Dr. Dolman, of the University of British Columbia, who had formerly worked in the Connaught Laboratories, greeted him in Vancouver); friends from his old unit overseas (a dozen representatives of the 13th Field Ambulance were also awaiting him at the Vancouver railway station); members of "onety-seven" (his old friend, Bill Tew, in London). Everywhere he went he assiduously gathered information for the Committee, while Stewart made careful notes. Everywhere he stimulated interest, fired ambition and revealed with a sure instinct for promising men the latent skills and energies which he knew to abound in the least likely places. He was prospecting, as it were, for the gold of half-revealed talent, the precious intellectual ore which he considered by far the most important of Canada's natural resources.

Writes Dr. George Hunter, Department of Biochemistry, University of Alberta:

Before he visited here towards the end of 1938 he desired to have some arrangements made for him to meet the medical students. He gave perhaps the most inspiring address they had ever listened to, on the subject of medical research. His other purpose here was to find what facilities we had for research. That has also borne fruit in the shape of financial assistance which has aided in the training of certain young people and yielded a modest harvest of new and useful knowledge.

An ambitious young man, provided he was neither brash nor opportunist, could usually succeed in kindling Banting's interest; Banting, conversely, could almost always, with a few pertinent questions or an apt suggestion, actuate a laggard purpose and give definition to a vaguely realized wish. The impression he made upon the young, particularly medical students, was vivid and incisive, and his influence was invariably heartening. He was seldom sententious and he never "talked down."

In Fredericton, New Brunswick, he was approached by a youthful reporter who had prepared himself carefully for the interview, reading whatever he could lay his hands on relative to Banting's accomplishments and arming himself with a list of intelligent queries. Banting was won over. The reporter, who looked like a high-school boy, eagerly scribbled the replies. In addition to these he was able to take down some extra bits of information which Banting offered as premiums toward the writing of a good story. Finally the boy closed his notebook, expressed his thanks and turned to go, more than content with his interview.

"Just a minute," said Banting, "I think it's time you gave *me* a turn at asking questions." And he proceeded, with the most genial and whole-hearted interest, to inquire into the education, prospects and ambitions of the gratified young journalist. He exhorted him not to be content with a ten-dollar-a-week job. He urged him to submit special articles to metropolitan newspapers. Without appearing to sermonize, he thus pointed up the boy's predelictions and fed his sprouting ambition with hope.

With the magical extract, insulin, he had given new life to diabetics; with the magical elixir, encouragement, he gave new fire, new ardour to the aspirations of the young.

Of Banting's relations with the newspapermen generally, Stewart gives eye-and-ear-witness testimony that they were cordial. He commonly received the reporters in his hotel room on arrival, often before he had had a chance to wash up after a train journey. He was patient and courteous in answering questions except when the newsmen displayed what he always considered an unwarrantable curiosity about his personal affairs; his private life was the only subject "out of bounds."

Sometimes when they pressed him too hard or too long he turned them over to Stewart, and whenever he gave a speech or granted an interview touching on something he thought was likely to be misunderstood or misconstrued by the journalists, he required that the stories be checked for accuracy by the secretary before they were published. He once delivered an address on cancer before a body of laymen in which he referred to quack healers and the nostrums and manipulations by which they professed to cure malignancy, saying that he had never seen anyone benefit from a so-called "cancer-cure." The latter statement, removed from its context and deprived of the inverted commas obviously meant to enclose the expression "cancer cure," was twisted by an obtuse reporter into the startling assertion that Banting had never seen a case of cancer cured. This carried the implication that surgery, X-ray and radium were all of no avail and that cancer of any type was incurable, an idea very far from the truth. Stewart naturally refused to sanction the printing of this stupid and disheartening article until it had been completely revised.

Stewart feels that Banting was probably more patient and more willing in his dealings with newsmen than he might otherwise have been, because he was travelling as an agent of the government at the expense of the tax-payer, an ambassador of good will from men of science. This is in keeping with the fine-edged sense of his public responsibility which he never allowed to grow dull.

On their journey through western Canada they were joined at Winnipeg by Dr. Thorlakson, a well-known surgeon of that city and a member of the Committee. Many aspects of medical research and of other kindred topics were exhaustively debated as their train sped over the prairies. As they were passing from the foothill country into the majestic presences of the Rocky Mountain summits, Stewart, a native of Prince Edward Island and a first-time visitor to the West, lost interest in the conversation as he gazed from the train window at the changing spectacle of mountain scenery. Banting and Thorlakson were deep in an earnest discussion.

Suddenly, "Stewart," said Banting, "change seats with me." They exchanged seats and Stewart was pleased to find that on facing in the opposite direction he had a much better view of the passing landscape. With the murmured comment, "I've been through the Rockies before," Banting resumed his conversation with Thorlakson. This, asserts Stewart, was typical of the unstudied consideration with which Banting treated his associates.

During the many long train journeys which his tour involved, he sometimes amused himself by making pencil sketches. On several occasions Stewart discovered that he was being caricatured by his travelling companion, but Banting always refused to let him see the drawings, gravely avowing that his features were so nicely balanced, with no predominance of any one, that he was an impossible subject. Sometimes, too, Sir Frederick's attention was distracted from the profundities a learned scientist or other pundit might be declaiming by a prominent nose or beetling eyebrows which seemed to be expressly made for the cartoonist; he was once caught in the act of caricaturing a distinguished professor while talking to him, under the pretence of taking notes on a tiny scratch-pad cupped in his hand; fortunately the professor was not too dignified to be amused. In Edmonton, at a formal dinner, he was up to his old tricks, drawing caricatures on the menu; when the dinner was over, an Edmonton lady presented him with a comic portrait of himself which she, meantime, had been sketching; Banting was quite delighted to have the tables turned and was very much pleased with the drawing.

The survey of Canada's research facilities was not complete until early in 1939. It was a thorough piece of work and Banting's findings formed the basis for subsequent allotments by the National Research Council. His was the unifying, synoptic vision which later gave form and coherence to wartime research activities in the Dominion; the grasp of the general situation and the detailed knowledge of men and means which he obtained on his nation-wide tour immediately before the war contributed in no small degree to the excellence of this result.

PART XIV
The Last Campaign: 1939-1941

. . . And many a darkness into the light shall leap,
And shine in the sudden making of splendid names,
And noble thought be freer under the sun,
And the heart of a people beat with one desire;
For the peace, that I deem'd no peace, is over and
      done,
And now by the side of the Black and Baltic deep,
And deathful-grinning mouths of the fortress, flames
The blood-red blossom of war with a heart of fire.

Let it flame or fade, and the war roll down like a
      wind,
We have proved we have hearts in a cause, we are
      noble still,
And myself have awaked, as it seems, to the better
      mind.
It is better to fight for the good than to rail at the
      ill;
I have felt with my native land, I am one with my
      kind,
I embrace the purpose of God, and the doom assign'd.

ALFRED, LORD TENNYSON.

1

IN THE FAMOUS rectorial address, *Courage,* delivered at St. Andrew's University in 1922, Sir James Barrie, referring to the lesson of the war, admonished the students in these words: "Do not be too sure that we have learned our lesson, and are not at this very moment doddering down some brimstone path."[1]

The words have an air of prescience, of Celtic clairvoyance. After the first World War a succession of well-meaning politicians doddered (as he said) along a perilous track, beguiled by such catch-words as "lebensraum," "non-intervention" and "appeasement."

Banting, who was a staunch Imperialist, was at the same time a believer in the need for an authoritative League of Nations, equipped with "teeth." The wavering policies of the democratic powers filled him with uneasiness. We are told that after 1935 or thereabouts he realized the inevitability of another war and began to set up in Canada the research machinery which would be necessary. It is doubtful, however, if this object was really in the forefront of his mind at so early a date. It is the opinion of several of those close to him that his prescience has been exaggerated; probably chance remarks have since been invested with greater meaning than they had.

On the other hand, it seems well attested that by the time of the Munich agreement in the autumn of 1938, he had made up his mind that there was no way out.

"Don't believe it," he is quoted as saying when he heard of the Chamberlain declaration. "There is not going to be peace in our time. Let's all get ready for war."

Repeatedly he expressed his alarm over day-to-day and week-to-week developments in the international scene and his conviction that a titanic struggle was in the making.

In the autumn of 1938, Major A. A. James, R.C.A.M.C., R.C.A.F., discussed with Banting the need for medical research in relation to military medicine and proposed that the Depart-

[1]*Courage* was one of Banting's favourites. I am transcribing the quotations from his own copy of the book.—L. S.

ment of Medical Research should study the physiological problems of speed and altitude. Banting at once initiated a series of discussions with his colleagues at the Institute; without further ado he plunged his department into grappling with the tremendous physiological difficulties incident to aerial combat in modern aircraft capable of developing very high speeds and of flying at altitudes approaching the stratosphere. He was quick to see that an intimate and exact knowledge of the physiological stresses besetting the airman was a prerequisite to formulating a research programme. While the lot of the civilian pilot was by this time fairly safe, the special hazards imposed by military conditions on the airman were many and dangerous.

But this was too big a job for any one laboratory. Banting felt that the National Research Council, of which he had been a member since 1935, should use its resources for the purpose. The Associate Committee on Medical Research had recently been formed and what work could more urgently require attention? He consulted Major-General McNaughton, then President of the N.R.C., and Air Vice-Marshal Croil. He was asked to prepare a memorandum. After further discussions with McNaughton, James, Professor E. A. Bott of the Department of Psychology, and others whose opinions he valued, he drew up a statement and submitted it to Air Vice-Marshal Croil. There were further conversations and a definite plan began to take shape.

With the war-clouds looming in Europe Banting had envisaged a change in emphasis from civil to military medicine. In order to make possible the broadest basis for research in aviation medicine he urged the formation of a Federal committee to deal with all such problems and succeeded in having it established. It was originally a Committee of the Department of National Defence and the first meeting was held in Ottawa in June, 1939. This original committee was subsequently dissolved and its successor, the Associate Committee on Aviation Medical Research, was established by the National Research Council, a Privy Council Committee receiving reports from the latter. This action enjoyed the full support of Dean C. J. Mackenzie, then Acting-President of the N.R.C.

Banting was asked in 1938 to act as chairman of the Associate Committee on Medical Research. He respectfully declined on the ground that he already carried too many executive responsibilities. His objections were overruled, however, and he was "drafted" for the job. General McNaughton, in a personal interview, listened patiently to his demurrer that he was not suited for the post. Then with a penetration keener and more effective than praise, the General challenged him thus:

"Banting, it makes no difference in the world whether you deserve your reputation or not. The simple fact is that you have it, and I ask you, whether or not you will use it for a great service to medicine in Canada."

"Banting's face set," recounts a witness to the interview. "He stiffened almost to attention, paused only a second, and said: 'Yes, sir, I will.' "

When the Associate Committee on Aviation Medical Research was established he assumed the second chairmanship. Through the mechanism of this committee, on which service personnel and civilians exchanged ideas as equal partners, all of the early work on aviation medical research was organized and supported. Throughout the entire war, work on aviation medicine was carried out in the Royal Canadian Air Force and in university research laboratories under the auspices of the Associate Committee.

Several months before the outbreak of hostilities Banting had thus created a powerful weapon for waging the war in the air.

2

Before the sky darkened and the thunder of warfare began, there was an idyllic interlude. The relenting gods brought a gift of happiness to one whom they had harried for so long with changing and uncertain fortune.

On June 2, 1939, Banting was married to Miss Henrietta Ball. Before her marriage, Lady Banting, a Mount Allison graduate, had been occupied in research work at the Institute on chemotherapy and tuberculosis. Although the marriage had long been planned, only their immediate relatives and intimate friends knew the secret. The ceremony was simple and was performed with few attendants.

On June 6, Banting wrote from the Temogami to a friend in Toronto:

I wonder if you have ever been up here? . . . This is a marvellous lake. We were out for three hours in a canoe this afternoon—and plan to go all day tomorrow. . . . If I am not back inside the two weeks don't blame me.

During the golden weather of the summer before the war, he was surrounded for the last time in his life by happiness and peace, untroubled by the demands of military duty and the thronging tasks that awaited him. In the trying months which followed fast, Lady Banting gave unfailing support to her husband in his arduous wartime labours for Canada.

3

At the end of August Banting watched the newspaper accounts of last-minute negotiations in Europe with the utmost anxiety. He listened, as did everyone else in those breathless days at the beginning of September, to radio newscasts of the latest developments. When the fateful news at last was announced, he must have sighed with extreme regret, as one who knew the terrible cost of war from lurid personal experience, and yet with some sense of relief that the unavoidable decision had been reached and that the time of "appeasement" was over.

"The end will indeed have come to our courage and to us," Barrie had written, "when we are afraid in dire mischance to refer the final appeal to the arbitrament of arms."

Sir Frederick had not delayed, however, for Canada's declaration of war. Nor even for Great Britain's. He was on the reserve of officers as a Captain, and while not in the Non-Permanent Active Militia, had always taken a very great interest in the Medical Corps, visiting the camp when annual training exercises were in progress and attending mess functions during the winter.

He heard through Headquarters in Toronto that his friend and classmate, Cecil A. Rae, was being asked to form and mobilize No. 15 Canadian General Hospital. He knew that Rae was driving to Toronto from Muskoka, where he had been spending his vacation, to see Lieutenant-Colonel C. P. Fenwick (afterwards Major-General) who was the Assistant District Medical Officer of Military District No. 2. As it happened, Colonel Fenwick lived just across the street from the Banting home in Rosedale, and as Rae drew up in his car at midnight on the thirtieth of August, he found Banting waiting for him, pacing about excitedly in a dressing gown.

"Cecil," he said determinedly, "I am going to war with you. I don't give a damn what as, or in what rank, but I am going!"

"I can think of nothing that would suit me better," was the answer. "You can be my pathologist and that will carry the rank of Major."

His eyes gleaming, Banting vehemently replied, "I don't give a couple of blankety blanks about the rank, so long as I go!"

"So it was agreed," writes Colonel Rae,[2] "and there was no keener officer in the unit and no better soldier in those busy days of mobilization. . . . It has always been a source of pride with the unit that Fred was one of our original members. He was, as you can well believe, the very best of comrades and was beloved by all."

Although he did not serve for long in the capacity of pathologist, the story illustrates his extreme eagerness to be "in at the start," to waste not a moment in delay. He joined the Army September 1, 1939, nine days before Canada declared war.

4

"I am going to war!" he had said. He was forty-eight. A little heavier, a little more stooped, than when he had last worn khaki. Would he be accepted for service in the field? He was strong and vigorous, in better health than he had been ten years before. Still . . . he was forty-eight. No longer young.

[2]Personal communication.

Nonsense! He was a better man than most of his juniors. He was accustomed, moreover, to get what he wanted. What he wanted was active service in the fullest sense—service on the field of battle.

Meantime (for there was no fighting as yet) what required most pressingly his immediate attention? Having long foreseen the coming of war, having visualized clearly the importance of research in a vast conflict of land, sea and air forces, all requiring highly technical equipment, having, in fact, laid plans for the development of wartime research and made a start toward their realization, Banting was ready with a well-considered scheme for harnessing Canadian science to the war machine and galloping off into action. A memorandum which embodied not only his own ideas but those common to the whole group of forward-looking scientists with whom he kept close contact had been despatched at once to Ottawa.

The second week in September found him in the capital, whence he wrote:

> *Chateau Laurier, Ottawa, Ont.*
> *September* 12, 1939.

My dear Hall:

I have just finished dinner and what a day I have had! (1) 9.15 *Cathcart* re neuropsychology (2) 9.50 *Powers* . . . He said . . . that I should stay at research. . . . Powers wants to see a copy of our memo. (3) 1.30 McNaughton himself. We had a long talk. . . . I took up with him the business of Army Medical Research, Aviation Medical Research, etc. . . . He is all in favour of the general plan and thinks that it should be taken up at the meeting of the Associate Committee of Medical Research of the N.R.C. . . .

I came down very depressed but today's happenings have left me most optimistic. There is now no doubt in my mind but that research will be given its place in this war.

I am very tired, and am going to bed early in preparation for a big day tomorrow. . . .

Next day he wrote to Hall again, giving an account of further conversations with government officials:

I am sure that we will get a square deal. . . .

In the meantime urge Franks to continue his experiments, urge Lucas to formulate his plans and urge Irwin to consider the

Portrait by Milne Studios, Limited, Toronto.

DR. F. G. BANTING IN 1933

effect of toxic gases on the lungs, and finally urge James to wait until the Departments here are ready to participate in a large-scale research in aviation medicine—for it is coming.

Sincerely,

BANTING.

Urge. Urge. Urge. Still the sense of an overwhelming necessity for speed. In a few days he would be back in Toronto, but the message could not wait. Urge Franks. Urge Lucas. Urge Irwin.

Almost he seems to say: "Ottawa is giving us the green light. Let's shift into high and get going. Let's show them what we can do."

With all this there was the joyful persuasion that a large-scale effort, subsidized by the Government, would be worth a moment's pause— *"for it is coming."*

September 17, 1939.

MY DEAR HALL:

. . . This week has been a terror. However, things are coming along rapidly. . . .

The Asso. Comm. on Med. Res. meets tomorrow—what a day it will be! But I am better prepared in a matter of policy than I have ever been for former meetings and I think we will get things done.

Please do not decide or promise anything concerning your immediate future until I see you or until this new plan is formulated.

Sincerely,

BANTING.

Get things done. We must get things done. Was this driving force due entirely to the urgency of the war situation? That alone? Perhaps he felt, too, that he must get the wheels rolling on the right track before he himself turned to other things.

The final appeal to Hall was a reference to the latter's decision to enlist. If both of them joined the active forces then what of the Department? What of the master plan for research? Neither was indispensable, but would not the simultaneous withdrawal of both disrupt the smooth functioning of organized investigation? He was facing a curious dilemma. Hall's ultimate decision to join the R.C.A.F. was probably an important factor in deciding Banting's future course.

Throughout all his difficulties, Professor Duncan Graham was a wise and dispassionate counsellor. Sir Frederick was a frequent visitor in Dr. Graham's office in the Institute to consult him on matters of policy. Such a consultation preceded almost every major decision which Banting reached.

5

On November 16, he went overseas on a special mission, representing the Associate Committee on Medical Research of the National Research Council. No. 15 Canadian General Hospital would not be ready to sail until January, 1940. His attachment with his unit had grown tenuous. Nevertheless he had not yet quite given up the idea of front line duty.

When the dark shadow of war overtook Canada and the Empire (writes General McNaughton) he came overseas with the desire for service again with the forces in the field, but at my personal request he gave this up unselfishly to undertake the organization of research of far-reaching importance to us and which he alone could do. . . . Already [1941] we have felt the benefit of his endeavours, which will continue to bring comfort to us and confusion to our enemies.

In 1914 he had been anxious to give up his medical course and join the infantry, but had been persuaded that he could render greater service in a professional capacity and had eventually seen more action in the field than do many combatant officers. In 1939 he wanted to go back to his old post, but was persuaded of the paramount claim of other duties.

The position he was assuming might have seemed to others to be one of relative safety, but the responsibility was heavy, the toil was unremitting and the final price of his devotion to his job was life itself.

It was first reported that his headquarters in England would be the Canadian Red Cross Hospital then in process of erection on the estate of Lord and Lady Astor at Cliveden, where a special laboratory was allegedly being prepared for his use. It was announced that he planned to stay in England for the duration of hostilities. Actually, however, his scope was to be wider than this. He was to organize research in Canada and he was to act as liaison officer between British and Canadian scientists in wartime medical research.

The work of organizing and administering a comprehensive research programme was not entirely to his taste. He felt that he had been ensnared too long in what Mr. Churchill once described as the "briars of detail." It was therefore entirely from a sense of duty that he took up his task. But when he was once fully engaged by the manifold problems presenting themselves, the wind of his freshening enthusiasm blew strongly as of old and a score of laboratories in Great Britain and America were stirred and rallied by a sudden gust of fervour.

In London, in Liverpool, in Oxford—wherever medical research work was in progress—the khaki-clad scientist made his appearance. Every question they answered for him seemed only to provoke another. He was determined to take back to Canada the best and latest information on wartime medicine as the basis for new departures. He wished to be thoroughly acquainted with the directions research was taking in England and he hoped that co-operative administration would prevent reduplication of effort.

6

Shortly after his arrival in England he dictated the following letter:

Victoria Hotel, London, W.C.2,
December 2, 1939.

MY DEAR HALL:

We have been in London just one week tonight. My general conclusion is that they have done fine organization work both for civilian and military casualties—for example, blood transfusion, sulphanilamide treatment, empty hospital beds, inoculations

(voluntary even in the army) against tetanus, typhoid—vaccin-
ation, etc. (There was enough blood went to waste during the
first four weeks of the war to float a battleship.) Bacteriology
labs were set up all over England. Medical schools were moved
from London to outlying cities. Everything was disrupted. As
a consequence of all this research has suffered very greatly. Odd
jobs were commenced but nothing very much was done on the
larger problems.

Things are beginning to happen, however. We have not been
to ——— as yet but there have assembled Lovatt Evans, Sir
Joseph Barcroft and Douglas (of the bag[3]) and one may expect
something to come of a combination of that nature. As far as I
have learned there is nothing to surpass our own group when it
comes to aviation medicine. I met Barcroft for a moment last
Wed. . . . Monday I saw Air Marshal ——— and Air Commodore ——— but they would say nothing without a letter
from up the creek. It has now arrived and everything they have
is now open and welcome to us. Tues. I saw Mellanby and he
was fine. He gave us access to everything. . . . Thurs. I went with
A. V. Hill to a meeting of the Royal Society at Cambridge—Sir
Wm. Bragg, the President, motored up with us. We stayed for
club dinner and motored home in the dark. I met a great many
but will go to Cambridge again as I did not have a proper chance
to see labs, and have a real talk. Friday I spent at the N.R.C.
. . . Dale was as nice as he could be and gave me his full time
until after closing (they start at 8.00 and close at 4.00). . . . [He
gives a brief account of the work being done and the particular
problems of individual workers.] . . . E. J. and Mrs. King came in
for tea and dinner tonight and we had a long talk. [He mentions
a war research problem in which King was interested.] It may
be some time before he can start to work on it and he suggests
that our lab. also work on it. I think it worth trying. Mendel
might be interested—or Stevenson might take a shot at it. . . . It
is up to you.[4]

[3]An apparatus devised in 1911 by C. G. Douglas. It consists of a rubber-
lined bag and a flexible tube, fitted with a mouthpiece and a pair of valves;
the valves are so arranged that the subject's inspired air is drawn from the
room while his expired air is directed into the bag. The total volume of
expired air is measured and samples are analyzed for carbon dioxide and
oxygen.—L. S.

[4]A second letter, dated December 4, repeats the request for consideration
of the same question. "You might discuss this matter with the group in
the laboratory." Having "flushed" an idea, Banting was loath to lose sight of
it. This was an important part of his function.—L. S.

[The next paragraph is devoted to an abortive research by an English bacteriologist who endeavoured]

. . . to mix sulphanilamide with substances which would slow up absorption—so that he could give one large single does instead of the q4h procedure[5] as advocated after wounding in France. He has not had any luck—and he leaves the work shortly. Lucas might have some suggestions. It is like zinc protamine. . . .

All in all the week has been strenuous but I think a good deal has been accomplished. . . . It takes a little while to get into the graces of the Englishman.

They are certainly going thro' hell with constant dreads, blackouts, taxes, etc.—but they are full of courage, cheerfulness and hope. They are a wonderful people. . . .

Sincerely,

F. G. B.

With an inquisitive mind and an apperceptive eye, Banting journeyed from one laboratory to another, ever desirous to find something newer, something better, than he had left at home, and ever alert for problems to which members of his own group might be specially qualified to contribute. He ranged over England like a bird dog, picking up likely scents and pointing the game.

Canada House, London, S.W.1,
December 23, 1939.

MY DEAR HALL:

I cannot remember the exact time of my last letter to you, but I have spent the whole of the last week on Aviation Medical Research. I saw Professor ———— at ———— last Monday, and as far as I can ascertain, they have been spending most of their time and energy in devising and manufacturing new types of apparatus for the testing of pilots. They seem to be greatly concerned in deciding at an early date whether or not a given individual will make a fighter or a bomber. They have some very elaborate and complicated apparatus for the performance of these tests. I asked ———— if similar apparatus could be made in their machine shops for our use but he replied that their mechanics had more work ahead of them than they could properly do. . . .

[5]Administration every four hours.—L. S.

. . . On Tuesday I visited Halton, where there is a large camp for training ground workers. They accept boys of good families of from fifteen to eighteen years of age for three years' training and twenty-five years' service. The feature of greatest interest was the hospital. . . .

During the following two days I visited the flying squadron at Debden and the bombing squadron at Mindenhall, and found out more about Spitfires and Wellington bombers than about research. These visits were made in company with Wing Commander Corner, who is the clinical psychologist for the Royal Air Force. We talked to a number of the pilots, Wing Commanders and Group Captains, and found that there was the usual amount of army grouching, but no evidence of fatigue.

On Friday I had a long talk with Group Captain ———— of ————. [He] has been trying to get the money necessary for the construction of an accelerator for some months, but has not yet succeeded. He estimates the cost of an accelerator at approximately $15,000, but the higher authorities consider this amount excessive for the present, although they supplied him with a $50,000 aeroplane and a specially trained pilot for preliminary experiments on blackout. This has held up his work very greatly. [It] is a defended area. As a consequence they cannot fly when there are clouds because any aeroplane above the clouds is considered as an enemy, and no aeroplane can with safety cross over the area boundary. Weeks have now passed without a single observation.

[He] is preparing for me a complete outline of his plans for research, and his ideas on blacking out. During the conversation, he told me of his hope to construct an apparatus almost identical with that proposed by Franks some weeks ago. . . . [He] is very anxious for whole-hearted co-operation with reciprocation of ideas and research results.

Last evening I had a long talk with Major-General McNaughton and discussed with him the one problem that I have been unable to settle in my mind. . . . I had planned to sail on December 29, but McNaughton has practically ordered me to write a memorandum on this subject so that it may be submitted to the army authorities. . . .

I hope that all the work of the laboratory is progressing satisfactorily. Might I strongly urge that the work of Franks and your own group be carried on as rapidly as possible? In regard to Air Medical Research I feel that we are as far on in Canada as they are here. . . . I hope you will transmit the information of this letter to James, Bott, Franks, and others of the group.

On December 15, Wing Commander ———— took me to ————to see his work on the effect of mustard gas on the eyes of rabbits. The method which he has followed has been to place one mgm. of pure mustard gas in the eye of the rabbit. He has tried a number of mild alkaline washes, etc., but he finds that the best treatment to give these rabbits is an intravenous injection of ———— . . . I saw the group of animals so treated and was able to compare them with the control animals, and certainly the result was phenomenal. The eyes of the treated animals after eight days appeared almost normal, whereas the eyes of the untreated animals were exuding pus, and there was marked conjunctivitis, with a semi-translucent cornea. The mode of action of ———— has not yet been investigated. I think you should tell Irwin, Lucas and McRea about these experiments. . . .

I think that gives you a summary of what I have been doing recently. I hope to spend my Christmas preparing the memorandum . . . and hope that you and your family will have had a merry Christmas and a happy New Year.

With kind personal regards, I remain,

Yours sincerely,

BANTING.

He added a postscript to relate that "on Sunday I had tea and a long talk with Sir Edward Mellanby," who told him that a certain officer "had done nothing in two years" on his specific research job and "hence he was being 'promoted' away from the work and that our lab. would be asked to take up the problem."

Banting's military rank, along with his title, combined to make up a strange cognomen in title-conscious England. Sons of the nobility, it is true—and many with fancier appellations than his— were serving in minor capacities and even in the ranks. But that a scientist of world-wide fame, knighted by his King for imposing achievement, should be sent overseas in such a capacity seemed inexplicable to his British hosts. At a public banquet of scientists where he sat in the company of generals, brigadiers and colonels innumerable, he was the only major. The distinguished chairman could not refrain from remarking that Canada seemed to be more cautious and economical than Great Britain in distributing commissions and assigning ranks. And yet Banting to the time of his death never advanced beyond a majority. Nor had he any desire to do so.

The object of his service was perfectly clear. "I am here in London," he told reporters in the capital, "because the Empire is fighting Hitlerism and Hitlerism is my enemy too." It was with the aim of combating Hitlerism, of outdoing Nazi scientists and providing Allied fighting men with the means of victory, that he pressed forward determinedly against the enigmas of aviation medicine and of wartime medical research in general.

His work became complicated and prolonged. Week succeeded week and still he could see no end to it. Early in the new year he wrote the following letter to his ten-year-old son in Toronto:

> *Office of the High Commissioner for Canada,*
> *Canada House, London, S.W.1,*
> *January 6, 1940.*

My dear Bill:

It is some time since I wrote to you and it is a much longer time since I heard from you. In fact I have not seen your handwriting since the last evening of spelling.

I hope you have done better in all your examinations this last time.

Well, your daddy has been very busy since coming here. I hoped that I would be on my way home before this but I really do not know when I will be home. When one is in the army one has to do as one is told.

I hope you will act like a soldier, but I cannot hope that you will have to be one.

I hope you had a good Christmas and holiday—but you will have almost forgotten about it by the time you get this letter.

Keep up your homework and be a good boy. I'll be home as soon as my duties will permit.

I hope you are looking after the snow shovelling and other things about the house. Carry on, Bill, while I am away.

> Love,
>
> Dad.

His voluminous correspondence with Dr. Hall in Toronto still continued.[6] He received closely written reports of the activities

[6]At the same time he was corresponding frequently with Dr. C. J. McKenzie, Dr. Duncan Graham, and others.

of the Department and wrote long and detailed replies. Interspersed among the longer epistles there was a succession of brief notes, hurriedly scribbled.

From Canadian Military Headquarters in London he wrote:

> 2 Cockspur Street (Trafalgar Square),
> London, S.W.1,
> January 15, 1940.

MY DEAR HALL:

I don't know if you saw the latest paper by Air Commodore Whittingham, so I am enclosing a copy, which I hope you will pass on to Majors James and Tice for their information, also.

> Yours sincerely,
>
> BANTING.

And again:

MY DEAR HALL:

Enclosed please find a copy of Notes for Medical Officers on the Psychological Care of Flying Personnel, for use in M.D. 2. I am also sending a copy to Stewart.

> Yours sincerely,
>
> F. G. BANTING.

Thus he kept the Canadian group in close touch with developments in England. Much of the information he transmitted had not yet reached print. Much of it was "top secret." For example:

> Office of the High Commissioner for Canada,
> Canada House, London, S.W.1.

DEAR HALL:

There is a mail out this p.m. I enclose ——— in as far as I have got copied ——— the minutes of the Aviation Committee. The rest will follow. They are *strictly* and *absolutamlutly* confidential.

> F. G. B.

Canada House, London, S.W.1,
January 18, 1940.

SECRET AND CONFIDENTIAL

Dr. G. E. Hall,
Department of Medical Research,
University of Toronto,
Toronto, Canada.

MY DEAR HALL:

Enclosed please find copies of the remaining minutes of the meetings of the Flying Personnel Research Committee. Again, I would ask you to be very strict in the observation of precautions, because these are considered to be of the greatest secrecy. I do not think that you should let them out of your possession, but the contents could be used if necessary in the discussions which take place at your meetings.

Yours sincerely,

BANTING.

Such confidential information crossed the Atlantic in the sacrosanct diplomatic pouch from Canada House and was forwarded to Hall from Ottawa. It was transmitted by Hall to the workers immediately concerned and was made available, with suitable precautions to prevent leakage, to research experts of the N.R.C. Banting was, of course, in intimate contact also with Stewart, the secretary of the Associate Committee.

7

A letter of great interest was written to another friend in Toronto on the eighteenth of January:

I am glad to be able to tell you that I have been able to get out of a rut, and find that I want to do things, and have the power to do them, in a manner and to an extent that I have not possessed for many years. Nor can I explain even to myself the way in which it has all come about. I have lost cynicism, suspicion, jealousy, and have gained tolerance, trust and faith. I am afraid, however, that my happiness is associated with accomplishment, and that once a thing is accomplished the happiness passes off until I take on some other task.

Since September 1 all my energy has been on war medicine. During the two months here I have done nothing but work. On Sundays I have different work for I have started to write. As you know, it has been possibly my greatest ambition for many many years. I am writing a book on medical research, but it is a thing that one can only work at when one is in a particular mood, and it is going more slowly. I am also writing the history of insulin, giving all the details and the interesting things that happened in those stirring times. I have got closer to things than I have ever been able to accomplish before. Fancy, I have written about two hundred pages (handwritten, not typed) on the story. It is the first draft but I find myself remembering things I had long since forgotten. I have a lot more to do before even the first draft will be completed and furthermore I have to do a lot more at it when I get home and have available the records which are on file in the laboratory. But it is on the way.

Thus, I have been working hard (maybe I should call it play for it gives pleasure and happiness). I have always considered work as a protective mechanism. One does not deserve credit for it, for it happens when one allows oneself to be driven by a force or urge from within. Work occupies the mind and body and keeps one's energies directed into useful and purposeful channels. . . . That set me on a line of thought and I have just written five pages on research. . . .

Keep up the battle. It is the fighting that counts. No one wins a war nowadays.

It appears, however, that Banting had won his own war, for he had overcome the forces of discord in his heart and mind and had gained not only a fresh impetus to work but also an inner unity such as he had never known.

A colleague who was associated with him at this time has written that "he was as energetic and active as before, but more tolerant, more sympathetic than ever."

8

He returned to Canada early in 1940, full of new ideas and so dynamic, enterprising and impatient that the processes of research, necessarily deliberate, smartened their pace. He had come back to correlate and combine, to suggest and advise, to get into the work himself. "He is a key man," said Dean Mackenzie later, "in the research work of the Empire."

As his ship steamed homeward in January across the cold stretches of the Atlantic, it was passed by other vessels going east, one of which was the *Empress of Britain,* carrying No. 15 Canadian General Hospital. His comrades were off to the wars, while Banting, much against his will, proceeded under orders in the opposite direction.

Despite his desire to get on with the job assigned to him, the event has an overtone of wistfulness. Two great vessels, one going east, one going west, passed each other distantly in mid-Atlantic, and a dream vanished softly in the mist above the waters.

His battles henceforward were to be on the research front, where action sometimes proceeded with blitzkrieg swiftness, sometimes crept forward slowly, but where no gunfire sounded, no banners flew, and where much of the work was patient drudgery. Drudgery of the kind which once caused Thomas Carlyle to speak scornfully of the "beaver sciences." Drudgery lightened, it is true, by the pleasures of intellect, and yet at times galling enough to the would-be man of action.

It was fate. There was nothing he could do about it. He accepted it gracefully. Not only gracefully but with voracious and increasing gusto.

On the first day of February, 1940, he was attached for duty to National Defence Headquarters in the directorate of Director General of Medical Services. Thereafter he divided his time between Toronto and Ottawa.

9

At the second meeting of the Aviation Medical Research Committee (later reorganized and renamed) Dr. G. E. Hall had read a memorandum proposing problems for clinical investigation. Banting had had a letter from Dr. Mellanby suggesting that Canadian scientists study fatigue in air personnel and this problem had therefore been added to the list. Banting had also outlined the programme of Dr. W. R. Franks for the design and construction of a semi-rigid jacket to prevent "blacking out," a grant from outside sources having been made for the purpose.

Most of the scientists interested in aviation medicine happened to be in Toronto. A grant had been made to Professor E. F. Burton for work on portable oxygen apparatus and a grant to Professor E. A. Bott for work on methods in the choice of air personnel. The others were chiefly members of Banting's Department. The work was therefore centralized in Toronto and Banting had an excellent opportunity to show his powers "of successful organization, of holding a body of workers together and of maintaining a comprehensive hold of a diversity of ideas contributing to a common goal." [7]

At the end of October, 1939, Banting had called a meeting of the Toronto workers in his office and a programme had been sketched out. This programme, like the one presented by Hall to the Committee in Ottawa, had been tentative; some of the problems had later to be dropped, new ones introduced. Banting had arranged for several of those interested to visit research centres in the United States. Franks had subsequently visited the famous laboratories at Wright Field, where he had talked with Dr. Harry G. Armstrong, director of the research unit, about decompression chamber studies (masks, anoxia, "bends") accelerations and stratosphere suits; Drs. Bott, Franks and Doupe had gone to Boston, where Dr. McFarland of the Harvard Fatigue Laboratory had given them information on pilot selection tests and Dr. Dill had discussed problems of anoxia. Throughout all the work

[7] These words are borrowed from the obituary notice by Dr. E. J. King, already quoted in part elsewhere.

which followed there was reciprocation of ideas not only with British but also with American scientists.

Just before he had departed for England Banting had called a second meeting in his office and a definite programme, in physiology, psychology and physics, had been laid down. During the three months of his absence, Dr. Hall (at this time Captain, R.C.A.M.C., R.C.A.F.) had been acting head of the Department. Banting had been kept fully abreast of developments by means of regular and detailed letters. He was therefore ready on his return to plunge immediately into the work.

A small decompression chamber (the first to operate in Canada) had been built at the Institute by Banting's direction for the purpose of animal research. In December, while he was still overseas, a delegation of American scientists had visited the laboratory, and Hall and Major Tice had returned the visit and had studied a larger chamber at the Mayo Clinic. Hall had thereupon arranged for the construction of a large chamber, suitable for the observation of physiological changes in humans at simulated high altitudes, to be installed in the Institute.

It was in this chamber that Banting insisted on experiencing the effects of barometric decompression to increasing "heights" until the barometric pressure approached that of the stratosphere. A few similar studies had been conducted in Great Britain and the United States. Banting was the first person in Canada to subject himself to a simulated altitude of 40,000 feet ($7\frac{1}{2}$ miles) for a period longer than an hour. Naturally his colleagues were loath to see him carry out what was then an heroic experiment and they tried to dissuade him, for they felt that this was a chore for a young man. The unwitting mention of this was taken up by him as a challenge. The result was that he carried out this experiment on Boxing Day of 1940. On this and other "flights" he experienced the dreaded and disabling effects of decompression-sickness, also known as "aviator's bends" or aeroembolism (bubbles in the blood). However, just as many an airman has been forced to do to complete a mission in the actual substratosphere, Banting endured this strange new type of pain doggedly and persisted in his experiment beyond the planned duration of the simulated flight.

From these preliminary observations made by Banting and his

associates on decompression-sickness, important experimental projects were initiated in Canada on this limiting factor of human flight. The subsequent studies were carried out at London, Ont., Toronto, Regina and Halifax, on civilian volunteers and R.C.A.F. personnel.

Banting's own part in the decompression studies was carried out in association with Dr. Edgar C. Black, a brilliant Canadian who had left a teaching position in the United States to work with Banting on the latter's telegraphed invitation. His previous studies on the respiration of fishes had established him as an authority on oxygen exchange at low pressures and he was invited by Banting to join the Toronto group at the suggestion of Dr. Colin C. Lucas. He became a valued member of the Department, leaving it since Banting's death to become Professor of Physiology at Dalhousie University. Dr. J. K. W. Ferguson also collaborated with Banting and Black in studying respiratory exchanges at high altitudes.

The work done in London began in an unusual way. The London Association for War Research was founded on May 23, 1940, by a public-spirited group of citizens, chiefly physicians and business men, and Banting was approached for suggestions. On his advice the new organization became affiliated with the Associate Committee on Aviation Medical Research of the National Research Council, although remaining financially independent. It was at his suggestion, too, that a decompression chamber was purchased and was installed in the Medical School of the University of Western Ontario, where he had once been a demonstrator. The work in this chamber was done in collaboration with the Clinical Investigation Unit (Research) of the R.C.A.F. So impressed was Banting with the patriotism of the London Association and the generous and democratic manner in which it was displayed that he consented to attend a dinner meeting in London and make a speech. This was an uncommon signal of esteem from one who disliked speech making and was already overburdened with work. After 1939 he seldom spoke in public.

Not all of Sir Frederick's experimental flights were simulated. Through arrangements with the R.C.A.F. he proceeded to experience the special physiological conditions of actual flying. In a fighter plane at Trenton he underwent the effects of sudden changes in gravitational forces (due to curvilinear accelerations) which lead to a sudden draining of blood from the eyeballs, brain and other parts of the head to the lower levels of the body. These changes lead to dimming of vision, then total loss of vision (temporarily) and, if prolonged, complete loss of consciousness, a phenomenon known as "black-out." Banting gloried in his stamina and he was proud of the fact that younger men, airmen moreover, sometimes "blacked out" before he did. He also personally experienced the effects of lack of adequate oxygen encountered at altitudes above 10,000 feet.

10

While still concerned with Banting's insistence "On Being One's Own Rabbit,"[8] we may deviate for a moment from aviation medicine and recall another such experiment. Fearing that the enemy might resort, as he had done in the last war, to the use of vesicant gases, Allied scientists determined to be prepared, and a part of the work entailed was performed at the Banting Institute. When a method of neutralizing the effect of mustard gas was being investigated, Sir Frederick requested that mustard gas be applied to the skin of his leg to test out the effect of the treatment. On his insistence this was done, although his colleagues were very dubious. It was a Saturday afternoon, late in March, 1940, when his leg was anointed with the blistering gas, and soon afterwards he left for home, taking a supply of the antidote with him. (Mustard gas does not take effect instantly and a short interval may safely be allowed before starting treatment.) But when Banting reached home he found that a grass fire was threatening his fence and in the excitement of fighting the fire, which took some time to control, he forgot about the necessary treatment until it was too late. A deep mustard gas burn resulted which must have caused him considerable discomfort.

[8]The title of one of J. B. S. Haldane's fascinating essays in *Possible Worlds*. Professor Haldane observes that not even the most intelligent rabbit can tell you very much about what he feels and that this is one of the reasons that a scientist sometimes experiments on himself. He records one of his own adventures in this perilous type of research.

"It was impossible," writes Dr. Norman M. Wrong,[9] who was given charge of the case, "to persuade him that bed rest was essential, and he continued to work with a badly swollen leg. The burn took six weeks to heal and left a considerable scar."

It must be confessed that scientific progress was not greatly furthered as a result of this burn, but at least, "it was demonstrated," as Dr. Wrong observes, "that an extensive mustard gas burn would not incapacitate a man who had the desire to carry on."

11

About the time that Banting's committee was re-constituted as an Associate Committee of the National Research Council, the facilities of the Department of Medical Research, previously offered to the Royal Canadian Air Force, began to be used for physiological tests of the first group of aircraftsmen to be trained under the British Commonwealth Air Training Programme. Major G. E. Hall, still with the Department, supervised this work, with the help of Mr. J. E. Goodwin and others. An effort was made to find better pre-selection criteria for aircrew personnel. Electrocardiograms, electroencephalograms, spirometer tracings, blood pressures, pulse rates, etc., of subjects on a tilt table were carefully recorded. The airmen were also taken for "flights" in the decompression chamber to a "height" of 30,000 feet to teach them the symptoms of anoxia and the resulting loss of efficiency, how to wear a mask and the benefits of oxygen, and how to ventilate their ears to avoid pain on rapid descent. From April to October, 1940, over 1,400 aircraftsmen received these special tests in the Department. By March of the following year the training records of about 500 were available and Mr. John E. Goodwin did a great deal of work in an attempt to correlate the findings of the physiological tests of airmen with their records in subsequent training. Many of the tests showed statistical but not individual correlation.

While this work was in progress the smoke-blue uniforms of the R.C.A.F. were almost constantly to be seen in the rooms and

[9]Personal communication.

corridors of the Banting Institute. One of the young aircraftsmen who underwent the tests recalls most vividly his first meeting with the head of the Department. A group of the boys had come to the Institute, prepared to be deeply impressed by the famous scientist for whom it was named. They asked a stray character they met in one of the corridors to point out Sir Frederick Banting for them. The stray character grinned. He was dressed in a "lab." coat with abbreviated sleeves and was wearing tennis shoes. It presently dawned upon the boys that this was Sir Frederick himself!

Although they had looked for someone more imposing, they decided after chatting with him for a time that they liked their great scientists informal. So this was the wonderful "Sir Frederick" of whom they had heard so much! It was not long before they began to refer to him among themselves as "Sir Fred." When this reached Banting's ears we are told that he was not displeased.

"Sir Fred," says the aircraftsman who tells the story, "was a great guy. Really a great guy." And of all the many tributes paid to him, some of them eloquent, some of them fulsome, this would not have been the least pleasing to the ever-youthful "Sir Fred."

When the Clinical Investigation Hut at Eglinton was completed and ready for use, the special physiological tests of aircraftsmen were henceforth performed there. More space was made available in the Department and the academic investigations in which Banting was interested began to proceed more rapidly.

12

One of the most brilliant of Banting's group of workers was Dr. W. R. Franks, who had been a member of the Department since its days in the old Pathology Building. Dr. Franks (at that time Lieutenant, R.C.A.M.C., R.C.A.F.) had presented to Banting as early as September, 1939, a memorandum entitled "Problems Arising from the Effects of Manœuvring in Space at High Speeds." The effect on the human body of forces due to acceleration was a limiting factor in the use of high-speed modern aircraft and the problems to be solved in overcoming the limitations of flesh and blood were discussed in the memorandum. Experiments were described in which mice were whirled in a centrifuge at speeds up to 150 "G" (where G=gravitational force). By means of interposing a fluid system between the animal body and the supporting structure the animals were enabled to survive even this terrible force. The effect was independent of the amount of fluid, which in practice could be minimal.

This suggested the possibility of designing a semi-rigid suit containing a fluid system which might protect fliers from the blacking-out experienced in high speed manœuvres. There were many practical difficulties to be overcome but by March of the following year Banting received a second memorandum from Franks reporting completion of his preliminary studies. By the middle of May he was able to report that six modifications of the original suit had been effected and tested. These had been worn by Lieutenant Franks during test flights in a Fleet aircraft. Early in June an experienced test pilot, Wing Commander D'Arcy Greig, R.A.F., tried out an improved suit in a Spitfire and gave an encouraging report. Even in the most harsh manœuvres a feeling of normality had been experienced, especially with regard to the movement of limbs and respiration. During the following nine months many improvements in design were effected and in April, 1941, Franks went to England with a number of suits of various sizes to have them tested under service conditions.

Franks had also proposed the construction of an "accelerator," a stationary apparatus capable of producing the effects of acceleration in a laboratory. This apparatus offered many unexpected engineering difficulties in its manufacture and operation but with the help of Professor H. W. Price of the Department of Electrical Engineering, University of Toronto, these problems were eventually overcome. The huge and complex machine was located in a special hut at No. 1 Initial Training School, Eglinton.

All this work Banting followed with avid interest, backing it forcefully through the Associate Committee on Aviation Medical Research and taking great pride in its continued development.

13

In the midst of his preoccupations, Banting was not too busy to write a letter to Bill, who was visiting his Uncle Thompson on the farm near Alliston, the farm where his father was born.

205 *Rosedale Heights Drive,*
Toronto, Ontario,
July 7, 1940.

DEAR BILL:

How are you getting along on the farm? I hope that you are a help to them now during their busy season. You must work as much as you can for in order to win the war Canada must supply England with food from the farms, as well as soldiers, planes and guns. So you see, by working you can help win the war.

I hope you have been in to visit your grandmother. There has not been any word yet about our war guest children, but we are ready for them.

Be a good boy and do as you are told—and do not leave jobs half done.

Love,

DAD.

A war guest, David Howarth, an English lad approximately the same age as Bill, arrived soon afterward at Rosedale Heights.

The hope expressed in the letter that Bill had visited his grandmother requires explanation. Her husband was dead, and old Mrs. Banting having slipped and broken her hip was carried away from the fine town house they had built for their retirement and lay long in hospital in Alliston. Every week there was a fresh bouquet of flowers from Fred.

But the mists were closing fast around her, soon to give way to darkness.

14

Banting brought several trained scientists into his department to augment his staff carrying out war research. The most senior of these was Professor H. C. Bazett, head of the Department of Physiology, University of Pennsylvania. Professor Bazett had been one of the principals who had carried out medical research as a medical officer in the Royal Air Force during the latter part of the Great War, 1914-18. The wisdom of Banting's action in selecting an investigator of Dr. Bazett's invaluable experience was shown on many occasions.

Dr. Harry G. Armstrong, on a year's leave of absence from the United States Army Air Corps, did research in collaboration with Dr. A. C. Burton on the physiological effects of the cold experienced at high altitudes. Dr. Armstrong was the author of the only English language textbook on aviation medicine available at the outbreak of War. His work in Toronto was interrupted by his recall but he was able to demonstrate conclusively that the breathing of cold air has no effect on body temperature.

A low temperature decompression chamber, not yet complete at the time of Armstrong's departure, was installed at No. 1 I.T.S., where Dr. A. C. Burton studied heat loss from the human body at different pressures and temperatures and with different types of flying clothes. An "artificial man," made of papier mâché and electrically maintained at body temperature, was used in similar studies and to assess accurately the insulating properties of flying suits. Data of considerable practical value were obtained. Once again Dr. Hall, at whose instigation Armstrong had been invited to Toronto, was intimately concerned in the work.

15

Studies were made by members of the Department, or by those associated with it, of almost every conceivable aspect of aviation medicine. Decompression, anoxia, aeroembolism; acceleration and black-out; heat loss; suits, gloves, masks, even goggles.

(There was a study of agents to prevent or diminish fogging of goggles and turret windows.) Nor were the psychological aspects forgotten.

Banting played a presiding rôle, much as he had done in the silicosis research. He also kept up the Ottawa end, spending about half of every week in the capital. He presided at meetings, knocked at doors, talked, argued, conferred and confided, and funds were forthcoming.

But unlike his participation in the silicosis work, there was also active experimentation. The decompression studies have already been mentioned and these were his chief personal interest. Elsewhere his usual common sense was constantly apparent. A single instance affords a clear illustration.

His practical mind envisioned the necessity for testing equipment under other conditions than can be obtained with a static decompression chamber. Early in the war a commercial oxygen mask, which showed certain desirable features when tested in the chamber, was being considered for use in the R.C.A.F. One look was enough. He decided that this oxygen face-piece would not be very secure when used in military aircraft, particularly if a pilot suddenly found his wind-shield torn away. Banting arranged to have the mask tested in the wind-tunnel of the National Research Council and noted, not without a gleam of satisfaction, that when the wearer turned his head the mask was ripped from his face by the force of the blast.

Another of Banting's great contributions was that as director of the Department of Medical Research, he continually and persistently drew back his colleagues and associates from their many "flips into fancy," from their pet schemes, from the side-alleys of so-called pure research, and back from all similar academic distractions to the central problem as he saw it—the wellbeing and comfort as well as the efficiency of fighter pilots and bomber aircrew. This steadfast consideration of the comfort and efficiency of the human was the constant yardstick by which he measured all projects presented to him and by which he judged the worth of such research work.

Many of his associates in his Department took up the prosecution of research on problems connected with military aviation.

Some of them continued to work as civilians, but two of his senior colleagues, Dr. G. E. Hall and Dr. W. R. Franks, joined the Royal Canadian Air Force Medical Branch (via the R.C.A.M.C.) in order to be able to attack these problems more effectively from within the Service. Both have organized and prosecuted major experimental projects on aviation medicine in the R.C.A.F., and it is interesting to note that first Group Captain Hall, A.F.C., and later Wing Commander Franks, O.B.E., held the senior administrative office in charge of research for the Directorate of Medical Service of the Air Force.

Banting's major personal contribution to aviation medicine was the organization of his Associate Committee, a national vehicle for the work. This service he carried out with his characteristic vigour.

It should be mentioned that the Associate Committee on Aviation Medical Research acted as a clearing house for all scientific data accumulated by Canadian investigators. These data were transmitted to the appropriate war committees in Great Britain, the United States, Australia, New Zealand and the Union of South Africa through the National Research Council of Canada. Similarly, essential information coming to Canada from these sources was directed through the Associate Committee on Aviation Medical Research to the appropriate groups of Canadian workers.

But the mails were not entirely satisfactory for the purpose. Banting liked to see for himself the progress of work on both sides of the Atlantic. It is frequently difficult to describe such experiments precisely; complicated apparatus is often hard to visualize. There was also the added factor that much of the information was highly secret. As a personal liaison officer, as a gatherer of information to relay to his workers and as a purveyor of a knowledge of their contributions to their counterparts in Great Britain, he was able to perform an essential service.

16

Early in 1941 he began to feel that another transatlantic journey was required of him. A great mass of data had been accumulated. Liaison was defective. The personal touch was again required. To save time he would travel by air.

Part of his last evening in Toronto was spent in the home of his cousin, Dr. F. W. W. Hipwell. Dr. Hipwell, an expert amateur photographer, took several pictures of Sir Frederick. He was apparently light-hearted for he was smiling happily. Yet to one or two of his Toronto friends he expressed a vague foreboding. For no apparent reason his stout heart momentarily misgave him. It is useless to speculate of presentiments but whatever was passing in his mind seemed somehow to cast a shadow.

In Montreal he had a lengthy conversation in his hotel room with Professor Collip. Chiefly about the work of the N.R.C., of which both were members. But again Banting voiced an obscure, illogical presentiment. What was wrong?

When Collip asked if he were dressed warmly enough for the flight, Banting admitted that he had no suitable gloves. Collip offered to lend him a pair and later in the day he left them at the hotel desk. They were warm, sheepskin gloves and Banting departed on his journey wearing them.

Later on, much later, the gloves came back under tragic circumstances. They were no longer warm. They would never be warm again. They were chill with the touch of death.

PART XV
Tragedy in Newfoundland

By his death the world has lost a great benefactor, Canada a great citizen, the medical profession a most potent force in research, and the National Research Council an indefatigable worker. . . .

C. J. MACKENZIE.

1

In mid-February, 1941, the R.C.A.F. Station at Gander Bay in Newfoundland, the take-off point for wartime transatlantic air travel, consisted of extensive runways and a group of hangars and hutments; it could be said to interrupt, rather than to relieve, the desolation of the landscape.

The Senior Medical Officer of this lonely Station was Flying Officer (afterwards Squadron Leader) Clifford S. Wilson, of Kitchener, Ontario. In mid-February, his notes record, the routine of his duties was pleasantly varied by the arrival of a visitor.

February 17, 1941 (Monday). Dr. Knapp of Lewisport knocked at my door in the evening and said that Sir Frederick Banting was at the Eastbound Inn and wished to meet the M.O.'s. So we went down (Dr. Knapp, Kent Irwin and myself) and found Sir Frederick, who greeted us with a hearty handshake and an affable smile. We returned to my quarters. Knapp and Kent went on to the party later and we chatted until midnight. Walked back to the lodge with him.

February 18, 1941 (Tuesday). First thing when I stepped out in the morning I met Sir Frederick, not knowing what to do with himself, so he walked to the R.A.P. with me. He fixed a B.L.B. oxygen mask with adhesive tape while I made rounds. . . . Then to the new hospital building. . . . Later, after supper, Sir Frederick came in looking for Buckinghams.

February 19 (Wednesday). . . . At 7.00 p.m. Sir Frederick joined me. We chatted, Saw movie, "Stardust," with Linda Darnell and Roland Young. Then Kent, Sir F. and I had an interesting chat for two hours re the origin of aviation medicine, research, war, etc.

February 20 (Thursday). A dull grey sky with tendency to blow and snowflurries. About 10.30 a.m. Sir Frederick came in and sent his wife a wire which I despatched for him. Then we had a long talk about hobbies, homes, wives and families, etc.— and the future. He has a definite yen for a home in the country and retirement. He said, "I have never been happier in my life." In the afternoon . . . picked up Sir F., who was immersed in my

409

book, *How To Fly A Plane,* which he had borrowed, and we walked to the new camp site. At suppertime I prepared two covers with Newfoundland one cent to ten cent stamps and had them postmarked. Sir F. addressed the outer covers. One is to be returned via Clipper and the other in the diplomatic mail. When I went down and gave them to him he gave me a letter for Lady Banting which I mailed.

Something else that Banting said remained in the Medical Officer's mind. The foreboding he had experienced in Toronto and in Montreal had now sharpened.

"Wilson," he said, with a strange mingling of lightness and gravity, "Wilson, I'm *scared!*"

In the hangar later I helped him into his Teddybear suit and was the last to shake his hand when he ran for his plane which was being hauled to the runway.

"Happy landings, Sir!" said Flying Officer Wilson.
"Oh, we'll have those!" said Banting.
He grinned, waved and disappeared into the plane.

2

The pilot of the big Hudson, assigned to fly Sir Frederick to Great Britain, was 33-year-old Captain Joseph Creighton Mackey,[1] of Kansas City, a civilian ferry-pilot with the R.C.A.F. Mackey was a flier of long and varied experience, who had operated an airport at Findlay, Ohio, for four years, had participated in many air races, was a winner of the Freddie Lund Trophy for precision stunt flying, had written a book on sky writing, and had been a U.S. Army instructor at Kelly Field, San Antonio, and a test pilot at Kansas City before coming to Canada in 1940 to ferry bombers to England. He had been described by the famous Captain Roscoe Turner as one of the best pilots he had ever

---

[1]Excerpts from Capt. Mackey's narrative are quoted with the permission of *The Toronto Star,* in which it originally appeared.

known. The navigator was Flying Officer William Bird, "with whom," said Mackey, "I had no previous experience," but who was acknowledged a skilled and reliable officer. The radio operator was William Snailham, "with whom I was well acquainted."

I was instructed (wrote the pilot) to take aboard as passenger Sir Frederick Banting. . . . I had no opportunity to make the acquaintance of Sir Frederick. In the preparation of my ship for the flight I was introduced to him and he boarded the plane. . . .

Very shortly after taking off I discovered that it would be necessary for us to return.[2] My first act was to jettison our main fuel cargo and I informed my three companions in the rear compartments of the plane of my intention to return. I asked them to throw overboard all the baggage and every item they could find that would reduce our weight for the possibly powerless return flight to land.

It was dark and snowing. By the time I had reached what I was certain to be land, I instructed Snailham, who was in the radio compartment immediately behind me, to order the others to bail out. Snailham and I had been working together for some time, and I knew he was thoroughly familiar with the situation and how to meet it.

It never occurred to me to think that they would not bail out. . . . I felt what I thought to be a definite change of balance in the ship and assumed that they had gone. I then devoted my attention to making the best possible landing entirely by instrument, as, of course, I was unable to see the ground at any time. I gambled that as half of the surface of Newfoundland was frozen lake, I might have the luck to strike one of them.

In actual fact, my wing struck the one large tree in that whole area. I came within a few feet of making a safe landing. I do not recollect anything whatever of the crash.

In the final article of the series which begins with the above narrative, Mackey returned to the question of why his companions failed to jump.

[2]It was reported that one engine failed and that while the aircraft was flying back inland the other engine faltered and the wireless ceased to function. Late in the day, the Newfoundland air station received a communication from the ship, reporting that it was turning back. Snailham asked for a bearing, which was given. No other message was ever received.—L. S.

My orders to jump were given to Snailham and were acknowledged. I did not give those orders until I was sure we were over the land. They were given at a normal altitude at which such orders are given, about 2,500 feet.

From that moment on I was much too occupied with flying the ship to pay attention to whether the order was obeyed or not. I took it for granted the order was obeyed. . . .

Whether they preferred to take their chance by riding on down with the ship to jumping over what they knew to be at least the winter wilderness of Newfoundland, if not the ocean, is the merest speculation and anybody's guess is as good as mine. It is my opinion now that if they had jumped they would have been saved.

It is true they would not have been together. The ship would have gone on a distance of perhaps six or seven miles. The three would have fallen some distance apart, depending on how quickly they had followed one another. But it is my belief they would have fallen within calling distance of one another and despite the cold and the long night that would have been ahead of them, they could have contrived some way of contacting the searching 'planes the following day.

This, of course, is a dubious proposition. Sufficient difficulty was experienced in finding the wreckage of the plane, together with the lone survivor, to offer any assurance that the others, had they jumped, would have been discovered in time, or discovered at all, by the searching aeroplanes. It was largely due to chance that Mackey himself was found.

Be that as it may. The speculation is an idle one. Whatever their reason, the navigator, the radio operator and the distinguished passenger did not "bail out," but plummeted down through the night with the luckless Hudson to violent and terrible deaths.

Why, it may be asked, did Captain Mackey stay with the plane? Why did he not jump himself? The answer, presumably, is that he was trying to save the ship. Gambling on the rare good fortune that had seen him safely through a score of dangers and mishaps, feeling himself free of the obligation of passengers, and hoping against hope that Lady Luck would drop him on a treeless surface (Newfoundland, as he said, was half lakes), he rode the ship down. His luck was still strong enough to bring him through alive, but not quite strong enough to bring his companions with him.

Reaching a malignant arm from the silent darkness beneath, a great tree clutched disastrously at his wing. The plane crashed helplessly and with terrific impact, and following a momentary tremor and a flash and flurry of snow, the frigid wilderness enclosed the broken plane and the broken men in its cold, blind silence.

Mackey regained consciousness with the awareness that he had sustained a head injury.

I woke to consciousness as you wake from sleep, wide awake, and I found that I had already tied my handkerchief around my head which was bleeding profusely.

I then looked at my watch and realized it had been one hour since my last wholly conscious moment. All the cabin lights were still burning brightly. I sat in my seat for several minutes trying to collect my thoughts. A pleased feeling crept over me momentarily as the realization that I had been able to avert fire became complete.

As my head wound was bleeding. . . . I realized I must bandage myself and I reached for the first-aid kit beside me. It was missing. I climbed from my seat to go back into the cabin. This was my first look backwards into the ship. And, to my utter amazement and horror, a body was visible lying between the main cabin and the radio cabin.

Having given orders for them to jump by parachute. . . . I was certain I was alone in the final stages of the flight. I found that the body was that of Snailham. He was dead, and had obviously been killed on impact. I went on back in the cabin, dreading what I might find. And found Sir Frederick still alive but unconscious, with a severe head wound, his left arm broken and other injuries. I went on to the back of the cabin and found Flying Officer Bird also dead and presumably killed on impact.

The pilot returned to Banting and made a further examination of his injuries. They appeared to be severe. He got him into a sitting position, talked to him and finally succeeded in rousing him to semi-consciousness.

He was able to help me move him from the cabin floor into the bunk in the cabin, where I covered him with several folds of a silk parachute. I had no knife, but by tearing another parachute by snagging it on a broken projection of the wrecked interior of the plane I got enough silk to make a sling for his broken arm and a new bandage for my head.

Captain Mackey has reiterated the statement that "while Sir Frederick lived for about sixteen to twenty hours after the crash he did not consciously suffer from his injuries. When I found him he was unconscious. He regained consciousness and lost it from time to time. But at no time during his apparently conscious moments was he really aware of his plight."

I think he was rendered delirious by his head injuries. I cannot figure out where he thought he was. But such was his force and energy that he spoke and acted throughout these periods of apparent consciousness as though he were a military officer on duty or perhaps a professor in a clinic. He commanded me to take down his dictation.

Throughout the first night of our crash and all through the first morning Sir Frederick roused himself time after time and in a strong and what seemed a perfectly lucid condition dictated rapidly letters, memoranda, and statements, everyone of which was to me merely . . . wholly unintelligible technical, medical phraseology which I . . . could not possibly take down.

The Captain has suggested the possibility that "scientific and medical information of the most priceless character was lost in those hours," and has written of "the struggle of a great mind to fight against death in a race to record his last thoughts." This is not wholly consistent with the assertion that Sir Frederick was quite unaware of his plight. In any case the absence of a medical stenographer has doubtless deprived us of little, for he was not the sole repository of the secrets he carried to England, and as for other technical information, it was almost certainly scattering and incoherent.

But how vividly Mackey has pictured for us the disordered but still unextinguished zeal which thus flared out with intermittent energy in the concluding hours of the scientist's life! How bravely he fought! With what dogged persistence he returned to the hopeless attempt to body forth some wavering and obscure conception, something half-formed and vaguely defined but burning hotly in his brain! A great mass of facts which kept dissolving and regrouping in his clouded consciousness were marshalled at his lips into a brave semblance of meaning. Was not the pilot right after all? Was he not struggling, with all his old ardour, all his old stubbornness, to accomplish something he had wanted very much to do? If he was not aware, in the ordinary sense, that night was closing round him and death was near, might not some deeper stratum of his mind have been dimly conscious of a deepening darkness, an increasing chill, and have filled him with a sense of urgency? The powerful engine of his will, which had driven through so many obstacles, attacked without hesitation the last, insurmountable barrier. Whatever he wanted to do, whatever he wanted to say, whatever impulse stirred him at the last, his resolution was never at fault. He went down fighting, and his last thought, obviously, was of duties not yet fulfilled.

. . . But at no time did Sir Frederick show the slightest recognition of the fact that he was gravely injured in a plane crash. Not once did he give any sign that he recognized in me the pilot of the plane. . . .

I made various excursions outside to look over the ground. It was cold. There was five feet of snow on the ground. We had struck a tree—the largest tree in sight on that desolate area as I saw later—and by only a few feet I had missed a landing on a snow-covered lake that might have turned out differently.

I turned off the lights in the plane, all save one, and devoted myself to attending to Sir Frederick. . . .

There was little that Mackey could do. He tried to make the scientist lie down and rest. But after a few minutes of rest he would insist on rising to a sitting position again and commence once more his dictation.

His entire bearing and attitude were military. He seemed to feel he was carrying on at a post of duty. [Mackey thought his speech seemed coherent] but on medical problems beyond my comprehension. At times I went through the motions of writing down his words in order to quiet him.

When morning came I went outside the plane and tried to figure what chances there were of our being spotted from the air, for I knew there would be planes searching for us. But it had been snowing, and as we had crashed against the edge of the lake, our wreckage might not show up amidst the rocks and the bush.

After waiting until noon, I decided that Sir Frederick's condition was such that he could not survive if he did not have immediate medical attention. He had by this time become completely unconscious. I had no proper plan in mind. I was weak from shock and my injuries, but I thought I might explore the immediate neighbourhood. I covered Sir Frederick well with coats . . . and then I started out.

After going only about twenty yards, I realized it would be hopeless for me to try to go anywhere in the five-foot deep snow. The woods were thickety and dense and full of little gullies. I had to stay in the open spaces.

The strongest of men could not wade through five-foot snow, so I returned to the ship and took the map board and broke it in halves by banging it on a rock. With friction tape, I rigged up a plausible imitation of snowshoes out of these two eighteen-inch square pieces of plywood and bound them to my feet. . . .

That first exploration trip might very easily have ended in disaster complete. . . . At the most, I do not think I travelled two miles from the plane. I set off for what I thought would be the seashore. Stumbling and floundering on the makeshift snowshoes, I grew terribly weary after a little while. I began to see mirages. I thought I could see houses. I even imagined I could see windows. But when I reached them they were merely snow-covered trees and rocks.

In this way, blundering along through the snow, Captain Mackey came to a frozen expanse which he believed to be a river. He had to decide which way to go, to the right or to the left. The wind was blowing strongly. If he went with the wind, it would be easier. But if he went against the wind, it would be easier to come back. He chose to go into the wind. After following the river bed for some distance he came to the realization that he could not go farther and that he had to get back to the plane. Of the return trip he wrote that "so long and grim was the struggle that I gave up completely half a dozen times."

Slowly my energy would creep back and rouse me to one more try. I set myself little tasks. I did not think of the plane. That seemed miles away. I set myself merely that next hillock, that next rock or bush. . . . Then I would set myself a new goal. . . .

The two miles I travelled that first afternoon took from shortly before noon until dusk. When I reached the plane, I found Sir Frederick dead. By some immense effort, he had got himself off the bunk in the wrecked cabin and had got outside. He lay fifteen feet from the wreck.

A final surge of that tremendous vitality which had never deserted him. A final confused and heroic effort to escape the fate which pressed him down.

Did he think himself abandoned? Did he wake in the dim cabin, wondering what had happened? Did he grope his way to the door and look out across the pitiless snowfields, vast and austere, realizing at last the measure of the calamity that had befallen him? Did he then set off, with unimaginable courage, to find a way out? Or was he merely floundering about in the snow, perplexedly looking for someone, alone and puzzled, like a lost child?

Collapsing in the snow—the shining snow he had so loved to paint with the flake-white from his palette, the cruel and beautiful snow with its deathly embrace—he again lost consciousness.

The snow. The snow. How the wind had whipped the snow, raising it into towering drifts, along the third concession of Essa. How the snow had fallen graciously, but cruelly too, on the sombre fields of France. How the snow stood gleaming on Ellesmere, and how it made patterns on the fields and roofs at St. Fidele and Ste. Irenée.

And here, in the midst of the desolate wilderness of Newfoundland, the snow at last received him. Banting was dead.

3

Captain Mackey was by now in a sorry case. He had sprained his ankle in the crash and after his fruitless and difficult exploration of the snow-locked terrain it had become severely swollen and very painful. He began the second night of his ordeal in the lowest spirits.

Here was a great enterprise in ruin in the midst of an immeasurable wilderness. Here lay dead a great man, a man I did not know, but a man of importance in the world. He had been the only other living thing, speaking to me in urgent riddles. Now he was still. And I was in this hole in the snow, beside the wreckage.

[With an engine cover of canvas under him and two overcoats over him, he tried to sleep in the snow beside the ship.] The snow that had been falling the night of our crash had all but hidden its wreckage. It was up against brush and trees, where its shape would not easily be recognized from the air.

He did not lack food, however, for in the wrecked plane he found sandwiches, oranges, and numerous tins of emergency rations. These were frozen solid, but he succeeded in eating the sandwiches and some of the oranges. The oranges he took to bed with him, placing them against his body during the night and so partially thawing them out by morning. Water was another matter, and "one thing that pressed me terribly all through my four-day experience was thirst."

On the second morning he made a list of everything he had and set about studying his map and considering what he should do. He decided that he would stay by the ship two days more, if the weather remained flyable, in the hope that he might be sighted from the air. If the weather were not flyable he would set out next day in a westerly direction. To the best of his figuring he could intercept a railway approximately twenty-five miles due west. The village of Musgrave Harbour showed clearly on his map and was only about ten miles distant, but he chose the longer trek, when planning this attempt, because he would be able to travel along a frozen river bed which was flat and relatively clear of obstructions, whereas the other way was over hills and rocks, through woods and gullies, and was almost certain to prove impassable to one so little experienced in the wild, so ill-equipped and in such poor physical condition. "I calculated that with a new set of snowshoes, made with the plyboard map locker of the ship and with a toboggan made of the metal cowling of one of the engines, I could make five miles a day." This estimate he afterwards doubted, and doubted indeed if he could have made the trip at all.

During the second day many planes passed within hearing and a few within sight. "I had rigged up a signal fire by dragging together what trees I could of those I had struck down in the crash, pouring gasoline over them. During this second day, I lit this signal fire three times, when planes passed in the distance." Alas! the gasoline burned brightly, a pale sheet of flame, but the trees and twigs were too filled with frost to ignite. His signal fires flickered out after only a few moments, and the searching planes droned off into silence. They were succeeded by others, and still others; these, too, faded sadly away, until the taunting, iterative fugue of the sonorous motors, never quite near enough for their pilots to see him, lost all its hope and all its meaning. He almost ceased to listen. He had no axe, no knife, no other implements for preparing wood and building a proper fire. What was the use of staying on? The overland trek would be arduous indeed, but it promised a fighting chance.

Nevertheless, he resolved to stick to his plan and wait a reasonable time for the planes to find him. He knew that his chances of reaching civilization afoot, hampered by his injured ankle and his head wounds, would be slight at the best. Meantime he made what preparations he could. Among the articles he found in the ship were two red flares which he decided to take along for signals to stop trains, should he be able to reach the railway. He spent much of the second day and part of the third in removing one of the two compasses from the ship and calculating the error which resulted from damaging it on removal. He gathered together the food, the extra clothing and all the other articles which he thought would be necessary for his journey. Then he composed himself to wait.

Somehow the time dragged by. Hope still pricked his heart whenever he heard the sound of a plane, but always, as during his previous vigils, he heard the plane turn back, and listened despondently till it was only a murmur, and till even the murmur died away.

The day arrived which was to be his last before setting out from the wreck. His toboggan was packed. Why should he wait longer? It was a great temptation to start at once. But he still held back, to give one more chance to searching aircraft to spot the crippled Hudson.

Just before noon he heard a plane coming. Nearer and nearer it approached. The murmur became a drone. The drone became a roar. Could it really be? Was it possible, after so many disappointments, that one of the roaming planes at last had noticed the ruins of his ship? Using gasoline, seat cushions, a life preserver and a grease-soaked engine cover, he endeavoured to set a signal fire that would create smoke. But to no avail. He saw the plane fly straight over him, about six hundred feet up, without any indication of recognition. It headed toward the horizon. With sinking heart he listened once again to that ominous, retreating murmur which he had come to know so well. It came back to him *diminuendo* from the distance, as if a note that had been sounded by plucking a string were lessening and dissolving in the blueness of air.

He seized the hauling rope of the metal toboggan and started. He gave up, for once and all, any hope of being found by aircraft.

He had gone about three hundred yards when he heard the plane returning. "So complete was my feeling of lost hope," he writes, "that I did not even pause in my stride, though the engine grew louder and louder."

Right overhead the plane flew. As he looked up he saw it dip one wing and heel over to let the pilot look down. Mackey waved madly, he flung his arms and shouted. But the pilot overhead had not seen him. Something else had attracted his attention. Was it the Hudson? Round he banked his plane, closer and closer to the wreckage, and then, as the frantic Captain leaped and waved, he saw him. The plane came very near—near enough for Mackey to recognize the pilot, an old friend named Jim Allison. Allison dropped a message: "Bringing help." Then he climbed to gain sufficient altitude to clear his wireless signals.

Circling round and round, he never lost sight of the spot. In an incredibly short time the air seemed full of planes. They dropped a sleeping bag, provisions, medical kits, tools—a veritable rain of supplies. "Despite my almost hysterical condition I realized they didn't know the truth. So I tramped out my name in big fifty-foot letters in the snow. 'Joe,' I wrote. Then 'three dead.' "

One of the cases they dropped burst open. There was a can opener among the goods, and canned pineapple juice. Mackey drank one can without stopping. Then another. "I never tasted anything so glorious in all my life."

But now he was exhausted and trembling from rushing about in the deep snow. And though the sky was full of planes he knew they could not land. How long would it be before actual help arrived? He crept into the sleeping bag to wait.

Two miles away, one of the many planes that gathered had spotted two men hauling a sled across a lake. These were Walter Hicks and Dalton Abbott of Musgrave Harbour. On their sled they had about fifty rabbits they had trapped during their week away from the village. Two miles farther away, following a lake shore to check over their snares, were two other companions, Harold Hicks and Tobias Moland. These men had surmised that there was something strange happening because of all the aircraft they had seen in recent days. But they had no word of the wreck.

Down on Walter Hicks and Dalton Abbott dove a plane and dropped them a message, telling them that two miles away in the direction indicated by the flight of the plane was a wrecked plane and men in need of help.

From what I have since learned, Hicks and Abbott simply dumped all their rabbits, guns and gear off their sled and started. On their snowshoes, they must have flown across the ridges and gullies intervening, following the sounds of the planes diving and circling above where I lay.

. . . It could not have been fifteen minutes that they took to reach me. They spotted the wreck first and went to it. I saw them appear, going at incredible speed on their snowshoes, and examine the wreck. Then they shouted. I sat up and shouted back. If ever I need help again, I hope to see men coming as those two came. They slackened their pace for an instant and then came on faster than ever. It seems to me they flew over the snow.

For Captain Mackey, who had quite despaired of rescue, the wilderness was wilderness no longer. But crumpled in the awkward attitudes of death, the dead lay silent and forlorn.

4

How was it, after so many would-be rescue planes had passed over the site of the tragedy without seeing it, that it was finally spotted and that help came? A curious factor—one of those elements of pure chance, seemingly of whimsy, which sometimes intervene when least expected—was responsible. This factor was a sea marker.

A sea marker is a sort of flask of aluminum powder which is carried by all planes crossing water for the purpose of estimating an aeroplane's drift. We drop the flask on to the water and the aluminum powder spreads in a bright patch, which we watch and by it calculate the amount of drift we are subject to.

I had six of these sea marker flasks in my plane when we crashed. Five of them burst on the impact. . . . When I waked from unconsciousness and looked around the plane that first hour, the whole scene was one weird and ghostly spectacle of silvery aluminum. Everything was powdered with it, the wreckage itself, the figures of my companions. Though the plane was badly wrecked, by some miracle the cabin lights, fed by battery, still glowed. And all shone in this strange unearthly glare of the aluminum from the five burst sea markers. During that unforgettable first night when Sir Frederick tried so desperately to communicate something to me, and I tried so hard to quiet him and force him to lie down and save his ebbing force, he and I and all about us were bathed in that silvery glare.

Yet it was the one unbroken sea marker that brought about my rescue. For now I know that it was not the wreckage of the plane that Jim Allison saw when he passed over me. It was not me, ploughing along with my toboggan. It was a black streak on the snow.

Among the things I had found, when I searched the wreckage for materials to make smoke with, was this one unbroken sea marker. The third day, when cushions, life-preservers and other things had failed to make a smoke fire, I had taken this flask over to my rock and burst it on the stone in the hope that it would make a silver shine on the rock. The wind took the powder and flung it out from the rock on the snow in a long streak. What looks like silver on the sea looks black on snow. It was that queer black streak that caught Jim Allison's eye when he flew over. It was that streak that caused him to bank steeply and turn and look. Then he saw the wreckage, the tail of the plane sticking out of the snow. And on his second circle, he saw me three hundred yards away, waving.

5

Meantime, at Gander Bay, anxiety had mounted sharply and had presently changed to despair. Flying Officer Wilson recorded the tension of waiting, watching, hoping, and finally the shock and sorrow of the news.

February 21 (Friday). Nasty day with snow flurries and heavy overcast. Ceiling four hundred feet. No word of Mackey's plane since request for position last night. . . . In the afternoon things cleared a bit and some planes got away. Searched for three hours with no luck. We are a doleful lot.

February 22 (Saturday). A fine clear morning and patrols got away. Planes returned at noon. Still no sign. Out again in afternoon—weather closing in—no sign of Mackey's plane. Begins to look quite hopeless. Rumour around radio of lost ship heard but it was one of our own giving position. . . .

On Tuesday, February 25, Wilson, wrote to his wife:

Yesterday morning as I returned from the R.A.P. I saw our chief wireless man on the tear for the hangar so I changed course for there and met him inside, where he told me Jim Allison in a Hudson had just located the plane. I hiked then for the control tower where the messages were coming in and just as I arrived Allison sent, "One man alive." Then followed a few position figures, then, "Send Digbys with food." So quick as a wink the operator picked up our machines and told them where to go. In a few minutes Allison said, "Still circling. Digbys coming up." Really it was a true miracle the way in which everything was done. The plane-to-plane telephone is amazing.

Soon one of the Hudsons came in and an R.A.F. chap rushed breathlessly to me and wanted to be passed for a parachute descent. He said, one man waved to them and the message he had tramped in the snow was signed Joe. His message: "3 DEAD—JOE."

The narrative is continued in Wilson's notes:

At 2.00 p.m. we took off and went directly to the scene. Plane lay with nose only into bush—port wing smashed to pieces—both motors out—fuselage ruined. No sign of life. While we turned and banked I snapped four pictures. . . .

The crash had occurred only twelve minutes' flying time from the Station at Gander Bay.

Wilson afterwards treated Captain Mackey, examined the bodies of the dead and regained the two "covers," sadly blood-stained, which Banting had promised to mail for him from overseas.

One final excerpt from his notes:

March 10, 1941. . . . Wrote Group Captain Ryan suggesting the new hospital be called "The Sir Frederick Banting Memorial Hospital." A final tribute to a great man.

6

On Sunday, February 23, the news had been released that Canada's most distinguished son was missing aboard the vanished plane. An official announcement described the aircraft as "a military aeroplane being delivered by a civilian organization." It added that three other persons were aboard the plane, and listed their names. Just where the plane on which Sir Frederick was a passenger had taken off, or where it was going, was not announced. The report said: "It was flying in favourable weather conditions, and as it had not arrived at its destination, and as no radio signal has been received from it since Friday morning,[3] it is feared it may have come down in the sea off the east coast, or on land remote from means of communication. An intensive and widespread search was commenced immediately and is still in progress." The British United Press added on Monday that the search was believed to be concentrated in the Newfoundland area.

[3]Actually the last signal was received on Thursday night.—L. S.

The news was a profound shock to the whole Dominion and was received with dismay in the United States, in Great Britain and indeed throughout the world. Banting had been little in the news of late, working obscurely and silently as he preferred to do, but now his name flashed once more into the headlines, headlines no longer triumphant but deeply tragic. A score of portraits, old cuts and new, were hurried into the press, and his pictures were printed in a thousand newspapers with what seemed to many readers a new poignancy, a tragic intensification of his familiar facial expressions. Public anxiety revealed itself in a multitude of speculations. Faith was avowed in public prayers for his safety; in many homes all across the continent sincere and silent prayer was passionately offered. It is impossible to conceive that a similar report of any other man, however important, however famous, could have perturbed the whole nation, and other nations than his own, so generally and so deeply. Banting was more than a mere celebrity. To Canada he was a beloved son. To those who had the country's war effort in charge he was a valued adviser, and much more than an adviser—a leader on the research war-front. To a million diabetics the world over he was a direct and powerful benefactor, and seemed almost a personal friend. To scientists he was an inspiration. It was hard to imagine that he might be lost, to imagine the terrible void which would be left if he were really gone. His relatives and intimate friends were joined by his associates in the University of Toronto, the Banting Institute, the National Research Council and numerous other organizations, and by the great mass of his well-wishers and admirers, in the ardent hope that all might yet be well.

There followed a painful interval of waiting. Mercifully it was short. The Canadian House of Commons was in session at Ottawa, and early in the afternoon of February 24, the Honourable C. D. Howe, replying to a question from Opposition Leader Hanson, announced that the missing plane had been located. He told of the writing in the snow as seen by aerial searchers. The writing—there was no indication of its message at this time—raised hopes that possibly more than one of those aboard the plane had survived.

The Minister could say no more, but as the day wore on

further news came in. Late in the afternoon the Honourable
J. L. Ralston, Minister of National Defence, informed a still
assembly of Sir Frederick's death. He read the following message
from Wing Commander Gordon in Newfoundland:

The pilot Mackey is alive—the others are dead. Two trappers
are at the aircraft. Aircraft dropped more emergency rations to
party. Moth ski-plane *en route* from St. John's, Newfoundland,
to Newfoundland Airport.
The Moth ski-plane will proceed to the scene of the crash as
soon as possible. Two ski-planes from Ottawa Air Station are
also proceeding to Newfoundland to bring out the pilot and
deceased.

A sigh swept through the House. The lofty chamber seemed
suddenly to be darkened with a sense of profound oppression. A
spiritless pause, a silence eloquent of dismay, succeeded the Minister's words. Then gravely, in stiff, formal phrases, Colonel
Ralston proceeded to pay tribute to the dead scientist:

For the Department of National Defence I wish to express the
deepest regret at the passing of Sir Frederick Banting, who was
himself an officer of the Department.
He has been rendering invaluable professional services to
Canada, and he has also been serving the country by devoting to
its cause his outstanding abilities in research. . . .

While members of Parliament vied with one another in
laudatory speeches, the melancholy tidings from Newfoundland
were beamed around the world by radio. And everywhere,
with universal agreement, lamentation was mingled with golden
opinions, swelling into a glorious pæan of praise, as in the
wonderful early days when Banting and insulin were young. But
for those who spoke and those who listened, for those who wrote
and those who read, the praises were robbed of all joy by the tone
of elegaic sadness, by the dreadful finality of the appalling fact that
Sir Frederick was no longer "missing," but beyond question and
beyond hope was "killed in action."

7

Back in the wastes of Newfoundland, the bodies of Sir Frederick, Snailham and Bird lay silently among the frozen drifts, untouched by the clamour of grief and unconcerned with the frantic search which had been made to find them.

Meanwhile, the Newfoundland trappers who had reached the spot were making strenuous preparations for the rescue of the only survivor. "Almost before I could understand what was taking place," writes Captain Mackey, "one of them was speeding off on his snowshoes to get his other two companions, while the other took his axe and went into the bush near by. It could hardly have been five minutes before the one returned dragging three trees with him, which he proceeded to cut to poles to lash to their sled for a stretcher. . . ." In what Mackey feels sure was less than half an hour, the other trapper returned with his two companions, Harold Hicks and Tobias Moland. "Without a single instant's delay they set to like sailors in a storm to lift me and lash me aboard the sled. . . ."

It was just about noon Jim Allison spotted me. You can figure for yourself how these men worked when I tell you that it was just two o'clock when we started off on the sled—they had been located, had come to find me, had returned for their companions, had cut the poles and prepared me for the journey, all in less than two hours.

In my sleeping bag, I was lashed aboard the little sled fixed up with poles to support me. . . . The runners would break through snow crust, the sled would strike boulder or stump, but not once did they upset me, not once did they hurt me or permit any slightest harm to come to me. They had to cut trails through gullies, over ridges. They had to lift me over windfalls. It is no exaggeration whatever to say that much of that furious journey across ten miles of extremely rugged wilderness these four bighearted men carried me bodily.

"Make Smith's Pond before dark," endlessly urged the leader of the four. Because, as I learned after, they had a trail cut from Smith's Pond into the village of Musgrave Harbour. And make Smith's Pond we did, just before dark, where nearly fifty men from Musgrave Harbour met us on their way out. . . .

I understand my flying friends in the rescue planes gave Musgrave Harbour a fright. They had come diving furiously, dropping messages and leaflets, and for an instant Musgrave Harbour
thought there was a bombing attack in progress. But that wonderful little community . . . went into action to the last person.
It was just dark when we arrived at Smith's Pond and met the
big rescue party coming out. They had sleds and implements
of every sort. You would suppose our exhausted party would
have stopped on meeting these friends, in order to discuss the
news. What impressed me, and a thing I never can forget, is that
when our parties met we ploughed straight on, and as we went
the newcomers ran beside us and plans were made on the run for
the big party to follow our trails back to the plane and bring out
the bodies of my companions.

It was about 11.00 p.m. that we arrived in Musgrave Harbour.
It was only about 2.00 a.m., three hours later, that this larger
party, following our trail in and out, returned to Musgrave
Harbour with the bodies of Sir Frederick, Snailham and Bird.

Nurse Parsons, the public health nurse, attended Captain
Mackey. The following day, suspecting infection in his head
injuries, she sent out by radio for an air force surgeon.

"A sensational event crashed into the quiet life of Musgrave
Harbour," which in winter is completely cut off, except by radio,
from the outside world. "They handled it with courage and
complete humanity."

8

Two ski-equipped aeroplanes presently dared a landing on
the lake, though the weather had made flying difficult and there
was some delay before their arrival. They had come for the
bodies of Banting and his two companions. On the afternoon
of February 27, the bodies were taken to the village church, where
the Rev. Mr. Michelson officiated at a ten-minute service, rever-
ently attended by the villagers. Then the bodies of Sir Frederick
and Snailham were placed aboard a sled, draped in a Union Jack.
While pallbearers in dark clothing, wearing white arm bands,
marched beside the bodies, others pulled the sled to a spot on the

frozen lake where one of the planes was waiting. A procession a quarter-mile long proceeded over the snow-covered trail, winding over frozen muskeg and swampland between great drifts. As the bodies were placed in the machine, a bugler sounded the notes of the "Last Post." A Salvation Army band played a hymn and then "God Save the King." Eight hundred persons crowded around the plane.

Thick weather intervened to prevent the take-off, and the men of Musgrave Harbour brought out sails from their fishing boats to protect the planes from a snowstorm. Fifty stalwart men lifted each of the three-ton planes in turn, so that they could be supported on blocks overnight to prevent their skis from freezing into the ice.

Next morning the weather was much improved. The body of Flying Officer Bird was moved to one of the planes, accompanied by another procession. The planes were now ready to leave. Sixty abreast the Musgrave villagers walked through the snow on the lake to tramp down a runway for the machines. With a roaring of motors the aircraft swept down the lake and lifted slowly into the morning sky. In Musgrave Harbour the bell of the village church was solemnly tolling.

By 11.00 a.m. the planes had travelled the fifty miles to Newfoundland Airport. Shortly afterwards a T.C.A. plane took off for Musgrave Harbour to bring in Captain Mackey; it carried a group of officials going to inspect the wreckage. An inquest was held at Newfoundland Airport in the afternoon and next day the bodies were flown to Canada. Bird and Snailham were buried in Halifax.

9

On the evening of March 2, the entire area of Malton Airport, Toronto, from the front gates of the civilian and air observation fields to the distant boundary fences, was cleared of visitors and placed under guard. Just after sunset, as the airport lights were beginning to reflect from the ice-covered fields, a camouflaged bomber appeared from the east, landed in front of the R.C.A.F. training post and taxied up to the apron.

In the presence only of the bomber's crew and a handful of civilian officials, the body of Sir Frederick was carried from the plane to a hearse. As it was driven up the lane through the air training establishment, airmen on guard at the gate and drawn up on each side of the road came to rigid attention and saluted. The car drove off through the night.

10

In the Department of Pathology of the University of Toronto, in the Banting Institute on College Street, Professor W. L. Robinson performed a post-mortem examination of the body.

He was a very dear friend of mine (writes Professor Robinson)[4] and it was with great regret that I had to perform this duty. . . . My examination of the remains, after they arrived in Toronto, showed that he had received a number of bruises over the left side of the face and forehead. The one on the left forehead measured $3'' \times 3\frac{1}{2}''$, that in the left malar region about $1'' \times 2\frac{1}{2}''$, and the one on the left chin $2'' \times 4''$. There was hæmorrhage into the left upper eyelid. There was a bruise on the outer aspect of the left upper leg about half-way between the hip and the knee. There were two small bruises back of the left first finger and the nail of that finger was missing. The end of the first finger of the right hand was torn away and the nail of the second finger was gone. Both hands were swollen from B. Welchii infection. There were a number of brush burns on the outer, inner, and anterior aspects of the right foot.

Internally, I found hæmorrhage into the left temporal muscle, with subcutaneous hæmorrhage over the left parietal and frontal regions. There was subarachnoid hæmorrhage of the left temporal region. There was a dislocation of the left humerus downwards and inwards. This had crushed the chest and produced a depressed fracture of the left third and fourth ribs. One of these fractured ribs had punctured the left lung and there was some blood in this pleural cavity.

I have a feeling that the injuries to the head would probably

[4]Personal Communication.

have knocked him unconscious and that the dislocated shoulder and fractured ribs, in themselves, were not serious, but the punctured wound of the lung no doubt led to the hæmorrhage and, finally, his death.

It is hard to resist the thought that if Sir Frederick had had immediate expert medical attention his life might have been saved, but lost as he was out in the barren wastes of Newfoundland, there was not much hope for his recovery even though he was a strong, virile, healthy man.

A terrible duty.
A sad conclusion.

11

On Tuesday morning thousands of visitors filed through Convocation Hall, where Sir Frederick's body was lying in state. Twenty-four years previously in the same great Hall Banting had received his degree as a bachelor of medicine.

The funeral service in the afternoon was a very simple one.

Afterward the flag-draped coffin was carried through the streets on a caisson drawn by an armoured car. At the cemetery there was a brief committal service. Three volleys were fired over the grave, and the thin notes of the "Last Post" carried clearly and mournfully over the snow-whitened acres.

Epilogue

PROFESSOR DUNCAN GRAHAM, head of the Department of Medicine at the University of Toronto, was appointed a member of the National Research Council for a period of three years, filling the vacancy left by the death of Banting. He succeeded also to the chairmanship of the Associate Committee on Aviation Medical Research. Dr. J. B. Collip, Director of the Research Institute of Endocrinology at McGill University, became chairman of the Medical Research Committee. Professor C. H. Best took over direction of the Banting-Best Department of Medical Research at Toronto. Professor Bazett was asked to lead the civilian group engaged in aviation medical research in the Department. The ranks closed and the work went on.

In the autumn of 1941, Lady Banting registered in the second year of the medical course at Toronto (as Mrs. H. E. Banting) and graduated early in 1945. Another "Dr Banting" had joined the fellowship of medicine.

During the years since Sir Frederick's death his deeds have been commemorated in many ways. His Alma Mater has established a Memorial Lectureship. The Canadian Medical Association has set up a scholarship foundation to be known as the Banting Memorial Fund. An R.C.A.F. hospital has been named for him. Even a liberty ship, launched from the Bethlehem-Fairfield shipyard in Baltimore in 1943 was christened *The Frederick Banting*. Yet these posthumous honours—and the honours and awards that were showered upon him during his lifetime—will have less effect in keeping his memory green than the labours of his own mind and heart and the radiance of inspiration that shines so clearly from his life. The sort of immortality he would value most is "on lips of living men" and in the achievements of youthful scientists spurred forward by his example. Scholarships and fellowships are of undoubted value for the encouragement of needy workers; no one realized this more clearly than he. But the added fillip that kept the front advancing, the touch of the empyrean element that gave courage and resolution to all who worked beside him, was his particular gift.

433

Something of Banting's philosophy of life can be gleaned from his admiration for, and attempts to emulate his old preceptor, the late Dr. C. L. Starr. . . . Sir Frederick regarded the young surgeons developed by his professor as the greatest monument to Dr. Starr's memory. Banting's interest in, and encouragement of research-minded young people was his idea of handing on the torch given to him by Dr. Starr. The broad base of such a monument to his memory has been laid by the achievements of those who enjoyed the privilege of association with him; the ultimate proportions of the monument rest with those left to carry on.[1]

Banting's death was in a generous sense a fulfilment of his life, a life devoted to service and concluded abruptly and tragically, yet somehow triumphantly, in the mid-progress of a serviceable act. It had likewise its element of frustration: frustration not only of his immediate purpose but of his plans for future work. At fifty, in the fullness of his matured abilities, his life was destroyed. The mind that had striven toward fuller and clearer light was suddenly extinguished in darkness, like an eclipse at noon. Had he foreknown his fate, he might perhaps have rejoiced that he was never to be reduced to gradual insignificance; that the course was to terminate by crisis rather than by lysis. But how bitterly he would have regretted the princely forfeit of work-enriched and splendidly energetic years that his inheritance and his vigour had seemed to promise. Although anxious to retire from official duties, he had many plans for other work: his personal research problems, his painting, his projected writing, his farming, gardening and travelling.

When Pierre Curie met his end in the Rue Dauphine beneath the wheels of a carter's wagon, the event seemed doubly tragic because it was adventitious and meaningless. Death struck him *en passant*. This was not the case with Banting. As a soldier he had undertaken a dangerous mission; as a soldier he met his fate. He died on active service, and in this at least he would not have quarrelled with his fortune.

Enough of death. A spirit so restless and wakeful is not to be dismissed. The source of the energy is darkened, but the energy is in part transmitted and resolved.

Banting's secret was two-fold: he was possessed, almost

[1]Irwin, D.A., *Op. cit.*

inflamed, by his interest in the workings not only of disease but of life itself; and he followed the track where his interest led him with gusto and determination and with a stout heart.

His life is an amazing, invigorating, humbling example of what the will to achieve may accomplish surpassingly and what faith and persistence may do to set the tardy old world spinning gaily on its axis. The dry bones of truism seem clothed in reality and surprise. The familiar axioms are seen to be functioning here in the recognized features of human flesh. A man did thus and so, never abating the will to work, and the outcome, gloriously, was not self-containing and self-consuming virtue, but centripetal power. Hard work was his creed and his practice. And yet, like Benjamin Franklin, he was greater than his precepts, for "he showed men that achievement comes less by hard work than by keeping one's eyes open."

Banting fought the good fight, died gallantly, and endures with joy translated in the myriad lives he blessed and saved through the miracle of insulin. The story is not finished: it has no end. In every hospital and clinic in the world, in millions of homes and offices and shops, a new chapter is written every day. To such a tale as this it is not possible to write a conclusion. It still goes on.

Appendix

APPOINTMENTS HELD

Resident Surgeon, Hospital for Sick Children, Toronto, 1919-1920.
Assistant, Department of Physiology, Western Ontario University, London,
Canada, 1920-1921.
Lecturer, Pharmacology, University of Toronto, 1921-1922.
Senior Demonstrator in Medicine, University of Toronto, 1922-1923.
Professor of Medical Research, University of Toronto, 1923-1941.
Honorary Consulting Physician, Toronto General Hospital.
Honorary Consulting Physician, Hospital for Sick Children, Toronto.
Honorary Consulting Physician, Toronto Western Hospital.

DEGREES

M.B. (Toronto), 1916.
M.D. (Toronto), 1922.
L.R.C.P. and M.R.C.S., 1918.
LL.D. (Queen's), 1923.
D.Sc. (Toronto), 1923.
F.A.C.P., 1923.
LL.D. (University of Western Ontario), 1924.
Sc.D. (Yale), 1924.
F.R.S.C., 1926.
F.R.C.S. (England), 1930.
F.R.C.S. (Canada), 1931.
D.Sc. (University of the State of New York), 1931.
F.R.S., 1935.
F.R.C.P., 1936.
D.Sc. (McGill), 1939.

TITLE

Knight Commander of Civil Division of Order of British Empire, June, 1934.

SCHOLARSHIPS AND PRIZES

Starr Gold Medal, University of Toronto, 1922.
George Armstrong Peters Prize, University of Toronto, 1922.
Charles Mickle Fellowship, University of Toronto, 1923.
Reeve Prize, University of Toronto, 1923.
Nobel Prize, 1923.
John Scott Medal, Philadelphia, 1923.
Rosenberger Gold Medal, Chicago, 1924.
Cameron Prize, Edinburgh, 1927.
Life Annuity of $7,500 voted by the Parliament of Canada, 1923.

Banting and Best Chair of Medical Research, established by the Board of
Governors of the University of Toronto, 1923, for the support of
which $10,000 per year was voted by the Legislature of the
Province of Ontario, 1923.
Flavelle Medal, Royal Society of Canada, 1931.
Apothecaries' Medal (London), 1934.
F. N. G. Starr Gold Medal (Can. Med. Association), June, 1936.

ASSOCIATIONS AND SOCIETIES

Honorary Fellow, Academy of Medicine, Toronto, 1923.
Honorary Member, Ontario Medical Association.
Canadian Medical Association.
American Society for Pharmacology and Experimental Therapeutics.
British Physiological Society.
Alpha Omega Alpha Honorary Medical Fraternity.
Association of American Physicians.
Canadian Chemical Association.
Foreign Correspondent, La Societa Medico Chirurgica de Bologna, 1924.
Honorary Member, Chemists' Club, New York, 1929.
Académie Royale de Médicine de Belgique (Foreign Correspondent, 1930,
Honorary Member, 1935).
Corresponding Honorary Member, Royal Society of Medicine (Section of
Therapeutics and Pharmacology), 1932.
Member, Imperial German Academy of Natural Sciences, 1932.
Honorary Fellow, New York Academy of Medicine, 1933.
Honorary Member, Norwegian Medical Society, Oslo, 1933.
Corresponding Member, Royal Medical Society of Budapest, 1938.
Honorary Member, Canadian Club, Toronto, 1923.
Honorary Member, Canadian Club, New York, 1923.
Honorary Member, Canadian Club of Great Britain, 1923.
Arts and Letters Club.
Caduceus Club.

Bibliography

Banting, F. G. and Best, C. H.: Internal secretion of pancreas, *J. Lab. & Clin. Med.*, 7: 251-266, Feb., 1922.

—— and Best, C. H., Collip, J.B., Campbell, W.R. and Fletcher, A. A.: Pancreatic extracts in diabetes, *Can. M.A.J.*, 12: 141-146, March, 1922.

—— Pancreatic extracts, *J. Lab. & Clin. Med.*, 7: 464-472, May, 1922.

—— and Miller, F. R.: Cerebellar stimulations, *Brain*, 45: 104-112, June, 1922.

—— Effect of pancreatic extract (insulin) on normal rabbits, *Am. J. Physiol.*, 62: 162-176, Sept., 1922.

—— Effect of insulin on experimental hyperglycemia, *Am. J. Physiol.*, 62: 559-580, Nov., 1922.

——, Campbell, W. R., and Fletcher, A. A.: Insulin in treatment of diabetes mellitus, *J. Metabolic Research*, 2: 547-604, Nov.-Dec., 1922.

——, Campbell, W. R. [*et al.*]: *Insulin in the treatment of diabetes mellitus*, 545-985, Morristown, N.J., 1922.

—— Best, C. H., Collip, J. B., and Macleod, J. J. R.: The preparation of pancreatic extracts containing insulin, *Tr. R.S.C.* (3rd series), XVI, Sec. V: 27-29, 1922.

—— Best, C. H., Collip, J. B., Macleod, J. J. R., and Noble, E. C: The effect of insulin on normal rabbits and on rabbits rendered hyperglycæmic in various ways, *Tr. R.S.C.* (3rd series), XVI, Sec. V: 31-33, 1922.

—— Best, C. H., Collip, J. B., Hepburn, J., and Macleod, J. J. R.: The effect produced on the respiratory quotient by injections of insulin, *Tr. R.S.C.* (3rd series), XVI, Sec. V: 35-37, 1922.

—— Best, C. H., Collip, J. B., Macleod, J. J. R., and Noble, E. C.: The effect of insulin on the percentage amounts of fat and glycogen in the liver and other organs of diabetic animals. *Tr. R.S.C.* (3rd series), XVI, Sec. V: 39-41, 1922.

——, Best, C. H., Collip, J. B., and Macleod, J. J. R.: The effect of insulin on the excretion of ketone bodies by the diabetic dog, *Tr. R.S.C.* (3rd series), XVI, Sec. V: 43, 1922.

—— Best, C. H. [*et al.*]: The effect produced on diabetics by extracts of pancreas, *Tr. Ass. Am. Physicians*, 37: 337-347, 1922.

—— Best, C. H., and Noble, E. C.: Pancreatic extracts in the treatment of diabetes mellitus. *Bull, Battle Creek San. & Hosp. Clin.*, 18: 155-170, 1922-23.

—— The value of insulin in the treatment of diabetes, *Proc. Inst. Med., Chicago*, 4: 144-157, 1922-23.

——, Campbell, W. R. and Fletcher, A. A.: Clinical experience with insulin in diabetes, *Brit. M.J.*, 1: 8-12, Jan. 6, 1923.

—— Insulin, *J. Michigan M. Soc.*, 22: 113-124, March, 1923.

Gilchrist, J. A., Best, C. H., and Banting, F. G.: Observations with insulin on Department of Soldiers' Civil Re-establishment diabetics, *Can. M.A.J.*, 13: 565-572, Aug., 1923.

McPhedran, A., and Banting, F. G.; Insulin in treatment of severe diabetes, *Inter. Clinics*, 2: 1-5, 1923.

McPhedran, A., and Banting, F. G.: Insulin in treatment of severe diabetes, *Tr. Ass. Am. Physicians*, 38: 370-373 [Discussion]: 405-410, 1923.

Best, C. H., Scott, D. A., and Banting, F. G.: Insulin in blood, *Tr. R.S.C.* (3rd series), XVII, Sec. V: 81-85, 1923.

Banting, F. G., Cammidge, P. J., [*et al.*]: Discussion on diabetes and insulin. *Brit. M.J.*, 2: 445-451, Sept. 15, 1923.

—— The use of insulin in the treatment of diabetes mellitus. The Nathan Lewis Hatfield lecture. Lecture V., *Tr. Coll. Phys. Phila.*, 45: 153-164, 1923.

Macleod, J. J. R., and Banting, F. G.: *Antidiabetic functions of the pancreas and the successful isolation of the antidiabetic hormone—insulin.* The Beaumont Foundation Lectures, Series No. 2, 69 p., Mosby, St. Louis, 1923.

Banting, F. G., and Best, C. H.: The discovery and preparation of insulin, *Univ. Toronto M.J.*, 1: 3: 24-28, February, 1924.

Banting, F. G., and Gairns, S.: Factors influencing production of insulin, *Am. J. Physiol.* 68: 24-30, March, 1924.

—— Glandular therapy; pharmacologic action of insulin, *J.A.M.A.*, 83: 1,078, Oct. 4, 1924.

—— Canada's record in research, *Macleans*, 37: 22: 22, 44-46, Nov. 15, 1924.

—— Insulin, *Inter. Clinics*, 4: 109-116, Dec., 1924.

—— Medical research, *Inst. Quart.*, Springfield, Ill., 15: 11-18, 1924.

—— Medical research and the discovery of insulin, *Hygeia*, 2: 288-292, 1924.

Macleod, J. J. R., and Banting, F. G.: *The antidiabetic functions of the pancreas and the successful isolation of the antidiabetic hormone—insulin.* 69 p., Kimpton, London, 1924.

Macleod, J. J. R., Banting, F. G., and Wilder, R. M.: Glandular therapy, pancreatic gland preparations, *J.A.M.A.*, 83: 1077-1079, 1924.

Banting, F. G.: Medical research, *Ann. Clin. Med.*, 3: 565-572, March, 1925.

—— Insulin, *Proc. Internat. Conf. Health Probl. Trop. Am.* 1: 728-743, 1925.

—— *Diabetes and insulin: Nobel lecture delivered at Stockholm on September 15, 1925*, 20 p., P. A. Norstedt & Fils, Stockholm, 1925.

Boyd, Gladys L., and Stalsmith, Marion D.: *Manual for diabetics.* Introduction by F. G. Banting, M.D., 90 p., Funk and Wagnalls, New York and London, 1925.

Banting, F. G.: Diabetes and insulin, *Can. M.A.J.*, 16: 221-232, March, 1926.

—— and Gairns, S.: Suprarenal insufficiency, *Am. J. Physiol.*, 77: 100-113, June, 1926.

—— Medical research, *Can. M.A.J.*, 16: 877-881, Aug., 1926.

—— History of insulin, *Edinburgh M.J.*, 36: 1-18, Jan., 1929.

—— With the Arctic patrol, *Can. Geograph. J.*, 1: 1: 19-30, May, 1930.

—— and Gairns, S.: Antitryptic properties of blood serum, *Am. J. Physiol.* 94: 241-246, July, 1930.

——, Gairns, S., Lang, J. M., and Ross, J. R.: Study of enzymes of stools in intestinal intoxication, *Can. M.A.J.*, 25: 393-399, Oct., 1931.

—— Medical research, *New York State J. Med.*, 32: 311-315, March 15, 1932.

—— and Gairns, S.: Immunity to rous sarcoma, *Tr. R.S.C.*, 27 App. B, CLXVI, 1933.

—— and Gairns, S.: Resistance to rous sarcoma, *Can. M.A.J.*, 30: 615-619, June, 1934.

—— and Gairns, S.: Study of serum of chickens resistant to rous sarcoma, *Am. J. Cancer*, 22: 611-614, Nov., 1934.

Irwin, D. A., Gairns, S., Banting, F. G.: Study of rous sarcoma tissue grafts in susceptible and resistant chickens, *Am. J. Cancer*, 22: 615-619, Nov., 1934.

Banting, F. G.: The early story of insulin, *Lilly Res. Lab. (Dedicat. Vol.)* 14-20, 1934.

Banting, F G.: Silicosis, *J. Indiana M.A.*, 28: 9-12, Jan., 1935.

Armstrong, A. R., and Banting, F. G.: Site of formation of phosphatase of serum, *Can. M.A.J.*, 33: 243-246, Sept., 1935.

Fallon, J. T., and Banting, F. G.: Cellular reaction to silica, *Can. M.A.J.*, 33: 404-407, Oct., 1935.

Fallon, J. T., and Banting, F. G.: Tissue reaction to sericite: *Can. M.A.J.*, 33: 407-411, Oct., 1935.

Hall, G. E., Ettinger, G. H., and Banting, F. G.: Experimental production of coronary thrombosis and myocardial failure, *Can. M.A.J.*, 34: 9-15, Jan., 1936.

Banting, F. G.: Science and the Soviet Union, *Can. Business*, 9: 2: 14-15, 67-69, Feb., 1936.

—— Ivan Petrovitch Pavlov, 1849-1936, *Am. J. Psychiat.*, 92: 1481-1484, May, 1936.

Ettinger, G. H., Hall, G. E., and Banting, F. G.: Effect of repeated and prolonged stimulation of vagus nerve in dog, *Can. M.A.J.*, 35: 27-31, July, 1936.

Banting, F. G.: Silicosis research, *Can. M.A.J.*, 35: 289-293, Sept., 1936.

—— Early work on insulin, *Science*, 85: 594-596, June 25, 1937.

—— and Hall, G. E.: Experimental production of myocardial and coronary artery lesions, *Tr. A. Am. Physicians*, 52: 204-209, 1937.

Manning, G. W., Hall, G. E., and Banting, F. G.: Vagus stimulation and production of myocardial damage, *Can. M.A.J.*, 37: 314-318, Oct., 1937.

Banting, F. G., Hall, G. E., Janes, J. M., Leibel, B., and Lougheed, D. W.: Physiological studies in experimental drowning (preliminary report), *Can. M.A.J.*, 39: 226-228, Sept., 1938.

Hall, G. E.: Physiological studies in experimental insulin and metrazol shock; composite preliminary study by members of Department of Medical Research, Banting Institute, University of Toronto, *Am. J. Psychiat.*, 95: 553-566, Nov., 1938. [For Banting's contribution to this composite paper see p. 328.]

Banting, F. G.: Walter Ernest Dixon memorial lecture, resistance to experimental cancer, *Proc. Roy. Soc. Med.*, 32: 245-254, Jan., 1939.

Index

441